# Constructing Paul

THE CANONICAL PAUL
*volume 1*

# Constructing Paul

Luke Timothy Johnson

WILLIAM B. EERDMANS PUBLISHING COMPANY

GRAND RAPIDS, MICHIGAN

Wm. B. Eerdmans Publishing Co.
4035 Park East Court SE, Grand Rapids, Michigan 49546
www.eerdmans.com

26  25  24  23  22  21  20      1  2  3  4  5  6  7

ISBN 978-0-8028-0758-8


**Library of Congress Cataloging-in-Publication Data**

Names: Johnson, Luke Timothy, author.
Title: Constructing Paul : the canonical Paul / Luke Timothy Johnson.
Description: Grand Rapids, Michigan : William B. Eerdmans Publishing Company, 2020.
   | Includes bibliographical references and index. | Summary: "First of a two-volume
   work providing a framework for understanding the life and thought of the apostle
   Paul"— Provided by publisher.
Identifiers: LCCN 2019036811 | ISBN 9780802807588 (hardcover)
Subjects: LCSH: Bible. Epistles of Paul—Criticism, interpretation, etc.
Classification: LCC BS2650.52 .J64 2020 | DDC 225.9/2—dc23
LC record available at https://lccn.loc.gov/2019036811

# CONTENTS

## PART 3: THE ELEMENTS

# PREFACE

This is the first of two volumes dedicated to the canonical Paul. The canonical Paul is the term I use for the thirteen letters under his name that have been read in the church's worship and have been the basis for the church's debates over Christian belief and behavior. These thirteen letters should be what Christian readers mean when they speak of "Paul," because, apart from the Acts of the Apostles, they alone provide secure access to the historical circumstances of their composition, and they alone address present-day readers as the words of God's chosen vessel to bring the good news to the gentiles, among whom we stand. This first volume takes up in the form of essays all the questions pertinent to the canonical Paul as a set of compositions, only at the very end making a case for why this Paul ought to be heard today as a liberating rather than oppressing voice.

The second volume consists of a series of specific studies of each canonical letter, excepting only Philemon, which gets treated in the present volume. These studies do not purport to provide an adequate interpretation of each letter; exegetical studies of that sort can be found in many places, including my own interpretation of the New Testament. Instead, each study tries to demonstrate how many and different questions can be put to each letter, and how rewarding to thought and life the serious engagement with each writing can be. Far from being exhaustive, the essays show the possibilities for further and better inquiry into these amazing compositions, once we abandon the silly notion of finding and fixing a single "Paul" who can be abstracted from the actual compositions that he (almost surely together with others) wrote, and turn gladly to the compositions themselves—all the compositions—as an arena for thought and debate.

The circumstances under which this volume was written were difficult, but I hope that clarity in thought and expression did not suffer as a result. I dedicate this book to my late wife, Joy, who was unstinting in her support of all I have done. Special thanks for the encouragement and support of colleagues like Carl Holladay and Steven Kraftchick, who don't agree with much of what I have to say, but seem to enjoy the way I say it. Talented doctoral students, who have feigned interest when afflicted with passages read aloud, have been a sustaining presence throughout many years. Among recent implicit collaborators (or silent victims) are Bo Adams, Brandon Wason, Chris Holmes, Michael Suh, Jennifer Wyant, Jenny Pietz, Jarrett Knight, and especially David Carr, whose intellectual and practical assistance would be difficult to measure.

LUKE TIMOTHY JOHNSON
*Emory University*
*December 31, 2018*

# ABBREVIATIONS

| | |
|---|---|
| AB | Anchor Bible |
| *ABD* | *Anchor Bible Dictionary.* Edited by David Noel Freedman. 6 vols. New York: Doubleday, 1992 |
| ABRL | Anchor Bible Reference Library |
| AnBib | Analecta Biblica |
| *ANF* | *Ante-Nicene Fathers* |
| *ANRW* | *Aufstieg und Niedergang der römischen Welt: Geschichte und Kultur Roms im Spiegel der neueren Forschung.* Part 2, *Principat.* Edited by Hildegard Temporini and Wolfgang Haase. Berlin: De Gruyter, 1972– |
| *Bib* | *Biblica* |
| BZNW | Beihefte zur Zeitschrift für die neutestamentliche Wissenschaft |
| *CBQ* | *Catholic Biblical Quarterly* |
| ConBNT | Coniectanea Neotestamentica or Coniectanea Biblica: New Testament Series |
| FAT | Forschungen zum Alten Testament |
| FRLANT | Forschungen zur Religion und Literatur des Alten und Neuen Testament |
| *HTR* | *Harvard Theological Review* |
| HTS | Harvard Theological Studies |
| Ign. *Eph.* | Ignatius, *To the Ephesians* |
| Ign. *Magn.* | Ignatius, *To the Magnesians* |
| Ign. *Phil.* | Ignatius, *To the Philadelphians* |
| Ign. *Pol.* | Ignatius, *To Polycarp* |
| Ign. *Rom.* | Ignatius, *To the Romans* |
| Ign. *Smyrn.* | Ignatius, *To the Smyrnaeans* |

| | |
|---|---|
| Ign. *Trall.* | Ignatius, *To the Trallians* |
| *JAAR* | *Journal of the American Academy of Religion* |
| *JBL* | *Journal of Biblical Literature* |
| *JSNT* | *Journal for the Study of the New Testament* |
| JSNTSup | Journal for the Study of the New Testament Supplement Series |
| *JTS* | *Journal of Theological Studies* |
| LCL | Loeb Classical Library |
| LNTS | The Library of New Testament Studies |
| NABRE | New American Bible Revised Edition |
| NIGTC | New International Greek Testament Commentary |
| *NovT* | *Novum Testamentum* |
| NovTSup | Supplements to Novum Testamentum |
| NRSV | New Revised Standard Version |
| *NTS* | *New Testament Studies* |
| Pol. *Phil.* | Polycarp, *To the Philippians* |
| RSV | Revised Standard Version |
| SBLDS | Society of Biblical Literature Dissertation Series |
| SBLSBS | Society of Biblical Literature Sources for Biblical Study |
| SCS | Septuagint and Cognate Studies |
| SP | Sacra Pagina |
| StPB | Studia Post-biblica |
| SUNT | Studien zur Umwelt des Neuen Testaments |
| SVTP | Studia in Veteris Testamenti Pseudepigraphica |
| *TBT* | *The Bible Today* |
| *TDNT* | *Theological Dictionary of the New Testament.* Edited by Gerhard Kittel and Gerhard Friedrich. Translated by Geoffrey W. Bromiley. 10 vols. Grand Rapids: Eerdmans, 1964–76 |
| WBC | Word Biblical Commentary |
| WUNT | Wissenschaftliche Untersuchungen zum Neuen Testament |
| *ZNW* | *Zeitschrift für die neutestamentliche Wissenschaft und die Kunde der älteren Kirche* |

# INTRODUCTION

Since large books on the apostle Paul are both abundant and easily available, some case must be made for adding to the pile. Why burden bookshelves—and weary readers—with still another volume (or two) on Paul?[1] I hope that this introduction will make clear that there is room for a different kind of approach to the apostle than the ones most often taken.

Saint Paul commands our attention for at least five reasons. First, beginning as a persecutor of the primitive church, he personally experienced the resurrected Lord and became a firsthand witness to the resurrection. Second, being sent as an apostle by the risen Lord, he founded communities of believers in Asia Minor, Macedonia, and Achaia, and was the head of an extensive missionary endeavor that had an even wider scope. Third, he was a pivotal figure in the mission to the gentiles, and vigorously defended the legitimacy of the gentile mission. Fourth, he was the first, and arguably the most important, interpreter of the story of Jesus. Fifth, his letters formed the basis of what became the New Testament canon and, as part of that

---

1. Just within the last decade, a partial list of "big" books on Paul would include the following: Fredriksen, *Paul*; Porter, *Apostle Paul*; R. Longenecker, *Paul, Apostle of Liberty*; E. Sanders, *Paul: The Apostle's Life*; Boccaccini and Segovia, *Paul the Jew*; Bird, *Anomalous Jew*; Thiselton, *Living Paul*; Sumney, *Paul*; Campbell, *Deliverance of God*; Barclay, *Paul and the Gift*; Bird, *Introducing Paul*; Engberg-Pedersen, *Cosmology and Self*; B. Longenecker and Still, *Thinking Through Paul*; Childs, *Church's Guide for Reading Paul*; Wright, *Paul: In Fresh Perspective*; and Wright, *Paul and the Faithfulness of God*. Even the Vatican weighed in; see Benedict XVI, *Saint Paul the Apostle*. And if the (partial) list is extended back only about five more years, it would include the following: Schnelle, *Apostle Paul*; Gorman, *Apostle of the Crucified Lord*; Crossan and Reed, *In Search of Paul*; Griffith-Jones, *Gospel According to Paul*; Harink, *Paul among the Postliberals*; Meeks and Fitzgerald, *Writings of St. Paul*. Imagine the size of the list if works in languages other than English were included!

canonical collection, have had a critical role in shaping Christian theology down to the present.

The first four of these reasons are historical in character, and although they generate vigorous debate concerning details, they enjoy broad recognition. The fifth reason—the place of Paul's letters in the canon—has been and continues to be the basis for contention, precisely because the influence of these letters (whether regarded as positive or negative) persists to the present day. The Paul of the letters is not simply a figure of the past. His letters continue to be read aloud in the liturgical assembly; they are taught in seminaries; they are pondered in Bible study groups; they feed private reflection. When his letters are read, his voice speaks to the minds and hearts of contemporary readers.

Precisely because of that existential significance, the study of Paul's letters has never been a simple matter of historical inquiry; interpreters of Paul—including those who approach him from outside the Christian tradition—are never entirely neutral in approach, are never completely free of bias or prior assumptions. Certainly, I bring to the study of Paul my own set of prejudices. Some of them I recognize, while others probably operate implicitly outside my consciousness.[2]

Here are three of my own biases of which I am conscious. First, I am aware that I approach Paul not first of all as a critic but as an admirer and advocate. Although my scholarly work has centered mostly on non-Pauline materials,[3] Paul has always been for me personally the true heart of the New Testament and the framework for my self-understanding as a Christian. I read and have always read Paul as passionately as a neurotic might read Freud or Jung. I seek in his letters the best understanding of my own commitment to the risen Lord Jesus.

Second, when I compare myself to other New Testament scholars, it is clear to me—and will quickly become obvious to the reader—that I am also unusually cautious and conservative concerning the dating and authorship of compositions. This tendency is not, I think, due to a deficiency of a critical spirit. Rather the opposite: my close study of the so-called critical methods often employed in the study of the Bible has led me to conclude, first, that the conclusions to which they lead are more often wrong than right, and,

---

2. A healthy pluralism within scholarship enables such unconscious biases to be brought to light through diverse constructions and mutual criticism.

3. I have worked primarily on questions concerning the historical Jesus, Luke-Acts, and the Letter of James.

second, that the application of such methods has done little to enhance the understanding of New Testament compositions themselves.

Third, I am also aware that my reading of Paul is very much affected by my allegiance (uneasy but steadfast) to the Roman Catholic Church, as a "cradle Catholic" who eventually became both a Benedictine monk and ordained priest, before becoming a lay professor, husband, and father. My reading of Paul has therefore been affected by the rich resources of the Catholic tradition, including patristic authors like Origen, Augustine, and Chrysostom; theologians from Aquinas to Rahner; monastic authors like Dom Columba Marmion; and Catholic biblical scholars like Lucien Cerfaux, Jacques Dupont, John McKenzie, and Joseph Fitzmyer.

An emphasis on the sacramental, ecclesial, and mystical elements in Paul's letters has consequently appeared to me as "obviously" correct, while certain other aspects (forensic justification, atonement, apocalyptic) have had a harder time gaining my attention. Likewise, my instinctive understanding of the "faith of Jesus" as his trusting obedience to God has undoubtedly been affected by the importance of the Letter to the Hebrews among Catholics. I carry all these influences lightly, however, and resist the notion that there is a specifically "Roman Catholic" understanding of Paul.[4] I do think, though, that it is consistent with the longer catholic tradition, or catholic sensibility, to read all the canonical letters as Pauline in some real sense.

I am, to be sure, not alone in bringing predispositions and prior assumptions to the study of the apostle. An important stream of Pauline interpretation since the Protestant Reformation was, after all, shaped by the specific theological commitments of the Reformation. Within that broad stream is a distinctive "Lutheran" approach to Paul's thought,[5] an interpretive tradition that not only generated an amazing amount of literature but also governed the shape of much Pauline study over the course of several centuries, becoming *de facto* if not *de jure* the dominant paradigm for responsible Pauline scholarship, so dominant, indeed, that only when challenged did it begin to appear as something other than the natural and obvious way to study the apostle.[6]

---

4. Thus my discomfort with my assigned essay "The Paul of the Letters: A Catholic Perspective," in Bird, *Four Views on the Apostle Paul*. In that essay, and here, I understand "Catholic" as representing a broadly capacious embrace of Paul in contrast to a narrowly selective one.

5. The perspective is wonderfully illustrated by Bultmann, *Theology of the New Testament*, and the review of Bultmann's work by Dahl, "Rudolf Bultmann's Theology."

6. A good sense of this approach is provided by Schreiner, "Paul"; see also his *Paul,*

In a development roughly corresponding to biblical scholarship's shift to a secular academy, scholars have increasingly embraced other explicit theoretical perspectives on Paul. The so-called New Perspective rejects the "Lutheran" (vertical) view of Paul for a more sociological (horizontal) view—not the salvation of the individual soul from sin but the healing of humanity from social division and hostility is now thought to be Paul's main concern.[7] Not surprisingly, this "new" perspective quickly generated in turn a "post-new perspective."[8]

Today's biblical scholars have increasingly joined their academic colleagues (above all in the humanities) by defining their investigations in terms of such theoretical starting points. Thus, some adopt an aspect of Paul's own cultural context as the key to unlocking his thought. Some privilege the Jewish side: Paul is read within the framework of Jewish apocalyptic literature,[9] or deciphered through the clues offered by the "covenantal nomism" of Second Temple Judaism,[10] or understood within the categories of Hellenistic Judaism.[11] Some privilege the Greco-Roman side: Paul is read in terms of one or the other version of philosophy, whether Stoicism, Epicureanism, or an eclectic "popular" philosophy of the early Roman Empire.[12] Still other contemporary scholars read Paul through the lens of present-day cultural concerns, whether scientific[13] or ideological; the latter tend to employ a hermeneutics of suspicion and focus on texts that are regarded as harmful to humans.[14] Thus, we meet African American,

---

*Apostle of God's Glory in Christ*. For a thorough and balanced exposition, see Westerholm, *Perspectives Old and New on Paul*.

7. For the so-called New Perspective see the important work of E. P. Sanders, *Paul and Palestinian Judaism*, which was enthusiastically embraced by N. T. Wright and many others.

8. See, e.g., Campbell, "Christ and Church in Paul"; and Tilling, *Beyond Old and New Perspectives*.

9. Whether under the rubric of "eschatological" or "apocalyptic," this approach goes back at least to Schweitzer, *Mysticism of Paul the Apostle*, and includes Käsemann, *Perspectives on Paul*; Beker, *Paul the Apostle*; and Campbell, *Deliverance of God*.

10. This approach is classically represented by W. Davies, *Paul and Rabbinic Judaism*; and with more refinement by Sanders, *Paul and Palestinian Judaism*; and most recently by Nanos, "Jewish View," and Nanos, *Paul within Judaism*.

11. See, e.g., Schoeps, *Paul*; Sandmel, *Genius of Paul*.

12. For Epicureanism, see DeWitt, *St. Paul and Epicurus*; for Stoicism, see Engberg-Pedersen, *Paul and the Stoics*; for Greco-Roman moralists, see Malherbe, *Paul and the Popular Philosophers*.

13. See, e.g., the application of anthropological categories to Paul by Neyrey, *Paul, in Other Words*.

14. The term "hermeneutics of suspicion" derives from Ricoeur, *Freud and Philosophy*,

feminist, and queer approaches to Paul, as well as (the most recently popular) a "postcolonial" perspective.[15] Such ideologically defined perspectives can also be found in combination.[16]

The more explicit the attachment to a specific perspective, however, and the narrower the scope of that perspective, the more there is the danger of elevating a part of Paul into the whole, while simultaneously missing much of the full range of the concerns addressed in his letters. Take, for example, the debate between the so-called "old" and "new" perspectives on Paul: whatever the validity of the arguments made for each approach, it is clear that either one is helpful only with regard to a small portion of Paul's correspondence. In letters other than Galatians, Romans, and a single chapter in Philippians, it is as difficult to find "justification by faith" as it is to find "Jew and gentile together"—that is, unless one included Colossians and Ephesians. Each perspective leaves 1 and 2 Thessalonians, Philemon, and 1 and 2 Corinthians outside its scope. A perspective that provides insight only into three letters, and these only in part, cannot be considered an adequate apprehension of the apostle's correspondence.

But here is a more significant point: the narrowing effect of theoretical perspectives is less obvious to some scholars because they have long ago accommodated themselves to an earlier reduction in the number of Pauline letters that count as Pauline. Most critical scholars today accept as dogma the position that the authentic Pauline corpus consists of only seven letters (Romans, Galatians, 1 and 2 Corinthians, 1 Thessalonians, Philippians, and Philemon). This means that six of the letters ascribed to Paul in the New Testament canon effectively vanish from view (Colossians, Ephesians, 2 Thessalonians, 1 and 2 Timothy, Titus). For the vast majority of the studies on Paul, slightly more than half of the canonical letters count as "Pauline."[17]

---

and has entered into common parlance; it can be applied with equal accuracy to the classic historical-critical approach, which began with suspicion concerning the surface account of biblical writings.

15. An overview of African American interpretation is provided by M. Brown, *Blackening of the Bible*; Blount et al., *True to Our Native Land*; and Wimbush, *African Americans and the Bible*. For a sense of feminist perspectives, see Newsom, Ringe, and Lapsley, *Women's Bible Commentary*; Levine, *Feminist Companion to Paul*; Bernadette J. Brooten, "Paul's Views on Women"; and Castelli, *Imitating Paul*. For queer approaches, see, e.g., S. Moore, *God's Beauty Parlor*; Townsley, *Straight Mind in Corinth*. For the postcolonial perspective, see S. Moore, *Empire and Apocalypse*; and Segovia and Sugirtharajah, *Postcolonial Commentary*.

16. See, e.g., Tinsley, *Re-Reading of Colossians*; Marchal, *Politics of Heaven*.

17. Out of all the books on Paul listed in my first footnote above, for example, only Gor-

Within this reduced core, in turn, it is not unusual for scholars to rely on only five of the letters—the so-called great letters of Galatians, Romans, 1 and 2 Corinthians, and Philippians—for their construal of Paul, leaving 1 Thessalonians and Philemon out of serious consideration. And not a few interpretations of "Paul" turn out to rely almost entirely on Romans, because, with its systematic argument and patently theological themes, it provides a control over the far more scattered evidence in the remaining letters that are actually being used.[18]

The simple fact is that every interpretation of Paul also involves a construction of Paul, with the two activities occurring simultaneously and with mutual effect. What do I mean by "constructing" Paul? I mean that the figure we call Paul is not simply *there* for our analysis in an obvious and indisputable fashion. He must be fashioned from the far-from-complete bits of evidence offered from ancient sources, thus "constructed." But because these sources themselves resist easy analysis—they are fragmentary and they offer any number of challenges to the premise that they agree with each other or are even internally consistent—every approach to Paul demands decisions concerning the building blocks used for construction.

## Constructing the "Historical Paul"

The most fundamental decision concerns what Paul is being sought. Most contemporary studies, for example, seek to construct "the historical Paul," by which they mean Paul's life and his thought in its original context. All critical scholars dedicated to this task begin, quite properly, by eliminating from consideration later apocryphal writings about Paul (as legendary), in favor of New Testament compositions (as relatively more historically reliable). Then for constructing Paul's life, scholars tend to prefer his so-called

---

man, Schreiner, Bruce W. Longenecker, and Benedict XVI treat all thirteen of the canonical letters rather than the seven "undisputed" letters.

18. The dominant role played by Romans in constructing Paul's theology is equally visible, for example, in Bultmann's *Theology of the New Testament* and in Dunn's *Theology of Paul the Apostle*. Among the books listed in my first footnote, Bird's *Anomalous Jew* deals entirely with Galatians; Barclay's *Paul and the Gift* focuses exclusively on Galatians and Romans; Wright's *Paul and the Faithfulness of God* is entirely dominated by Galatians and Romans. And Campbell's massive (1218-page) tome, *Deliverance of God*, is in reality a study of Galatians and Romans. He devotes fifteen pages to Philippians 3, and fourteen pages to four passages in 1 Corinthians, 2 Corinthians, and 1 Thessalonians, under the rubric "loose ends"!

authentic (or undisputed) letters as firsthand, primary sources, in preference to the New Testament secondhand source, the Acts of the Apostles, even though it is impossible to provide anything close to a satisfactory "life" of Paul without recourse to the narrative of Acts.[19] So-called critical treatments of Paul's life/ministry therefore usually end up being based on a judicious use of Acts and the undisputed letters, while leaving the disputed letters out of consideration.[20] Even with such fastidiousness, portraits of Paul are notoriously various,[21] since not even so simple a question as the sequence of his letters (and therefore a full chronology) can absolutely be secured.[22]

Contemporary studies of Paul's "thought" or "theology," in turn, deal with the source question crisply, holding that only compositions actually written by Paul should be taken as sources for his thought. Acts can consequently be ignored completely, since it expresses the thought of Luke the Evangelist rather than of Paul; the speeches attributed to Paul in Acts are samples of Luke's rhetoric and convictions placed in the mouth of the literary character Paul. So far, so good.[23] But now the question of which letters are to be considered becomes more significant.

The vast majority of scholars, as I have indicated, follow the convention that only seven of Paul's letters can be taken as the basis for his "thought." The remaining letters in the canonical collection are ascribed to some sort of Pauline "school" or "schools" arising after his death. Beginning in the early nineteenth century, considerable effort has been expended to demonstrate the inauthenticity of these six letters, with arguments stressing the supposed differences between them and the hypothetically authentic Pauline core.[24] So much energy has gone into this effort, indeed, that they are as rigidly excluded from considerations of Paul's theology as is Acts. Very seldom is it

---

19. The study by Knox, *Chapters in a Life of Paul*, succeeds mainly in showing how little can really be stated about Paul's life if one holds strictly to the undisputed letters alone.

20. For a serious effort to use only the letters, but one that ends up using quite a bit of Acts, see Murphy-O'Connor, *Paul*. In contrast, conservative scholars have sometimes tried to fit Paul's life and letters completely within the framework of the Acts narrative; see Ramsay and Wilson, *St. Paul the Traveler*, and J. A. T. Robinson, *Redating the New Testament*.

21. Allowing such extreme makeovers as that offered by Maccoby, *Mythmaker*, and A. Wilson, *Paul*.

22. See the efforts by Jewett, *Chronology of Paul's Life*, and Lüdemann, *Paul, Apostle to the Gentiles*.

23. I am totally in agreement with this position; see, e.g., L. Johnson, *Septuagintal Midrash*. For a recent demonstration of the Lukan character of Paul's rhetoric in Acts, see Wason, "'All Things to All People.'"

24. This history will be summarized in chap. 1.

asked whether these six letters, even if "inauthentic," could be read as legitimate expressions of Paul's own thought, or even as important developments of his thought, which might, in fact, throw important light on elements in his undisputed letters.

Deciding on a core of seven letters, alas, does not make things easier. The question of Paul's life, which we thought we could leave behind, rudely returns. Is there any connection between elements in Paul's life and his letters? Is his experience in any way significant for his theology? Is there any development in his thought? Such questions become even more difficult when the historical itch leads scholars to destabilize even the seven letters they accept as Pauline. Thus, some scholars ask what elements in these letters might have been taken over from an earlier tradition (that Paul may have emended); how do such fragments of non-Pauline material figure in an assessment of his thought?[25] Other scholars purport to discern interpolations that were added by later writers or editors; those who hold such views would exclude these putative interpolations from Paul's thought as being non-Pauline or even anti-Pauline in character.[26] Finally, some scholars hold that some of the extant seven letters lack literary integrity, being edited composites of separate Pauline fragments.[27]

But even when the reduced Pauline corpus of seven letters is acknowledged to have literary integrity, a disciplined examination of them reveals that they are remarkably diverse in character, resisting efforts to construct a consistent "Pauline theology" on their basis. To take only a single example: it is simply not the case that the seven undisputed letters reveal a single, coherent Pauline eschatology; 1 Thessalonians and 1 Corinthians come closest to agreement, but 2 Corinthians, Philippians, and Romans each offer quite different (and even incompatible) scenarios, while Galatians and Philemon lack any significant future eschatology. The same test for consistency can be applied to matters of composition across the seven-letter sample: it is not the case that in them Paul consistently quotes and interprets Scripture; that

25. See, e.g., B. Meyer, "Pre-Pauline Formula in Rom 3:25-26a"; Bornkamm, "Understanding the Christ Hymn"; Vawter, "Colossians Hymn."

26. See, e.g., Gamble, *Textual History*; Pearson, "1 Thessalonians 2:13-16"; D. Schmidt, "1 Thess 2:13-16"; Murphy-O'Connor, "Non-Pauline Character"; Wire, *Corinthians Women Prophets*; and Betz, "2 Cor 6:14-7:1."

27. The champion fragmenter of Pauline literature is Schmithals, *Paul and the Gnostics*; for fragment hypotheses on Philippians, see Rahtjen, "Three Letters of Paul"; Reumann, "Philippians 3:20-21"; Koester, "Purpose of the Polemic"; for a comprehensive analysis of the complex fragment theories for 2 Corinthians, see above all Stegman, *Character of Jesus*.

characterization applies splendidly to Romans, Galatians, and (to a slightly lesser degree and manner) 1 Corinthians. But the lengthy 2 Corinthians has only a handful of citations or allusions to Scripture, while 1 Thessalonians, Philippians, and Philemon have none. Similarly, it is inaccurate to characterize the style of the seven undisputed letters as "diatribal." Romans certainly fits the description as a form of scholastic diatribe.[28] But the stylistic elements of the diatribe are only occasionally present in Galatians and 1 Corinthians, and are absent from 2 Corinthians, 1 Thessalonians, Philippians, and Philemon.

The so-called undisputed letters are, in fact, remarkably and irreducibly diverse in style, argument, and theme. Such intractable diversity, even in the Pauline core, in turn, helps drive the search for some organizing theme or principle that might give the appearance of coherence, or for a single letter (Romans) that might be used as the key to the unification of Paul's thought. Scholars writing books on Paul share the distinctively Western preference for the one over the many, for unity over diversity. Their intellectual struggle comes from attempting to realize such a unified vision with material so diverse and refractory.

To speak of the diversity in the Pauline collection of letters, however, is to speak of only half the problem facing all interpreters of the apostle's letters. Together with obvious diversity, there are equally very real patterns of similarity. Actually, the canonical collection considered as a whole falls into distinct family clusters. Everyone acknowledges that the so-called Pastoral Letters (1 Timothy, 2 Timothy, Titus) are, despite real differences among them, a distinct group.[29] The same family resemblance is patent as well in the case of Colossians and Ephesians, giving rise to suggestions of literary dependence or even copying.[30] The cluster of Colossians/Ephesians, moreover, is easily distinguished from the cluster of the Pastorals in terms of style, argumentation, perspective, and themes. The similarities between the two clusters require greater work to uncover. This set of observations supports the common hypothesis that there were at least two Pauline "schools" writing after his death, one responsible for the Colossians/Ephesians cluster, the other the Pastoral cluster. Each cluster is somehow "Pauline," but distinct both from each other and from the other Pauline letters. All true.

28. The essential work on this is Stowers, *Diatribe and Paul's Letter to the Romans.*
29. Classically stated by P. Harrison, *Problem of the Pastoral Epistles.*
30. See Cadbury, "Dilemma of Ephesians 1"; Coutts, "Relationship of Ephesians and Colossians." For a full display of similarities and differences, see Lau, *Politics of Peace.*

The situation gets a little more complex in the case of the Thessalonian correspondence. Once more, the similarity between the two letters is so strong as to give rise to theories of literary copying, with 2 Thessalonians being written in imitation of 1 Thessalonians.[31] But because 1 Thessalonians is universally regarded as "authentic" (that is, written by Paul himself) and 2 Thessalonians is most often regarded as pseudonymous (without very good reason), the fact that the two letters together form another—a third— distinct cluster within the Pauline collection goes largely unobserved. But the plain fact is that 1 and 2 Thessalonians resemble each other much more than either resembles any other Pauline letter. If one places either Thessalonian letter next to Romans or Galatians, the differences leap to the attention.

Speaking of Galatians and Romans, however, leads us to another distinct cluster—a fourth. Once more, the similarity between the two letters is great and universally recognized. What is less often acknowledged is the distinctive nodule they form within the collection. As striking as is the similarity between Galatians and Romans (together with real differences), there is almost as great a distance between the two together and the other letters in the collection. Not much argument is required, in turn, to show that Paul's two letters to the Corinthians represent a fifth cluster, clearly close to each other in a variety of ways, suggesting authorship by the same hand and, however complexly, reflecting a sequence of moments in the relationship of the author and the Corinthian community. Yet in any number of ways, these two letters also distinguish themselves from the Galatians/Romans cluster—and, for that matter, the Thessalonian cluster, and the Pastorals cluster, and the Colossians/Ephesians cluster. Five distinct epistolary clusters, then, are found in the canonical Pauline collection, leaving only Philippians and Philemon as outliers.

The importance of these observations can scarcely be overstated for the conventional way of approaching the Pauline corpus—that is, in the quest for the historical Paul. It is simply not the case that the seven letters usually regarded as authentic are so uniform in style, argument, theme, and perspective as to form a measuring stick against which the "divergence" of six letters (the Pastorals, Colossians/Ephesians, and 2 Thessalonians) can be judged as non-Pauline. The case is just the opposite: the clusters of letters combining similarity to each other with difference from other letters obtain across the entire corpus. There exists no "core" by which to judge authenticity and inauthenticity, at least not if one wants to be honest in assessing

31. See, e.g., J. Bailey, "Who Wrote II Thessalonians?"

the data. A neutral statement of the facts on the ground is that the canonical corpus contains five distinct clusters that represent "Paul"—and, if we add Philippians and Philemon, two outliers to further complicate the situation.

The attempt to construct a "historical Paul" that begins with the elimination of some canonical letters on the assumption that they are too "different" to be authored by Paul, and then seeks a thematic or propositional heart to his thought within an undisputed core of letters, or seeks a single element of the symbolic world of the ancient Mediterranean as the key to that thought, is, therefore, essentially a flawed construction based on false assumptions.

Worse, such constructions of a "historical Paul" serve to fix such a constructed Paul statically in the reader's mind, thereby obstructing a more flexible and various engagement with the actual letters. An analogy can be drawn to the study of the ancient philosopher Plato. Any number of college students have been exposed in philosophy classes to something called "Platonism," which is defined in terms of certain categories (epistemology, cosmology, metaphysics, ethics, politics), and which can be compared to other philosophical schools on the same points.[32] But the few students who decide to push past their class notes and textbook to an actual reading of the dialogues attributed to Plato discover, usually with some surprise, that it is difficult to find that synthetic "Platonism." They begin to realize that the "Plato" they have been taught has been abstracted from certain dialogues and arranged into a logical system that is nowhere to be found as such in the dialogues themselves. More than that: when they actually begin to read the dialogues in all their particularity and complexity, they begin to discover how much exciting and challenging thought has escaped the usual categories; above all, they find that the true significance of the dialogues lies not in their containing certain doctrines but in their capacity to challenge the mind and give rise to thought.

I am convinced that the same thing happens in historical constructions of "Paul." The construction itself draws evidence selectively from a small subset of letters, and shapes that evidence into a "Paulinism" that is difficult to find in the letters taken as a whole. And, as with the artificial construction called "Platonism," this historical construction misses entirely the true excitement to be found in a direct engagement with Paul's actual arguments, which force readers to perform the difficult task of thinking.

---

32. The habit of so synthesizing ancient teachers and their teachings goes back at least to the biographies of Diogenes Laertius, in his highly influential *Lives of Eminent Philosophers* (ca. third century CE).

By pointing out the deficiencies built into the historical construction of Paul, I by no means want to suggest that we abandon the study of history altogether when reading his letters. To the contrary, a thorough knowledge of the historical circumstances (including the social conditions) attending the composition of Paul's letters is absolutely necessary, if only for the obvious reasons that they were written in a different language, used a rhetoric, employed arguments, and addressed issues of nascent Christian communities in the first-century Mediterranean world. But there is a real difference between studying history in order to better comprehend ancient literature (which is what I advocate) and using bits of ancient literature as sources for the reconstruction of a history (such as the "life" or "thought" of the ancient figure Paul).

Before making the case for the approach I take in this book, it is important to note another sort of construction of Paul within contemporary scholarship, which also uses history in a way distinct from the construction of the historical Paul and takes the canonical Paul—the letters traditionally accepted by the church—as its starting point. The "history of reception" or the "history of interpretation" of various biblical authors and writings has come increasingly to the fore in recent years and represents an extraordinarily important contribution to Christian discourse.[33] In such study, Paul's letters become an element in an intellectual (theological) history: the point is discovering precisely how his writings were understood by later Christian thinkers. Thus, the Paul of Irenaeus, of Origen, of Augustine, of Chrysostom, of Aquinas, of Luther, and of Barth is studied, not in order to freshly engage his letters, but in order to see how his letters functioned within the thought of the respective historical figures, or the life of the church. Tracing such historical development may or may not involve attention to the literary shape and arguments of the letters themselves; it is certainly not necessary in order for the study of the later figures to have integrity.

## Constructing the Canonical Paul

In this work I propose a third sort of construction, not of the life and thought of the "historical Paul," nor of Paul's thought as understood or used by later ecclesiastical commentators and theologians, but of the elements required

---

33. A small sample from a rapidly growing field of study: Mitchell, *Heavenly Trumpet*; Mitchell, *Paul, the Corinthians, and the Birth of Christian Hermeneutics*; Wilken, *Spirit of Early Christian Thought*; F. Young, *Biblical Exegesis*; Blackwell, *Christosis*.

for a responsible reading of the letters ascribed to Paul in the New Testament canon. My effort will be not to fix Paul in the past but to liberate his letters for the present. The essays in this first volume undertake an assessment of all the elements needed for a reader to do serious study of these letters.

Any number of historical questions will come into play in these discussions. But the point in each instance is not to single out any element as singularly critical for understanding Paul's letters, but to provide a sense of how a wide variety of elements must be kept in play when reading his letters. The goal is not to replace such reading but to encourage and enable a direct engagement with his difficult but exhilarating arguments. In the second volume, I provide a sample of such engagements with all of Paul's letters—not in the quest for a synthesis but to illustrate how Paul's letters resist synthesis even as they stimulate thought.

You can legitimately ask how this is a construction of "Paul." In fact, it is not such a construction, if by "construction" we mean a stable entity that can replace the actual reading of his letters. But it *is* a construction in the sense that all of the elements here identified and discussed appear as dimensions of the "life" and "thought" of the assumptive author of all the canonical letters ascribed to him. My aim is to construct a framework within which all of Paul's letters can be read responsibly and profitably, and then playfully to "deconstruct" that framework through a detailed analysis of specific passages and problems within those letters.

Why do I choose the canonical letters as this framework?[34] Because they represent the apostle who has been read and interpreted by the church, not only until the start of the nineteenth century—when the authenticity of letters was first questioned—but even until today. The canonical Paul is the lectionary Paul, the preached Paul, the Paul of theology among those not captive to the dogmas of historical criticism. For the church, the authority of any New Testament composition does not rest on its authorship but on the fact of its canonization.[35] For the church, it does not matter in the slightest whether 1 Timothy was composed by the historical Paul or by a disciple after his death. For the church, 1 Timothy is as much a "letter of Paul" as is Romans or Galatians. The Paul of liturgical reading and preaching is not

---

34. Childs, *Church's Guide for Reading Paul*, appears from its title to be doing much the same thing as I seek to do; in fact, however, Childs in this volume pursues his own vision of what "canonical criticism" means, rather than providing a framework for the reading of the canonical collection. Childs and I do agree on the importance of the terms "canon" and "church" and "Pauline corpus" (or "collection").

35. See L. Johnson, "Authority of the New Testament" and "Bible's Authority."

the "historical Paul" constructed by scholars but the Paul disclosed by such reading and preaching in the assembly.

In this obvious sense, then, the canonical Paul is the "apostle of the church." But he is so in another sense as well. Paul's canonical letters, taken individually and as a collection, reveal a consistent concern for the assembly of believers and pursue the goal that believers become a community with a certain definite character. This concern is obvious in the letters that are explicitly directed to a community readership (Romans, Galatians, 1 and 2 Corinthians, Philippians, Colossians, Ephesians, 1 and 2 Thessalonians). But it is evident as well in the letters addressed to individuals (Philemon, 1 and 2 Timothy, Titus), which all have a semipublic character: a larger community is part of the intended readership. Only 2 Timothy among the canonical letters is a genuinely personal letter, and even 2 Timothy is concerned with the character of Paul's delegate as a teacher of the community. Thus, Paul is the "apostle of the church" also in this thematic sense. Indeed, the capacity of Paul's letters not only to reveal the problems of ancient communities but to shape the Christian identity of subsequent communities through the ages is, in all probability, a major—if largely implicit—reason for his letters being collected and canonized in the first place.[36]

The canonical Paul as the apostle of the church is, then, this book's framework for reading the Pauline collection. I ask my reader to keep constantly in mind that I do not propose to construct a static portrait of "Paul's personality," or "Paul's life," or "Paul's thought." Just the opposite: even as I examine the elements that must go into any responsible reading of Paul's letters, I will do my best to insist that it is the reading of the letters in all their particularity and complexity that is the point. Thus, I will devote chapters to some of the standard topics found in Pauline studies: the sources, what can be said of his life and ministry, the character of his correspondence, aspects of his symbolic world, thematic elements in the letters. In each such discussion, the point will be informing the mind of the reader, rather than supplying a definitive portrait of a historical figure.

And just as my approach resists reducing the Pauline corpus to a subset of letters or reducing the elements of Paul's symbolic world to a single explanatory key, so does it resist elevating one theme within his letters to singular significance. My effort throughout will be to argue for a polythetic rather than monothetic approach to these compositions. I hope to provide the conditions for a fresh and vigorous engagement with each of the letters

36. See L. Johnson, "New Testament as the Church's Book."

in the canonical collection, an engagement that will lead to new discoveries and new questions. I emphatically do not seek to replace such an engaged reading of the letters with a synthesis of my own that already determines what can be found in the letters and answers all questions.

## The Plan of This Work

In the second volume of this work, as I have already stated, I develop a series of studies of Paul's letters ranging across the complete canonical collection. These studies are intended to stimulate precisely the sort of questioning and analysis that can, possibly, give rise to new insight into and a deeper appreciation for the whole range of Paul's letters. They do not provide a complete introduction to or exegesis of each letter. I have done that for each of Paul's letters in my New Testament introduction[37] and, in much greater detail, in several commentaries devoted to Paul's letters.[38] Instead, I want to show how it is possible to push past even such "standard" readings and reach fresh insight through the bold interrogation of texts that are all too familiar.

The present volume serves as an introduction to the studies found in the second volume, but also stands on its own. The essays in this volume deal with most if not all the critical issues pertinent to any genuinely scholarly reading of the canonical collection. With the exception of the discussion of sources, which necessarily demands decisiveness and a certain amount of closure, I mean these essays to provide some orientation for readers while not burdening them with a mountain of detail, and to be suggestive rather than definitive. In the best of fantasies, readers would be able to move back and forth between the essays on diverse aspects of the Pauline letters in this volume and the discrete studies on specific letters in the second volume. Just as the essays in volume 1 provide a framework that guides the reading of volume 2, so do the studies in volume 2 provide substance and depth to the essays in volume 1.

I begin this volume with a set of essays that I think of as a preliminary scaffolding for the construction of Paul (part 1). In these essays the role of historical study will be obvious. First, I work through the issues of sources

---

37. In *Writings of the New Testament*, 227–401, I provide a sketch of Paul's ministry and correspondence and an exegetical engagement with each of the canonical letters.

38. L. Johnson, *Invitation to the Letters of Paul*; *First Timothy, Second Timothy, Titus*; *Letters to Paul's Delegates*; and *First and Second Letters to Timothy*.

from the ground up, considering the apocryphal as well as the canonical writings, and sorting out the question of Acts and the letters, as well as the disputed and undisputed letters. The next essay takes up the question of what we can actually know about Paul's life and ministry, in each case placing an emphasis not on detailed chronology or development but on the character of the elements about which we can have some confidence. The third essay takes up the question of Paul's correspondence, providing an initial sketch of the letters individually and in relation to one another. The fourth essay deals with Paul's place in nascent Christianity by considering three main questions: Can Paul better be understood as the "founder" of Christianity or as a faithful interpreter of the tradition? How many and of what sort were the "opponents" dealt with in his letters? And in what sense is it appropriate to speak of a Pauline "school"?

The second set of essays (part 2) is devoted to aspects of Paul's symbolic world as they are disclosed in the canonical letters. I inquire first into the question of Paul's Jewish identity, which reveals perhaps unexpected complications, and second into the ways in which Paul engages Scripture. Turning to Greco-Roman culture, I ask about Paul and rhetoric, philosophy, and religion, in the process suggesting the level of Greco-Roman education revealed by the canonical letters.

The third set of essays (part 3) takes up elements of content within the letters, treating first the all-important role of experience in Paul's letters, and then considering the dialectic between experience and Paul's modes of discourse. By way of transition to the second volume, I then take up an actual canonical letter, seeking the "voice of Paul" through an appreciation of the Letter to Philemon, read within its canonical context. Finally, I attempt to answer the question pressed by critics of Paul since the eighteenth century and ever more loudly today—namely, whether Paul is an oppressive voice. I take the position that, responsibly read—and such responsible reading is the entire point of my exercise—Paul is more properly understood as a powerful liberating voice within Scripture.

*Part 1*

# PRELIMINARY SCAFFOLDING

# Chapter 1

# Assessing the Sources

In contrast to Jesus and James of Jerusalem, who have at least minimal attestation from extracanonical sources,[1] Paul is not mentioned by any ancient outsider source, a fact that reminds us that we ought not to confuse Paul's canonical dominance and subsequent influence with the impact he had in his own time.[2] There are, however, multiple sources for Paul outside the canonical writings that deserve attention, if only to clear the way for a closer consideration of the sources in the New Testament. Besides providing useful ground-clearing, a cursory look at extracanonical sources also establishes background for a discussion of the critical issues concerning the New Testament Acts and Letters.

The case of James, in fact, offers a helpful point of reference for analyzing the extracanonical sources concerning Paul. In the New Testament, James appears as the author of a letter, briefly in the narrative of Acts (12:17; 15:13–21; 21:18–25), and passingly in Paul's letters (1 Cor 15:7; Gal 1:19; 2:9–12). But a substantial amount of lore concerning James developed in later Christian circles. Some was straightforwardly encomiastic, such as the several accounts of James's martyrdom.[3] But some was also plainly ideological,

---

1. For Jesus, see Josephus, *Antiquities of the Jews* 18.3.3; for James, *Antiquities of the Jews* 20.9.1.

2. It is remarkable both how common and how little noticed this basic fallacy is. The fact that Paul dominates the second portion of the Acts narrative, that he has thirteen letters ascribed to him, and that he is mentioned by 2 Peter 3:15–16 does not justify the position (central since at least the time of F. C. Baur) that Paul was the pivot around which everything in nascent Christianity turned.

3. It is James's death that is recounted in Josephus, *Antiquities of the Jews* 20.9.1. Eusebius reports inconsistent accounts of the martyrdom from Clement of Alexandria (*Ecclesiastical History* 2.1.5) and Hegesippus (*Ecclesiastical History* 3.23.10–18). Even more complexity

advancing a particular vision of Christianity through its depiction of James. One ecclesiastically centered stream of tradition, for example, portrays James as the first bishop of Jerusalem;[4] a set of gnostic compositions sees him as a privileged recipient of revelations;[5] and in the pseudo-Clementine literature, James appears as the champion of a law-observant Christianity, whose opponent is a certain Simon, possibly a stand-in for Paul, described as an opponent of the law and therefore of the Christianity supposedly represented by James.[6] None of these traditions, remarkably, seem to have had the least connection with the canonical letter ascribed to James.

## Traditions about Paul

The earliest—and particularly precious—testimonies concerning Paul come from Clement of Rome (ca. 95), Ignatius of Antioch (ca. 110), and Polycarp of Smyrna (between 110 and 140). They provide evidence for the circulation of Paul's letters and "fill in gaps" of his life and death. Clement writes to the church in Corinth that Peter and Paul together are "righteous pillars of the church [who] were persecuted and contended unto death" (1 Clem. 5.2). Concerning Paul in particular, he writes, "Through jealousy and strife Paul showed the way to the prize of endurance; seven times he was in bond, he was exiled, he was stoned, he was a herald both in the East and in the West, he gained the noble fame of his faith, he taught righteousness in all the world, and when he had reached the limits of the West he gave his testimony before the rulers, and thus passed from the world and was taken up into the Holy Place—the greatest example of endurance" (5.5–7).[7]

Clement also refers explicitly to 1 Corinthians, telling his readers to "take up the epistle of the blessed Paul the Apostle," which Paul wrote to them "at

---

is added by the account in Pseudo-Clementine *Recognitions* 1.70–71, by the Manichaean *Psalms of Heracleides* 192.8–9 and *Psalms of Sarakoth* 142.25–26, and by the gnostic tractate *Second Revelation of James* 61–62.

4. See Eusebius's citations from Clement of Alexandria's *Hypotyposes*, book 6, in *HE* 2.1–3.7, and Hegesippus in *HE* 2.23.4, as well as his own statement that "James was first elected to the throne of the bishopric of the church in Jerusalem" (*HE* 2.1.2).

5. See the gnostic *Gospel of Thomas* 12; *Secret Book of James*; *First Revelation of James*; and *Second Revelation of James*.

6. For this complex literature, see L. Johnson, *Letter of James*, 102–6, and for its connection to Paul, see below.

7. English translation by Lake, *Apostolic Fathers*, 17.

the beginning of his preaching," and displays knowledge of the letter's content (1 Clem. 47.1–4).[8] If the conventional dating of 1 Clement is accepted, this letter from an elder in Rome testifies to the spread of at least one of Paul's letters to that city within about forty years of its composition and about thirty years of Paul's probable death. More fascinating, it takes Paul's journey to Spain and second defense as something of which the Corinthians would be aware. The nonchalance of the notice suggests that such an oral tradition had circulated before Clement's time, and if the tradition was based on guesswork from Romans and 2 Timothy, it supports the position that these letters were already known and associated with Paul.

Ignatius of Antioch mentions Paul twice. In *To the Ephesians* 12.2, he speaks of martyrs and would-be martyrs like himself as "fellow initiates with Paul, who was sanctified, who gained a good report, who was right blessed, in whose footsteps may I be found when I attain to God, who in every epistle makes mention of you in Christ Jesus." As in Clement, Paul is praised for his character and witness. The reference to Paul mentioning the Ephesians in "every epistle" is clearly erroneous if we take the entire canonical collection into account, but it suggests that Ignatius had some group of Paul's letters in which Ephesus is in fact mentioned.[9] In *To the Romans* 4.3, Ignatius urges the church against preventing his martyrdom, stating, "I do not order you as did Peter and Paul; they were apostles, I am a convict; they were free, I am even until now a slave." We note here the similarity to the contrast that Clement had drawn between Paul's generation and his own (1 Clem. 47.4–5).

Sometime before the middle of the second century, Polycarp of Smyrna had been asked by the Philippian church to send them a collection of Ignatius of Antioch's letters. Polycarp composed a missive of his own to accompany that collection, *To the Philippians*, the entire set of compositions delivered by Polycarp's delegate, Crescens (Pol. *Phil.* 14.1). Polycarp speaks of Paul as a model of endurance together with "the other apostles" (Pol. *Phil.* 9.1), and alludes to Paul's praise of the Philippians "in the beginning of his epistle" to them (Pol.

---

8. Without explicit citation but with unmistakable allusion, Clement's letter also reveals knowledge of the Letter to the Hebrews and the Letter of James; see L. Johnson, "Reception of James."

9. Translation by Lake, *Apostolic Fathers*, 187. There are possible allusions or echoes to these letters in Ignatius: 1 Cor 1:20 (Ign. *Eph.* 18.1); 1 Cor 2:10 (Ign. *Phil.* 7.1); 1 Cor 6:9 (Ign. *Phil.* 3.3; *Eph.* 16.1); 1 Cor 3:16 (Ign. *Eph.* 15.2); 1 Cor 5:7 (Ign. *Magn.* 10.2); 1 Cor 9:27 (Ign. *Trall.* 12.2); 1 Cor 10:16–17 (Ign. *Phil.* 4.1); 1 Cor 15:8–9 (Ign. *Rom.* 9.2); 1 Cor 15:12 (Ign. *Trall.* 9.2); Rom 1:3 (Ign. *Eph.* 18.2, 20.2; *Rom.* 7.2; *Smyrn.* 1.1); Phil 4:13 (Ign. *Smyrn.* 4.2); Eph 2:16 (Ign. *Smyrn.* 1.2); Eph 4:2 (Ign. *Pol.* 1.2); Eph 5:25 (Ign. *Pol.* 5.1).

*Phil.* 11.3). But Polycarp also characterizes Paul's ministry and provides a florilegium of Pauline texts. He states, "I write to you concerning righteousness, not at my own instance, but because you first invited me. For neither am I, nor is any other like me, able to follow the wisdom of the blessed and glorious Paul, who when he was with you in the presence of the men of that time taught accurately and steadfastly the word of truth, and also when he was absent wrote letters to you, from the study of which you will be able to build yourselves up into the faith given you" (Pol. *Phil.* 3.1–2).[10] Polycarp proceeds to weave together a set of moral instructions, which he regards as coming from Paul's letters, and in which we can detect loose citations or allusions to many of them (Galatians, Romans, Philippians, 1 and 2 Corinthians), including ones that scholars dispute as authentic (2 Thessalonians, Colossians, Ephesians, 1 and 2 Timothy). Only 1 Thessalonians, Philemon, and Titus are not represented.

The use of Paul changes in the middle of the second century, when his letters are appropriated by Marcion of Sinope (ca. 85–160) as the basis for what he claimed was the only true form of Christianity,[11] using all of Paul's letters—except for the Pastorals, which he rejected[12]—against the Old Testament (sponsored by the evil creator god) and the "Judaizing" elements of the New Testament, a dialectical stance illustrated by his *Antitheses*.[13] In his rebuttal of Marcion, Tertullian (ca. 212) plays the good lawyer and carefully refrains from employing the Pastoral Letters that Marcion rejects, but otherwise draws from all the other letters in the canon; and in his other writings, Tertullian uses the Pastoral Letters as well, considering them authentically Pauline. Similarly, in his massive response to Marcion and the gnostics—among Valentinians, in particular, Paul was popular[14]—Irenaeus of Lyons (ca. 180) employs all the letters attributed to Paul in the canon, including the Pastorals, omitting only Philemon.[15] These exchanges are the beginning of a long history of theological debate in which Paul's canonical letters play a central and controverted role. However fascinating that history is to follow, our present interest is in traditions about Paul himself as sources of knowledge concerning the apostle and his writings.

---

10. Translation by Lake, *Apostolic Fathers*, 287.

11. The best ancient source for Marcion and his teachings is Tertullian, *Against Marcion*, written ca. 212; English text available in *ANF* 3:269–475; the classic study is by Harnack, *Marcion*; see also Lieu, *Marcion*.

12. Tertullian, *Against Marcion* 5.21.

13. See Meeks and Fitzgerald, *Writings of St. Paul*, 286–88.

14. For a sample, see Meeks and Fitzgerald, *Writings of St. Paul*, 272–83.

15. Irenaeus of Lyons, *Against Heresies*; English translation in *ANF* 1:315–567.

Before turning to apocryphal writings attached to Paul, then, we can quickly note further positive statements. The second-century (?) Epistle of the Apostles has the risen Jesus instructing the apostles about the conversion and ministry of Paul.[16] The second-century Acts of Peter repeats the belief we saw already in 1 Clement that Paul preached in Spain before a second trial before Nero.[17] Clement of Alexandria (ca. 215) concludes from Paul's reference to "my true companion" (Phil 4:3) that he was married.[18] Ambrosiaster (late fourth century) argued Paul worked harder than any other apostle because he practiced his trade as well as preached.[19] John Chrysostom (ca. 390) devoted a series of encomiastic homilies to Paul as the exemplar of virtue.[20] Jerome can appropriately conclude this list with his entry on Paul in his *On Illustrious Men* (late fourth century), which once more states that Paul preached in the West before having a second trial and being beheaded under Nero in the year 68; Jerome lists all thirteen of Paul's letters, carefully distinguishing the Letter to the Hebrews on the grounds of "style and language," supposing it to be the work of Barnabas, or Luke the Evangelist, or Clement of Rome. He notes that "some read one also to the Laodiceans, but it is rejected by everyone."[21]

As I noted earlier, however, not everyone praised Paul. He was criticized by some Hellenistic critics of Christianity,[22] but even more severely by Jewish Christians who saw him as "the enemy" whose liberating message for gentiles was perceived as inimical to their own law-observant version of the gospel. It is important to emphasize, despite some scholarly opinion, that the canonical Letter of James should not be read as an anti-Pauline

16. Text in J. K. Elliott, *Apocryphal New Testament*, 576–77.

17. Text in J. K. Elliott, *Apocryphal New Testament*, 399–401.

18. Clement of Alexandria, *Stromateis* 3.53; Clement also passes on a tradition that has Paul making use of the *Sibylline Oracles* in *Stromateis* 6.5; for text, see Meeks and Fitzgerald, *Writings of St. Paul*, 216.

19. For the short excerpt from Ambrosiaster's *Commentary on 2 Corinthians*, see Meeks and Fitzgerald, *Writings of St. Paul*, 213.

20. John Chrysostom, *In Praise of Saint Paul*, translated and analyzed by Mitchell, *Heavenly Trumpet*.

21. For text, see Meeks and Fitzgerald, *Writings of St. Paul*, 210–11.

22. The earliest was Celsus (late second century) in his *True Word* (to which Origen responded with *Against Celsus*), although he did not make Paul his particular target—apart from mocking the Christians' preferring foolishness to wisdom (see 1 Cor 1:18–25). Paul is more of a target in the fourth-century attacks by Julian, *Against the Galileans* 106 a–c, 327 a–b, and Porphyry, *Against the Christians*; for excerpts in translation, see Meeks and Fitzgerald, *Writings of St. Paul*, 265–71.

composition.[23] Epiphanius (ca. 375) reports on the Ebionites that they "slander Paul, using certain charges trumped up by the malice and error of their pseudo-apostles."[24] By far the most important (and most difficult to disentangle) Jewish-Christian hostility to Paul is expressed in the so-called Pseudo-Clementine literature, which is a complex set of novelistic compositions from sometime before the fourth century[25] but possibly containing earlier sources.[26] Among such hypothetical earlier sources is The Ascents of James, found within the *Recognitions*.[27] It pictures James as leading a debate with Jewish leaders and almost winning them over, before "the hostile man"—later identified as Paul—disrupts the meeting and almost kills James by throwing him from the steps of the temple.[28] There are also sections of the Pseudo-Clementine *Homilies* that contain Peter's polemic against "Simon Magus," which some scholars take to be a veiled attack on Paul.[29] With the Pseudo-Clementine writings, however, we find ourselves entering into another category of sources for Paul—namely, apocryphal literature.

Before turning attention to the Acts and Apocalypses and letters that seek to portray Paul—all more positively than the hostile witnesses I have just reviewed—through such acts of imaginative art, it is helpful to review what has been learned from the first set of witnesses surveyed. First, apart from his martyrdom, the earliest traditions about Paul are largely dependent on the canonical letters; even the modest "filling in of the gaps" (such as Paul having a wife, or working long hours, or preaching in Spain) are drawn by inference from hints in his letters, and the more extravagant portrayal of opposition between Peter (and James) and Paul could derive from an ideologically driven reading of the letters. Second, with the exception of his champion Marcion on one side and his enemies the Jewish Christians on the other, Paul is less noted as a theologian than as a moral teacher and model of endurance (see above all Polycarp). Third, again with the exception of Mar-

<hr/>

23. Contra Martin Hengel's attempt to make it so in "Der Jakobusbriefe" (translation in Meeks and Fitzgerald, *Writings of St. Paul*, 242–53), a position rejected even by the earliest Tübingen critics; see, e.g., Kern, *Der Charakter und Ursprung des Briefes Jacobi*; see the discussion in L. Johnson, *Letter of James*, 58–63, 143–55.

24. See *Panarion* 28.5.1–3, 30.16.6–9; translation in Meeks and Fitzgerald, *Writings of St. Paul*, 229–30.

25. For the complex composition, see L. Johnson, *Letter of James*, 103–5.

26. See F. Jones, "Pseudo-Clementines."

27. See *Recognitions* 1.33.3–69.8, 1.70.1–71.6.

28. For English translation and analysis, see Van Voorst, *Ascents of James*.

29. See, e.g., Strecker, *Das Judenchristentum in den Pseudoklementinen*, 187–96.

cion, these sources affirm the canonical collection, including the Pastorals, while denying the Pauline authorship of Hebrews on the grounds of style and rejecting the Letter to the Laodiceans altogether. In short, the sources so far considered build on but do not significantly add to what is stated or implied by the canonical sources.

## Apocryphal Compositions

### Apocalypses

Two extant compositions called "apocalypses" feature Paul as one who ascends the heavenly realms through a visionary experience. Each is plainly based on Paul's own account in 2 Cor 12:1–4 of having gone up into the third heaven—"snatched into paradise"—and heard words he was not able to express.[30] The first is the *Visio Pauli* or Apocalypse of Paul, probably composed in the mid-third century.[31] Paul plays the passive role of seer. The descriptions of the fate awaiting those who had died had a significant impact on later descriptions of the afterlife,[32] but the composition adds nothing helpful to our store of knowledge about Paul. The second is the much shorter Revelation of Paul in Coptic found in the Nag Hammadi codices (V, 2).[33] This vision also depicts the fates of sinners but has Paul ascend to the tenth heaven, where he is at the end united with the twelve apostles. Like the *Visio Pauli*, the gnostic apocalypse fills in the gap opened by Paul's allusive account in 2 Cor 12:1–4.

### Acts

In the second and third centuries, narrative accounts of several apostles were produced, among the earliest being the Acts of Paul.[34] The three largest co-

---

30. For the interpretation of the passage in the Greek patristic tradition, see Wallace, *Snatched into Paradise*.

31. Translation in J. K. Elliott, *Apocryphal New Testament*, 616–44.

32. See Henning, *Educating Early Christians*.

33. Introduction and translation by George W. MacRae and William R. Murdock in J. M. Robinson, *Nag Hammadi Library in English*, 239–41.

34. In *On Baptism* 17 (ca. 180), Tertullian says it was written by a presbyter in Asia who (on the basis of Thecla) advocated ministry for women. The other compositions devoted to the deeds of the apostles are the Acts of Thomas, the Acts of Peter, the Acts of Andrew,

herent sections of the composition are (1) the Acts of Paul and Thecla, which circulated independently in association with the cult of the female saint; (2) a Corinthian Correspondence, containing a letter from the Corinthians and an answering letter by Paul (more on which below); and (3) the Martyrdom of Paul, which also circulated independently. The remainder of the material in the Acts of Paul relates Paul's travels and wonders, from Damascus to Rome.[35] Like the other narratives about apostles composed in the same time frame, the Acts of Paul owes something to the precedent set by the canonical Acts of the Apostles, but more closely resembles the Greco-Roman novels that were popular in the same period.[36]

The narrative has a number of distinctive features in addition to providing a physical description of Paul (Acts of Paul 3).[37] As in the canonical Acts, Paul is a wonder-worker: he has visions, heals the sick, exorcizes demons, escapes prison, baptizes a lion, raises from the dead; at his beheading, milk spills on the executioner's tunic. Paul preaches in the form of beatitudes that emphasize the purity of the body: "Blessed are the bodies of the virgins, for they shall be well pleasing to God, and shall not lose the reward of their chastity" (Acts of Paul 6). He is portrayed as a disrupter of households, precisely because his message of continence leads young women to forsake marriage (Acts of Paul 9, 12, 15). The narrative is striking most of all for the positive and powerful role given to Thecla, who is bold and courageous (Acts of Paul 25–28, 33, 37), baptizes herself, cuts her hair, dresses like a man, and declares her intention to preach; only at the end does Paul respond to her, "Go and preach the word of God" (Acts of Paul 40–41).

The Acts of Paul most surprises by its apparent familiarity with the Pastoral Letters. The place name Iconium and the character names Onesiphorus, Demas, Hermogenes the coppersmith, and Titus recall especially 2 Timothy, as does the strange echo of 2 Tim 2:18 in the declaration of Demas and Hermogenes that "we shall teach you about the resurrection which he says is to come, that it has already taken place in the children and that we rise again, having come to the knowledge of the true God" (Acts of Paul 14).

---

and the Acts of John. For translation of the Acts of Paul, see J. K. Elliott, *Apocryphal New Testament*, 350–89; for discussion of the religious sensibility found in the several Acts, see L. Johnson, *Among the Gentiles*, 172–83, 365–71.

35. See the analysis by J. K. Elliott, *Apocryphal New Testament*, 350–57.

36. See Thomas, *Acts of Peter*. To be sure, the canonical Acts also has some traits of the ancient novel; see Pervo, *Profit with Delight*.

37. See Malherbe, "Physical Description of Paul."

The Acts of Paul reverses the position in the Pastorals: here the ascetical Paul subverts traditional marriage and the domestic order, whereas the Paul of the Pastorals affirms both (1 Tim 2:15; 4:3–4; 5:14; Titus 2:2–5). The difference is so striking that some scholars propose that the Pastorals and Acts of Paul represent an ideological battle within a later Pauline tradition concerning the role of women in the church: Should they be active and preach, or stay within the household?[38] This is not the place to rehearse those arguments.[39] Certainly the Paul of the "undisputed" letters is ambiguous enough on the role of women, but postulating a direct conflict between the Pastorals and the Acts of Paul on a single subject oversimplifies.[40]

More pertinent to the present survey is the status of the Acts of Paul as a source for the life or thought of the apostle. Its overall novelistic character, its hagiographical portrayal of Thecla, its failure to convey even an echo of the concerns of Paul found in the canonical letters, its lack of genuine knowledge concerning Judaism or Paul's Jewish context, its romantic portrayal of the politics of the Roman Empire, and its clumsy effort to imitate Paul's correspondence all locate the Acts of Paul and Thecla as an act of imagination that has only the loosest connection to historical realities. The same is true of three other apocryphal writings associated with Paul composed in the fifth century or later: the Acts of Timothy,[41] the Acts of Titus,[42] and the Epistle of Pseudo-Dionysius the Areopagite to Timothy Concerning the Deaths of the Apostles Peter and Paul.[43]

## Letters

There are actually fewer extracanonical letters ascribed to Paul than one might expect. In the Acts of Paul, which had earlier offered a sample of Paul's preaching that sounds more like Jesus (6), we also find a letter from the Corinthian community to Paul and a letter from Paul to the Corinthians (designated 3 Corinthians). It has a few echoes of Pauline phrases recognizable from the canonical collection: "become alive by adoption" (8), "not children of righ-

38. See, e.g., D. MacDonald, "Virgins, Widows, and Paul"; S. Davies, *Revolt of the Widows*; Bassler, "Widow's Tale."

39. I take up the question in L. Johnson, *First and Second Letters to Timothy*, 259–76.

40. See especially the nuanced and responsible approach of Hylen, *Modest Apostle*.

41. Translation and discussion by Concannon, "Acts of Timothy."

42. Translation and discussion by Pervo, "Acts of Titus."

43. Translation and discussion by Eastman, "Epistle of Pseudo-Dionysius."

teousness but of wrath" (19), "how much more will he raise you up, who have believed in Christ Jesus, as he himself was raised up" (31), "let no man trouble me" (34), "I bear his marks" (36). But the bulk of the letter contains language and ideas reflective of a later period. The purported letter, after all, takes the form of answering questions posed by the Corinthians concerning doctrinal points some are denying. Thus, Paul is asked to address whether Jesus came in the flesh and was born of Mary (14), and Paul responds, "Our Lord Jesus Christ was born of Mary of the seed of David, the Father having sent the spirit from heaven into her" (6). Discussing the resurrection, the letter uses the analogy of seeds (as Paul does in 1 Cor 15:38) but combines it with the example of Jonah and the whale (found in Matt 12:39–41). In short, the letter offers few reasons to take it seriously as a production of Paul himself, and many reasons to regard it as a composition of a significantly later date (late second century?) by someone having some rough awareness of Pauline diction.

A classic example of an apocryphal writing seeking to "fill the gaps" in canonical compositions is the Epistle to the Laodiceans.[44] In Col 4:16 Paul makes reference to a letter he wrote to the Laodiceans, wanting the Colossian community and the Laodiceans to exchange letters. It is not in the canonical collection, so the way was open for some pious admirer of Paul to supply the want. The extant text may be from as early as the second century (the Muratorian Canon mentions such a letter). In contrast to 3 Corinthians, this composition reveals genuine knowledge of some of Paul's letters and weaves together Pauline phrases drawn especially from Galatians and Philippians.[45] It consequently has no distinctive voice of its own—there is no discernible argument—and its entire goal is expressed in its last line, "And see that (this epistle) is read to the Colossians and that of the Colossians to you" (20). Being in effect a florilegium drawn from Paul's letters, it adds nothing to our knowledge of the apostle.

Finally, the charming set of compositions known as the Correspondence of Paul and Seneca[46] exploits the opening provided by the facts that Paul and the Roman philosopher were contemporaries, both wrote letters, and both had contact with the emperor Nero. Eight of the short letters—actually notes—are from Seneca to the apostle, and six from Paul to the philosopher. Probably composed in the fourth century, the fictional letters presuppose a Pauline corpus: Seneca tells Paul, "I enjoyed reading your letters to the Galatians, to the

---

44. Translation and discussion in J. K. Elliott, *Apocryphal New Testament*, 543–46.
45. E.g., Gal 1:3, 11; 6:18; Phil 1:2, 3, 12, 13, 18, 19–20, 21; 2:2, 12, 13, 14; 3:1; 4:6, 8, 9, 22, 23.
46. Translation and discussion in J. K. Elliott, *Apocryphal New Testament*, 547–53.

Corinthians, and to the Achaeans" (7); Paul notes, "I ought, as I have often claimed, to be all things to all men" (10). The philosopher sees Paul as having a superior wisdom (2, 7, 12), but criticizes his style of writing: "I do wish you would obey me and comply with the pure Latin style" (13). The apostle in turn encourages Seneca to preach to the imperial court: "You must make of your-self a new herald of Jesus Christ by displaying with the praises of rhetoric that blameless wisdom which you have almost achieved" (14). Taken as a whole, the correspondence seeks to demonstrate the superiority of the Christian way by having one of Rome's most respected philosophers pay it court.[47]

A few summary remarks on the apocryphal Pauline literature are appro-priate. First, both external (textual) evidence and internal references within these compositions place them between the middle of the second century to the fifth century or even later. Second, the two apocalypses in which Paul figures as visionary are both based on the account of Paul's ascent in 2 Cor 12:1–4. Third, the Acts of Paul is a novelistic account (much like the other Acts of the apostles) that tells a completely different story than does canonical Acts; it ignores completely any Jewish context for Paul's life; it fails to give any sense of the content of his preaching or teaching found in the canonical sources; and it lacks any of the historical verisimilitude (and partial verifiability) of the canonical Acts. Finally, the apocryphal letters as-cribed to Paul are—with the partial exception of Laodiceans—stylistically at a great distance from the canonical letters; they evince no engagement with local circumstances or persons in the manner of all the canonical letters apart from Ephesians; they lack any Jewish context or employment of Scripture; and, apart from the "fill the gaps" piety of Laodiceans, they reflect signifi-cantly later concerns, such as Christianity's relationship to pagan philosophy and correct doctrine concerning the incarnation and Mary.

Scholars are quite right, then, to dismiss the apocryphal writings as im-portant sources for Paul's life and thought. In taking the time to assess these sources, however, we remind ourselves of an important point: the accep-tance or rejection of any composition is a matter of judgment and the careful application of criteria. It ought not to be a matter of taste or, worse, majority opinion that guides such judgment. In the case of the sources we have been surveying, such judgment is fairly easy and enjoys universal approval. But confirming a judgment that a source is spurious rather than authentic (as with the apocryphal letters) still requires something more than lazy assent. The point becomes more pertinent as we turn to the canonical sources.

---

47. See Malherbe, "'Seneca' on Paul as Letter Writer."

## Canonical Sources

### The Acts of the Apostles

The two-volume composition commonly referred to as Luke-Acts consists of the Gospel of Luke and the Acts of the Apostles.[48] They are written by the same author, conventionally designated as the evangelist Luke, and together form a literary whole, a narrative that stretches from the hill country of Galilee to the city of Rome, from the birth of Jesus to the captivity of Paul, across a period of decades. The story of Jesus in the Gospel anticipates the account of the church in Acts, and the account of Jesus's prophetic successors in Acts constantly echoes the portrayal of Jesus as the prophet who brings God's visitation to the people. The narrative of Luke-Acts works out a theological argument concerning on one side God's extension of salvation to the gentiles and on the other side God's fidelity to his promises to Israel.[49] It is within this overall argument that the portrayal of Paul appears in Acts 8:1–9:30; 11:25–30; 13:1–28:31; like Jesus and the other apostles, Paul is portrayed in prophetic terms: he is filled with the Holy Spirit, he proclaims the Word of God, he works signs and wonders, and he creates responses of both acceptance and rejection.[50] The very nature of Luke's overall presentation therefore has Paul play a role that is coordinated with that of other witnesses, and in continuity with the work of Jesus himself.

Such attention given to the gentile mission and to Christianity's relationship with Judaism immediately sets Luke-Acts apart from the apocryphal Pauline literature, where neither concern is evident, and makes plausible a dating of the composition within decades of the death of the apostle. The literary unity of Acts and Luke's Gospel points to a single author, and given the conventional dating of the Gospel of Luke around 85 CE, a similar date for Acts is not unreasonable.[51] The prologue to the Gospel (1:1–4) presents the entire work as a form of history: the author knows of earlier narratives, has used sources, and has done his own research. Allowing for the *kind* of history Luke writes—a form of apologetic for the Christian movement, for

48. The designation took hold especially because of the pioneering work of Cadbury, *Making of Luke-Acts*.

49. For orientation to Luke-Acts, see in particular the introductions to L. Johnson, *Gospel of Luke*, and *Acts of the Apostles*.

50. L. Johnson, *Prophetic Jesus, Prophetic Church*.

51. A second-century dating for Acts has been advanced by, among others, Pervo, *Dating Acts*, but I find the reasons given for that dating unpersuasive.

Paul, and above all for the faithfulness of God[52]—there is every reason to regard it as no less historical in character than the similarly interested writings of Josephus.[53]

As for Luke's sources, we are able to detect his use of Mark and Q in the Gospel part of his narrative, simply because we have Mark and Matthew for comparison; if they were not extant, we would not be able to find them within Luke's seamless prose. In the case of Acts, the quest for specific sources employed by Luke has proven mostly frustrating.[54] The first eight chapters of Acts consist of a handful of specific incidents given a sense of amplitude through the generous use of speeches and summaries. The parts of Acts dealing with Paul have more detail and circumstantial detail, suggesting the use (at least) of an itinerary as a source.[55]

The truly critical question is whether Luke knew or used Paul's letters in the composition of the Acts narrative. Those who assign Acts to the second century understandably also argue that Luke used some of the letters: the consonance between his account of Paul's movements in chapter 16–21 and the movements and plans in 1 Thessalonians, 1 and 2 Corinthians, and Romans is, in fact, notable. But Galatians, Philippians, and Philemon (leaving aside the disputed letters) don't fit within the Acts framework, and even when the basic movements recounted in the letters and Acts agree, the many small discrepancies between them argue more for Luke's independent knowledge than a use of Paul's letters. Strikingly, Luke never suggests that Paul even wrote letters. In short, Acts is better regarded as an independent source of knowledge about Paul from the late first century, rather than a second-century composition that used his letters in the shaping of its narrative of Paul.

How reliable is Acts as a historical source, bearing in mind its religious purposes and literary shaping? In general, it is impressively accurate in matters of local detail. Luke knows the correct titles, functions, and times of tenure of local officials. He conveys the local color of different regions. The practices he describes correspond to the practices we know about from other

---

52. See Sterling, *Historiography and Self-Definition*.

53. Contemporary critics are fully aware of the biases displayed in Josephus's *Against Apion*, *Jewish War*, and *Antiquities of the Jews* (written between 75 and 100 CE), while still regarding these compositions as indispensable sources for our knowledge of Judaism in the first century CE.

54. See Dupont, *Sources of Acts*.

55. The shift from third-person to first-person narration in the so-called we passages suggests, but does not prove, the participation of an eyewitness; see Cadbury, "'We' and 'I' Passages"; Praeder, "Problem of First-Person Narration."

sources.[56] In these respects, Acts is recognizably more grounded in the facts of the first-century Mediterranean world than are the apocryphal Acts. As we shall see in the next chapter, moreover, when Paul's movements in Acts are compared to those reported in his letters, they provide a reliable if partial framework for reconstructing parts of Paul's career; we will look also at the two major discrepancies between the sources concerning important events: the decision of the church concerning the gentiles, and Paul's collection.

On the question of historical accuracy, however, three cautionary remarks are necessary. First, the speeches put in Paul's mouth are entirely Lukan inventions and cannot be taken as evidence for Paul's own views.[57] Second, Luke's literary invention places Paul in settings and scenes evocative of Hellenistic models,[58] and his characterization of Paul is shaped by prophetic imagery drawn from Scripture. Third, we must remember the difference between getting Paul's world right and recounting his story accurately in every respect. The imaginative evocation of time and place, after all, is a feature of good historical fiction as much as it is of sober historiography. But we must also remember that if history aspires to be something more than a sheer chronicle, it also must employ fictional techniques in the construction of a narrative.

In sum, Acts is an invaluable secondhand primary source for knowledge of Paul's life and ministry, but not for his thought, written within decades of Paul's death, providing an essential narrative framework within which some of Paul's letters can be located; and even when it diverges on certain points from those letters, it offers a portrait of the apostle that is, in broad terms, historically more plausible than any of the apocryphal writings.

## Non-Pauline Letters

Although the opinion that the Letter of James was from the first an anti-Pauline polemic is extreme and indefensible,[59] a long scholarly tradition

---

56. See esp. Marshall, *Luke*; Hemer, *Book of Acts*.

57. See Dibelius, "Speeches in Acts"; L. Johnson, *Septuagintal Midrash*; Wason, "'All Things to All People.'"

58. At Lystra, Paul and Barnabas are taken to be Hermes and Zeus (Acts 14:8–18), a scene that recalls Ovid's tale of Baucis and Philemon (*Metamorphoses* 8:613–738); Paul's speech in Athens echoes Plato's and Xenophon's accounts of the trial of Socrates (*Apology*); Paul's reception by the natives of Malta recalls a similar scene in Dio Chrysostom's *Euboean Discourse (Oration 7)*.

59. See Hengel, "Der Jakobusbriefe." As Joseph B. Mayor sagely observes, given their

reads James as a reaction to an "antinomian" tendency within Paulinism, requiring an assertion of the necessity of both faith and works.[60] If such were the case, then James would represent a canonical witness to Pauline controversies after the death of the apostle. But besides erroneously reducing Paul to Galatians and Romans, and James to the thirteen verses where the language of faith and works occurs (2:14–26), careful analysis suggests that the Letter of James is at least as early as Paul's letters and that James's language about faith and works does not directly counter Paul's position. James and Paul should therefore be read independently of each other.[61]

The Second Letter of Peter is certainly a pseudonymous composition and probably the latest composition included in the New Testament canon, though it is not necessary to date it later than the first decade of the second century.[62] Telling his readers that they should consider the "patience/long-suffering" (*makrothymia*) of the Lord as salvation (2 Pet 3:15), the author continues, "So also our beloved brother Paul wrote to you according to the wisdom given him, speaking of this as he does in all his letters.[63] There are some things in them hard to understand, which the ignorant and unstable twist to their own destruction, as they do the other scriptures" (3:15–16). The statement is quite remarkable on three points: first, it speaks of "all his letters," assuming at least some sort of collection; second, it is aware of a tradition of disputed interpretation; third, it implicitly identifies Paul's letters as having the same authority as "other scriptures" (*tas loipas graphas*). The statement supports the relatively late dating of 2 Peter, but even as it aligns the author with Paul and "all his letters," it does not offer anything significant to our knowledge of Paul's life, ministry, or correspondence.

## Canonical Pauline Letters

Thirteen letters are attributed to Paul in the New Testament canon: Romans, 1 and 2 Corinthians, Galatians, 1 and 2 Thessalonians, Philippians, Ephesians, Colossians, 1 and 2 Timothy, Titus, and Philemon. The process

---

respective positions in the first century, it is just as logically possible to imagine that Paul was responding to James! See Mayor, *Epistle of Saint James*, xci–cii, clxxxiii–clxxxviii.

60. See the succinct statement of the position by Jeremias, "Paul and James."

61. For full discussion, see L. Johnson, *Letter of James*, 58–63, 111–14, 156.

62. See L. Johnson, *Writings of the New Testament*, 437–47.

63. Although this is not entirely correct, Paul does speak of *makrothymia* in Rom 2:4; 9:22; 2 Cor 6:6; Gal 5:22; Eph 4:2; Col 1:11; 3:12; 1 Tim 1:16; 2 Tim 3:10; 4:2.

of canonization did not entirely lack critical discernment.[64] The Letter to the Laodiceans, for example, while by no means heretical, was rejected as spurious, as was the Acts of Paul.[65] And the Letter to the Hebrews, thought by many to be by Paul, even appearing after Romans in our earliest manuscript of Paul's letters (P 46), was eventually attributed to one of several candidates other than Paul, precisely on the grounds of style.[66] It is worth noting that the ancient speakers and readers of Greek who detected such divergence in the case of Hebrews never caviled with respect to any of the other thirteen letters.

No challenge was put to the Pauline authorship of the canonical collection, in fact, until the nineteenth century. Not even the highly skeptical critics of the Enlightenment, who vigorously disputed the Letter of James, found any reason to challenge the authorship of Colossians, Ephesians, or the Pastorals.[67] Reformation interpreters, likewise, read all thirteen letters as thoroughly Pauline. Martin Luther was keenly sensitive to the differences between Paul and James, leading him to dismiss the Letter of James from the "proper books" of the New Testament.[68] But he found no conflict between 1 Timothy and Galatians on the question of the law, commenting on 1 Tim 1:5, "Now these are deep and genuinely Pauline words, and because they are very rich, we must explain them somewhat in order that we may understand it a little and become accustomed to his language."[69]

The challenge to the Pauline authorship of the entire canonical collection began with Friedrich Schleiermacher's questioning of the authenticity of 1 Timothy—by comparing it to 2 Timothy and Titus![70] Schleiermacher's critique was quickly extended by J. G. Eichorn, W. M. L. de Wette, and F. C. Baur to include other canonical writings;[71] in his monograph on Paul, Baur concluded that only four of the letters ascribed to Paul were actually by him (Romans, 1 and 2 Corinthians, Galatians), while 1 and 2 Thessalonians, Co-

---

64. For the process, see Mitton, *Pauline Corpus*; Trobisch, *Paul's Letter Collection*.

65. See the Muratorian Canon and other documents pertinent to canonization conveniently gathered in Holladay, *Introduction to the New Testament*, 941–51.

66. See Eusebius, *Ecclesiastical History* 6.25.3–14.

67. See the review of patristic and medieval interpretation of the Pastorals in L. Johnson, *Letters to Timothy*, 26–35.

68. Luther, "Preface to the New Testament (1522)."

69. Luther, "Sermons on the Sum of Christian Life."

70. Schleiermacher, *Über den sogenannten Ersten Brief des Paulos*.

71. Eichorn, *Einleitung in das Neue Testament*; de Wette, *Historico-Critical Introduction*, 298–304; Baur, *Die sogennanten Pastoralbriefe*.

lossians, Ephesians, Philippians, and Philemon, in addition to the Pastorals, were of doubtful authenticity.[72] The floodgates of criticism were open, and despite vigorous responses to the challenge,[73] scholars even more radical than F. C. Baur challenged the Pauline authorship of all the letters ascribed to him: they all came from the century, but they were all forgeries.[74] Such a sweeping conclusion left little that could be considered nascent Christianity, and nothing that could be regarded as genuinely Pauline. Bruno Bauer represents an extreme, but his radical position indicates how, once the process of dismantling is begun, it does not have any natural stopping point.

A compromise position was adopted by more moderate scholars, which enabled them to claim the title of critics while still retaining the Paul that they most treasured: the four letters accepted by F. C. Baur plus Philippians, Philemon, and 1 Thessalonians were accepted as genuine (or "undisputed"); Colossians, Ephesians, and 2 Thessalonians were placed in the "disputed" category; and the Pastorals were definitively excluded from the Pauline corpus. The great authority of H. J. Holtzmann helped secure this compromise position, which continued to represent scholarly orthodoxy to the present time.[75] Although arguments continued to be made for the authenticity of all Paul's letters (often by great scholars), the compromise position—so serviceable for the dominant framework of New Testament studies—hardened to what is sometimes called a scholarly consensus, but may more accurately be designated an academic dogma, since the majority of those now holding it have not actually done the hard work of examining and testing the arguments for and against it.[76] Albert Schweitzer accurately summarized the predictable consequences:

> Not even the most conservative of critics had the boldness to place all the letters which have come down under the name of Paul on a footing of equality. Even those who regarded the Epistles to the Ephesians and Colossians as genuine did not fuse the ideas of these Epistles with the system extracted from the four main Epistles, but presented them separately; and any who

72. Baur, *Paulus, der Apostel Jesu Christi.*

73. Most impressively by Wiesinger, *Biblical Commentary.*

74. Above all, see B. Bauer, *Kritik der paulinischen Briefe.*

75. Holtzmann, *Lehrbuch der historisch-kritisch Einleitung.*

76. The dogmatism of this statement by Jack T. Sanders is not exceptional: "That Colossians, Ephesians, 2 Thessalonians, 1 and 2 Timothy, Titus, and 1 Peter are pseudonymous and imitate Paul's style and thought is not to be debated here but rather accepted as the assured result of critical historical scholarship." *Ethics in the New Testament,* 67.

were not converted to the rejection of the Pastorals at all events took the precaution to give a separate chapter to the Pauline theology of these writings. If only the personal references might be saved, these Epistles were as completely excluded from the presentation of the Pauline system as if they had been pronounced wholly spurious.[77]

The criteria for judging a composition Pauline or non-Pauline have not changed since the first challenges by Schleiermacher and Baur: (1) fit within the ministry of Paul as reconstructed from the (uncontested) letters and Acts; (2) style of composition; (3) nature of opponents; (4) organization of the church; and (5) consistency in theme, embracing law and faith, salvation, eschatology, and ethics. At this point in the history of Pauline scholarship, few critics bother examining either the formal or material validity of the criteria, since the "consensus" obviates any such need. But it is important, especially for any adopting a non-consensus position, to assess the strength and weakness of the arguments arranged under these criteria.

Only the first criterion is actually "hard": if we had a complete account of Paul's movements, and a letter claimed to come from a time or place contrary to what we knew, then we could disqualify it. But, in fact, we do not have such a complete account of Paul's movements. Take two examples. First, Acts tells of Pauline captivities in Philippi (16:24–34), Caesarea (23:35–26:32), and Rome (28:16–31), and Paul himself speaks of multiple imprisonments (2 Cor 11:23); but none of these provides a fully satisfying location for even the "undisputed" captivity letters, Philippians and Philemon, so that some scholars have actually invented an Ephesian captivity (for which there is no positive evidence) to support a theory of multiple exchanges between Paul and the Philippians.[78] Second, the criterion is unevenly applied: neither Acts nor the other letters can provide a compelling date or location for the Letter to the Galatians, yet it is so universally acknowledged as Pauline that the question of its fit within Paul's ministry is waived; conversely, according to the other criteria usually applied, the "authenticity" of 1 Thessalonians might easily be challenged, but because its internal evidence overlaps so nicely with that in Acts, it is universally accepted as genuine.

The criterion of style can include diction, grammar, syntax, mode of citation, and manner of argumentation. We have seen that the early church decided that Hebrews could not be by Paul on these grounds. Remarkably,

---

77. Schweitzer, *Paul and His Interpreters*, 27.
78. See, e.g., Duncan, "Paul's Ministry in Asia."

no other of the canonical letters was so challenged before Schleiermacher, and he only caviled at a handful of word choices in 1 Timothy. The criterion is notoriously subjective, especially when applied by people who learned Greek laboriously and partially in seminary rather than as a native language. It also pays insufficient attention to four things: (1) the diversity of style even within the undisputed letters (compare Romans to 1 Thessalonians); (2) the influence of subject matter and situation on modes of epistolary discourse; (3) the ancient rhetorical ideal of *prosōpopoiia* ("writing in character"), which employed distinctive modes for diverse audiences and settings; and (4) the complex character of Pauline compositions (more on this in the next chapter).[79]

The two criteria of opponents and church order can be dealt with quickly, since both are based on false premises. On the opponents, the Tübingen School saw the authentic Paul as engaged in an ongoing battle against a unified front of "Judaizers" representing James and Peter, whereas the inauthentic letters showed a battle against gnostics of one form or another.[80] That picture is inadequate. First, in some circumstances it is not clear that Paul is combatting actual living opponents (see Galatians, Colossians) so much as local deviations. Second, greater knowledge of both Jewish Christianity and Gnosticism has complicated the too simple schema adopted by Tübingen and its followers.[81] As for church order, the classic trajectory from a charismatic community (the authentic Paul) in the first century to an institution (the Pastorals) in the second century that is so confidently sketched by historical critics,[82] not only is sociologically naive, but fails to reckon with the elements of institution found in the undisputed letters, which are not at all discordant with those found in the Pastorals.[83]

The most frequent criterion applied by contemporary commentators, especially by those who have not thoroughly examined the issue as a whole, is thematic consistency, which can include the topics of salvation, law, faith, eschatology, and ethics.[84] The disputed composition is said to

79. For more on this, see L. Johnson, *Letters to Timothy*, 68–72.

80. For a sampling, see Baur, *Die sogennanten Pastoralbriefe*; Mangold, *Die Irrlehrer der Pastoralbriefe*; Georgi, *Opponents of Paul*; Jewett, "Agitators and the Galatian Community" and "Conflicting Movements"; Meeks and Francis, *Conflict at Colossae*.

81. On Jewish Christianity, see R. Brown, "Not Jewish Christianity." On the complexities of "Gnosticism," see Bianchi, *Le Origini dello Gnosticismo*; Layton, *Rediscovery of Gnosticism*.

82. See Campenhausen, *Ecclesiastical Authority*; Brosch, *Charismen und Ämter*.

83. See L. Johnson, "Rise of Church Order."

84. A sample: Mitton, *Ephesians*; Best, *Epistle to the Ephesians*; Lohse, *Colossians and*

be divergent in one respect or another from Paul's usual position in the undisputed letters, and therefore to be reckoned as inauthentic. There is, no doubt, some formal validity to the criterion: if a composition were flatly to deny or distort one such element found in another letter, that would certainly raise questions. If, for example, a putative Pauline letter argued against faith, hope, and love, or if it were to advance the proposition that observance of the law were sufficient for salvation, then serious doubts as to its Pauline origin would be legitimate. The discrepancies identified in the disputed letters fall far short of these obvious cases and represent variations on Pauline themes rather than deviations from them. The premise of absolute consistency in theme is, however, dubious in the case of an apostle who wrote letters in response to local circumstances rather than composed systematic philosophical tractates. In any case, as I have already indicated in my introduction, there is significant diversity on many Pauline themes even within the undisputed letters.

In fact, the entire disputation concerning the authorship of Paul's letters has been haunted by a glaring but unacknowledged error, which can be called the fallacy of false grouping. The seven undisputed letters are formed into a group, to which other letters are compared. The assumption is that the seven letters represent a uniform and consistent Paul in terms of style and theme. The very real differences even among the undisputed letters are ignored for the purpose of establishing such a Pauline "norm" against which deviance can be measured. But, in fact, this norm is abstracted from the specific letters precisely in the interest of providing a foil for comparison. Then this abstraction is compared to another abstraction representing the letters thought to be deviant. Thus, the "Pastorals" as a group are compared to the seven "undisputed letters" as a group, with no recognition of either the differences among the three letters to Paul's delegates or the differences among the seven undisputed letters.[85] This is simply bad science.

Nevertheless, partly on the basis of such criteria, and partly on the basis of scholarly inertia, the conventional approach to the canonical collection, as we have seen, is to distinguish between disputed and undisputed letters, or, to be more candid, authentic and pseudonymous letters. Seven letters (Romans, Galatians, 1 and 2 Corinthians, 1 Thessalonians, Philippians, Philemon) are taken as authentically Pauline. Three letters (2 Thessalonians,

---

*Philemon*; Schweizer, *Letter to the Colossians*; M. MacDonald, *Colossians and Ephesians*; Dibelius and Conzelmann, *Pastoral Epistles*; Bassler, *1 Timothy, 2 Timothy, Titus*.

85. See L. Johnson, *Letters to Timothy*, 63–64.

Ephesians, Colossians) are disputed—with some scholars still arguing for their authenticity—but mostly regarded as inauthentic. Three letters (1 Timothy, 2 Timothy, Titus) are designated as inauthentic by all but a tiny minority of critics.[86] The six canonical letters designated as non-Pauline in the strictest sense are recognized as "Pauline" in a weaker sense—that is, as productions of one or more Pauline "schools" operating after the apostle's death and producing letters in his name. The only evidence for such schools, to be sure, are these very compositions.[87]

Such is the present framework for the scholarly analysis of Paul, a framework that leaves out six of the letters traditionally ascribed to him and contained in the canon. I have already quoted above Schweitzer's canny observation on the consequences: those letters discarded as non-Pauline are eliminated from theological discussions altogether, since even proponents of a larger Pauline corpus can only engage others on the basis of the reduced body of evidence. The need for a thorough reexamination of the history and the consequences of Pauline scholarship on the issue of authorship is long overdue.[88] Such a reexamination will need to deal with a set of factors that go beyond the set of explicit "criteria" that I have here identified, and that exercise greater influence than the criteria.

The first factor is the power of construal, which is closely linked to the social construction of ideology.[89] It is striking that, for nineteen hundred years, readers who assumed Pauline authorship of all the letters were able to make sense of all of them as Pauline, down to and including Enlightenment critics. In similar manner, for two hundred years, the dominant opinion that some letters are inauthentic, reinforced as it is by classroom instruction and scholarly focus, has become a virtually unassailable dogma. Now the burden of showing the "Pauline" character of, say, Colossians falls on the individual reader, who must engage not only the evidence but the great weight of fos-

---

86. The best place to see the dominant position—as well as the weak arguments adduced in its favor—is introductions to the New Testament; see, e.g., Kummel, *Introduction to the New Testament*; Marxsen, *Introduction to the New Testament*; Koester, *Introduction to the New Testament*; R. Brown, *Introduction to the New Testament*; Holladay, *Introduction to the New Testament*.

87. For discussion, see R. Collins, *Letters That Paul Did Not Write*; and on the larger issue of Christian pseudonymity, see Aland, "Problem of Anonymity"; Meade, *Pseudonymity and Canon*; Metzger, "Literary Forgeries."

88. I have attempted this with respect to the Pastoral Letters in L. Johnson, *Letters to Timothy*, 20–102.

89. See Berger and Luckmann, *Social Construction of Reality*.

silized opinion. The social construction of reality is real, and it is powerfully operative in this matter.

The second factor is the understandable, if distorting, desire to find a usable Paul. The Holtzmann compromise regarding authorship enabled Protestant scholars to claim the mantle of criticism while at the same time keeping the Paul they most desired, the Paul they considered the defender of righteousness by faith.[90] By the same token, those arguing for the authenticity of the disputed letters are also motivated theologically: it is not a surprise to find such defenders primarily among more conservative scholars who embrace what they consider traditional values concerning gender and social structure. But the quest for an apostle who supports the theology of the scholar is a search that is less than disinterested.

The third factor is the tendency to equate authenticity with authority. If Paul did not write Ephesians, some seem to think, then its value is diminished; if he did not write the Pastorals, they can be dismissed. The tendency is found on both sides of the debate: if liberal scholars seek to deny authenticity in order to save Paul from what they perceive to be distortions, conservative scholars seek to establish authenticity in order to preserve the authority of threatened compositions. But the equation is simply wrong. The letters of Paul gain their authority not from the fact of his having written them but from the fact of their being canonized by the church. For the church, Colossians is read as Scripture whether Paul wrote it or not, just as the Gospel of Mark is read as Scripture even though its authorship remains undetermined. To think otherwise is to displace ecclesial discernment with historical criticism.

A better and more comprehensive assessment of Paul's letters must include two elements missing from the standard discussions. The first is the candid admission that the premise of a uniform Pauline "core" is wrong, together with the acknowledgment of multiple clusters within the canonical collection, groups of letters bound together by common style and theme, yet noticeably distinct from other groups. Thus, the Thessalonian letters, the Corinthian letters, Galatians and Romans, Colossians and Ephesians, and the letters to Paul's delegates (the Pastorals) form five such clusters, with Philippians and Philemon being outliers. These clusters pose a fundamental problem concerning the unity and diversity of the Pauline correspondence.

---

90. It is to the credit of Holtzmann, *Die Pastoralbriefe*, that, while devoting 282 pages to the question of inauthenticity, he recognizes the specific Protestant theological agenda involved in this sort of historical criticism (see 280 82).

Second is a theory of composition that more adequately accounts for such unity and diversity than the conventional appeal to the passage of time or a theory of development that is theologically driven.[91] I will propose such a theory of composition in chapter 3. In the meantime, there are no sound literary or historical grounds for dismissing any of the canonical letters as inauthentic, and every reason to attend to each of them as a source for Paul's life and thought.

91. Campenhausen makes it clear: "In the course of these three centuries the ideal to which Christianity had originally been committed was impaired in various ways: not only do we find rigidities in attitude, curtailment of aspiration, distortion of insight, but also in every department—and indisputable trivialization" (*Ecclesiastical Authority*, 3). At one end of this development, Campenhausen places "Paul," and at the other end, the "Pastorals" (301).

*Chapter 2*

# Paul's Life and Apostolic Ministry

A consideration of Paul's life and ministry—which involves recognizing what we do not know as well as what we know—is important because the canonical letters are ascribed to a specific individual and are addressed to specific communities and persons. Letters are not narratives about the past that allow authors (like the evangelists) to withdraw modestly within their stories. Letters speak to present circumstances and implicate the perspectives of the one writing. The more we can grasp of the circumstances of the canonical letters—if not in detail, then in general—the more responsible readers we can be. Certainly, some grasp of Paul's overall life and ministry is a necessary starting point for such historical contextualization.[1]

### Evaluating the Sources

Having determined that the Acts of the Apostles and the canonical letters are the best available sources for a genuine knowledge of Paul, it is possible now to enter into a critical comparison of those compositions before laying out what we can and cannot know about Paul's life and ministry. Acts introduces Paul as a persecutor of the church in 7:58–8:3, recounts his conversion and first encounters with believers in 9:1–30, relates his recruitment by Barnabas and (with him) his embassy to Jerusalem in 11:25–26, 30; 12:25, and tells of his first missionary efforts in 13:1–14:28. After the Jerusalem Council (Acts 15:1–35), Luke devotes all of his last thirteen chapters (16–28) to Paul. I earlier suggested that Luke can be considered as a generally reliable historian

---

1. The basic material in this chapter can be found as well in L. Johnson, *Writings of the New Testament*, 227–47.

(by ancient standards), especially when checked against Paul's letters. But a more detailed analysis is needed.

Considered as historical evidence, Acts is a secondhand primary source for the life and thought of Paul. It is also a later source. Even if we date it (as I do) around the year 85, it looks back over some two decades on Paul's activity as something past (see, e.g., 20:17–35). In contrast, Paul's letters must be considered as firsthand primary sources, written contemporaneously to the events they mention. Paul speaks in some detail of his past and present activities especially in 1 Thessalonians, 1 and 2 Corinthians, Galatians, Romans, Philippians, and 2 Timothy; only incidental information can be drawn from 2 Thessalonians, Colossians, Ephesians, 1 Timothy, and Titus.

By ordinary historiographical standards, the letters would be considered far more valuable as sources. Three considerations, however, caution against a hard choice for Paul instead of Acts. First, Acts is required for a relative, much less an absolute, chronology; the letters do not date themselves or provide their sequence. Second, Paul was less concerned with biographical accuracy—with the exception of Galatians, where he takes an oath on one point (1:20)—than he is with the development of his argument. Third, Paul cannot be considered a disinterested reporter; his autobiographical statements (especially in Galatians and 2 Corinthians) have a polemical edge.

Nevertheless, Paul's letters must be given great weight, particularly in the case of discrepancies between them and Acts. If the sources agreed completely on what Paul did and said, there would be no problem. In fact, however, there are three major kinds of divergence between the sources that force readers to make choices between them or to suspend judgment: chronology, apostolic style, and theology.

## Chronology

Only because of the fortuitous correlation between an archaeologically recovered inscription from Delphi and the report of Acts 18:12 that Gallio was proconsul of Asia when Paul encountered him in Corinth can historians work toward an absolute as well as a relative chronology for Paul.[2] The narrative of Acts, moreover, is indispensable even for a relative chronology for the apostle. The attempt to construct a chronology on the basis of the letters

---

2. See the discussion of Murphy-O'Connor, *Paul*, 15–22.

alone is futile,[3] for their internal evidence is insufficient to support lines of development or causal connections between letters.[4] Only the narrative of Acts 16–19 enables us plausibly to date 1 Thessalonians,[5] 1 and 2 Corinthians, and Romans.

How wide is the disparity between Acts and the letters concerning what happened and in what order? After his account of Paul's call/conversion (Acts 9:1–9), Luke has Paul preach in Damascus (9:10–25); make a first visit to Jerusalem, where he is sponsored by Barnabas (9:26–27); and preach first in Jerusalem, then in Cilicia and Antioch (9:28–30; 11:25–26). After being recruited by Barnabas, Paul was sent with him by the Antiochean church with a collection for Jerusalem (11:29–30; 12:25). Then he and Barnabas are commissioned by the church in Antioch for a "first missionary journey" (chaps. 13–14). Paul made a third visit to Jerusalem for the council concerning the admission of gentiles (15:1–29). He and Silas then embark on a "second missionary journey" overland through Asia Minor into Europe (15:36–18:21). He makes a fourth trip to Jerusalem to greet the church (18:22). He then began a "third missionary journey" from Antioch, once more through Asia Minor to Europe (18:23–21:14). His fifth and final visit to Jerusalem leads to his arrest, a transfer to Caesarea for a two-year imprisonment, a long sea voyage to Rome, and a final two-year house arrest there (21:15–28:31).

From Luke's account, we see the apostle making well-structured missionary journeys, interspersed with visits to the Jerusalem church. He touches base with Jerusalem a total of five times, so that Jerusalem appears to be the center of his missionary endeavors as it was for the other witnesses (cf. Acts 8:4–25; 11:1–18).

The information provided by the letters is sparser. Paul's call to be an apostle (Gal 1:15–16) is not immediately followed by a trip to Jerusalem; instead, Paul spends three years preaching in Syria and Arabia (Gal 1:17), which is then followed by a short trip to Jerusalem (Gal 1:18–20). Paul next preaches for eleven years in "the regions of Syria and Cilicia" (Gal 1:21). Then he goes on a second trip to Jerusalem—the "after fourteen years" can variously be computed[6]—for a meeting with "the pillars" of the Jerusalem community, Peter, James, and John (Gal 2:1–10). This meeting is followed

---

3. Against Knox, *Chapters in a Life of Paul*.

4. It can be argued, to be sure, that 1 and 2 Thessalonians as well as 1 and 2 Corinthians do suggest such connections and sequence.

5. I would include 2 Thessalonians in this list, since I regard it as following shortly after 1 Thessalonians.

6. See Jewett, *Dating Paul's Life*, 33–62.

by his activity in Galatia, Asia, Macedonia, Achaia, and possibly Dalmatia, as indicated by oblique references to his movements in Galatians, 1 and 2 Corinthians, and Romans. He planned to visit Jerusalem a final time with a collection for the saints that he had taken up from his churches (Rom 15:25–32), and then visit Rome to be equipped for a journey to Spain.

In contrast to Acts, Paul emphasizes his independence from Jerusalem with respect to his apostolic call and the gentile mission (Gal 1:11–12; 2:5–11). Still, the three visits to Jerusalem (two made and one anticipated) that he mentions testify to the importance he accorded that church. Likewise, it is difficult from Paul's letters to detect the sort of organized "missionary journeys" charted by Acts. The letters give the impression that Paul used various urban centers as the base for his activities for greater or lesser periods of time, with Acts 18:11 and 19:10 supporting that picture. By the measure of ancient histories, the divergence between the sources in the matter of Paul's movements is not remarkable and tends to confirm more than it calls into question.[7] But two cases of divergence pose more serious problems.

The first concerns what is sometimes called the "apostolic council" that decided the legitimacy of the gentile mission without requiring circumcision and the observance of the law. Was there such a formal meeting in the first generation? If so, who took part? And when did it occur? In Gal 2:1–10 Paul says that a conference took place after he had preached independently for fourteen years. Acts, at least on the face of it, would suggest a much shorter period of time between Paul's call and the meeting. In Acts, Barnabas and Paul are sent to Jerusalem as part of an Antiochean delegation. According to Galatians, Paul's companion is Titus, and the two of them went up to Jerusalem in response to a revelation (Gal 2:1–2). Was there a full gathering of the church (Acts 15), or was it a private meeting among peers (Galatians)? Even more critically, did such a meeting come *before* the encounter between Peter and Paul in Antioch (recounted in Gal 2:11–14) or *after* that contentious meeting? Galatians could actually be construed either way. If it came after that encounter, then Acts and Paul would agree that the meeting in Jerusalem resolved issues raised by the Antiochean dustup (see Acts 15:1–2). If before, then Paul sees that the meeting had not resolved the fundamental issue of table fellowship, concerning which he and Peter came into subsequent conflict.[8] Finally, did the conference issue a decree concerning dietary

---

7. The strength of positivistic studies such as Ramsay and Wilson, *St. Paul the Traveler*, and more recently Hemer, *Book of Acts*, is in making just such specific material connections.
8. As argued by Achtemeier, *Quest for Unity*.

regulations (Acts 15:23–29) or only an agreement concerning areas of missionary endeavor (Gal 2:7–10)?[9] These questions have resisted easy solution. It should be stressed, however, that precisely the differences in the accounts tend to confirm the basic historicity of the central point: sometime in the first decades of the Christian movement, Paul and other leaders met in Jerusalem and struck an agreement concerning the validity of the gentile mission.

The second major discrepancy concerns Paul's collection of money for the church in Jerusalem. According to his letters, this collection was a major undertaking in the latter part of his ministry (Gal 2:10; 1 Cor 16:1–4; 2 Cor 8–9). He was planning to bring the collection to Jerusalem before heading to Rome for his proposed expedition to Spain (Rom 15:25–29). In its account of Paul's fateful last journey to Jerusalem, however, Acts mentions nothing of such a collection for the church, even though it says that Paul was accompanied by delegates from the very places where the collection was taken up (20:4–5), and that he was in possession of a large amount of money as a gift to "my nation" (24:17, 26). More striking, although Paul clearly saw the collection as an act of reconciliation between gentile and Jewish churches, Acts has James suggest to Paul upon his arrival in the city that he undertake quite another sort of act of reconciliation, which equally involved money (21:23–25)! Yet Acts does have Paul take part in a monetary collection for the church in Jerusalem: he and Barnabas are sent by the community in Antioch with a collection taken up by the Antiochean Christians. This collection is placed by Luke at the start, rather than the end, of Paul's ministry.[10] It is impossible to reconcile these accounts. Once more, however, the paradoxical effect of the divergence is to confirm the basic historicity of Paul's taking part in a collection from gentile believers to the Jewish believers in Jerusalem.

Finally, Acts and the letters are of limited value in establishing the dating or sequence of Paul's letters. Letters such as 1 and 2 Thessalonians, 1 and 2 Corinthians, and Romans fit well within the Acts narrative. Those written from captivity, however—Colossians, Ephesians, Philippians, Philemon, 2 Timothy (more than a third of the canonical collection)—could come from Paul's two-year imprisonment in Caesarea (Acts 24:27), or his two-year captivity in Rome (Acts 28:30), or even from another detention that Acts does not mention (see 2 Cor 11:23–27).[11] Still other letters are virtually impossible to locate with any confidence within the Acts narrative

---

9. See Öhler, *Aposteldekret und antikes Vereinswesen*.

10. See L. Johnson, *Literary Function of Possessions*, 29–36.

11. See Murphy-O'Connor, *Paul*, 175–79, on the hypothesis of an Ephesian captivity.

(Galatians, 1 Timothy, Titus). All this means is that the letters and Acts alike have other interests than furnishing an exhaustive biography. A more telling point is that, in all of Acts, Paul is never said to write a single word. Paul the preacher and witness, Paul the founder of churches, is Acts' interest. And this brings us to the next category of comparison.

## Apostolic Style

The differences between Acts and the letters with respect to Paul's way of being an apostle have frequently been noted, and sometimes the differences have been exaggerated. In his letters, Paul says he has little eloquence (1 Cor 1:17; 2 Cor 11:6), but Acts presents him as a master orator in every setting, whether addressing Jews in the synagogue (13:16–40), sophisticated philosophers in Athens (17:22–31), or elders of the church (20:17–35), or appearing before rulers in self-defense (26:2–23).[12] Although the Paul of the letters is not shy about the signs and wonders he has done as an apostle (Gal 3:1–4; 2 Cor 12:12; Rom 15:19), or his ecstatic mystical experience (2 Cor 12:1–5), or his speaking in tongues (1 Cor 14:18), he characteristically subordinates such wonder-working to the message of the cross (1 Cor 2:1–5) and imitating the self-emptying obedience of Jesus (Phil 3:7–11).[13] In Acts, by contrast, Paul works many signs and wonders, performing both healings and exorcisms (19:11–20; 20:7–12; 28:1–10), and shows himself resourceful in responding to every circumstance (16:25–30; 27:21–25), even as he declares that "through many tribulations we must enter the kingdom of God" (14:22).

Acts stresses Paul's relationship with and even his dependence on Jerusalem; in his letters, Paul minimizes both. In Acts, Paul is an observant Jew: he takes a vow (18:18); he purifies himself in the temple (21:24–27); he even has his close follower Timothy circumcised (16:3). In his letters, Paul affirms that he is a "Jew to the Jews" (1 Cor 9:20–23), but he also refuses to circumcise Titus when that act might be construed as a capitulation to the demands of Torah (Gal 2:3), and he resists the pressure from a Jerusalem delegation to break off table fellowship with gentiles (Gal. 2:11–14).

These are significant differences. They must be placed, however, within the intentions and literary conventions of the respective sources. Luke-Acts

---

12. See now Wason, "'All Things to All People.'"

13. See Georgi, *Opponents of Paul*. It goes too far, however, to claim that Luke advanced a "theology of glory," in contrast to Paul's "theology of the cross."

portrays Paul as part of a prophetic tradition that expresses the good news through signs and wonders, and speaking God's word with boldness.[14] In contrast, Paul in his letters emphasizes his suffering as a counter to the arrogance of those who oppose him. He therefore minimizes his rhetorical skill (even as he practices it) and his miracles (even as he works them) in favor of the paradoxical weakness in strength of the cross (1 Cor 1:18–31; 4:9–13; 2 Cor 4:1–18; 11:5–33; Phil 2:1–3:11; 2 Tim 2:8; Col 1:24).

## Theology

Acts contains little of Paul's most distinctive theological themes, although more subtle affinities than are sometimes supposed can be detected.[15] It is light work to highlight differences on specific points, such as the treatment of what is sometimes called "natural theology," or the ability of humans to seek and find God even apart from special revelation: Acts 17:27 is markedly more optimistic in this respect than is Paul in Rom 1:18–32.[16] Similarly, we hear in Acts 13:39 only the faintest echo of Paul's argument concerning righteousness by faith in Galatians: "By him everyone who has faith is freed from everything from which you could not be freed by the law of Moses" (adapted).

Such point-by-point comparisons lead us to a single, fairly obvious conclusion: the Paul of Acts, like the Peter and Stephen of Acts, does not speak in his own voice but in Luke's voice. Paul's speeches express the religious perceptions and convictions—the theology—of Luke. Through the speeches of his major characters, Luke functions as a proper Hellenistic historian, providing words that are appropriate (through the technique of *prosōpopoiia*) to the circumstances, while interpreting for the reader the narrative within which the speech is embedded.[17] Given the prophetic characterization that Luke uses for all Christ's witnesses in Acts, a characterization that minimizes individual traits in favor of a common literary presentation, the small element of the distinctively Pauline that does emerge is actually more impressive.

14. L. Johnson, *Prophetic Jesus, Prophetic Church*.

15. See, e.g., Descamps, *Les Justes et la Justice*; L. Johnson, "Social Dimensions of *sōtēria*."

16. See Vielhauer, "Zum 'Paulinismus' der Apostelgeschichte."

17. Plümacher, *Lukas als hellenistischer Schriftsteller*.

By now it should be clear that any effort to sketch Paul's life and ministry must make use of both his letters and Acts. Both sources need to be read critically, but overall they tend to converge on the most important things even as they tend to diverge on the details. In the following sketch, therefore, I seek to respect the vast tracts about which we have little or no knowledge, and seek the solid points of convergence on the elements the sources actually provide.[18] My sketch of Paul's life and ministry will consequently be just a sketch, but it is enough to provide a meaningful context for his letters.

Establishing a chronology for Paul's life and ministry requires correlating the indicators of time and place in his letters and in Acts, together with a handful of pertinent external markers. I have already mentioned the Delphi Inscription, which places Gallio as proconsul in Corinth in 51–52 CE. Others include the expulsion of Jews from Rome under Emperor Claudius (Acts 18:1–2), the time of Paul's escape from Damascus under King Aretas (2 Cor 11:32–33; see Acts 9:23–25), and the tenure of the procurators Felix and Claudius (Acts 23:24–25:1).[19] Taking into account also Paul's reference to himself as "an elderly man" (*presbytēs*) in Philemon 9, and the designation of Paul as a young man (*neanios*) at the time of Stephen's martyrdom in Acts 7:58,[20] and the early tradition that Paul was executed under the emperor Nero (54–68 CE), it is possible to come up with a rough chronological framework.

Paul was born around the beginning of the first century CE, perhaps a few years before, perhaps a few years after.[21] His conversion took place around 33 CE. His death under Nero was sometime between 64 and 68, preceded by at least four years of captivity (in Caesarea and then in Rome); if a first release and subsequent work in Spain and again in the East is figured in, the date of 68 is more probable. The years of his active ministry therefore extended from roughly 33 to 60, a period of twenty-seven years. Our extant letters written while Paul was in active ministry date approximately from 49 to 57. Letters from captivity, as I have suggested, are harder to place within the framework but probably were written in the last period.

---

18. Despite, or perhaps because of, his minute attention to detail, Murphy-O'Connor slips into such speculation; see *Paul*, 199, 205, 211, 245, 252, 282, 331.

19. Murphy-O'Connor, *Paul*, 4–8, 22–23.

20. Philo (*On the Creation of the World* 103–5) quotes Hippocrates to the effect that the designation *neaniskos* is appropriate roughly for the ages 21–28, while a *presbytēs* is appropriate for the ages 49–56; after that, one is a *gerōn* (old man).

21. Murphy-O'Connor, *Paul*, 1–4.

## Paul's Early Life

According to Acts 22:3, Paul was born in Tarsus, the capital of Cilicia, which was in fact "no mean city" (21:39).[22] It was a center for Hellenistic culture. Popular philosophers and rhetoricians preached in its streets.[23] Important Stoic teachers such as Athenadoras, the tutor of Caesar Augustus, lived and taught there.[24] Mystery cults were also present.[25] In Tarsus, the diaspora Jew Paul was exposed to the same Hellenistic environment as his older contemporary Philo of Alexandria. It was his Jewish identity, however, that Paul stressed, having in his view a particularly impressive pedigree: "I was circumcised on the eighth day, of the people of Israel and the tribe of Benjamin, a Hebrew of Hebrew origins" (Phil 3:5, author's translation; see Rom 11:1). And he was defensive when his heritage was challenged: "Are they Hebrews? So am I. Are they Israelites? So am I. Are they descendants of Abraham? So am I" (2 Cor 11:22; cf. Acts 22:3; 24:14-16; 26:4-8).

According to Acts, Paul was born with the privilege of citizenship in the city of Rome, which astonished his jailer, who had purchased his own citizenship (16:37-39; 22:25-28; 23:27). On this status Paul based his appeal to be heard by Caesar (25:11-12). While Roman citizenship was considerably extended during the first century,[26] it still would have been unusual for Jews in a provincial city like Tarsus to possess it for two generations. If Acts is correct, then Paul's family had some social prominence. A sense of his original social status may give some edge to Paul's appreciation of all he gave up for the Messiah (Phil 3:8), and to his complaints about his manual labor (1 Cor 4:12; 1 Thess 4:11; 2 Thess 3:7-9).[27] During his ministry, Acts portrays Paul as working as a tentmaker, a trade he practiced with his companions Aquila and Priscilla (18:3). Such manual labor was practiced by early rabbinic teachers as well as by Cynic philosophers who did not want to take payment for their

---

22. Luke's use of litotes corresponds to the straightforward characterization of Tarsus as "great" by Xenophon (*Anabasis* 1.2.23) and Dio Chrysostom (*Oration* 33.7)

23. Dio, *Oration* 33.3-4; Strabo, *Geography* 14.5.13.

24. Lucian, *Octogenarians*; Plutarch, *On Stoic Contradictions* 1033D.

25. See Ulansey, *Mithraic Mysteries*, 40-45.

26. See Goodfellow, *Roman Citizenship*; Sherwin-White, *Roman Citizenship*.

27. See Dahl, "Paul and Possessions." Paul's claim to work with his hands is echoed in Acts 20:34: "You yourselves know that these hands ministered to my necessities, and to those who were with me."

teaching.[28] Such labor enabled Paul to claim self-sufficiency (Phil 4:11) and to share with others (Acts 20:34–35).

Paul's religious allegiance was to the strictly observant Jewish sect known as Pharisaism:[29] "as to the law a Pharisee, . . . as to righteousness under the law blameless" (Phil 3:5–6). His dedication to that fellowship and its ideals was intense, even fanatical: "I advanced in Judaism beyond many of my own age among my people, so extremely zealous was I for the traditions of my fathers" (Gal 1:14). The importance of Paul's Pharisaic background can hardly be overestimated. It involved both the perception that the punctilious observance of the commandments was the absolute measure of righteousness before God, and the perception that the study of Torah was the source and frame of wisdom. Paul was professionally committed to the knowledge and practice of the symbolic world of Torah.[30] Of all first-century believers, he was uniquely positioned to perceive the issues posed to the Jewish symbolic world by a crucified and raised Messiah.[31]

If the Pharisaic movement was centered in Judea, the question arises how a diaspora Jew like Paul—according to his own witness—attached himself to that sect. This brings us to the question of where and how Paul was raised and educated. Did he come to Jerusalem as a youth and receive technical scribal training, in the manner that gentile youths (such as Cicero and Aelius Aristides) would travel to Athens to receive an education in rhetoric and philosophy? Acts 22:3 has him claiming so: "I am a Jew, born in Tarsus of Cilicia, but I was brought up in this city [Jerusalem]. Here I sat at the feet of Gamaliel and was educated strictly in the laws of our fathers" (author's translation). This would be Gamaliel I, the successor of Hillel, about whom we know little, but whose tenure in Jerusalem roughly corresponds to the Lukan claim.[32] Does Paul's statement in Gal 1:22 argue against this: "I was still not known by sight [*en prosōpō*] to the churches of Christ in Judea"? Not really, for even first-century Judea was sufficiently populous for a for-

---

28. For rabbinic practice, see Avot of Rabbi Nathan 6; Pirke Avot 4.14; b. Shabbat 49b; b. Bava Batra 132a; b. Pesahim 34a; for Cynic practice, see Hock, *Social Context*.

29. For the Jewish sects in the first century CE, see G. Stemberger, *Jewish Contemporaries of Jesus*; Saldarini and VanderKam, *Pharisees, Scribes, and Sadducees*. For the Pharisees in particular, see Neusner, *From Politics to Piety*; Finkelstein, *Pharisees*.

30. For the language of "symbolic world," see L. Johnson, *Writings of the New Testament*, 1–18.

31. Paul's Jewish identity will be explored more thoroughly in chap. 5.

32. Murphy-O'Connor, *Paul*, 55–56.

mer scribal student and persecutor, however notorious, to be unknown "by sight" to small messianic communities.

Taking all the evidence into account—the overall agreement between Acts and Paul concerning his background; the use of technical biographical terminology by Luke in Acts 22:3;[33] the further indication that Paul had relatives in Jerusalem (Acts 23:16); the greater probability of scribal training being available in Judea than in the diaspora, together with the plain fact that Paul uses such scribal technique in some of his letters—the probability is that Paul went to Jerusalem as a young man, joined the Pharisees, studied Torah there, and because of his zeal became a persecutor of the nascent church there (Acts 7:58).

Did he also marry? The question does not seem to be of great importance to Paul in his letters. He asserts to the Corinthians that he had the right to travel with a wife as did "the other apostles and the brothers of the Lord and Cephas" (1 Cor 9:5) but does so in a manner that makes clear he does not make use of the right (9:15). His earlier statement to the same community that, concerning marriage, "I wish that all were as I myself am" (7:7) continues, "To the unmarried and the widows I say that it is well for them to remain single as I do" (7:8). At the time of writing this letter, then, Paul is clearly single. Whether he had ever married, as would have been the norm in Judaism, cannot be determined; certainly, it goes well beyond the evidence to suggest that the death of his wife was a factor in his becoming a persecutor![34]

Determining Paul's place of upbringing and education has often been considered important because it was thought to provide insight into the relative strength of cultural influences on his thought. Those who understand Paul in apocalyptic or rabbinic categories would like to locate him in Palestine. Those emphasizing Hellenistic elements in his thought would like to place him exclusively in the diaspora.[35] In fact, however, while certain phenomena are predominantly if not exclusively Palestinian, such as

---

33. See Van Unnik, *Tarsus or Jerusalem.*

34. An example of the speculative tendency is Murphy-O'Connor, *Paul,* 62–65.

35. The alignment of geography and culture was a staple for the history of religions school's reconstruction of Christian expansion: Palestinian Christianity was "Jewish" and "apocalyptic"; in the diaspora, Christianity became a "Christ cult" under the influence of Hellenistic mysteries; Paul joined this form of Christianity and elaborated and refined it. See, e.g., Heitmüller, "Zum Problem Paulus und Jesus" (English translation in Meeks and Fitzgerald, *Writings of St. Paul,* 424–33); Bousset, *Kyrios Christos*; Bultmann, *Theology of the New Testament.*

Pharisaism and apocalyptic, the influence of Hellenism has been shown to be as pervasively present in Palestine as in the diaspora.[36] Geography and symbolic worlds don't neatly align in the first-century Mediterranean. In any case, like Philo but even more dramatically, Paul creatively reshapes the multiple and overlapping elements in his symbolic world as he responds to the complex needs of a diaspora community. No single aspect of the world he was born into or in which he was educated adequately explains Paul, for his creativity consists precisely in his realignment of those symbols. And the chief factor in this process of reinterpretation is the personal experiences that distinguished Paul among all other followers and proclaimers of Christ. He was a persecutor of the messianic movement who then became its passionate advocate. The complete reversal in the direction of his life happened because he experienced the resurrected Jesus as Lord. Paul is paradigmatic for the way in which religious experience can re-create a symbolic world.

## Persecutor

That Paul actively sought to destroy the Christian movement is emphasized both by his letters and Acts. Paul states flatly, "You know how I persecuted the church of God violently and tried to destroy it" (Gal 1:13, author's translation; see Phil 3:6). Even decades after his call, he finds it remarkable: "I am the least of the apostles, unfit to be called an apostle, because I persecuted the church of God" (1 Cor 15:9). Paul contrasts the mercy shown him in his call to Jesus's service with his former behavior as the first of sinners: "I formerly blasphemed and persecuted and insulted him; but I received mercy because I had acted ignorantly in unbelief" (1 Tim 1:13).

According to Acts, Paul colluded in the stoning of Stephen (Acts 7:58), persecuted followers of Jesus in Jerusalem (8:3), and was traveling to Damascus to continue his persecution of "the Way" (9:2) when he encountered the risen Lord. Paul's defense speeches in Acts elaborate on his behavior. Before the crowd in Jerusalem, Paul states, "I persecuted this Way to the death, binding and delivering to prison both men and women, as the high priest and the whole council bear me witness. From them I received letters to the brethren, and I journeyed to Damascus to take those also who were there and bring them in bonds to Jerusalem to be punished" (Acts 22:4–5). Before

---

36. So Lieberman, *Greek in Jewish Palestine*; Hengel, *Judaism and Hellenism*; Fischel, *Rabbinic Literature* and *Talmudic Literature*.

Agrippa he states, "I myself was convinced that I ought to do many things in opposing the name of Jesus of Nazareth. And I did so in Jerusalem; I not only shut up many of the saints in prison, by authority from the chief priests, but when they were put to death I cast my vote against them. And I punished them often in all the synagogues and tried to make them blaspheme; and in raging fury against them, I persecuted them even to foreign cities" (Acts 26:9-11). The details provided by Luke—especially concerning Paul acting as an agent of the Sanhedrin—are impossible to verify[37] and may represent rhetorical flourishes by Luke, but our two sources massively agree on the central point, that Paul sought the extermination of Christians.

Why did Paul persecute the church? The best clues are provided by his self-description as one "zealous" for the law—"as to the law a Pharisee, as to zeal a persecutor of the church" (Phil 3:5-6)—and his subsequent arguments against the ultimacy of Torah (see esp. Gal 3:10-4:10; 5:1-4). By the norms of Torah, the claim that Jesus was Messiah (much less "Lord") could be considered blasphemous and a direct assault on the authority of Torah since, according to a strict reading of Torah, Jesus's death by crucifixion must be considered as one cursed by God (see Deut 21:23), a text explicitly cited by Paul in Gal 3:13. Thus, as he tells the Corinthians, Christ crucified is a "stumbling block to Jews" (1 Cor 1:23).

If God was truly at work in Jesus, if Jesus was indeed the Messiah and Lord proclaimed by Christians, then, in Paul the Pharisee's eyes, the whole symbolic framework of Torah was threatened: if this sinner was the righteous one, then Torah could not be the ultimate norm of righteousness. Either Torah must fall, or this blasphemous movement must be destroyed. For one "zealous/jealous" for Torah, the choice was easy and could be regarded as obedience to God. Before Paul's call and after, the categories remain the same; they are simply and radically transvalued. No wonder his theology is markedly dialectical, and that his habitual contrast is between the then and now, for such was the shape of his own experience.

## Encounter with the Risen Lord Jesus

The experience that turned Paul from persecutor to apostle is not easy to define. It can legitimately be termed a "conversion" if that term signifies a turn from one direction to another, or a shift of allegiance from one Jewish

37. Murphy-O'Connor, *Paul*, 65-70.

sect (Pharisaic) to another (Christian).[38] But our primary sources speak of it as a prophetic call and as a direct encounter with Jesus as Lord. In Gal 1:15–16 Paul says, "He who had set me apart before I was born, and had called me through his grace, was pleased to reveal his Son to me [or: in me], in order that I might preach him among the Gentiles."[39] Paul stresses that his call came not through human agency but directly from God, "by revelation from [or: of] Jesus Christ" (Gal 1:12, author's translation).[40] Paul speaks of it as a resurrection appearance in his recital of such appearances: "Last of all, as to one untimely born, he appeared also to me" (1 Cor 15:8). He asks the Corinthians, "Am I not free? Am I not an apostle? Have I not seen Jesus our Lord?" (1 Cor 9:1). Paul's experience almost certainly provides the backdrop for the remarkable statement in 2 Cor 4:6: "It is the God who said, 'Let light shine in the darkness,' who has shone in our hearts to give the light of the knowledge of the glory of God in the face of Christ" (adapted).

The turn of Paul from persecutor to apostle is so dramatic and unexpected that Acts recounts it three times, once in direct narrative (9:1–9) and twice more in Paul's defense speeches (22:6–11; 26:12–18). Although the accounts differ in detail,[41] they agree that the call was the result not of logical calculation but of a sudden and shattering collision. They agree that it was an encounter with Jesus as a "Lord," who identified himself with the church that Paul was persecuting, so that what Paul did to believers, he did to Jesus (9:5; 22:8; 26:15). They agree that the experience issued a call to service (9:6), specifically to preach to the nations (22:21; 26:16–18). In sum, Acts and the letters agree on the basics: Paul experienced the risen Lord Jesus and was commissioned by him to preach the good news to the gentiles. For Paul the Pharisee to be assigned this specific task was deeply paradoxical: one whose duty had been to avoid fellowship with gentiles, or even with those associating with gentiles, is now assigned a mission to them by the very Messiah he had scorned. But Paul takes up the challenge and spends his life carrying it out (see Rom 1:5; 11:13; 15:16; Eph 3:1; Col 1:27–28; 1 Tim 2:7; 2 Tim 4:17).

The direct result of Paul's experience is obvious: it impelled him on the task of proclaiming Jesus as Messiah and Lord. But the experience also profoundly shaped his interpretation of that proclamation. Paul's starting

---

38. See the learned and thoughtful study by Segal, *Paul the Convert*.

39. The Greek *en emoi* is best translated "in me," suggesting an encounter that was interior as much as (or more than) exterior.

40. The genitive construction *apokalypseōs Iesou Christou* can be understood either objectively (a vision of Jesus Christ) or subjectively (a vision from Jesus Christ).

41. See Hedrick, "Paul's Conversion/Call"; D. Stanley, "Paul's Conversion in Acts."

point in his letters is never the memory of Jesus's words or deeds but the transforming experience of the risen Lord: "Even if we once knew Christ according to the flesh, we no longer so know him" (2 Cor 5:16, author's translation). To know Jesus only according to the flesh—that is, in the merely human terms employed before his experience—is to see him as cursed by God: "No one speaking by the Spirit of God ever says 'Jesus be cursed!'" The knowledge given by the Spirit is the opposite: "No one can say 'Jesus is Lord' except by the Holy Spirit" (1 Cor 12:3). For Paul, Jesus is not the deceased founder of a messianic community but the present source of its life and power: "Now the Lord is the Spirit, and where the Spirit of the Lord is, there is freedom. And we all, with unveiled face, beholding the glory of the Lord, are being changed into his likeness from one degree of glory to another; for this comes from the Lord who is the Spirit" (2 Cor 3:17–18). Because the risen Lord is its life force, the community is the Messiah's "body" (1 Cor 12:12–27; Eph 4:12–16), "the fullness of him who fills all in all" (Eph 1:23); it is also the "temple of the Lord" sanctified by the presence of his Holy Spirit (1 Cor 3:16; 2 Cor 6:16; Eph 2:21).

Paul was plunged in a moment from hostility to a false Messiah to belief in an exalted Lord. His thought was therefore dominated by the turning of the ages. What he and his fellow Jews had longed for was now accomplished in the resurrected Jesus. But the fulfillment of their expectation was both more profound and paradoxical than they could have anticipated. Jesus did not inaugurate an age of righteousness and messianic rule within Israel alone—indeed, it could be argued, not at all. Paul grasped that through the resurrection and exaltation of Jesus, God had inaugurated a renewal of humanity itself, even of the world: "If anyone is in Christ, there is a new creation; the old has passed away, behold, the new has come" (2 Cor 5:17, adapted; see 1 Cor 15:42–50; Rom 5:12–21; Eph 1:9–10; Col 3:10–11). And for Paul the Pharisee, who had measured all righteousness within the scale of Torah, there was the severe cognitive dissonance that needed to be resolved between faith in a crucified and raised Messiah and the words of Torah, which were "holy and just and good" (Rom 7:12).

## Patterns of Paul's Ministry

We are once more captive to our sources when it comes to tracing Paul's activity as an apostle. Much of what we would like to know they simply do not tell us. Neither Acts nor the letters tell us much about the important years before Paul began his collaboration with Barnabas. Did he found communities or even write letters to them? For that matter, neither source is helpful on how Paul actually founded communities; Acts is preoccupied with prophetic preaching and the turn from Jew to gentile; Paul himself writes letters to churches already in existence. Did he preach in public like the sophists (Acts 17:22–31); did he begin in the local synagogue (Acts 13:13–16; 14:1–7); did he evangelize households (Acts 16:14–15, 33–34); did he use all of these approaches? Certainly, we can detect traces of the "Jew first, then gentile" perspective on the mission as a whole (see Rom 1:16; 11:11–12; 1 Cor 9:20; Eph 1:11–14; 2:11–15), but we do not know if this stemmed from or affected Paul's own practice.

The sources do, however, converge on some significant patterns of Paul's ministry. Thus, we can state with a high degree of probability that Paul's work was primarily if not exclusively in urban settings. He tended to use the most important city of a territory as his base of operations, sometimes also accepting from churches of that city financial support for the work of evangelization. According to Acts, Antioch on the Orontes was the sponsor of Paul and Barnabas's first expedition to the West (13:1–3), and they reported back to that church (14:26–28). Acts also has Paul remain in Corinth eighteen months (18:11) and in Ephesus for two years (19:8–10). From the letters we learn that Philippi, his first European community (see Acts 16:11–15), was active in his financial support (Phil 4:15–16; 2 Cor 11:8–9), and that Paul hoped to find Rome an equally committed sponsor of his mission to Spain (Rom 1:13; 15:28–16:2). Paul worked with his hands to support himself (1 Thess 2:9; 4:11; 2 Thess 3:7–12; Acts 20:34–35), but the work of his mission required considerable support. Travel and lodging for missionary teams were expensive; the support of churches was critical to the mission going forward.

Our sources also agree that Paul did not operate alone, but rather as the head of an extensive network of coworkers. Acts lists these significant associates: Barnabas (13:2), John-Mark (13:5; 15:37), Timothy (16:3), Priscilla and Aquila (18:2–4), Apollos (18:24–28), Erastus (19:22), Sopater, Aristarchus, Secundus, Gaius, Tychicus, and Trophimus (20:4)—thirteen people. Paul also makes frequent mention of associates and coworkers. He had never visited the Roman church, yet in Rom 16:3–16 was able to greet by name twenty-six people,[42] designating nine of them explicitly as workers for the

---

42. Prisca and Aquila, Epaenetus, Mary, Andronicus, Junias, Ampliatus, Urbanus,

gospel.[43] He extends greetings to that church from eight others who were presently with him (16:21-23),[44] while also recommending Phoebe as a deacon and financial patron (Rom 16:1-2). The Corinthian congregations could recognize references to these workers for the mission: Cephas (1 Cor 1:12; 9:5), Apollos (3:6; 16:12), Barnabas (9:6), Sosthenes (1:1), Timothy (4:17; 16:10), Aquila and Prisca (16:19), Titus (2 Cor 2:13; 8:16), as well as other traveling workers (2 Cor 8:23).[45] The Philippians knew Timothy (Phil. 1:1; 2:19) and the fellow workers Epaphroditus (2:25; 4:18), Euodia, Syntyche, and Clement (4:2-3).

Paul's letter to the Colossians mentions Epaphras (1:7), Luke and Demas (4:14), Tychicus and Onesimus (4:7-9), Aristarchus (4:10), Nympha (4:15), and Archippus (4:17). Philemon speaks of Timothy (1), Apphia and Archippus (2), Onesimus (10), Epaphras (23), Mark, Demas, and Luke (24). Ephesians makes mention only of Tychicus (6:21), while 1 and 2 Thessalonians have only Silvanus (1 Thess 1:1; 2 Thess 1:1). Second Timothy adds Onesiphorus (1:16), Demas and Crescens (4:10), Titus, Luke, Mark, and Tychicus (4:11-12), as well as Priscilla and Aquila, Erastus, Trophimus, Eubulus, Pudens, Linus, and Claudia (4:19-21). Titus mentions Artemas, Tychicus, Zenas, and Apollos (3:12-13). This impressive list includes only those who can be considered fieldworkers rather than local authorities, although at this distance it is impossible to distinguish them adequately and they may have moved from one role to another. The list is therefore a rough one, but given the random character of the evidence, it must be considered conservative. We can therefore estimate that Paul's mission network involved at least forty people, both male and female.

Although they differ markedly in details, as we have already noted, Acts and the letters agree that Paul (and his team) engaged in collaborative efforts with other leaders and churches. Luke places Paul's participation in the Antiochean collection for the relief of the Jerusalem church before the beginning of his active mission (Acts 11:29-30; 12:25), and Paul speaks of the collection from gentile churches for Jerusalem as an effort he undertook during the period of his Aegean ministry (Gal 2:10; 1 Cor 16:1-4; 2 Cor 8-9;

---

Stachys, Apelles, Aristobulus, Herodian, Narcissus, Tryphaena, Tryphosa, Persis, Rufus, Asyncritus, Phlegon, Hermes, Patrobas, Hermas, Philologus, Julia, Nereus, Olympias.

43. Prisca and Aquila, Mary, Andronicus, Junias, Urbanus, Tryphaena, Tryphosa, Persis.

44. Timothy, Lucius, Jason, Sosipater, Tertius, Gaius, Erastus, Quartus.

45. For a prosopographical analysis of the names in the Corinthian congregation, see Meeks, *First Urban Christians*.

Rom 15:25–29). But they agree that he worked with gentile believers for the material assistance of an impoverished Jerusalem community.[46] Similarly, attention is usually paid to the manifest disparities between the account of a Jerusalem Council in Acts 15:1–29 and Paul's report of a meeting with the "pillars" James, John, and Cephas (Gal 2:1–10).[47] But the accounts converge on the basics: Paul and other leaders met in Jerusalem in the first generation and decided the legitimacy of the gentile mission. They also confirm that Paul knew James the brother of the Lord, Cephas, and John personally.

The energy, effort, and organizational ability required to coordinate the work of so many collaborators, and to carry out such extensive projects, must have been considerable. After listing a catalogue of hardships he had experienced, Paul ends climactically, "And, apart from other things, there is the daily pressure upon me of my anxiety for all the churches" (2 Cor 11:28). Given the complexity of his mission and the problems within communities he needed to address, we should take the statement at face value. He was not only the founder of churches, he was a pastor, and such work invariably has a wearing effect on those who do it—even when they are not dealing with powerful rivals or recalcitrant congregants! A corollary of his extensive ministry is that Paul could not do everything himself. Although his preferred mode of communication with his churches was the personal visit (Rom 1:10–13; 15:24; 1 Cor 4:10; 16:2–3; 2 Cor 1:15–16; 2:1; 13:1; 1 Thess 2:17–18; 3:6; 1 Tim 4:13; Phlm 22), he frequently employed delegates to handle important and delicate matters when he himself could not make a visit (see 1 Thess 3:2; 1 Cor 4:17; 2 Cor 8:23; Eph 6:21; Phil 2:19, 25; Col 4:7–8; 1 Tim 1:3; Titus 1:5).[48] As we shall see, his letters were a third (and definitely tertiary) mode of mediating his personal presence to his communities.

At the risk of repeating what has already been noted, the state of the evidence does not permit a precise chronology of Paul's ministry or correspondence. Acts and some letters overlap sufficiently to allow a plausible insertion of some letters within the Acts narrative. Because of the coincidence of Paul's sojourn in Corinth (from the winter of 50 to the spring of 52) and of Acts' close attention to his movements before and after that period of time, the following letters can be dated between 52 and 58 and in a reasonable sequence: 1 and 2 Thessalonians, 1 and 2 Corinthians, and Romans. These are, however, only five out of thirteen letters. The letters written from

---

46. On the collection, see Georgi, *Remembering the Poor*; Joubert, *Paul as Benefactor*.
47. On the council, see Wall, "Jerusalem Council."
48. See Mitchell, "New Testament Envoys."

captivity, as we have seen, could possibly derive from a Caesarean (Acts 24:27) or Roman (Acts 28:30) imprisonment, or from some earlier detention about which Acts is silent. It is therefore impossible to give a precise date or sequence to Philemon, Colossians, Philippians, and 2 Timothy. Three remaining letters presuppose Paul's active ministry but contain too little circumstantial information to place them confidently in the Acts narrative or in relation to the other Pauline letters: 1 Timothy, Titus, and Galatians. The largest part of the canonical collection, in sum, cannot be located certainly within what we know of Paul's career.

There are two reasons, therefore, why it is impossible from the extant evidence to trace "development" in Paul's practice or thought. The first is that our first extant letter was written some dozen years after he began preaching; it is highly likely that his basic ideas were already firmly in place. The second is that, apart from the five letters that fall in an eight-year range, we cannot pinpoint the date of the remaining eight canonical letters.

It is surely possible that Paul experienced changes in attitude and perception. Age, imprisonment, rejection, and suffering have left their mark on the writings of others. But our evidence does not allow us to make such determinations. And as we shall see, factors other than the passage of time or psychological adjustment can account for the differences in Paul's letters.

A final point on Paul's ministry. He not only worked with others and collaborated with those who were apostles before him (like Cephas and James); he also had available to him the community traditions of his own and other churches—both Palestinian and diasporic. Thus, Acts has him associating with the brothers in Damascus and Jerusalem and Antioch (9:17-19; 13:1-3), and Paul speaks of traveling to Jerusalem to confer with Cephas for fifteen days, three years after his call (Gal 1:18).[49] As the head of a complex and extensive missionary endeavor, Paul could not be, and his letters do not reveal him to be, purely charismatic and freelancing. We shall see how he employs earlier traditions in his letters. But we see as well that he disliked disorder. In choices between spontaneity and structure, Paul chooses structure with perhaps surprising frequency (see, e.g., 1 Cor 5:1-5; 7:17; 11:16; 14:33-36; 2 Cor 6:14-7:1; Gal 6:7-10; Titus 1:3).[50] In the same way, Paul is concerned

49. I translate the term *historēsai* as "confer"; it can mean "meet or make acquaintance" or "to get information from," which is the more likely sense here; see Kilpatrick, "Galatians 1:18 *historesai Kephan*."

50. In this chapter I deal only with general patterns; for the specific circumstances of each letter, see L. Johnson, *Writings of the New Testament*.

for the establishment of local authority in his churches. Acts reports that Paul and Barnabas "appointed elders . . . in every church" (Acts 14:23), and has Paul direct a farewell discourse to the elders of the church in Ephesus (Acts 20:17–35). Paul's letters generally support the presence of local leaders to teach, direct, and exhort others (1 Thess 5:12; 1 Cor 12:28; 16:15–18; Rom 12:7–8; Gal 6:2; Eph 4:11; Phil 1:1; 1 Tim 3:1–13; 5:17–20; 2 Tim 2:1; Titus 1:5).

## Conclusion

Paul's encounter with the risen Lord did not effect only a momentary change; it completely restructured his existence. From a zealot filled with rage at those following the way of Jesus Christ, he became, paradoxically, the most passionate advocate for the crucified Messiah. He did so, we see, not as a free agent or as a solo performer but as the head of a complex missionary effort, encompassing fellow workers, delegates, and local leaders. He was, on the evidence, fully invested in the faith and the faithful to whom God had called him. His correspondence, to which we turn next, emerges out of this passionate pastoral practice.

*Chapter 3*

# The Pauline Correspondence

W e learn of and from Paul most directly through his letters. They are remarkably direct and vivid, written in a Koine Greek that is vigorous even when it is not entirely clear. Nothing in these letters is obvious or banal. Nothing in them suggests the aesthete or dilettante; they everywhere evince high moral purpose and earnestness. They everywhere communicate a level of passion for the Lord Jesus Christ that is at once personal and profound. Paul's letters, however, are far from the outpouring of raw emotion. They are carefully constructed and display ancient rhetorical conventions. Above all, they require of the reader—even belated and indirect readers such as we are today—the ability to inhabit the same symbolic world that Paul simultaneously constructs and inhabits, and the willingness to think with the author through difficult and sometimes alien conceptions.

In a very real sense, everything that follows in this volume and the next deals with these canonical compositions, as I move in and out of Paul's letters at a variety of angles. But mindful of the need to establish things that many other treatments of Paul assume are already known, I ask the reader's patience as I lay out in this chapter some basic considerations concerning the letters that are the foundation for all constructions of Paul—large or small, plausible or incredible—offered to a world that has seldom actually worked through the primary texts in English translation, much less in the original Greek. In this chapter, then, I place the Pauline correspondence in the context of ancient epistolary practice, note some of the characteristics and formal elements of the Pauline collection, and then return to the puzzle proposed in my introduction concerning the combination of diverse and similar "clusters" within his correspondence, before proposing a theory of authorship that better accounts for the data than the conventional solution.

First, though, some basic prefatory remarks. In the Greek New Testament and all translations, Paul's letters are arranged in order of length, in two groups; the letters written to churches run from Romans to 2 Thessalonians; those written to individuals run from 1 Timothy to Philemon. Such an arrangement based on stichometry forbids drawing theological conclusions from "canonical arrangement," such as have sometimes been drawn from the arrangement of Old Testament books.[1] Romans may be considered the most important of Paul's letters on other grounds, but it cannot be on the ground of its heading up the collection. Several conventional categories are used to organize the canonical collection. I have already addressed in general the distinction between "undisputed" letters (Romans, 1 and 2 Corinthians, Galatians, 1 Thessalonians, Philippians, Philemon) and "disputed" letters (2 Thessalonians, Colossians, Ephesians, 1 Timothy, 2 Timothy, Titus). Letters written during Paul's active ministry are sometimes called "travel" letters (1 and 2 Thessalonians, 1 and 2 Corinthians, Galatians, and Romans); 1 Timothy and Titus also belong in this group. Captivity letters are those written from a place of imprisonment (Philippians, Philemon, Colossians, Ephesians, 2 Timothy). The designation "Pastoral Letters" is usually applied to 1 Timothy, 2 Timothy, and Titus; a better descriptor would be "letters to delegates." Finally, the term "great letters" is sometimes applied to Romans, 1 and 2 Corinthians, and Galatians, partly on the basis of their length, and partly because of their substance.

## The Epistolary Context

Paul's cultural context was one in which the art of writing letters (Gr. *epistolai*, Lat. *epistulae*) was both esteemed and highly developed.[2] Philoso-

---

1. See, e.g., Childs, *Old Testament as Scripture*. This is not to say that the overall canonical arrangement of the New Testament cannot give rise to interesting inquiries; see L. Johnson, "John and Thomas in Context."

2. For an overview, see Stowers, *Letter Writing*; J. White, *Light from Ancient Letters*.

phers like Seneca,[3] statesmen like Cicero,[4] and poets like Horace[5] all used the letter as a medium for moral and aesthetic exposition. Such efforts were often self-consciously literary and sometimes aimed at an audience beyond the addressee; posterity was as much in view as the correspondent. Rulers from emperors to governors used the form of letters—even when inscribed on stone for public viewing—to commission delegates and provide instruction for local circumstances.[6] Jewish leaders also wrote letters to communities located in the diaspora.[7] Not only the learned and the powerful wrote letters. Archaeologists have unearthed thousands of letters that were scrawled on papyrus or even clay shards (ostraca) to communicate the whole range of personal and business affairs across the Mediterranean world.[8] The difference between the "literary" epistles composed as aesthetic or philosophical exercises and "nonliterary" or "real" letters has been used to support a sociological distance between the elite and the non-elite: literature belongs to the elite; pragmatic business letters belong to the crowd.[9]

On the basis of that distinction, Paul's letters, which are manifestly "real," in the sense that they are composed for contemporary readers in specific circumstances rather than for posterity, have been considered as popular letters, with the early Christian movement correspondingly charac-

3. Seneca's 124 letters to Lucilius are known as his *Moral Epistles*; see Seneca, *Epistles*. Plato had thirteen letters ascribed to him, although the authenticity of most of them is questioned; see Hamilton and Cairns, *Collected Dialogues of Plato*. In book 10 of his *Lives of Eminent Philosophers*, Diogenes Laertius includes three letters that Epicurus wrote to his followers concerning some of his teachings. Widely regarded as pseudonymous are the so-called *Cynic Epistles* ascribed to early teachers in the Cynic movement like Diogenes; see Malherbe, *Cynic Epistles*.

4. Cicero was a prolific correspondent, with thirty-seven books of his letters extant and another thirty-five lost. The extant letters include "Letters to Atticus," "Letters to Brutus," "Letters to Friends," and "Letters to His Brother Quintus"; for a sample, see Cicero, *Letters to Atticus*. Pliny the Younger also wrote hundreds of letters, of which 247 survive, including his correspondence as governor of Bithynia with the emperor Trajan; see Pliny the Younger, *Complete Letters*.

5. Horace innovated when he wrote two books of letters in the form of verse, taking up in them philosophical issues; see Horace, *Satires, Epistles and Ars Poetica*. The poet Ovid also wrote four books of letters, the *Letters from the Black Sea*, while in exile.

6. See Welles, *Royal Correspondence*.

7. Doering, *Ancient Jewish Letters*.

8. See Grenfell and Hunt, *Oxyrhynchus Papyri*; Hunt and Smyly, *Tebtunis Papyri*; Deissmann, *Light from the Ancient East*.

9. See esp. Deissmann, *Light from the Ancient East*, 1–61.

terized as proletarian.[10] Such classification encouraged the neglect of rhetorical aspects of Paul's correspondence. The distinction is, in any case, overly sharp: literary expression and social standing do not match up so neatly.[11] Whether literary or nonliterary, letters served a variety of functions, some of them intensely practical. Greeks, Romans, and Jews, for example, all wrote letters of commendation to accompany delegates. So did the early Christian communities (see 2 Cor 3:1), examples of which can be found in the New Testament (see Rom 16, Philemon, 3 John). But perhaps the most universal function of letters was to make the writer present to the reader or readers in a very real way; this sense of the other's presence would be enhanced by an oral delivery of the letter.[12]

Even everyday correspondents sought to follow the rhetorical conventions appropriate to the respective social location of the correspondents and the function of the letter.[13] Later rhetorical handbooks, like those of Pseudo-Demetrius and Pseudo-Libanius, helpfully categorized such letter types, describing their character and offering examples. Did one want to write a letter of rebuke, or a friendly letter, or a letter of consolation, or offer advice or encouragement? The handbooks offered samples of the appropriate conventions and stylized expressions to be used in each. Pseudo-Libanius, for example, describes a "paraenetic letter" as one written to "exhort someone, advising him to pursue something and to abstain from something," and goes on to provide a short sample of such a letter: "Always be an emulator, dear friend, of virtuous men. For it is better to be well-spoken of when imitating good men, than to be reproached by all for following evil men."[14] The classic example of such paraenetic discourse in antiquity is Pseudo-Isocrates's *To Demonicus.* Among Paul's letters, 2 Timothy perfectly fits within the frame of a paraenetic letter.[15]

Among ancient corpora of correspondence, Paul's letters are marked by unusual variety. Of the letters written to individuals, Philemon is clearly a letter of commendation, easing the return of the slave Onesimus to his owner, while 1 Timothy and Titus fit the form of *mandata principis* letters, instructing Paul's delegates in the field.[16] Second Timothy, as I have already

---

10. See Deissmann, *Paul,* 1–51.

11. See the discussion of Deissmann's position in Malherbe, *Social Aspects,* 29–59.

12. See the classic essay by Funk, "Apostolic Presence."

13. See Stowers, "Social Typification."

14. Translation by Malherbe, "Ancient Epistolary Theory."

15. L. Johnson, *First and Second Letters to Timothy,* 319–24.

16. See Fiore, *Function of Personal Example;* Wolter, *Pastoralbriefe als Paulustradition.*

noted, is a personal paraenetic letter, with elements of protreptic encouraging Timothy the teacher. In contrast to these individual letters, Ephesians is the most public of epistles, most general in its scope, in all likelihood written as an encyclical to a number of churches, delivered by Paul's delegate, Tychicus (Eph 6:21–22).[17] Colossians and Romans are written to churches founded by others and unknown to Paul firsthand. In contrast, Philippians fits the form of a friendly letter, directed to Paul's dearest and closest community.[18] Galatians is a letter of rebuke and persuasion. The two Thessalonian and two Corinthian letters come closest to being genuinely "pastoral letters," in the contemporary sense of that word, meaning that their contents are determined above all by the current needs of the addressees.

## Common Characteristics

Despite their variety, the Pauline letters share some features that not only link them together but also distinguish them from other ancient letters about which we have some knowledge. First, they all (even Ephesians) are in some degree occasional; that is, they are written in response to real-life, contemporary circumstances. In this sense, Paul's letters are "real letters," in contrast to epistles written for the ages. Paul had no sense of writing "Scripture": what he proclaimed to churches could be called "the word of God" (1 Thess 2:13), but Paul does not so name his letters. Most often the occasion is trouble, conflict, or misunderstanding in a local church (Galatians, 1 and 2 Corinthians, 1 and 2 Thessalonians, Philippians, Colossians, 1 Timothy, Titus). But in some cases a moment in Paul's own life stimulates composition (Romans, Philemon, 2 Timothy). None of his letters, however, show signs of having been dashed off in haste; all have elements of rhetorical art; all display careful construction. The occasional nature of his correspondence, however, poses a perpetual caution against all efforts to turn Paul into a systematic thinker for whom letters were only an opportunity to develop this aspect or that of his vision.[19] Even Romans, by far the most carefully constructed composition in the collection, is motivated

17. L. Johnson, *Writings of the New Testament*, 359–71.

18. See the essays in Fitzgerald, *Friendship*.

19. Thus, the strength of Mitchell's *Paul and the Rhetoric of Reconciliation* is to highlight the topoi concerning harmony that Paul deploys throughout the letter; the weakness is in downplaying the influence of the specific issues in eliciting those topoi.

by Paul's present situation and future plans, and develops themes already adumbrated in Galatians and 1 Corinthians.[20]

At the same time, Paul's letters are also official religious literature. This feature above all sets his letters apart from the epistolary cultural context, for nowhere else (outside the New Testament, to be sure) do we find a collection of letters from an apostle to the churches. In none of the letters ascribed to him does Paul write only as a colleague or a friend. He writes as one sent with a commission by God and the risen Lord Jesus to assemblies gathered by the call of God. With the *possible* exception of Philemon and the Letters to Timothy and Titus, moreover, his letters were intended to be read aloud within those assemblies, probably by the delegate who delivered the missive to the church (see 1 Thess 5:27; 2 Thess 2:2, 15), and even to be exchanged by churches (Col 4:16). Paul's subject matter is also unrelievedly religious in character. Even news about himself and his delegates is placed within a religious framework (see, e.g., 1 Thess 2:18; 2 Cor 1:8–14; Phil 2:19–30; Col 4:10–17).

Paul's letters represent his third—and least favored—mode of personal presence to his communities. As stated in chapter 2, Paul preferred always to visit a church in person. Failing that, he would send a delegate to represent him—and we remember that a delegate represented the sender completely. When the Corinthians dealt with Timothy, they dealt with Paul at a remove: "I sent to you Timothy, my beloved and faithful child in the Lord, to remind you of my ways in Christ, as I teach them everywhere in every church" (1 Cor 4:17). Disrespecting the delegate is equivalent to disrespecting the apostle himself: "When Timothy comes, see that you put him at ease among you, for he is doing the work of the Lord, as I am. So let no one despise him" (1 Cor 16:10–11). Paul's letters arose out of the need to address a situation that could not be addressed in either of these preferable ways. Two corollaries attach to this fact. The first is that Paul's letters sometimes address situations that are already far advanced—1 Corinthians and Galatians are good examples, as is 2 Thessalonians—and require of Paul a certain level of social engineering as well as rhetoric, stretching thereby his already tenuous authority over some refractory communities. The second is that we belated and present-day readers must realize that in every case we are dealing not with the facts of the case but rather with the facts of the case as understood by Paul, perhaps reliant on reports of partisans or delegates (see 1 Cor 1:11; 5:1; 11:17).

20. See Dahl, "Missionary Theology."

Finally, Paul's letters not only serve the communication of news, correction, encouragement, rebuke, and affection from the apostle to his churches; they also work to create bonds of allegiance between the readers and Paul, among the readers themselves, and between the readers and Christ. Paul's use of "fellowship" (*koinōnia*) language encourages such unity, evoking the cultural resonance attached to friendship in antiquity.[21] Similarly, his use of kinship language helps create the sense of being a fictive family among readers: Paul depicts himself as a parent who has "begotten" churches and even individual believers; he addresses his readers as *adelphoi* ("brethren"),[22] and also as "children" (*tekna*), and refers to his delegates as "children."[23] The strength of such rhetoric is revealed in Paul's plea to Philemon concerning the returned slave Onesimus: "Perhaps this is why he was parted from you for a while, that you might have him back forever, no longer as a slave but more than a slave, as a beloved brother [*adelphos*], especially to me but how much more to you, both in the flesh and in the Lord. So if you consider me your partner [*koinōnos* = "friend"], receive him as you would receive me" (Phlm 15–17).

## Epistolary Structure

The structure of a Hellenistic letter was straightforward. The addressee's name was usually written on the outside of the papyrus roll. A greeting opened the letter itself; its normal form was "From A to B, greetings [*chairein*]" (see, e.g., 1 Macc 10:25; 11:30; 12:6; Acts 15:23; 23:26). The body of the letter followed.[24] A short statement of farewell usually consisted of

21. For cognates of *koinōnia*, see Rom 12:13; 15:26–27; 1 Cor 1:9; 10:16, 18–20; 2 Cor 1:7; 6:14; 8:4, 23; 9:13; 13:13; Gal 2:9; 6:6; Phil 1:5; 2:1; 3:10; 4:14, 15; 1 Tim 5:22; 6:18; Titus 1:4; Phlm 6, 17. For the connotations of these terms relative to ancient conceptions of friendship, see L. Johnson, *Writings of the New Testament*, 328–29.

22. The designation appears in all letters except Titus; see, e.g., Rom 1:13; 10:1; 16:14; 1 Cor 1:10; 6:5; 8:11; 15:1; 2 Cor 1:1; 2:13; 9:3; Gal 1:2; 6:18; Eph 6:21, 23; Phil 1:12; 2:25; Col 1:1; 4:7; 1 Thess 1:4; 4:1; 2 Thess 2:1; 3:1; 1 Tim 5:1; 6:2; 2 Tim 4:21; Phlm 1, 7, 20. Paul's letters never use Luke's characteristic gendered phrase "men brethren" (*andres adelphoi*, Acts 1:16; 2:29) and should be taken as broadly inclusive of all the readers.

23. For Paul as parent of the community, see 1 Cor 4:15; Gal 4:19; 1 Thess 2:11; as parent of individual believer, see Phlm 10. For the readers as children, see 1 Cor 4:14; 2 Cor 6:13; 12:14; Gal 4:19; Phlm 10; for delegates as children (*tekna*), see 1 Cor 4:17; Phil 2:22; 1 Tim 1:2; 2 Tim 1:2; Titus 1:4.

24. See J. White, *Body of the Greek Letter*.

a wish for good health or good fortune. Paul's letters share the same basic structure but display a certain amount of freedom in the expansion of this element or that.

In the *greeting*, for example, Paul changes the secular *chairein* to the more theologically fraught term *charis* ("grace" or "gift") and adds the normal Jewish greeting, *eirēnē* ("peace," i.e., *shalom*). This grace and peace, moreover, is not from Paul, the sender, but "from God our Father and the Lord Jesus Christ" (Rom 1:7; 1 Cor 1:3; 2 Cor 1:2; Gal 1:3; Eph 1:2; Phil 1:2; 2 Thess 1:2; 1 Tim 1:2; 2 Tim 1:2; Phlm 3). Three letters have slight variants: "grace to you and peace from God our Father" (Col 1:2); "grace and peace from God the Father and Christ Jesus our Savior" (Titus 1:4); and "grace to you and peace" (1 Thess 1:1)—although this last is preceded by "To the church of the Thessalonians in God the Father and the Lord Jesus Christ." In effect, Paul's letters begin with a greeting that is a blessing. Paul also will expand one of the other basic elements of the Hellenistic greeting. In some letters he expatiates on the senders (Rom 1:1–6; Gal 1:1–2; 1 Tim 1:1; Titus 1:1–3). In others he provides elaboration concerning the recipients (1 Cor 1:2; 2 Cor 1:1; Phlm 2) or the wish he has for the recipients (Gal 1:3–5). The point Paul chooses to elaborate can bear important clues to that letter's later thematic developments.

Paul characteristically follows the greeting with a *prayer of thanksgiving* or *blessing*. This innovation helps mark his letters as formally religious literature. He typically uses the singular or plural form of "give thanks" (*eucharistein*, as in Rom 1:8; 1 Cor 1:4; Phil 1:3; Col 1:3; 1 Thess 1:2; 2 Thess 1:3; 1 Tim 1:12; 2 Tim 1:3; Phlm 4). Twice he uses the familiar Jewish blessing formula "blessed be God" (*eulogētos ho theos*; 2 Cor 1:3; Eph 1:3); the blessing in Ephesians is followed by a thanksgiving (1:15–23). In only two letters does Paul omit the prayer (see Gal 1:6; Titus 1:5), and the alteration in each case is startling. The prayer often anticipates themes that Paul will develop in the body of the letter, and therefore functions rhetorically as instruction and persuasion as well as prayer.[25] Thus, the thanksgiving in 1 Cor 1:4–9 acknowledges the rich bestowal of spiritual gifts among the Corinthians—all speech and all knowledge (see chaps. 12–14)—while connecting these to the confirmation of the witness of Christ (see 1:18–2:16; 12:3; 15:1–8) and placing their gifts in the context of an eschatological reservation (see 3:10–15; 5:5; 15:1–58). It is not their own gifts and efforts but Jesus who will keep them guiltless in the day of the Lord. The conclusion to the prayer reminds them

---

25. See Schubert, *Pauline Thanksgiving*; O'Brien, *Introductory Thanksgivings*.

that the point is not their gifts but their relationship to each other in Christ: "God is faithful, by whom you were called into the fellowship of his Son, Jesus Christ our Lord" (1 Cor 1:9; see chaps. 8–11).

There is considerable variation in the length of Paul's opening prayers as well as their placement: the prayer in 1 Thessalonians takes up much of the first three chapters (of five!); in 2 Thessalonians there are two formal thanksgivings (1:3–4; 2:13–17); and in 1 Timothy the prayer follows a preliminary exhortation (1:12–17).

In the *body* of his letters, Paul addresses the specific difficulties of a community or develops his argument. This is the most variable element in his letters, as it is in ancient (and modern) letters generally. The body is introduced with one of a number of transition formulas, including "I exhort [*parakalō*] you" (1 Cor 1:10; 1 Thess 4:1; 1 Tim 1:3; 2:1; Phlm 9),[26] "we ask you" (2 Thess 2:1), "we do not want you to be ignorant" (2 Cor 1:8), "I want you to know" (Phil 1:12), and "on this account" (Eph 1:15; Col 1:9; 2 Tim 1:6; Titus 1:5). Similar formulas often introduce transitions within the body of the letter (see, e.g., 1 Cor 7:1; 8:1; 10:1; 12:1; 15:1; 16:1).

The body of the Pauline letter merges, sometimes imperceptibly, into the *final greetings* and *farewell*. Where they occur, the personal greetings are sometimes extensive (as in Rom 16, discussed in chap. 2) and reveal something of the complex and communal nature of Paul's ministry (see also 1 Cor 16:19–20; Col 4:10–17; 2 Tim 4:19–20; Phlm 23–24). It is notable, however, that as many letters lack such greetings by name altogether (Galatians, Ephesians, 2 Thessalonians, 1 Timothy) or are content with a general greeting to the readers (2 Cor 13:12–13; Phil 4:21; 1 Thess 5:26; Titus 3:15). The letters characteristically close with a prayer formula, wishing, with considerable variation, grace from God to the readers (Rom 15:33; 16:25–27; 1 Cor 16:23–24; 2 Cor 13:13; Gal 6:18; Eph 6:23–24; Phil 4:23; Col 4:18; 1 Thess 5:28; 2 Thess 3:18; 1 Tim 6:21; 2 Tim 4:22; Titus 3:15; Phlm 25).

Despite the great variety in the Pauline corpus—a topic to which I will shortly return—the letters share these formal markers, the consistency of whose presence also sets them apart among ancient letters, lending the canonical collection a certain recognizability as Pauline.[27] It is

---

26. See Bjerkelund, *Parakalô*.

27. Of the other canonical letters, Hebrews lacks any epistolary element apart from the final greetings and prayer (13:22–24); James has only the greeting common to Hellenistic epistles (1:1); 2 Pet 1:1–2 has an opening greeting similar to Paul's but nothing else, likewise 2 John and Jude. The manner in which 1 Peter matches the formal elements of the Pauline

perhaps worth noting that, among the apocryphal letters attributed to Paul, only *To the Laodiceans* makes any effort to capture these formal traits. It is also striking that, within the canonical Pauline collection, Galatians, a letter whose authenticity no one disputes, lacks more of these formal elements than any disputed letter (opening prayer, transition to body, personal greetings).

## Elements of Composition

Paul's letters could not be a direct outpouring of emotion, first because of the slow and probably indirect mode of epistolary communication, and second because of the complex elements involved in his correspondence. Paul can be said to "author" all his letters, in the sense that they were written under his authority and direction. But it is by no means certain how direct a role he played in the "writing" of specific letters. Several aspects of his correspondence that emerge from the evidence of the texts themselves deserve attention.

Writing on parchment or (more likely) papyrus was slow work and physically demanding, particularly in the case of some of Paul's longer letters. The job of actually writing a letter in Greco-Roman practice was often assigned to a trained secretary (amanuensis). Cicero, for example, often dictated his letters to Atticus (see, e.g., *Atticus* 7.13a, 8.13, 10.3a, 11.24, 13.15). His secretary, Tiro, took dictation but also deciphered Cicero's handwriting (*Atticus* 7.2). He also managed Cicero's table (*Letters to Friends* 11.22) as well as his garden (16.20) and even his financial affairs (7.5). He was, in short, a valued associate of the statesman. We know that Paul also used a secretary for at least some of his letters.[28] The scribe appears explicitly in Romans: "I Tertius, the writer of this letter, greet you in the Lord" (16:22). At other times, Paul indicates that he is penning the greeting in his own hand, suggesting strongly that he had dictated the rest of the letter (see 1 Cor 16:21; Col 4:18; 2 Thess 3:17; and possibly Gal 6:11). Why is this important? Because trusted secretaries could be given considerable latitude in the actual composition of letters. Given the main point to be made, they could work up an appropriate treatment

---

letter is well known and has led to various theories concerning that letter's dependence on the Pauline tradition; see Mitton, "Relationship."

28. On this, see Roller, *Das Formular der paulinischen Briefe*; R. Longenecker, "Ancient Amanuenses"; Richards, *Secretary in the Letters of Paul*.

consonant with the author's thought and often of his style as well. We have, to be sure, no direct evidence of this happening in Paul's correspondence, but the wide variety of styles within the Pauline corpus make this a factor to be taken seriously.

Many of Paul's letters, furthermore, were cosponsored. These letters are sent not only in his name but also in the name of Timothy (2 Cor 1:1; Phil 1:1; Col 1:1; Phlm 1), of Silvanus and Timothy (1 Thess 1:1; 2 Thess 1:1), of Sosthenes (1 Cor 1:1), or of "all the brothers" with him (Gal 1:2). Thus, eight letters bear the name of another sender with Paul. Only Romans, Ephesians, and the three letters to Paul's delegates Timothy and Titus were sent out with Paul's name alone. It is difficult to know exactly what such cosponsorship entailed. Was it purely formal, a gesture of solidarity? Or did it mean that the co-senders also had some hand in the shaping of the letter?

The questions concerning the contribution of others to Paul's letters is sharpened when we consider the social setting presupposed by some passages in his correspondence. Scholars have long recognized the presence of a diatribal style in parts of the letters, notably Romans and the Corinthian letters. The style is highly dialogical, with the direct address of readers, the frequent use of apostrophe and rhetorical questions, the employment of stock examples for illustration, and the use of stereotypical moral commonplaces, such as tables of household ethics, lists of vices and virtues, and polemics against opponents.[29] Such style was formerly associated with the sort of street-corner preaching of sophists and philosophers like Dio Chrysostom or Apollonius of Tyana,[30] but more recent study has shown that the diatribe is a style of teaching that has its home in the classroom, as in the *Discourses of Epictetus*.[31] Elements of the diatribe in Paul's letters therefore represent a literary transposition of the dialogical exchanges between teacher and student. The communal activity of study and teaching could have been the practice of Paul with Timothy and Titus and Sosthenes and Silas even at his workbench, in the manner of other ancient philosophers and rabbis.

Other portions of his letters contain examples of midrashim (see esp. Gal 3–4; 2 Cor 3–4; Rom 9–11) in which scriptural texts are carefully elaborated within a sometimes highly technical argument. For Paul's Pharisaic movement—from which rabbinic Judaism derived—the practice of mid-

---

29. See Malherbe, *Moral Exhortation*.
30. As in Bultmann, *Der Stil der paulinischen Predigt*.
31. Stowers, *Diatribe*.

rash was not a private but a communal activity. It was what teacher and students did together over the text of Torah.[32] It is highly likely, then, that in the portions of letters displaying such close and extended interpretation, we see set pieces worked out by Paul and his coworkers in their communal practice of midrash. As with the diatribe, so with midrash: Paul's letters evince the literary residue of a social practice. The corollary is that something very much like a Pauline "school" was operative during his ministry that quite possibly had a hand in the production of his letters. The social setting for the Pauline correspondence, in short, is as complex as for the Pauline mission.

Further complicating Pauline correspondence is the apostle's use of prior traditions. Such usage involves more than literary connections, however important; it also points to Paul's immersion in the wider Christian movement. The materials that Paul brings into his letters affect the style and vocabulary of the literary contexts in which he places them, since he not only cites, alludes to, and echoes prior traditions but also comments on or elaborates them. Of perhaps greatest importance is Paul's use of the Septuagint—a topic to which I will return in a later chapter. For now I simply note that when Paul engages Scripture, as he does especially in Galatians, Romans, and 1 and 2 Corinthians, he engages it vigorously, even passionately; the presence of scriptural citations makes a great difference in the shape of his discourse. But there are other letters in which Paul uses Scripture only slightly if at all (Ephesians, Colossians, 1 and 2 Thessalonians, 1 and 2 Timothy, Titus, and Philemon). This does not mean Scripture is utterly absent; its implicit presence can be detected in a number of cases.[33] But it does mean that the Pauline correspondence is at best uneven in its deployment of Scripture.

Paul's letters use other elements drawn from tradition. He makes use of confessional formulas (Rom 10:9; 1 Cor 12:3), kerygmatic statements (1 Cor 15:3–8; Rom 4:24–25; 1 Thess 1:9–10; Titus 3:4–7), hymns (Phil 2:6–11; Col 1:15–20; 1 Tim 3:16; 2 Tim 2:11–13), liturgical formulas (Eph 5:14; 1 Cor 16:22; Gal 3:28; 4:6), and even—occasionally—the words of Jesus (1 Cor 7:10; 9:14; 11:24–25; 1 Thess 4:15; 1 Tim 5:18). Paul works frequently with traditions

---

32. See Holtz, "Midrash"; Safrai, "Education and the Study of Torah." It is a practice that continues. In my PhD seminars with the great Judah Goldin at Yale (in 1971–72), students sat around the table, reading aloud in turn the unpointed Hebrew of the *Avot of Rabbi Nathan* and the *Sifre on Deuteronomy*, and expounding, under his guidance, the nuances of the texts.

33. See, e.g., Hays, *Echoes of Scripture*.

associated with the practice of baptism (see Rom 6:1–11; 1 Cor 1:13–17; 6:11; 10:2; 12:13; 15:29; Gal 3:27–4:6; Eph 4:5; Col 2:12; Titus 3:4–7) and once with the practice of the Lord's Supper (1 Cor 11:23–26). Perhaps most impressive is the way in which the story of Jesus—by which he means the pattern of Jesus's obedient faith toward God and self-emptying love for humans—governs his thought (see Rom 1:17; 3:21–26; 5:12–21; 6:3–13; 1 Cor 1:17; 2:16; 8:11–13; 11:23–32; 15:12–18; 2 Cor 1:18–22; 4:7–15; 5:14–21; 8:9; Gal 1:42; 2:16–21; Eph 2:1–22; 5:2, 25; Phil 2:4–11; Col 1:21; 2:20; 3:3; 1 Thess 4:14; 1 Tim 1:15; 2:6; 2 Tim 1:10; 2:8; Titus 2:14).

The use of secretaries, cosponsorship, the presence of social teaching practices (midrash and diatribe), and the use of prior traditions all point us to the conclusion that Paul's correspondence was both socially and literarily a complex process. It will not do to think of Paul sitting by lamplight alone in a tent, summoning vagrant thoughts and imaginations; his arguments are too disciplined, and his use of prior traditions too pervasive, for that model of authorship to work. But this subject can be pushed one step further.

## Clusters of Letters and an Adequate Model of Authorship

Having shown common elements in the canonical collection of Pauline letters, I now return to an issue I touched on in the introduction to this book—namely, the way that collection falls into distinct clusters, with groups of two or three letters having a strong family resemblance (together with a number of differences) that distinguishes them from other such groups. This phenomenon is too little noticed among Pauline scholars, but deserves close attention. Only a surface survey is possible within the constraints of space, but even such an inadequate account should suffice to support two critical points concerning Paul's correspondence. First, an honest assessment of all the data reveals that the premise on which the conventional authentic/inauthentic hypothesis is based is wrong: there is no consistent Pauline core (of style or content) against which other letters can be measured and adjudged pseudonymous. Second, the presence of multiple clusters (of style and content) within the Pauline collection demands a more adequate theory of authorship than the conventional one, which has Paul himself penning seven letters, leaving six letters to be composed by members of Paul's school after his death. I begin by describing each cluster and then advance an alternative theory of composition.

*Thessalonian Cluster*

First and Second Thessalonians are written to the same church by the same set of cosponsors (Paul, Timothy, and Silvanus). Both have an abbreviated greeting, and both lack any personal greetings at the end. They both assume gentile believers. The stylistic similarity between the two letters is sufficient to have generated theories of copying one from the other.[34] Both letters have extended discussions of a future parousia, although they present different scenarios concerning that event and differ in tone (1 Thess 4:13–5:4; 2 Thess 2:3–12). Further differences: in 1 Thessalonians Paul devotes considerable space to his past relations with the church and his present circumstances (1:2–2:14; 3:1–10), whereas 2 Thessalonians has only a brief reminder of his behavior among them (3:6–10); in 1 Thessalonians the death and resurrection of Jesus are pivotal (1:10; 4:14; 5:9–10), while in 2 Thessalonians they are absent; in 1 Thessalonians the community issue is grief and lack of hope (4:13), and in 2 Thessalonians it is panic and ceasing daily activities like work (2:1–3; 3:10–12). Still, the two letters clearly go together well, especially if 2 Thessalonians is read as the response to a crisis generated by Paul's own words in the first letter.[35]

But it is equally important to note what these two letters do not contain. Although the respective eschatological sections echo scriptural passages, there is a notable lack of explicit citation or interpretation of Scripture in either letter. Neither has any element of the diatribe. There is nothing in either about the law or circumcision, certainly not as opposed to grace or faith. The cross is not mentioned. There is no Jew-gentile issue; Jews are mentioned only briefly in 1 Thess 2:14–16 as the persecutors of the church in Judea and as killers of Jesus.[36] There are no references to baptism or the Lord's Supper. Although the Holy Spirit is present in both letters—and prophecy is encouraged in 1 Thess 5:20—there is no elaboration of spiritual gifts and absolutely no sense of the Spirit as indwelling power for transformation: the ethical instructions in 1 Thess 4:1–12 touch on external behavior more than internal dispositions.

---

34. See J. Bailey, "Who Wrote II Thessalonians?"; Roose, "2 Thessalonians."

35. See L. Johnson, *Writings of the New Testament*, 249–60.

36. I do not find the arguments for thinking of this passage as an interpolation convincing.

## Galatians/Romans Cluster

With this cluster, it is easier to begin with differences. Galatians is cosponsored; Romans is ascribed to Paul alone. Romans has a standard greeting and opening prayer; Galatians replaces the opening prayer with an explosive "I am astonished" (*thaumazō*, 1:6). Romans has the most extensive list of final greetings; Galatians lacks them altogether. Galatians is written to the local churches of a region that Paul had founded; Romans to a church in Rome that Paul did not found and does not know personally. Galatians remains fixed from beginning to end on the issue of community upheaval caused by ambitions among gentile converts concerning law, circumcision, and righteousness measured by the law (3:1–5; 4:21–31; 5:2–12; 6:13–15), and Paul's tone is highly polemical. Although Romans deals with the same issues, it does so not in response to local troubles but as part of a magisterial argument arising out of Paul's mission to Jews and gentiles. Both letters make Abraham key to their argument, but each letter deals with Abraham in a distinct fashion (Gal 3:16–22; Rom 4:1–25); both letters touch on the issue of table fellowship, but from different angles (Gal 2:11–15; Rom 14:1–23).

Despite such differences, there is no mistaking the family resemblance of the two letters. Stylistically, they are both strongly dialectical, with elements of the diatribe—Romans, indeed, is from start to end a scholastic diatribe in the form of a letter.[37] In Galatians and Romans, furthermore, we find the Jew-gentile issue paramount, with grace and faith and freedom and life set dialectically against works and law and slavery and death (Gal 2:16–21; 5:1, 13; Rom 6:15–8:4). In these two letters above all, we see Paul's most sustained and intense engagement with Scripture, not only through citation but also through sometimes technical forms of midrashic interpretation (Gal 3:6–18; 4:26–31; Rom 3:10–18; 9:1–11:36). Both letters are generous in reporting Paul's own life, whether past or present (Gal 1:11–2:15; 4:12–20; Rom 1:8–15; 15:14–33). In both letters, some anxiety concerning Paul's authority is displayed: in Galatians he must assert that authority to change minds and practices; in Romans he must insinuate that authority to win favor and future support. In both letters, the community practice of baptism plays a key role in Paul's argument (Gal 3:27–4:7; Rom 6:1–11). In both, Christ's faithful death is critical (Gal 1:4; 2:20–21; 6:14; Rom 3:21–26;

---

37. For an exposition of the diatribal argument, see L. Johnson, *Writings of the New Testament*, 305–19.

5:12–21), though only Galatians uses the language of cross and crucifixion (3:1; 5:11, 24; 6:12–14); and while Romans uses the language of resurrection extensively of both Jesus and believers (1:4; 4:24–25; 6:4–5, 9; 7:4; 8:11, 34; 10:9), Galatians does so only once with reference to Jesus alone (1:1). Galatians and Romans strongly emphasize the role of the Holy Spirit as an indwelling power for personal transformation and oppose "living according to the flesh" and "living according to the Spirit" (Rom 5:5; 7:6; 8:2–27; 15:13–19; Gal 3:2–5; 4:6, 29; 5:5–25). Despite the real differences between these two letters, then, they are clearly and powerfully linked by these thematic, stylistic, and rhetorical elements.

What does the Galatians/Romans cluster lack? Most striking is the complete absence of the eschatological urgency expressed in the two Thessalonian letters. Galatians speaks of the "Jerusalem above" (4:26) and of a "new creation" (6:15) but contains no reference to a future coming of Jesus. Romans' short evocation of creation's groaning for the revelation of God's children (8:18–23) bears no resemblance to the future parousia anticipated by the Thessalonian letters. To anticipate comparison with other clusters, Romans and Galatians lack any reference to the Lord's Supper, deal with no behavioral issues apart from those pertinent to Jew-gentile relations, pay no attention to household relations, and have only the briefest acknowledgment of local leadership.

Before turning to the description of other clusters, a short pause to consider what we have so far observed. Quite apart from the fact that the Thessalonian letters and Galatians/Romans manifestly reveal distinct (and internally consistent) "hands" at the stylistic level, and quite apart from the lack of Jew-gentile/law-faith issues in one cluster and its pervasiveness in the other, two major discrepancies command our attention. The first is the dominance of future parousia discourse in the Thessalonian letters and its complete absence in the Galatians/Romans cluster. The second is emphasis on personal transformation through the Holy Spirit in Galatians and Romans and the complete absence of that theme in the Thessalonian letters.

I submit that any reader capable in Greek, coming blind to these four letters from the outside and uninfected by theories of Pauline authorship, would with no hesitation place them in two separate piles and assign to them two different authors. Yet 1 Thessalonians, since it is magnificently capable of being coordinated with Acts, is universally accepted as Pauline, while 2 Thessalonians generally is not. Similarly, Romans, which corresponds so marvelously with Acts and the Corinthian letters, is (almost) universally taken to be by Paul, and Galatians, which is not at all capable of being inserted confidently in Paul's ministry,[38] is also read as Pauline, because of its family resemblance to Romans (not, we shall see, to all the other "undisputed" letters)! Our neutral but competent reader would, I think, be astonished to find that 1 Thessalonians, Romans, and Galatians are assumed not only to all be authentic but also to form part of the measure of what is authentically Pauline, by which other letters are judged.

### Corinthians Cluster

This cluster is in some respects the most difficult to characterize. The family connection is obvious, since both letters are written to the Corinthian church and can be read easily in sequence. Even the surface similarities, however, contain some small differences: 1 Corinthians is cosponsored by Paul and Sosthenes, while 2 Corinthians is sent by Paul and Timothy; 1 Corinthians is sent to the church of God in Corinth, "together with all those who . . . call on the name" (1:2), and 2 Corinthians to the church of God in Corinth "with all the saints in all of Achaia" (1:1, RSV adapted); the greeting in 1 Corinthians is followed by a prayer of thanksgiving, whereas in 2 Corinthians there is a prayer of blessing; 1 Corinthians contains final greetings by name, whereas 2 Corinthians ends with generalized greetings. These are, to be sure, minor differences.

Comparing the style of the two letters is more difficult. The language of 1 Corinthians is deeply affected by the multiple practical issues in the community Paul addresses: schisms and conflicts (1:10–16; 11:19), sexual behavior (5:1–13; 6:12–20; 7:1–40), lawsuits (6:1–8), disagreements concerning food (8:1–13), attendance at pagan shrines (10:1–30), discrimination at the Lord's Supper (11:17–34), and disorder in the practice of spiritual gifts (11:2–16; 12:1–14:39). The diatribal elements in 1 Corinthians are patent: rhetorical questions, direct address, examples, citation of texts, irony, recitation of hardships, sharp contrasts.[39] While vigorous and at times challenging, the Greek of 1 Corinthians is nevertheless relatively clear, especially when anchored in real-life matters.

---

38. Despite the efforts of Murphy-O'Connor, *Paul*, 180–84.

39. Rhetorical questions in 1:20; 3:4–5; 4:21; 5:2; 6:3–8; 9:1, 4, 6–7; 10:19, 30; 12:17, 29–30; 14:7, 15, 36; 15:35; direct address in 1:26; 10:18; citation of texts in 1:31; 2:9, 16; 3:19–20; 5:13; 6:16; 9:9–10; 10:7, 26; 14:21; 15:27, 45, 55; irony in 4:8; hardship catalogue in 4:11–13; contrasts in 4:10; 6:12; 15:12–19.

The Greek of 2 Corinthians is correspondingly more difficult because of the lack of specific grounding. The concrete references are to Paul's past: his frustrated journeying (1:15–22; 2:12–13; 7:5–6), letter (2:3–4, 9; 7:8–12), visits (2:1; 12:14; 13:1), sufferings (1:8–11; 6:4–10; 11:23–29), financial practices (11:7–11), and mystical ascent (12:1–10). Only his present efforts for the collection emerge with genuine clarity (8:1–9:15). Second Corinthians is at times simply hard to decipher. The letter has a handful of rhetorical questions (3:1; 6:15–16; 11:7, 22; 12:13), some direct address (7:2–3; 10:7; 11:1), paradoxes (6:8–10), extended lists of hardships (4:8–10; 11:23–29), and citation of texts (4:13; 6:2, 16–18; 8:15; 9:9–10; 10:17; 13:1), but as a whole, 2 Corinthians lacks the dialogical character of 1 Corinthians. The letter is driven, rather, by powerful and extended metaphors (e.g., 2:14–17; 3:1–17; 4:3–6, 7–11; 4:17–5:10; 8:9–10; 10:1–6; 11:2–3, 12–15).

Thematically, the greatest difference between 1 and 2 Corinthians is the treatment of eschatology. First Corinthians lines up most closely to the Thessalonian letters in expressions of future eschatology (1 Cor 1:7–8; 3:12–15; 7:29–31), although it presents a scenario of the eschaton that does not correspond to either of those offered in the Thessalonian letters. But in 2 Cor 4:16–5:10 Paul's eschatological language moves away from the grand portrayals of a communal future, to a more platonic reflection on "being with the Lord" when free of the body at death.[40]

The letters are bound most closely by their compelling and largely consistent witness to the developing (or deteriorating) relationship between Paul and the Corinthian community he founded. In the first letter Paul works hard to establish his authority to teach a restless community that is dividing on the basis of allegiance to rival teachers like Cephas and Apollo (1 Cor 1:10–16; 3:1–4), and seeks to show that he and Apollos, in particular, are colleagues rather than rivals (3:5–4:7), and that Paul and other preachers proclaim the same good news (15:1–11). In 2 Corinthians the rift between Paul and the Corinthians is so advanced that Paul must forge a rhetoric of reconciliation to persuade his refractory readers to join in his collection effort for Jerusalem (5:11–7:4); as for the rivals, they now appear as "false apostles, deceitful workmen, disguising themselves as apostles of Christ" (11:13) who, Paul suggests, preach another Jesus, a different gospel, than the one they received (11:4).

Accompanying this relationship crisis is the theme of boasting. In 1 Corinthians, Paul reminds his readers of the paradox of their call: they were

---

40. See esp. Dupont, *ΣΥΝ ΧΡΙΣΤΟΙ*; see also Plevnik, *Paul and the Parousia*, which can include only the Thessalonian letters, 1 Corinthians, and Philippians in its survey.

nothing in human terms, yet "the world or life or death or the present or the future, all are yours; and you are Christ's; and Christ is God's" (3:22–23). They are not therefore in a position to boast, for "no human being might boast in the presence of God" (1:29), but rather Paul says, in a quotation from Jer 9:23–24, "Let him who boasts, boast of the Lord" (1:31). Their arrogance (5:2) and boasting (5:6) are therefore all the more repellent, because they fail to exercise even the most basic moral discernment among themselves (5:1–6:20). In 2 Corinthians, Paul declares that the Corinthians ought to be the basis for his boasting as an apostle (1:12; 7:4; 8:24), but their abandoning him for rival preachers forces him to an extended (and admittedly embarrassing) boasting (10:1–12:13), even as he repeats the citation from Jeremiah, "'Let him who boasts, boast of the Lord.' For it is not the man who commends himself that is accepted, but the man whom the Lord commends" (10:17–18).

If we compare the Corinthian letters to the other clusters, we can see equally dramatic points of convergence and divergence. The two letters have little in common, stylistically or substantively, with the Thessalonian correspondence, even though, as I have noted, there is some agreement on the matter of a future eschatology in 1 Corinthians. With Galatians and Romans, the Corinthian correspondence agrees most, perhaps, in its emphasis on the Holy Spirit as a power interior to human freedom, and on both present and future human transformation. They also share an emphasis on both the death and resurrection of Jesus: the terms for "cross" (*stauros*) and "crucifixion" (*stauroō*) occur as often in them as in Galatians (1 Cor 1:13, 17–18, 23; 2:2, 8; 2 Cor 13:4).

The most startling contrast with the Galatians/Romans cluster is the complete absence of the tension between Jew and gentile in either letter; they appear together in 1 Cor 1:22–24; 9:20–21; 10:32, and in the baptismal formula of 12:13, but never as an issue within the church.[41] By themselves, gentiles are spoken of negatively (1 Cor 5:1; 10:20; 12:2) as outsiders. Despite the frequent use of citations from Scripture in both letters (1 Cor 1:31; 2:9, 16; 3:19–20; 5:13; 6:16; 9:9–10; 10:7, 26, 23; 14:21; 15:27, 45, 55; 2 Cor 4:13; 6:2, 16–18; 8:15; 9:9–10; 10:17; 13:1), and despite the elaborate midrashic interpretations of the exodus story in 1 Cor 10:1–11 and 2 Cor 3:7–17, each of which has the effect of a *qal va-chomer* argument,[42] Scripture is deployed

---

41. In 2 Cor 11:24 "the Jews" appear only as persecutors in Paul's table of hardships, as they had in 1 Thess 2:14–16; "gentiles" also appear only as a source of danger (2 Cor 11:26).

42. "From the light to the heavy," or "from the lesser to the greater" (see also Rom 5:11–21).

mostly as a straightforward authority for points made in Paul's argument, with specific texts attaching to specific situations. Except for the strange "Romans lightning bolt"[43] of 1 Cor 15:56, "the power of sin is the law," the term *nomos* ("law") is used entirely positively in 1 Corinthians (9:8, 20; 14:21, 34) and does not appear in 2 Corinthians at all. It follows that the term "works of the law" is absent as well: the term *ergon/erga* refers to deeds (1 Cor 3:13–15; 5:2; 2 Cor 10:11; 11:15), task (1 Cor 15:58; 16:10), or accomplishment (1 Cor 9:1; 2 Cor 9:8). It follows further that *peritomē* is "nothing" in 1 Cor 7:19 and is absent from 2 Corinthians. Paul's statement in 1 Cor 7:19, in fact, summarizes the positive view of the law: "Neither circumcision counts for anything nor uncircumcision, but keeping the commandments of God." And whereas "faithing" (*pisteuein*) and "faith" (*pistis*) occur throughout both letters, they are never opposed to the observance of the law. In short, First and Second Corinthians have some important points of contact with Galatians and Romans but are different from them in equally important ways. They form their own cluster within the Pauline collection.

## Colossians/Ephesians Cluster

Two of the letters written from captivity, Colossians and Ephesians are recognizably similar in style. They have no elements of the diatribe, with its characteristic dialogical elements. Instead, they feature relatively long hypotactic sentences, with extensive use of participles, and a tendency toward redundancy. This last feature characterizes Ephesians in particular, whose language has a certain liturgical cadence.[44] In places, the two letters use virtually identical phrases or clauses;[45] more often, similar terms are used in slightly different ways or in slightly different combinations.[46] A good example is Eph 5:19, which has the same words in the same order as Col 3:16 ("psalms," "hymns," "spiritual songs," "singing in your hearts to the Lord "), yet with a distinct effect, since the context of the series is different in each

---

43. I use the term by analogy with the expression "Johannine lightning bolt" applied by scholars to the language of Matt 11:25–30, as an indication of its unexpected appearance in that place.

44. See O'Brien, "Ephesians I"; Kirby, *Ephesians, Baptism and Pentecost*.

45. E.g., Eph 1:4/Col 1:22; Eph 1:15/Col 1:4; Eph 2:13/Col 1:20; Eph 4:2–3/Col 3:12–13; Eph 6:21–22/Col 4:7–8.

46. E.g., Eph 1:18/Col 1:9; Eph 2:15/Col 2:14; Eph 3:2/Col 1:25; Eph 3:16/Col 1:11.

case. Nevertheless, the style of the compositions is sufficiently alike to encourage theories of literary dependence.[47]

The letters share thematic elements as well. Both letters stress the divine status of Christ[48] and the reconciliation won through Christ's death and resurrection that represents a victory over cosmic powers,[49] creates a new humanity in which distinctions between Jew and gentile no longer create enmity (Eph 2:11–22; Col 3:10–11), and gives believers a participation in this resurrection life through the Holy Spirit (Eph 1:7, 19–23; 2:1, 5–10, 18; Col 1:12–14, 22; 2:13–15; 3:1–3). Both letters freely employ the language of mystery (*mystērion*) with regard to the church and God's plan to save gentiles (Eph 1:9; 3:3, 4, 9; 5:32; 6:19; Col 1:26–27; 2:2; 4:3), a plan that both connect to Paul's distinctive mission (Eph 3:1–13; Col 1:23–29; 4:3).[50] In both letters, the church is the body of Christ, whose head is Christ himself (Eph 1:22–23; 2:16–22; 3:6; 4:4, 12–15; 5:23; Col 1:18; 2:19).[51] Both letters use a table of household ethics in moral exhortation (Eph 5:21–6:9; Col 3:18–4:1).[52]

There are, to be sure, compositional differences. Colossians is sent from Paul and Timothy, and Ephesians from Paul alone; in Colossians the addressees are clearly indicated, while textual issues make the recipients of Ephesians obscure.[53] Colossians has a classic Pauline thanksgiving (1:3–7), whereas Ephesians has an opening prayer of blessing (1:3–14) followed by a thanksgiving (1:15–23). Although Colossians is written to a church founded by Paul's fellow prisoner Epaphras (1:7; 4:12) and not known to him personally, it is nevertheless full of incidental detail about that community's problems and contains a robust list of personal greetings to and from named individuals (4:7–17). In contrast, Ephesians lacks any reference to local circumstances and contains only the name of Paul's delegate, Tychicus (6:21; named also in Col 4:7). And whereas Ephesians

47. See, e.g., Goodspeed, *Meaning of Ephesians*; Coutts, "Relationship of Ephesians and Colossians."

48. Colossians speaks of the "beloved Son" (1:13) as "the image of the invisible God, the first-born of all creation; for in him all things were created" (1:15), and declares, "In him the whole fullness of deity dwells bodily" (2:9; see also 1:19). Ephesians declares that God chose them "in him [Christ] before the foundation of the world" (1:4).

49. Eph 1:20–23; 2:11–22; 3:10; Col 1:13, 21; 2:13–15; 3:1–4, 10.

50. See Caragounis, *Ephesian Mysterion*; Cerfaux, "Revelation."

51. Meeks, "'In One Body.'"

52. See Crouch, *Colossian Haustafel*; Sampley, *Two Shall Become One Flesh*.

53. For the textual problem (some manuscripts lack the name "Ephesians," yet the syntax seems to call out for a name), see Santer, "Text of Ephesians i. 1"; Batey, "Destination of Ephesians"; Best, "Recipients."

gives glancing attention to leaders in the church (4:11–12), Colossians is as silent as Galatians on this point.

The relationship between Colossians and Ephesians can be compared to that between Galatians and Romans. In Colossians, as in Galatians, Paul battles tendencies toward elitism and separatism in the local church of Colossae: certain people disqualify and judge others on the basis of their supposed greater maturity (perfection) given by circumcision, asceticism, and mysticism. Arguing on the basis of the experience of baptism, Paul insists that true maturity lies in ever-growing insight into the "truth of the gospel," which is transformation in the image of Christ.[54] The difference here is that Paul writes to a church he himself did not found, and does not use Scripture in the manner of Galatians; indeed, Colossians lacks any explicit reference to Scripture.[55] But as Romans picks up the themes of Galatians and works them into a larger theological reflection on God's work in Paul's mission, so does Ephesians raise the themes of Colossians into a theological reflection on God's work in the world, the difference from Romans being mainly the more explicitly cosmic character of the symbolism in Ephesians.[56]

The distance of the Colossians/Ephesians cluster from other letters in the collection should not be exaggerated. Language about "principalities and powers" (*archai kai exousiai*) used with reference to cosmic forces, for example, occurs several times in Colossians (1:16; 2:10, 15) and Ephesians (1:21; 3:10; 6:12), but is found also in Rom 8:38 (and possibly in 1 Cor 15:24 in one textual variant).[57] Colossians uses the equally obscure "elements of the universe" (*stoicheia tou kosmou*, 2:8, 20), found also in Gal 4:3, 9, but not in Ephesians. The term "surpass" (*hyperballein*) does not occur in Colossians but is a favorite in Ephesians (1:19; 2:7; 3:19) and is found even more frequently in 2 Corinthians (1:8; 3:10; 4:7, 17; 9:14; 11:23; 12:7). The repeated phrase "praise of glory" in Eph 1:6, 12, 14 occurs in a variant form in Phil 1:11. The two letters seem to be especially rich in language about knowledge and enlightenment, but closer analysis shows that the concentration is not unusual in a Pauline letter. "Knowledge" (*gnōsis*) occurs once in Col 2:3 and in Eph 3:19, but appears also in Rom 15:14; 1 Cor 1:5; 2 Cor 4:6; Phil 3:8. "Recognition" (*epignōsis*) is a favorite of Colossians (1:9, 10; 2:2; 3:10) and Ephesians (1:17; 4:13), but is used similarly in Rom 1:28; 3:20; 10:2; Phil 1:9;

---

54. See L. Johnson, "Ritual Imprinting."
55. Ephesians, in contrast, has direct citations of Scripture in 4:8, 25–26; 5:31; 6:2–3.
56. See Wild, "The Warrior and the Prisoner."
57. See Caird, *Principalities and Powers*; Schlier, *Principalities and Powers*.

1 Tim 2:4; 2 Tim 2:25; 3:7; Titus 1:1; Phlm 6. The term "enlighten" (*phōtizein*) occurs twice in Ephesians (1:18; 3:9) and appears also in 1 Cor 4:5 and 2 Tim 1:10. "Light" (*phōs*) is a metaphor for revelation in Eph 5:8–9, 13 and Col 1:12, but also in Rom 13:12; 2 Cor 4:6; 6:14; 1 Thess 5:5; 1 Tim 6:16.

Even when all appropriate qualifications have been made, there is no avoiding the conclusion that Ephesians and Colossians together make up another distinctive cluster within the Pauline collection. In this surface examination of such clusters, I have used eschatology as something of a test theme. We saw that the Thessalonian cluster had an intense expectation of a future parousia, which was completely absent from the Galatians/Romans cluster. The Corinthian cluster presented mixed evidence, with a future eschatological scenario provided by 1 Corinthians (but one not in agreement with either of those found in the Thessalonian letters), and a more individualistic, Platonic expectation of being with Christ when out of the body in 2 Corinthians. What, then, do we find in Colossians/Ephesians?

Colossians focuses completely on what God has already accomplished for the readers: the Father "has qualified us to share in the inheritance of the saints in light. He has delivered us from the dominion of darkness and transferred us to the kingdom of his beloved Son" (1:12–13). When Paul speaks of the readers being presented as holy and blameless and irreproachable before him, he means their persevering in faith (1:22–23): "As therefore you received Christ Jesus the Lord, so live in him" (2:6). God has already raised them up with Christ (2:12), and they should therefore "seek the things that are above, where Christ is, seated at the right hand of God" (3:1). The closest thing to a future expectation follows: "When Christ who is our life appears, then you also will appear with him in glory" (3:4).

Ephesians speaks of the seal of the Holy Spirit, "which is the guarantee of our inheritance until we acquire possession of it" (1:13–14). But like Colossians, its emphasis is on their now being made alive (2:1, 5), saved (2:5), and raised up to "sit with him in the heavenly places in Christ Jesus" (2:6), that his grace might be shown "in the coming ages" (2:7). The gift of the Holy Spirit is "for building up the body of Christ, until we all attain to the unity of faith and of the knowledge of the Son of God, to mature manhood, to the measure of the fullness of Christ" (4:12–13). Ephesians mentions the reward or punishment to be received (from God) by either master or slave doing good or evil (6:8–9). Ephesians closes in 6:10–20, however, with dense eschatological discourse casting believers in battle "against the principalities, against the powers, against the world rulers of this present darkness, against the spiritual hosts of wickedness in the heavenly places" (6:12). The imagery reminds us of 1 Thess 5:4–10 and 2 Cor 10:3–4, but it does not in the least resemble the expectation of a future parousia in the Thessalonian cluster and in 1 Corinthians.

*Letters to Paul's Delegates Cluster*

No great argument is required to establish the distinctiveness of this cluster. The Pastoral Letters, as they are usually designated, have been grouped together at least since the Muratorian Canon, which speaks of them as being written "for the regulation of ecclesiastical discipline" (lines 62–63).[58] Precisely the special character of these three letters encourages their nearly unanimous exclusion from the proper Pauline collection. The conventional position today regards them as pseudonymous compositions written by a single author in a single literary construction, not real letters but a fictional correspondence: 2 Timothy represents the aging apostle in a farewell discourse, while 1 Timothy and Titus anticipate the development of ecclesiastical church orders.[59] My delicate task in the next few paragraphs is to affirm the distinctive character of these three letters (they *are* a "cluster"), while not agreeing with the conventional categorization of them as obviously pseudonymous.

The first thing that distinguishes the three letters is that they are written to Paul's delegates Timothy and Titus, each of whom (according to other letters) played a significant role in Paul's ministry.[60] Whereas Paul's fourth personal letter was written to the "fellow worker" Philemon as a letter of commendation to ensure the safe return of his slave Onesimus, these three letters are written to two of Paul's close collaborators in the mission and

58. The origin of the designation "Pastoral Letters" is obscure. Thomas Aquinas already refers to 1 Timothy as *quasi pastoralis regula*, and 2 Timothy as *ad curam pastoralem*; see L. Johnson, *Letters to Timothy*, 13, 35.

59. The conventional position is elaborated by Redalié, *Paul après Paul*, and is reflected in such commentaries as Dibelius and Conzelmann, *Pastoral Epistles*, and Bassler, *1 Timothy, 2 Timothy, Titus*.

60. Timothy cosponsored six of the letters ascribed to Paul (Philemon, Philippians, 1 Thessalonians, 2 Thessalonians, 2 Corinthians, Colossians). He served as Paul's delegate to Thessalonica (1 Thess 3:2) and Philippi (Phil 2:19) as well as to the church in Corinth (1 Cor 4:17; 16:10–11; Rom 16:21). Titus was a Greek (Gal 2:3) who traveled with Paul to Jerusalem (Gal 2:1), and is linked especially to Paul's Corinthian ministry (2 Cor 2:13; 7:6, 13–14), playing a particular role in Paul's collection efforts (2 Cor 8:6, 16, 23; 12:18) as Paul's "partner" (*koinonos*) and "fellow worker" (*synergos*, 2 Cor 8:23).

concern their character and behavior as coworkers. As we have seen, the letters have the basic formal elements of other Pauline letters.

Taken together, the three letters exhibit a Greek style that is neither dialectical and diatribal (as in Romans, Galatians, and 1 Corinthians) nor ornate and rich in metaphor (as in 2 Corinthians, Colossians, and Ephesians). The koine of the Pastorals is "flatter" or "looser" than that in those letters. The three letters share a number of distinctive locutions: a preference for "Christ Jesus" over "Jesus Christ,"[61] a use of "in Christ" that is noteworthy,[62] and the citation of traditional material,[63] often introduced by a formula found only in these letters, "the saying is faithful" (*pistos ho logos*).[64] They also contain a large number of words that are otherwise unattested in the undisputed letters; such *hapax legomena* tend to occur in passages that deal with matters other than those found in the undisputed letters.[65] At the same time, the three letters have passages that sound just like the undisputed letters both in diction and syntax. The combination of similarity and difference has led to the theory that a pseudonymous author used fragments of authentic Pauline letters to lend credibility to his pseudonymous effort.[66]

The three letters are by no means identical. Their differences are as significant as their similarities. In terms of letter types, 2 Timothy is written from captivity and is a perfect example of a personal paraenetic letter (with protreptic elements),[67] while 1 Timothy and Titus assume Paul's active ministry and are examples of the sort of *mandata principis* letters written by superiors to delegates that combine community directives with personal advice. First Timothy and 2 Timothy each have a short burst of scriptural citations (1 Tim 5:17-19; 2 Tim 2:19), while Titus lacks any citation. Although each of the letters devotes space to polemic against false teachers in the manner of ancient philosophers,[68] neither the character of the opposition

61. The letters use "Christ Jesus" some twenty-seven times and use "Jesus Christ" only five times (1 Tim 6:3, 14; 2 Tim 2:8; Titus 1:1; 3:6). Compare the more evenly distributed thirteen to nineteen uses of the two terms in Romans, and the six to eleven distribution in 1 Corinthians.

62. See Allan, "'In Christ' Formula."

63. See Ellis, "Traditions in the Pastoral Epistles"; Gundry, "Hymn Quoted in 1 Tim 3:16."

64. See Knight, *Faithful Sayings*.

65. See, e.g., Grayston and Herdan, "Authorship of the Pastorals."

66. Classically argued by P. Harrison, *Problem of the Pastoral Epistles*; see also Miller, *Pastoral Letters*; Cook, "Pastoral Fragments Reconsidered."

67. See L. Johnson, *Letters to Timothy*, 137-43, 320-23.

68. Karris, "Polemic of the Pastoral Epistles."

nor the mode of response is identical in the three letters.[69] Compared to 2 Timothy, Titus and 1 Timothy are overwhelmingly focused on directives, with 1 Timothy concentrating on the appointment of worthy officers (3:1–13) and the solving of problems (2:1–15; 5:3–22; 6:1–3) in the assembly, and Titus concentrating on good order in the household (2:1–3:2).

The consistently practical and paraenetic-protreptic character of the three letters to Paul's delegates makes thematic comparison with other clusters more difficult. Certainly, many themes that are found in other letters are found in them as well: Paul's call to be an apostle (1 Tim 1:12–17), his mission to the gentiles (1 Tim 2:7; 3:16; 2 Tim 4:17), the suffering he underwent for the gospel (2 Tim 1:12; 3:11), Christ's redemptive death (1 Tim 2:3–6; 2 Tim 1:10; 2:11; Titus 2:14), Christ's exaltation (1 Tim 3:16), salvation for all humans (1 Tim 1:9–10; 4:10; 2 Tim 2:10), the gift of the Spirit (1 Tim 3:16; 4:1; 2 Tim 1:7, 14; Titus 3:5), and baptism (Titus 3:5–6). A prominent role is given to grace (1 Tim 1:2, 12–14; 6:1; 2 Tim 1:2, 9; 2:1; 4:22; Titus 1:4; 2:11; 3:7, 15) and to conscience (1 Tim 1:5, 19; 3:9; 4:2; 2 Tim 1:3; Titus 1:15). Faith is as prominent as it is in other Pauline letters,[70] as is love (eleven occurrences). The instructions concerning local leaders, furthermore, are not out of line with the scattered instructions in other Pauline letters, and conform to what is known about leadership within the synagogue.[71]

What about eschatology? The Pastorals present still another variant on this most various Pauline theme. They do not use the word *parousia*, but they use its near equivalent, *epiphaneia* ("appearance"). At times the term (or its verbal form) refers to saving events in the past or present (2 Tim 1:10;

---

69. In 2 Timothy, the opposition is characterized as charlatans who take advantage of vulnerable women and declare that the resurrection has already happened (2:16–18, 23; 3:1–9, 13; 4:3–5). In 1 Timothy, the opposition has ambitions to be teachers of the law, caught up in what is "falsely called knowledge" (6:20) and is entangled in myths and genealogies that do not advance faith, rejects conscience, forbids marriage and the eating of certain foods, and seeks wealth (1:3–7, 19–20; 4:2–3; 6:9–10). In Titus, the opposition comes from the circumcision party and teaches for gain Jewish myths and purity laws (1:10–15). In 2 Timothy, Paul's delegate is to shun the false teachers and correct them in the hope they will repent (2:24–26); in Titus, the superintendent (*episkopos*) appointed by Titus is to confute opponents and silence them (1:9–11), and if they do not listen after several admonitions, they are to be shunned (3:10); in 1 Timothy, Paul tells his delegate to charge "certain people" from teaching (1:3) and offers theological rebuttals to the opposition's positions (1:8–11; 4:3–5, 8–10; 6:6–8).

70. Occurring thirty-three times in these three letters; cf. twenty-two uses in Galatians, thirty-eight in Romans, and fourteen in both Corinthians letters.

71. See L. Johnson, *Letters to Timothy*, 74–76.

Titus 2:11; 3:4). But it is also used for a future "manifestation" of the Lord Jesus Christ (1 Tim 6:14; 2 Tim 4:1; 4:8) or "our great God and Savior Jesus Christ" (Titus 2:13). Second Timothy speaks repeatedly of a future "day" (1:12, 18; 4:8).[72] Both letters to Timothy can also refer to the present time of opposition as "in later times" (1 Tim 4:1), "in the last days" (2 Tim 3:1), and "the time is coming" (2 Tim 4:3). In brief, the eschatology of the Pastorals seems close to that of the Thessalonian letters and 1 Corinthians: a future appearance of the Lord is expected. At the same time, we find language of "eternal life" (1 Tim 1:16) "immortality" (1 Tim 6:16; 2 Tim 1:10), and "heavenly kingdom" (2 Tim 4:18).

All these elements of similarity and difference combine in such fashion as to make the letters to Paul's delegates a distinctive cluster within the canonical collection. It must be emphasized, however, that such similarity and difference applies to all the clusters; the Pastorals are no closer or more distant from Galatians and Romans as those two letters are to the Thessalonian correspondence.

### Philippians and Philemon

I have called these two letters "outliers" because they do not fit easily into any of the five clusters I have described. Philemon is simply too short and idiosyncratic to say a great deal about it stylistically or thematically, although its greetings align it most naturally with Colossians and Ephesians[73]—and I will devote a later chapter to Paul's voice in this letter. Philippians is another sort of case. It does not line up easily with any single cluster, yet it contains elements found in more than one of the clusters and challenges any oversimplified construal of the Pauline collection.

The authenticity of Philippians has not been seriously challenged since it was initially rejected by F. C. Baur;[74] no doubt its universal acceptance by historical-critical scholars owes much to the way in which Paul's spir-

72. Cf. Rom 2:16; 1 Cor 1:8; 5:5; 2 Cor 1:14; Phil 1:6.

73. The names in Phlm 1-2 and 23-24 correspond to those in Col 4:10-17. That so short and personal a letter was preserved in the first place is probably because it was part of a three- or four-letter packet delivered by Tychicus (Philemon as letter of commendation; Colossians as letter to a local church [together with the lost letters to the Laodiceans], and Ephesians as a circular letter/treatise); an analogy is provided by 1, 2, and 3 John. See L. Johnson, *Writings of the New Testament*, 337-45, 495-505.

74. Baur, *Paulus, der Apostel Jesu Christi*.

ited autobiographical material in chapter three connects to the issue of law and faith in Romans and Galatians.[75] Yet the letter has a number of features ordinarily associated with "disputed" letters. Stylistically, for example, it is "flatter," lacking the dialogical edge and liveliness of the diatribe. It lacks any scriptural citations,[76] and it has expressions found elsewhere only in other captivity letters, such as "the praise of glory" in Phil 1:11 (see Eph 1:6, 12, 14). Philippians in 3:20 calls Jesus "savior" (*sōtēr*), a title otherwise found only in the "disputed" letters (Eph 5:23; 2 Tim 1:10; Titus 2:13; 3:6). The description of Paul's sufferings in Phil 1:16–18 finds its best match in 2 Tim 1:8–12; 2:9.

The emphasis on the cosmic scope of Christ's resurrection corresponds most closely to Col 1:15–20 and Eph 1:19–23, but the letter equally stresses "Christ, the righteousness from God that depends on faith" (Phil 3:9; cf. Rom 3:22) and Christ the exemplar of obedient service (Phil 2:5–11; cf. 1 Cor 11:1; 2 Tim 2:8–13). Indeed, the argument of 2 Tim 1:15–2:13, which presents in sequence the examples of Onesiphorus, the soldier, the athlete, the farmer, Jesus Christ, and Paul, is strikingly similar to the sequence in Phil 2:1–3:17, which offers as examples Jesus Christ, Timothy, Epaphroditus, and Paul. Phil 1:1 mentions superintendents (*episkopoi*) and deacons (*diakonoi*) as local leaders, in agreement with 1 Tim 3:2, 8, 12; 4:6; Titus 1:7.

In contrast to Paul's claim elsewhere that he is independent of support from his churches and works with his hands (2 Thess 3:6–9; 1 Cor 9:15–18; 2 Cor 11:7–12), Paul here gladly acknowledges that from "the beginning of the gospel" he has been in a relationship of "giving and receiving" with the Philippian church (Phil 4:14–15). At the same time, he stresses his personal contentment and self-sufficiency (*autarkeia*) with respect to possessions (4:11–13).

The eschatology of Philippians is also complex. On one hand, Paul expresses a definite future expectation like that found in the Thessalonian correspondence and 1 Corinthians (Phil 1:10; 2:16; 3:11, 20–21), and even gives such expectation a note of urgency: "The Lord is near" (4:5 NRSV). On the other hand, he also expects, should he die, that he will then "be with" Christ (1:21–23), reminding us more of 2 Cor 5:1–5. To complicate things further, Paul speaks of the Christians' "homeland" in spatial rather than temporal terms: it is "in heaven" (3:20; cf. 2 Cor 5:1–2; Eph 6:9; Col 1:5; 4:1); but "from it" we also "await a Savior, the Lord Jesus Christ" (3:20).

What Philippians reminds us of above all, if we are careful readers, is just how complex and multifarious the Pauline correspondence truly is. If

75. See Holtzmann, *Lehrbuch der historisch-kritisch Einleitung*, 272–92.
76. Joining 1 and 2 Thessalonians, Colossians, Philemon, and Titus in this respect.

my identification of the five clusters (and two outliers) is accurate—and I have tried to be strictly descriptive—then we clearly need a more adequate model of Pauline authorship than is usually offered.

## A More Adequate Model of Authorship

The conventional understanding of Pauline authorship does not problematize the "undisputed" letters, only the disputed ones. It therefore does not deal straightforwardly with the complexity of the correspondence that I have here examined: Paul is taken to be author/writer of the seven letters in the same manner that Cicero is taken to be the author/writer of the *Letters to Atticus*. The six letters that—according to the standard criteria—are classified as disputed are ascribed (vaguely, to be sure) to Pauline "schools": one moving in a more mystical direction (Ephesians, Colossians), the other in the direction of institutionalization (1 Timothy, 2 Timothy, Titus). The perceived differences in the two groups of letters (authentic and inauthentic) are ascribed to different authors/writers working in different times. The Pauline correspondence is placed in a temporal framework, and historical/ecclesiastical developments account for discrepancies between authentic and inauthentic letters.

In chapter 1 of this book ("Assessing the Sources") I noted that the standard criteria failed to meet the standard of logical rigor at both the formal and the material level, and noted further that the proposed "schools" had only the literature assigned to them as evidence for their existence. In this chapter on Paul's correspondence, I have shown how an honest assessment of the data presented by the entire Pauline collection—above all, the way in which letters fall into distinct stylistic and thematic clusters—shows the emptiness of the usual premise concerning Pauline authorship, namely, that there is a recognizable consistency in style and theme in seven of the letters that is lacking in the other six. In the face of my analysis, which is strictly descriptive, one could certainly choose one of those clusters as "really" written by Paul himself—let us say, Galatians and Romans—but then one would have to offer an account of the appearance of the other eleven letters that is more complex than the one offered by the standard introductions and commentaries.

A more adequate model of Pauline authorship must account for the unity and the variety across the entire correspondence that are most striking when letters are placed in natural clusters. I do not consider appeals to biographical circumstances (captivity rather than active ministry, aging and suffering) as adequate explanations for the data as I have laid it out. And however tempting, an appeal to the ancient rhetorical ideal of *prosōpopoiia* ("writing in character") is likewise insufficient; a brilliant writer like Lucian of Samosata could compose dazzling satires (*The Eunuch, Dialogues of the Dead*) while also composing sober—and stylistically distinct—treatises (*On Writing History, The Syrian Goddess*), but all the works ascribed to Paul are letters, and they all display, as we have seen, the same formal features. The clusters are distinct, moreover, not only stylistically but thematically, as I hope my illustrative example of eschatology has demonstrated. What is needed is a model of authorship that is commensurate to the complexity of the correspondence as I have described it.

I propose, then, that we follow up on the intimations presented earlier in this chapter. That Paul used a secretary, that some of his letters were cosponsored, that his letters show diverse use of traditional materials, that some letters show the literary residue of social (scholastic) practice—all these suggest a more complex process of composition all through the correspondence than the simple distinction between "individual author" and "later school." What the product suggests, indeed, is a process of composition involving a Pauline "school" at work in all his letters, albeit in varying degrees.[77]

I by no means am suggesting that Paul himself did not "author" his letters, only that the process of "writing" them was probably more complex and socially located than is usually supposed. It is impossible to demonstrate how much or how little Paul himself physically wrote any of his letters—Philemon would seem to be the most obvious candidate for a note written by the apostle himself—but it is possible to affirm that he "authorized" all the letters that bear his name.

A present-day analogy may be helpful. The president of the United States of America delivers a formal address to congress each year. Typically, the president tells his staff what basic themes he wants to state. The staff, who know the president's ideas and often the rhythms of his speech, work on a draft. The president reads the draft and responds. The process may take weeks or even months for such a major address. In the whole process, the president may contribute ideas, phrases, or paragraphs that are incorporated into the succeeding drafts. Many minds and hands, in a word, shape the composition that will become "the President's address to Congress." But here is the crucial point: when the president stands before both houses of

---

77. As intimated already by Conzelmann, "Paulus und die Weisheit."

Congress and delivers the speech, it is his; he is the "author" and is answerable for what the speech contains, even if his contribution of actual words may have been minimal.

Thinking of Paul as the author but not necessarily the writer of his entire correspondence, and imagining his delegates and coworkers as participating in the formation of the letters that are sent out in his name (and therefore authorized by him), is a historically and sociologically more plausible model of composition, and one that helps account for the peculiar combinations of similarity and difference that characterize the collection as a whole.

*Chapter 4*

# Paul's Place in Early Christianity

We have just one more element of historical scaffolding to consider before engaging aspects of Paul's symbolic world and letters more closely. You will perhaps remember my comment at the beginning of chapter 1 that we should not equate Paul's historical importance with his canonical importance. There is no doubt that Paul dominates the New Testament canon. But what was his actual place within early Christianity? Just as the historian cannot assume, from the way in which the Gospels portray Jesus as galvanizing all Jewish attention during his ministry, that his activity in fact created such a commotion, so the historian cannot assume from Paul's place in Acts and the letters that everything after Jesus revolved around Paul.

Having sketched the elements of Paul's life and ministry, such as they can responsibly be known, and having provided an equally rudimentary sketch of the letters and their (probable) mode of composition, I am in a position now to address more directly the question of Paul's place in the earliest Christian movement by considering three classic questions: (1) Was Paul the real founder of Christianity? (2) Was Paul constantly opposed in his ministry, and if so, by whom? (3) Was there a "Pauline school" after his death?

## Paul as Founder of Christianity

This question arises because of the apparent gap between Jesus (as portrayed in the Gospels) and Paul (as revealed in his letters). In the Gospels, Jesus proclaims God's kingdom as an eschatological event that breaks into history with his words and deeds; in his letters, Paul proclaims Jesus as "Lord." In the Gospels, Jesus himself is baptized by John and shares a final meal with his disciples; in Paul, believers are baptized "into Christ" and participate in "the Lord's Supper," sharing his body and blood. In the Gospels, the fact that God was with Jesus is shown most of all in his words and powerful deeds of healing and exorcism; in Paul, the good news from God is revealed most of all in the death and exaltation of Jesus to the right hand of God, and his continuing presence in his "body" through the Holy Spirit. In the Gospels, Jesus is at the head of a band of disciples with no visible structure or hierarchy; in Paul, the church has boundaries, structure, and leadership. The difference was classically stated by Alfred Loisy: "Jesus announced the Kingdom and it was the church that arrived."[1]

Seduced by the canonical arrangement of the New Testament, many readers took "Jesus" and "Paul" as two historical figures in relation to each other, rather than as representations within discrete bodies of literature, and regarded "Paul" as the cause that changed the Jesus movement into Christianity.[2] Paul, then, should be regarded as the real "founder" of Christianity, rather than Jesus, simply because "Christianity" did not exist until after Jesus, who died as a Jewish leader of a messianic movement, not as the cult figure of a world religion.[3] Positively, Paul could be regarded as a religious genius who grasped the "essence" of Jesus's message and freed it from its "Jewish particularity," thus opening the way for gentile inclusion.[4] Negatively, Paul could be seen as a deeply conflicted fanatic whose inner psychological issues shaped Christianity into a world-denying and neurotic religion.[5] In either

1. "Jesus annonçait le Royaume, et c'est l'église qui est venue." Loisy, *L'évangile et l'église.*

2. The seduction takes two forms: first, the canonical arrangement places the Gospels before Paul, but in fact, the Gospels are written after Paul wrote his letters; second, Paul's canonical dominance is assumed to reflect his historical dominance.

3. "The history of the development of Christianity dates of course from the departure of Jesus from the world. But in Paul this history has a new beginning; from this point we are able to trace it not only in its external features, but also in its inner connection. . . . Paul the apostle takes up an attitude of so great freedom and independence . . . that one might be inclined to ask whether a view of his relation to the person of Christ can be the right one which would make the apostle Paul the originator and first exponent of that which constitutes the essence of Christianity as distinguished from Judaism." Baur, *Church History*; this passage is taken from Meeks and Fitzgerald, *Writings of St. Paul*, 400-401.

4. E.g., Harnack: "It was Paul who freed the Christian religion from Judaism" (*What Is Christianity?*, 173); see Meeks and Fitzgerald, *Writings of St. Paul*, 419-24. See also Pfleiderer, *Religion and Historic Faiths*, 267-69; Bousset, *What Is Religion?*, 247-49; Wrede, *Paul.*

5. See the passages from Friedrich Nietzsche and George Bernard Shaw in Meeks and Fitzgerald, *Writings of St. Paul*, 408-19; the tradition continues in screeds like Maccoby, *Mythmaker.*

case, Christianity is attributed to Paul even more than to Jesus.[6] But is this a sustainable hypothesis? Two lines of evidence suggest that it is not.

## Evidence of Paul's Letters

The first body of evidence comes from Paul's letters themselves. In a justly famous essay in the early twentieth century, Wilhelm Heitmüller shifted the conversation from "Jesus and Paul" to diverse early types of Christianity. Earliest Palestinian Christianity, Heitmüller asserted, derived from Jesus and his first followers, was Aramaic-speaking, law-observant, and apocalyptic in character. But the Christianity deriving from the "Hellenists" like Stephen was Greek-speaking and more universalist (less "Jewish") in character, finding success in the diaspora (see Acts 6:1–7:60; 11:19–26). Paul was initiated into this Hellenistic version of Christianity, which had already been influenced by the pagan culture of the diaspora and had already become a "Christcult": Jesus was there proclaimed as "Lord" (*kyrios*) and was regarded as a dying and rising savior; cultic acts like baptism were already performed.[7] Paul was therefore not the inventor of Christianity but rather the heir of this particular version of Christianity—already cultic and sacramental, already "doctrinal"—which he subsequently propagated and interpreted.

Now, there is much that is problematic about this historical analysis,[8] but its great and lasting value is that it correctly identifies Paul not as the creator of a cult but as an initiate into an already existing one, a point made abundantly clear already by Acts (see 9:10–19; 22:12–16), and which Paul himself confirms when he declares he submitted the gospel he preached among the gentiles to the leaders in Jerusalem, "lest somehow I should be running or had run in vain" (Gal 2:2), and when he states concerning the good news, "Whether then it was I or they, so we preach and so you believed" (1 Cor 15:11). This recognition, in turn, frees us to appreciate all the

---

6. This helps explain why, from the beginning, "historical Jesus" research began with the rejection of Paul; see L. Johnson, *Real Jesus*. A later chapter will consider more closely the identification of classic Christianity with Paul.

7. Heitmüller, "Zum Problem Paulus und Jesus"; English translation in Meeks and Fitzgerald, *Writings of St. Paul*, 424–33. This geographical/cultural schema was the basis for Bousset's *Kyrios Christos* and for Bultmann's *Theology of the New Testament*. Heitmüller himself built on observations made much earlier by F. C. Baur and by Pfleiderer, *Das Urchristentum*.

8. For a full-blown response to Bousset, in particular, see Hurtado, *Lord Jesus Christ*; also see L. Johnson, *Among the Gentiles*, 26–31, 298–300.

ways in which Paul's letters indicate reliance on prior tradition. We can consider two briefly: elements of worship, and Jesus traditions.

## Worship

Paul speaks of baptism as a ritual of initiation into the community that in the case of the Corinthians was, with some exceptions, administered by people other than himself (1 Cor 1:14–16); that he did not invent the ritual is obvious.[9] In Colossians 2:11–12 baptism is compared to the initiation ritual of circumcision. Aspects of the ritual practice are probably revealed in the symbolism of washing (1 Cor 6:11; Eph 5:26; Titus 3:5), taking off and putting on garments (Gal 3:27; Col 3:8–10; Eph 4:22–25), light (Eph 1:18; 5:8–9; 2 Tim 1:10), the laying on of hands (implied as sign of adoption; Gal 4:5–6; Rom 8:15), and the unification of opposites (1 Cor 12:13; Gal 3:28; Col 3:11). The understanding of baptism as a participation in the death and resurrection of Christ appears to predate Paul (Rom 6:3–11; Col 2:12; 3:3). Nowhere in any of his references to this ritual does Paul appear as its inventor; it is a practice of the community that he represents.

The Lord's Supper appears only in 1 Corinthians, in two key passages. In 11:17–22 Paul addresses abuses at the community meal: some were being filled while others went hungry, a situation that Paul terms "despising the church of God" (11:18–22). Paul applies to this situation words spoken by Jesus "on the night when he was betrayed," words that Paul "received from the Lord [which] I also delivered to you," designating the bread as his body and the cup as his blood (11:23–25).[10] Paul draws theological inferences from these words and this practice (11:27–32), but nowhere does he suggest that this ritual meal is one he invented. In 1 Cor 10:16, in a discussion of eating at the table of idols, Paul asks a rhetorical question that makes clear a community understanding of the table: "The cup of blessing which we bless, is it not a participation in the blood of Christ? The bread which we break, is it not a participation in the body of Christ?" Paul does not suggest that the understanding derives from his own suggestion.

Pliny the Younger described the Christians as "singing hymns to Christ as to a god" (*Letter* 10.96.7). Worship services undoubtedly included the singing

---

9. See Cullmann, *Baptism in the New Testament*; Betz, "Transferring a Ritual."

10. For Paul's use of the technical language for tradition (also 1 Thess 2:13; 4:1; 2 Thess 3:6; 1 Cor 15:1, 3; Gal 1:9, 12; Col 2:6; Phil 4:9), see Fee, *First Epistle to the Corinthians*, 548–49.

of songs, psalms, and hymns (1 Cor 14:26; Eph 5:19; Col 3:16). Through certain formal features, such as the use of an introductory relative pronoun and rhythmic strophes, it is possible to detect at least fragments of such hymns in Paul's letters (Phil 2:6–11; Col 1:15–20; 1 Tim 3:16),[11] which are usually regarded as pre-Pauline in character. Other elements of prayer likewise point to prior tradition. Paul uses the classic form of Jewish blessing (*berakah*) in Rom 1:25; 9:5; 2 Cor 1:3–7; Eph 1:3–14. A direct connection to Aramaic—and not Hellenistic—Christianity is found in the use of the caritative *abba* ("Father") in a ritual context (Gal 4:6; Rom 8:16),[12] the frequent employment of the Hebrew *amen* ("so be it"; see Rom 1:25; 11:36; 15:33; 1 Cor 14:16; 16:24; Gal 1:5; Eph 3:21; Phil 4:20; 2 Thess 3:18; 1 Tim 1:17), and—most striking—the Aramaic phrase *Marana tha* ("Our Lord, come!") in 1 Cor 16:22.[13]

### Jesus Traditions

The most obvious example of Paul's use of Jesus traditions is 1 Cor 15:3–11, where Paul repeats the basic kerygma of Christ's death and resurrection. When he declares that "I delivered to you as of first importance what I also received," he uses the technical language of tradition transmission.[14] Even though he is himself a witness to the resurrection (1 Cor 9:1; 15:8), he received from others the tradition concerning Jesus's death and rising and first appearances. It is on this basis that he can confidently assert, "Whether then it was I or they, so we preach and so you believed" (15:11). It is worth noting that such tradition came, not from a Hellenistic church of the diaspora, but from Cephas and James and the Twelve in Palestine (15:4–7).

Paul's letters reveal a perhaps surprising amount of additional information concerning Jesus—none of which would have resulted from a resurrection appearance, but would have come to Paul through community tradition. He asserts that Jesus was born in human fashion, was a Jew, and was sent to the Jews, when he declares, "God sent forth his Son, born of a woman, born under the law, to redeem those under the law" (Gal 4:4, RSV adapted; cf.

---

11. On the New Testament hymns, see, e.g., R. Martin, *Carmen Christi*; Vawter, "Colossians Hymn"; Wink, "Hymn of the Cosmic Christ."

12. Jeremias, *Central Message*.

13. The Aramaic can be read either as *marana tha* ("our Lord, come") or *maran atha* ("our Lord has come"); see discussion in Fee, *First Epistle to the Corinthians*, 838–39.

14. See the discussion and bibliography in Thiselton, *First Epistle to the Corinthians*, 1178–92.

Rom 15:8). Jesus was "descended from David according to the flesh" (Rom 1:3; cf. 2 Tim 2:8). Paul refers to the authoritative words of Jesus concerning divorce (1 Cor 7:10), payment for preaching the gospel (1 Cor 9:14; 1 Tim 5:17), and—perhaps—the end time (1 Thess 4:15).[15] Most impressive is the direct quotation of Jesus's words at the Last Supper that Paul identifies as words received by him and delivered to his readers (1 Cor 11:23–25).

Paul connects the death of Jesus to the Passover celebration of the Jews: "Christ, our paschal lamb, has been sacrificed" (1 Cor 5:7). He alludes to the trial of Jesus when he declares, "None of the rulers of this age understood this; for if they had, they would not have crucified the Lord of glory" (1 Cor 2:8). In 1 Tim 6:13, a trial before the Roman prefect is made explicit: ". . . Christ Jesus who in his testimony before Pontius Pilate made the good confession." That Jesus underwent abuse and humiliation is suggested by Paul's use of Ps 69:9 in Rom 15:3: "For Christ did not please himself; but, as it is written, 'the reproaches of those who reproach thee fell on me.'" In 1 Thess 2:14–16, as we have seen, Paul blames the Jews for the death of Jesus. That death was by crucifixion (1 Cor 1:23; 2 Cor 13:4; Gal 3:1; Phil 2:8; Col 2:14; Eph 2:16).

None of these statements about Jesus occur in a narrative. Without the Gospels, where they also appear, indeed, we would not recognize them as parts of a story. But as they stand, they attest to the antiquity as well as the ubiquity of the traditions Paul uses. I stress the term "ubiquity" as much as "antiquity": Paul can assume that the Roman church, which he had never met, was in as firm a possession of these basic aspects of the Jesus story as was his own Corinthian community. But Paul could also assume among his readers the basic narrative pattern concerning Jesus,[16] that his existence could be described in terms of his faithful obedience to God and his loving self-donation to humans (see Rom 3:21–26; 5:12–21; 15:1–3; Gal 1:4; 2:20; 2 Cor 1:19; 5:21; 8:9; 13:4; Eph 5:2, 25; Phil 2:5–11; Col 1:22; 1 Thess 5:10; 1 Tim 1:14–16; 2:6; Titus 2:14). Paul does not so much *relate* the narrative pattern as *allude* to it and *apply* it to the moral behavior of believers (see, e.g., Rom 15:1–3; 1 Cor 8:11–12; Gal 6:2). Such employment of traditions about Jesus further rebuts the notion that Paul somehow "created" Christianity.

15. The Greek of 1 Thess 4:15 (*hymin legomen en logō kyriou*) is ambiguous. Does it mean "we are delivering to you a word of the Lord"? Does "Lord" here refer to Jesus and his eschatological sayings? Or does it mean "we are speaking to you *in* or *by the authority of* the word of the Lord"?

16. Most important here is Hays, *Faith of Jesus*; Hays's insight is developed for Romans in L. Johnson, *Reading Romans*. See also Nicolet-Anderson, *Constructing the Self*.

## Evidence from Other Early Christian Literature

The thesis that Paul invented Christianity out of his own genius or pathology depends on either ignoring all other early Christian literature or dating it late and making it more or less derivative of Paul. Thus, Hebrews, James, and 1 and 2 Peter are all regarded as "Pauline" in the sense that they look the way they do because Paul preceded them and influenced them.[17] They thereby cease being independent witnesses to earliest Christianity and are instead testimony to the widespread effect of Paul's singular genius. The Heitmüller-Bousset-Bultmann positing of a pre-Pauline "Hellenistic" Christianity provides a welcome alternative, because it uses the evidence of these non-Pauline compositions to construct a picture of non-Palestinian belief and practice that Paul inherited and adapted.[18]

The result? Paul is not a solitary "inventor" of Christianity but a creative thinker within a broader movement. As I noted earlier, however, this "history of religions" approach has its own difficulties: it tends to downplay contributions from Palestinian Christianity, and to impose on "Hellenistic" Christianity a now-outdated understanding of Gnosticism and mystery religions.[19] It is nevertheless worthwhile to follow its lead in identifying the ways three quite disparate New Testament compositions share fundamental convictions with the Pauline letters, making it clear that Paul should not be designated as Christianity's "founder" in any sense.

### James

The Letter of James is perhaps our earliest extant Christian writing, with a Palestinian provenance.[20] It should be considered roughly contemporaneous to Paul, rather than dependent on him.[21] The historical/literary relationship

17. The supreme example of such literary stacking is Foster, *Literary Relations*. Foster has Ephesians depend on Colossians, James depend on Ephesians, and 1 Peter depend on James!

18. Thus, in his magisterial *Theology of the New Testament*, Bultmann decisively distinguishes between "The Kerygma of the Earliest Church" (1:33–62) and "The Kerygma of the Hellenistic Church Apart from Paul" (1:63–186), in each case drawing evidence from a variety of sources respectively located in Palestine and Diaspora.

19. See L. Johnson, *Religious Experience*, 1–37.

20. See L. Johnson, "James' Significance"; for James and Paul, see L. Johnson, *Letter of James*, 58–65.

21. For the date and place of James, see L. Johnson, *Letter of James*, 108–23.

between James and Paul usually posited is based on the use of language concerning faith and deeds (*erga*), righteousness and faith, and the example of Abraham in Jas 2:14–26 and Galatians/Romans. In fact, however, James and Paul do not stand opposed to each other; each of them states that righteousness comes from faith, and each of them states that faith must be expressed by deeds. Their way of dealing with the faith of Abraham and the faith of Christians is different, but so is the treatment of the same topos in the Letter to the Hebrews.[22]

James is unlike Paul most of all because it lacks any reference to the death and resurrection of Jesus or to the Holy Spirit. When it refers to "the Lord Jesus Christ" (1:1) and "our Lord Jesus Christ, the Lord of glory" (2:1), however, it clearly signals a belief in Jesus as sharing in the presence and power of God, as do the further uses of "Lord" that apply to Jesus in the letter.[23] James has a vivid expectation of the Lord's imminent parousia (5:8). The Jesus tradition is employed most vigorously by James in its citation of specific sayings in a form earlier than their appearance in the Gospels.[24]

What other elements in James point to its participation in the wider Christian movement, despite its minimal Christology (by comparison with Paul)? The letter is saturated with what can be called a developing Christian argot—that is, language that, while not unattested elsewhere, is used so pervasively by insiders that it can come to identify them as a group. James speaks of the poor, for example, as "heirs" of the "kingdom" that God had "promised" (2:5); while all of these terms are attested elsewhere in Jewish literature, they are found with particular intensity in New Testament compositions.[25] Similarly, James's use of "the name" in 5:10, 14 is characteristic Christian diction (cf. Acts 2:38; 1 Cor 1:2; 5:4; Phil 2:10; Col 3:17; 2 Thess 1:12), and the absolute use of *onoma* in 2:7 especially should be taken with reference to the name of Jesus: "Do they not blaspheme the noble name invoked over you?" (author's translation). Likewise, if Jesus is "Lord," then it makes sense that James designates himself as "a slave" (*doulos*, 1:1; cf. Rom 1:1; 2 Cor 4:5; Gal 1:10; Phil 1:1; Col 4:12; 2 Tim 2:24; Titus 1:1). James refers to the community as *synagōgē* ("synagogue," 2:2) and *ekklēsia* ("assembly," 5:14). Leaders in the

22. See R. Longenecker, "'Faith of Abraham' Theme."

23. Although a number of occurrences of *kyrios* probably refer to God (Jas 1:7; 3:9; 4:10, 15; 5:4,11), other uses apply most readily to Jesus (5:7, 8, 14, 15). As indicated above, Paul's use of *Marana tha* in 1 Cor 16:22 argues for the use of the title "Lord" even among Aramaic-speaking believers in Palestine.

24. See Hartin, *James*; L. Johnson and Wachob, "Sayings of Jesus."

25. For "kingdom of God" see Rom 14:17; 1 Cor 4:20; Gal 5:21; 2 Thess 1:5; for "heirs" see 1 Cor 6:9; Gal 5:21; Eph 5:5; for "promise" see Rom 4:13; 2 Cor 1:20; Gal 3:14.

community are *didaskaloi* ("teachers," 3:1; cf. 1 Cor 12:28–29; Eph 4:11) and *presbyteroi* ("elders," 5:14; cf. 1 Tim 5:17, 19; Titus 1:5).

James uses the kinship language characteristic of earliest Christianity. Members of the assembly are "brothers" (*adelphoi*) and "sisters" (*adelphai*, 2:15); three times James adds "beloved" (1:16, 19; 2:5). Remarkable in this short letter is the number of times the address is used (twenty times; cf. thirty-eight instances in 1 Corinthians and nineteen in Romans, both much longer letters), and the absence of the parental language adopted by Paul for communities he himself founded. The classic triad of virtues in earliest Christianity is faith, hope, and love (1 Thess 1:2–3; 1 Cor 13:13; 1 Pet 1:3–9). James does not use the term "hope," preferring language for "endurance" (*hypomonē*, 1:3, 12; 5:11) and "patience" (*makrothymia*, 5:7, 8, 10). But the letter is rich in its use of "faith" (*pistis*, 1:3, 6; 2:1, 5, 14, 17, 18, 20, 22, 24, 26; 5:15) and "faithing" (*pisteuein*, 2:19, 23), and strikingly speaks of faith as "saving" (2:14), a combination that is distinctively Christian and shared by Paul (Rom 10:9; 1 Cor 1:21; Eph 2:8). As for "love" (*agapē*), James calls the law of love of neighbor (Lev 19:18) the *nomos basilikos* ("royal law" or, more literally, "law of the kingdom," 2:8; cf. Rom 13:9; Gal 5:14). James speaks of God giving birth to humans through the *logos tēs alētheias* (1:18). The term can refer to creation itself, or to Torah, but is used elsewhere in the New Testament for the gospel message (2 Cor 6:7; Eph 1:13; Col 1:5; 2 Tim 2:15).

None of these expressions is sufficient by itself to persuade us that James and Paul drew from a common argot,[26] but cumulatively, the evidence is more than sufficient to convince us that Paul's convictions concerning the lordship of Jesus, his future coming, his role as judge, and the like were not drawn from his fertile (and perhaps ill) mind but were the common conceptions of believers in Palestine as well as in the diaspora.

## Letter to the Hebrews

Once considered a Pauline letter—and still treated as such by Thomas Aquinas[27]—this anonymous composition represents an independent witness to

26. One could add other terms found in other New Testament writings but completely absent from the LXX, such as "crown of life" (Jas 1:12; see Rev 2:10), "first fruits" applied to humans (Jas 1:18; see Rom 8:23; 11:16; 16:5; 1 Cor 15:20–23; 16:15; 2 Thess 2:13; Rev 14:4), and the distinctive terminology concerning "impartiality" (*aprosōpolēmpsia*; see Jas 2:1, 9; cf. Rom 2:11; Eph 6:9; Col 3:25; Acts 10:34).

27. See Aquinas, *Letter of Saint Paul to the Romans*, Prologue 7, and *Letter of Saint Paul*

Christianity roughly contemporaneous to Paul. Its specific resemblance to Pauline letters on a number of points is obvious: the conviction that Christ provides "access" to God (Heb 4:16; 10:19-22; cf. Rom 5:1; Eph 2:18); the understanding of Jesus's faith as obedience (Heb 5:1-10; cf. Rom 5:12-21); the attention given to the promise to Abraham (Heb 6:13-18; cf. Gal 3:16-18), and Abraham's response of faith (Heb 11:8-12; cf. Rom 4:1-25); and the comparison between the present generation and the wilderness generation (Heb 3:1-4:10; cf. 1 Cor 10:1-13).[28] But the Greek style, rhetorical argument, and above all Platonic worldview convince careful readers that this impressive composition comes from another than Paul.[29] Of interest here are the ways in which both the Pauline letters and Hebrews share in the common tradition of earliest Christianity.

Although Hebrews urges its readers to progress from the state of children to more mature knowledge of Christ (5:11-14; cf. 1 Cor 3:1-3), which involves especially its portrayal of Jesus as the great high priest that occupies the heart of its argument (7:1-10:31), it recognizes in 6:1-2 some of the basic elements already in possession of readers, including "repentance from dead works and faith toward God" (NRSV; cf. 1 Thess 1:9) and "instruction about ablutions" and "the laying on of hands," which is obscure but must refer to the ritual of initiation (see the language of "enlightenment" here and in 10:32; cf. Eph 5:15). The author declares that a second repentance is impossible for those "who have once been enlightened, who have tasted the heavenly gift, and have become partakers of the Holy Spirit . . . and the powers of the age to come" (6:4-5; cf. 1 Cor 12:3; Eph 3:19). Apostasy is tantamount to "crucify[ing] the Son of God on their own account and hold[ing] him up to contempt" (6:6).

Hebrews, in fact, displays the full range of the basic Christian tradition concerning Jesus: his preexistence (1:2; 10:5), his incarnation (2:14-18; 10:5-7), his sacrificial death (1:3; 2:9; 6:6; 7:27), and his resurrection (1:3). As for Paul, the resurrection is more than a coming-back-to-life; it is an

---

to the Hebrews. The mention at the end of the exhortation of "our brother Timothy" and "those who come from Italy" (Heb 13:23-24) encouraged the perception of the composition as Pauline.

28. See, e.g., C. Anderson, "Hebrews among the Letters of Paul"; Witherington, "Influence of Galatians on Hebrews."

29. The differences between Paul and Hebrews are well elaborated in Ellingworth, *Epistle to the Hebrews*, 3-12. Similarities between Hebrews and John are listed in Spicq, *L'Épître aux Hébreux*, 1:109-38. Connections between Hebrews and 1 Peter are listed in Attridge, *Epistle to the Hebrews*, 30-31.

exaltation of Christ to the presence and power of God; the enthronement imagery of the classic resurrection of Ps 110 runs throughout the composition (1:3; 5:6, 10; 6:20; 7:11, 15, 21). Finally, Jesus will return "a second time" for judgment (9:28; 10:25). Hebrews advocates the classic triad of Christian virtues: love (6:10; 10:24; 13:1), hope (3:6; 6:11, 18; 7:19; 10:23; 11:1), and above all faith (4:2; 6:1, 12; 10:22; and the twenty-three instances in chap. 11). Hebrews calls for practices we recognize as standard in the nascent Christian movement: prayer (13:15), hospitality (13:2), care for prisoners (10:34; 13:3), chaste marriage (13:4), sharing possessions (13:16), avoiding love of money (13:5), attendance at assemblies (10:25), and respect for leaders in the community (13:7, 17).

To the degree that Hebrews is regarded as independent of Paul, it gains in importance as a witness to shared Christian convictions in the same period as Paul, and serves as a strong rebuttal to the proposition that Paul was the inventor of Christianity.


The Book of Revelation

There can be no suspicion of Pauline influence in this early Christian composition, or of a Hellenistic setting.[30] Revelation is the classic expression of an apocalyptic genre and worldview.[31] Although the seer John writes from the Greek island of Patmos (1:9) and addresses "Spirit letters" to seven churches of Asia, including Ephesus and Laodicea (2:1–3:22), its symbolic world is far from that of Hellenistic Judaism, grounded instead in the apocalyptic, wisdom, and mystical traditions of Scripture and Palestinian Judaism.[32] Revelation therefore has considerable importance as a witness to shared Christian convictions, especially concerning Christ, that cannot be traced either to Paul or to a pre-Pauline Hellenistic Christianity.

Revelation speaks of God's rule (*basileia*) not only as something future (1:9) but as a reality in the present (cf. Rom 14:17; 1 Cor 4:20; 15:24, 50; Gal 5:21; Eph 5:5; Col 1:13; 1 Thess 2:12; 2 Thess 1:5; 2 Tim 4:1, 18). Jesus, the Lamb

---

30. It has been suggested, indeed, that the strictures against eating food offered to idols in 2:6, 14–15, 20 represent a covert anti-Pauline polemic; see Barrett, "Things Sacrificed to Idols."

31. See, e.g., Aune, "Apocalypse of John"; J. Collins, "Pseudonymity"; Rowland, *Open Heaven*, 403–41.

32. For the influence of Merkabah mysticism, see Gruenwald, *Apocalyptic and Merkavah Mysticism*.

who was slain but now lives (1:18; 5:6–14), shares the throne of God's power now (3:21). The Lamb is "Lord of lords and King of kings" (17:14; cf. 1 Tim 1:17; 6:15). He speaks powerfully with the voice of prophecy within the churches, for "the witness of Jesus is the spirit of prophecy" (19:10, author's translation; cf. 1 Cor 14:1–12). Although Jesus was crucified in Jerusalem (11:8), he not only has been raised but also raises up the righteous ones who bear witness to him (11:11–12; cf. 1 Thess 4:14). No writing of the New Testament puts more emphasis on the second coming of Jesus (1:8; 3:3, 11, 20; 22:7, 17), but Christ is not absent in the present: he stands among the seven churches and speaks to them (1:12–20), anticipating when "the salvation and the power and the kingdom of our God and the authority of his Christ have come" in full disclosure (12:10). The climax of God's victory will be when "death will be no more" (21:4 NRSV; cf. 1 Cor 15:26, 54–57), when God dwells with humans (21:3), when the heavenly Jerusalem comes down to become the city of God on earth (21:2; cf. Gal 4:29), when there will be a new heaven and a new earth (21:1), and the God who is the beginning and end of all things (1:8) can declare, "Behold, I make all things new" (21:5; cf. 2 Cor 5:17; Gal 6:15).

Even though the holy city of Jerusalem has "twelve foundations" on which were inscribed "the twelve names of the twelve apostles of the Lamb" (21:14; see 1 Cor 15:5), Revelation speaks of the church not in institutional terms—the only "elders" are around the throne in heaven (4:4, 10)—but in terms of radical commitment: the readers are to be holy ones (5:8; 8:3, 4; 13:7; 14:12; 17:6; 18:20) and slaves (1:1; 2:20; 7:3; 13:16; 15:3; 19:2, 18; 22:3, 6) and prophets (10:7; 11:10, 18; 16:6; 18:20, 24; 22:6, 9), and are to exclude all forms of immorality and irreligion (21:8; 22:15; cf. 1 Cor 6:9–11). Such radical commitment will entail suffering and even death at the hands of the forces representing Satan on earth (6:10; 7:14; 12:11; 16:6; 17:6; 18:24). Those who have died already share in the triumph of the Lord (6:9; 12:11). They are the "first fruits for God and the Lamb" (14:4). In the end, the union of Christ and the church can be imagined as the wedding feast of the Lamb and the Bride (19:7–9; cf. Eph 5:32).

The Letters of James and Hebrews, together with the book of Revelation, offer abundant evidence that Paul's most fundamental convictions were drawn not from his tortured psyche or religious genius. They were undoubtedly deeply influenced by his own experience of the resurrected one. But to a remarkable degree, Paul shares and interprets the language and perceptions of the Christian movement antecedent and contemporary to him. However much he deepens and expands Christian consciousness, he does not invent it.

## Paul's Opponents

The question of Paul's opponents—their identity and activity—has been a major contributor to the history of earliest Christianity for two reasons: (1) Paul's implicit or explicit response to such figures in the letters ascribed to him opens the door to speculation about what else was happening in the period of his ministry; (2) a change in the character of those opponents seems to provide evidence for development within the Christian movement.

The best example is found at the very beginning of critical historiography. The founder of the so-called Tübingen school was F. C. Baur (1792–1860), who conceived of the development of Christianity in terms of a dialectical process, in which the Pauline message of righteousness by faith was directly opposed by a Judaizing party (represented by Peter and James) that advocated observance of the law of Moses;[33] the conflict between these movements led to the synthesis called "Early Catholicism" (*Frühkatholicismus*).[34] Baur thought that both canonical and noncanonical writings could be arranged according to the stages of this dialectical process. The "thesis" was represented by the authentic letters of Paul (for Baur, only five: Romans, Galatians, 1 and 2 Corinthians, 1 Thessalonians). The "antithesis" of Jewish Christianity presented a problem, since it was known—according to Baur—primarily from Paul's own polemic; but he found in the Pseudo-Clementine literature a relic of what must have been earlier polemic against Paul. We remember from chapter 1 that this literature contains passages that speak of an "enemy" of James, whom scholars take to be a veiled reference to Paul. The "synthesis" of Early Catholicism is represented by the remaining canonical writings: the pseudonymous Pauline letters, Hebrews, James, and above all the Acts of the Apostles, which portrays Peter, Paul, and James as colleagues rather than opponents.

Thus, in this reading, the "historical" opponents of Paul in his authentic letters represent Jewish Christianity, and Paul's battle is one for the freedom of the good news against the servitude of the law. The battle is resolved by forms of Christianity that combine elements of Paul and his rivals: sacrament and institutionalization and strict morality come from the Judaizing side;

---

33. Baur first developed this theory in "Die Christuspartei in der korinthischer Gemeinde" and worked out his ideas more completely in *Paulus, der Apostel Jesu Christi* and *Church History of the First Three Centuries*. The dialectical process was worked out systematically by his student, Schwegler, in *Das nachapostolische Zeitalter*.

34. For a lively sketch of the Tübingen school and its importance in the shaping of Christian historiography, see Harris, *Tübingen School*.

conscience and love and faith from the Pauline side. The identification of opponents also assisted in locating compositions. Thus, it was Baur's perception (following Schleiermacher) that the Pastorals were combatting a form of second-century Gnosticism that helped him date those letters confidently in the mid-second century.[35]

Although the Tübingen theory is no longer maintained in its strict form, its legacy is obvious in subsequent developmental theories, in which a variety of opponents play a key role in reconstructions of early Christianity.[36] And even for those not pursuing a larger theory of development, the identification of Paul's opponents has seemed to be a necessary element in responsible exegesis. The literature is abundant for the study of Paul's opponents in general,[37] and in the several letters containing some evidence for them, especially 2 Corinthians,[38] Galatians,[39] Philippians,[40] Colossians,[41] and the letters to Paul's delegates.[42] The effort to reconstruct the opponents is thought to provide a better understanding of Paul's arguments in the respective letters and, as a bonus, a sense of the historical complexities of Christianity in the decades of Paul's active ministry—and after. One benefit of the close examination of each letter in the quest for the historical opponents is

35. Baur, *Die sogenannten Pastoralbriefe*, 8–39.

36. See, e.g., the influential study by W. Bauer, *Orthodoxy and Heresy*, and its successors, such as J. M. Robinson and Koester, *Trajectories through Early Christianity*.

37. E.g., Sumney, *Servants of Satan*.

38. See Georgi, *Opponents of Paul*; Kolenkow, "Paul and His Opponents"; Sumney, *Identifying Paul's Opponents*.

39. Schmithals, *Paul and the Gnostics*, 13–64; Jewett, "Agitators"; Lüdemann, *Opposition to Paul*, 97–103; Munck, "Judaizing Gentile Christians."

40. Jewett, "Conflicting Movements"; Schmithals, *Paul and the Gnostics*, 65–122; Klijn, "Paul's Opponents"; Koester, "Purpose of the Polemic"; Lüdemann, *Opposition to Paul*, 103–9; Telbe, "Sociological Factors."

41. See esp. the essays in Meeks and Francis, *Conflict at Colossae*; also see Francis, "Humility"; Arnold, *Colossian Syncretism*; Attridge, "On Becoming an Angel"; DeMaris, *Colossian Controversy*; Dunn, "Colossian Philosophy"; Hooker, "False Teachers"; Evans, "Colossian Mystics"; T. Martin, *By Philosophy and Empty Deceit*; Sumney, "Those Who 'Pass Judgment.'"

42. Since the Pastorals are taken to be a single pseudonymous composition, efforts to identify "the opposition" likewise seek to combine the quite disparate elements in the three letters. F. C. Baur thought the opponents were second-century gnostics (*Die sogenannten Pastoralbriefe*, 8–39), and that view still occasionally appears: see W. Bauer, *Orthodoxy and Heresy*, 222–28; Marxsen, *Introduction to the New Testament*, 199–215. For other composites, see Mangold, *Die Irrlehrer der Pastoralbriefe*; Lütgert, *Die Irrlehrer der Pastoralbriefe*; Goulder, "Pastor's Wolves."

that the sort of "unified field" theory of the Tübingen school simply must be abandoned: the notion of a well-organized Jewish opposition to Paul that underlies the polemic in each of his (authentic) letters does not correspond to the evidence the letters themselves present.

Efforts to identify Pauline opponents face at least four major difficulties. The first is that we are utterly dependent on Paul's perception of what is happening in a specific community, or the way he chooses to characterize what has been reported to him as happening in that community—or group of communities. We lack entirely any evidence of the opponents' voices themselves. The second is that our available evidence for non-Christian Jewish groups, or Jewish Christians in the time of Paul, or, for that matter, Greco-Roman philosophical and religious phenomena of the first century, generally is at best fragmentary. Attempts to construct a profile of Pauline opponents must necessarily seek to align obscure allusions in Paul with bits and pieces of historical knowledge. And the more knowledge we actually have of a group, the less attractive as candidates for the opposition they sometimes become. Before the discovery of the Dead Sea Scrolls in 1947, for example, scholars with some frequency offered up the Essenes as possible Pauline opponents, precisely because our lack of knowledge about them made them fit any number of possibilities. Actual knowledge of the Qumran sectarians has tended to eliminate the Essenes from the dance card.

The third obstacle to easy identification of Paul's opponents is the fact that, like other teachers in competitive contests, Paul makes use of the conventions of ancient polemic, which employed a variety of stereotypical slanders applied to all opponents: all rivals were called charlatans and hypocrites and were described as duplicitous and out for money, pleasure, power, or vainglory. To the degree that Paul makes use of such conventions, precise delineation of rival teachers is difficult.[43] Fourth and finally, the presence of discord and conflict within Pauline communities does not automatically demand "opponents" either from the outside or representing a different ideology. In 1 Corinthians, for example, the factions forming among believers seem to have much less to do with the actions or attitudes of Cephas and Apollos than with the rivalrous tendencies of the Corinthians. Similarly in Galatians and Colossians, whether or not there is an outside stimulus, the real issue in each community is the drive from within toward discrimination.[44]

---

43. See, e.g., Karris, "Polemic of the Pastoral Epistles"; Du Toit, "Vilification"; L. Johnson, "New Testament's Anti-Jewish Slander."

44. See L. Johnson, "Ritual Imprinting."

While recognizing such difficulties, it is possible at least to note what each letter actually tells us about opposition to Paul. Not surprisingly, we find more diversity than uniformity.

## First and Second Thessalonians

Although Paul draws a series of contrasts in 1 Thess 2:3–8, indicating that his preaching did not spring from error, uncleanness, or guile, that it did not seek to flatter, that it was not a cloak for greed, that it did not seek human glory, these are best read, not as an implied criticism of actual rivals, but as a standard form of self-encomium, such as is found in Dio Chrysostom's *Oration* 32.[45] In 2 Thessalonians, Paul speaks of those who are afflicting and persecuting the community from without: they "do not know God . . . do not obey the gospel of our Lord Jesus Christ" (1:6–9). Presumably, such enemies of the church are among those whom the lawless one has deluded with signs and wonders, and who refuse "to love the truth and so be saved," and who "had pleasure in unrighteousness" (2:8–12; 3:2). Everything in this description suggests outsiders to the Christian movement. Paul also deals with deviance within, since some are not living "in accord with the tradition that you received from us" by living in idleness and refusing to work (3:6–12). Paul advocates shunning one who disobeys his command to work: "Do not look on him as an enemy, but warn him as a brother" (3:15).

## First and Second Corinthians

Conflict among community members dominates 1 Corinthians, as disagreements concerning sexual behavior, dietary practices, and community worship cause divisions and even lawsuits in pagan courts (6:1–8). Much more difficult to determine is whether a consistent ideological difference drove the disputes between those Paul terms "the strong" and "the weak" (1:25, 27; 4:10; 8:7, 9, 10, 11, 12; 9:22; 10:22; 11:30; 12:22),[46] and to what extent,

---

45. See Malherbe, *Paul and the Popular Philosophers*, 35–48, 67–78.

46. For a sampling of efforts to make such connections, see Doughty, "Salvation in Corinth"; Horsley, "Spiritual Elitism in Corinth"; D. Martin, *Corinthian Body*; Pearson, *Pneumatikos-Psychikos*; Schmithals, *Gnosticism in Corinth*; Thiselton, "Realized Eschatology at Corinth."

if any, these behavioral conflicts are connected to the factions that align themselves with Cephas, Apollos, or Paul (1:10–14; 3:5–23).[47] Certainly, Paul makes every effort to show that he, at least, regards other preachers not as competitors but as collaborators (esp. 3:5–23; 16:12); indeed, he insists that he and other leaders preach the same gospel (15:11). At least in Paul's mind, then, there were no "opponents" to battle in 1 Corinthians, only wayward and self-deluded congregants.

The state of affairs reflected in 2 Corinthians is correspondingly the more shocking. Deciphering this complex and difficult letter is made more difficult by its literary angularity,[48] but although a precise sequence of events eludes us, we understand that Paul's relationship with the Corinthian church is now fragile if not broken. At least three factors have contributed to a state of alienation: Paul's handling of persons has generated resentment (2:1–11; 7:8–12), his efforts at a collection have aroused suspicion (7:2; 11:7–11; 12:14–18), and—of greatest interest here—rival teachers are gaining ascendancy among the Corinthians (11:1–12:13). Here, if anywhere, we seem to truly meet "opponents," yet Paul's fire is directed not so much at them as at the gullible Corinthians who are taken in by them. He characterizes them directly only in 11:13–15: "Such men are false apostles, deceitful workmen, disguising themselves as apostles of Christ. And no wonder, for even Satan disguises himself as an angel of light. So it is not strange if his servants also disguise themselves as servants of righteousness."

Who are they? There is no indication that the ones Paul here calls "super-apostles" (*hyperapostoloi*, 11:5; 12:11 NRSV) should be identified with either Cephas or Apollos. Although they claim a Jewish pedigree (11:22), the issue of circumcision or the observance of Torah never surfaces in the letter. Paul suggests that they may advance "another Jesus" or "different spirit" or "different gospel" than the one he preaches (11:4), but the scope of those differences he does not state. The real issue seems to be their claims to authority and the Corinthians' acceptance of those claims. They engage in self-commendation and measure themselves over against others (10:12); they also travel with letters of commendation from churches as validation for their authority (3:1). They say they work as Paul does, for free (11:12), but they accept payment

---

47. That these connections could be made was the basis of Baur's perception of early Christianity as a dialectical struggle between Pauline and Jewish forms of Christianity.

48. We remember that many scholars regard 2 Corinthians as an edited composite of Pauline letters to the Corinthian community: for a taste of such discussions, see Betz, "2 Cor 6:14–7:1"; Betz, *2 Corinthians 8 and 9*; Dahl, "Fragment and Its Context"; Bates, "Integrity of II Corinthians"; deSilva, "Measuring Penultimate and Ultimate Reality."

for their preaching (11:7–10), which makes them peddlers and tamperers of God's word (2:17; 4:2). Other characteristics must be guessed from emphases in Paul's own self-presentation. They were perhaps rhetorically gifted, placing stock in knowledge and speech (10:10; 11:6). They can work miracles to support their authority (12:12). They have mystical experiences (12:1–5). They are spiritual athletes who have endured great hardships as "servants of Christ" (11:23–27). They "boast" in all these things (11:21).

But do these stylistic traits amount to an ideological difference that challenges Paul's own gospel? The answer depends to a large extent on whether Paul's own insistence on linking his apostolic style with the truth of what he proclaims should be applied also to the rivals. Paul stresses the gap between the glory of what he proclaims and his own lowliness, which is based on the faithful obedience of the crucified Messiah: the power Paul exercises does not come from his own gifts but from the power-in-weakness of God as revealed in Christ; his suffering more than anything else recommends him (1:3–11; 4:1–6:10; 11:23–33; 12:7–10; 13:1–4). Do they, in contrast, proclaim a "Lord of glory" that corresponds to their own image of "divine men" in the Hellenistic manner? It is possible but by no means certain.[49] In the end, we learn more about the Corinthians' ability to be swayed by appearance and about their own disappointment in Paul than we do about "enemies" who sought to diminish or eliminate Paul.

### Galatians and Romans

Paul's letter to the churches of Galatia (1:2) appears to have opponents constantly in view. Paul speaks of "some who trouble you and want to pervert the gospel of Christ" (1:7), again using the term "a different gospel" (1:6). He puts anyone who would "preach to you a gospel contrary to the one which we preached to you" or "contrary to the one which you received" under a curse (1:8–9, adapted). The identity of these "certain people" (*tines*, 1:7, author's translation), however, is not certain. Paul himself does not seem

---

49. Building on the seminal work of Bieler, *Theios anēr*, this is the thesis advanced by Georgi, *Opponents of Paul*, 239–313, which became extremely influential in studies of conflict in Paul as well as in the Gospels; see, e.g., Talbert: "To some extent all of our canonical gospels are shaped so as to dispel a false image of the savior, and to provide a true one to follow" (*What Is a Gospel?*, 98). For criticism of the method, see Hickling, "Problem of Method"; for criticism of the *theios anēr* construct, see Tiede, *Charismatic Figure*; Holladay, *Theios Aner in Hellenistic Judaism*.

entirely sure when he asks, "Who has bewitched you?" (3:1), and "Who hindered you from obeying the truth?" (5:7). Are we to take these "certain ones" as outside agitators of the gentile community who seek to impose circumcision and the observance of the law on them? In that case, are they a continuation of the "certain ones from James" (author's translation) who challenged common table fellowship in Antioch (2:11–14)? This was certainly the view of Baur and the Tübingen school: the Galatian opponents would represent a Jewish Christianity counter to Paul.

That circumcision is the issue cannot be doubted. Paul speaks of members of the community who are "being circumcised" (5:2–4, author's translation). He says: "It is those who want to make a good showing in the flesh that would compel you to be circumcised, and only in order that they may not be persecuted for the cross of Christ. For even those who receive circumcision do not themselves keep the law, but they desire to have you circumcised that they may glory in your flesh" (6:12–13). But this characterization does not seem to fit outside, law-observant Jews. It sounds much more like members of the gentile community itself who wish to gain a greater perfection through circumcision, and impose it on others, so that they will not be persecuted— by Jews, who (like Paul had in his earlier life) persecute the church (1:13–14). Paul's vagueness on the actual identity of the agitators, and his otherwise positive portrayal of James here (1:19; 2:6–10) and in 1 Cor 15:7, make it more than likely that we have here no organized outside opposition preaching "a different gospel," but instead an inchoate movement from within that pushes for assimilation to the Judaism that Paul himself represents, possibly based on the desire to emulate the Pharisee Paul.[50] In this reading, Paul's account of his earlier life, his refusal to circumcise Titus, and his confrontation with Cephas all serve as paradigmatic for the manner in which the Galatians also should resist the "false brethren" (2:4) who seek to take away the freedom given by the Spirit for the bondage of the law (3:1–5; 5:1, 13).

Galatians serves best as evidence for the attractions of Judaism for a young and unstable gentile community, within which certain members compete for greater prestige, than as evidence for an organized opposition to Paul on the part of a rival Christianity based in Jerusalem and infiltrating Paul's churches in the diaspora.[51]

The only note of opposition to Paul himself in the Letter to the Romans occurs in his plea to his readers that they pray for him as he travels to Jeru-

---

50. See L. Johnson, "Ritual Imprinting."
51. Still one of the sanest analyses of Galatians is Munck, "Judaizing Gentile Christians."

salem with the collection, "that I may be delivered from the unbelievers in Judea, and that my service for Jerusalem may be acceptable to the saints" (15:30–31). The "unbelievers" (*apeithountōn*) here are distinguished from the "saints" (*tois hagiois*), making the reference more obviously to Jews hostile to believers (cf. 1 Thess 2:14–16) than to a party within the church opposed to Paul.

In Romans, the only sign of possible opponents comes at the end of the letter, when Paul warns his readers against troublemakers in their own community (16:17–20). The tone of this exhortation is quite different than the tone Paul employs when encouraging mutual acceptance rather than judgment and contempt in matters of diverse observance in 14:1–15:6. Paul's language here deserves attention particularly because it resembles another passage that is sometimes taken to be against opponents (Phil 3:2–21). He tells his readers to "observe" or "take note of" (*skopein*; cf. Phil 3:2, 17) those who cause "dissensions and difficulties" (*dichostasias kai skandala*) that are in opposition to the doctrine they had been taught (16:17; see 6:17), because such people do not serve the Lord Christ, "but their own appetites" (literally, "bellies" [*koilia*]; cf. Phil 3:19). They deceive the simple through "fair and flattering words" (16:18). Paul's language here is nonspecific, and its main point is to encourage his readers, of whose obedience he is assured, to be "wise as to what is good and guileless as to what is evil" (16:19). He assures them that God "will soon crush Satan under your feet" (16:20; cf. 1 Cor 5:5; 7:5; 2 Cor 2:11; 11:14; 12:7; 1 Thess 2:18; 2 Thess 2:9; 1 Tim 1:20; 5:15). The passage offers no evidence for opposition to Paul or his mission.

### Philippians

Philippians is sometimes considered as a composite of several short notes, and 3:2–21 as a polemical fragment concerning Pauline adversaries.[52] But the amount of actual polemic in this part of the letter is not extensive. In 3:2 Paul repeats three times the injunction to his readers to "look at" (*blepete*) the "dogs" (*kynas*), the "evil workers" (*kakous ergatas*), and the "mutilators of the flesh" (*katatomēn*). The NRSV translates the command as "beware of," but, as in other instances, *blepein* can here have the more neutral sense of "look at" or "observe" (see 1 Cor 1:26; 10:18; 2 Cor 10:7; Eph 5:15; Col 4:17). Paul then declares that "we are the circumcision, who

52. As in the works cited in note 40 above.

worship God in spirit, . . . and put no confidence in the flesh" (3:3, adapted), before reciting the reasons why he had confidence in the flesh and how he scorned all of them for the sake of Christ (3:4–16). He encourages his readers to imitate him and "look at" (*skopeite*) "those who so live as you have an example (*typon*) in us" (3:17). He then reminds them of those who live "as enemies of the cross of Christ" (3:18). But he does not speak of a counter-message to his own, but simply of immoral behavior: "their end is destruction [see 1:28], their god is the belly [*koilia*], and they glory in their shame, with minds set on earthly things" (3:19).[53] In contrast, Paul and his readers have a commonwealth in heaven (3:20).

The critical question with regard to this passage is whether Paul is speaking of a circumcision party that opposes him in Philippi, or he is presenting alternative models of behavior for the Philippians to "consider" and "imitate": one based on confidence in "the flesh" and one based on confidence in "the faith that is in Christ" (3:9, author's translation). The answer depends on whether Philippians has literary integrity and offers a coherent argument. In contrast to theories of fragmentation, the best analysis of Philippians demonstrates its literary integrity; chapter 3 therefore is not a haphazardly inserted fragment but part of a rhetorical strategy.[54] The section of the letter from 2:1–3:20, in fact, makes an argument for a "fellowship" in the Spirit that expresses itself in service to others in contrast to a spirit of envy that seeks only the interests of the individual, carried by the examples of Christ himself (2:5–11), Timothy (2:19–24), Epaphroditus (2:25–30), and lastly Paul (3:2–16): these are the ones Paul tells the Philippians to imitate, instead of those who seek only their own pleasure and power (3:17–19).[55]

This reading better accords with the evidence of the rest of Philippians, which shows Paul's concern in 1:15–18 for the good news being preached by some out of "envy and rivalry" (*phthonos kai eris*, v. 15) and "partisanship" (*eritheia*, v. 17), his command to do nothing in "grumbling and questioning" (2:14), and his exhortation to Euodia and Syntyche to work in harmony (4:2–3). In response to the spirit of envy that Paul detects among some of his readers, he writes a letter that highlights fellowship (*koinōnia*), which in ancient moral philosophy was synonymous with friendship, the oppo-

---

53. Note the similarity of the language in Rom 16:17–20.

54. See, e.g., L. Alexander, "Hellenistic Letter Forms"; Dalton, "Integrity of Philippians"; T. Pollard, "Integrity of Philippians"; Jewett, "Epistolary Thanksgiving"; Reed, *Discourse Analysis of Philippians*.

55. See esp. Kurz, "Kenotic Imitation."

site of envy.[56] The only firm evidence for "opponents" of the community is 1:28, where Paul tells the Philippians not to be "frightened in anything by [their] opponents" (*antikeimenōn*), who will face destruction (1:28; cf. 3:19); in context (1:12–30), the reference appears to be to persecutors rather than ideological contesters of Paul's gospel. Far from being an obvious and transparent witness to Paul's opponents, then, Philippians turns out to be more ambiguous and difficult than it at first appears.

### Ephesians and Colossians

As we would expect in a circular letter that is both generalizing and irenic, Ephesians contains only two brief and allusive references to possible opponents. In 4:14 Paul states that an effect of maturity in the fullness of Christ is that "we may no longer be children, tossed to and fro and carried about with every wind of doctrine, by the cunning of men, by their craftiness in deceitful wiles." And in 5:6 he says, "Let no one deceive you with empty words, for it is because of these things that the wrath of God comes upon the sons of disobedience. Therefore do not associate with them." The diction used in these short statements is thoroughly stereotypical.[57]

In contrast, Paul's letter to the Colossians is full of specifics. Unfortunately, as in the case of Galatians, which Colossians resembles in many ways, it is not clear—perhaps even to Paul—whether discord is caused by outsiders ("opponents" in the strict sense) or by members of the community itself (perhaps even the Archippus whom Paul rebukes at the end of the letter [4:17]).[58] Paul himself has not founded the church and is reliant on the reports he hears from his fellow prisoner and founder of the church, Epaphras (1:7; 4:12). Paul speaks of a "philosophy" based on human traditions according to "the elemental spirits of the universe" (*ta stoicheia tou kosmou*) and not Christ (2:8; see 2:20 and Gal 4:3, 9). It involves physical asceticism (2:20–22) and appears to represent some version of Judaism, since Torah (2:14) and circumcision (2:11) figure in Paul's response. Mystical experiences, perhaps of a Merkabah character ("visions," "worship of angels"), also play a part (2:18). No small amount of effort has been

---

56. See L. Johnson, *Writings of the New Testament*, 327–34.

57. *Kybeia tōn anthrōpōn, panourgia, methodeia tēs planēs* in 4:14 and *apatatō kenois logois* in 5:6.

58. See the indefinite "someone" (*tis*) in 2:8 and 2:16.

devoted to putting these puzzling pieces together into a portrait of the "Colossian Heresy."[59]

Paul is most concerned, as he is in Galatians, with the disruptive effect on the community. The agitators, whoever they are, are "judging" others (2:16) and even "disqualifying" them (as from a race [2:18]). Paul regards them with disdain: they are "puffed up without reason by [their] sensuous mind" (2:18); their "appearance of wisdom" is a cover for fleshly behavior (2:23). They seek to "defraud" (2:4, author's translation) members of the community and make them their "booty" (2:8, author's translation). But they are like people who offer a "shadow" rather than the "body" (2:17), because they "do not hold fast to the head" (2:19, author's translation), as those whom Paul exhorts should do (2:6-7).[60]

*Letters to Delegates*

First Timothy, 2 Timothy, and Titus all contain information about opponents. Unfortunately, scholars convinced that the letters are inauthentic and a literary fiction construct a composite portrait from all three letters, ignoring the very real differences among them. But consistency in approach demands that we treat each letter on its own terms.

1 Timothy

In 1 Timothy, Paul portrays troublemakers as members of the community who have "wandered away from the faith" (6:10; cf. 1:3; 6:21) or "shipwrecked their faith" (1:19, author's translation), naming Hymenaios and Alexander as among their number (1:20). But Paul also portrays Timothy as having authority over them: he is to "charge" them "not to teach a different doctrine" (*heterodidaskalein*, 1:3; cf. 6:3) and stay away from them (4:7). Paul himself has handed the two named persons over to Satan, "so they might learn not to blaspheme" (1:20, author's translation). Paul sees them as sponsored by deceitful spirits, teaching the doctrines of demons, with lying pretension (4:1-2). He associates them with "myths and endless genealogies," "speculations" (1:4), and "godless and silly myths" (4:7). If we cut through the

59. As in the studies cited in note 41 above.
60. L. Johnson, "Ritual Imprinting."

stereotypical polemic (as in 6:3–5) applicable to almost all opponents, we find that they are members of the community with intellectual pretension to "the contradictions of falsely named knowledge" (*antitheseis tēs pseudonymou gnōseōs*, 6:20, author's translation), desiring to be "teachers of the law" (*nomodidaskaloi*) without understanding what they are saying (1:7); they advocate physical asceticism (4:7), including forbidding marriage and avoiding certain foods (4:3). Paradoxically, they also see religion as a source of profit (6:3–5). Paul provides a substantive response to each of their false positions on law (1:8–11), asceticism (4:3–5, 7–10), and wealth (6:6–10).

## 2 Timothy

Consistent with its character as a personal paraenetic letter, 2 Timothy uses the description and condemnation of opponents as a foil for the positive exhortation of Paul's delegate. Thus, he contrasts the abandonment of him by Phygelus and Hermogenes as representing those "in Asia [who] turned away from me" in contrast to the loyal Onesiphorus, who sought him out and aided him (1:16), as contrasting models for his delegate (1:18). Paul complains that people in the coming days will select teachers to their own liking and wander into myths (4:3–4). Among such teachers are the "charlatans and wicked men" (3:13) who enter households and make captives of women eager to learn (3:6–9). In 2:16–18 Paul names Hymenaios and Philetus as representing the godless chatter that spreads like gangrene and upsets the faith of others; they have "swerved from the truth by holding that the resurrection is past already" (*tēn anastasin ēdē gegonenai*—or, "the resurrection has already happened"). Timothy is to avoid disputing about words (2:14) and should correct the opponents with gentleness in the hope that they might repent and escape the devil's snare (2:25–26). Second Timothy contains more conventional polemic than substantive description, and provides no doctrinal clarifications; the entire emphasis is on the contrasting character and manner of Paul's delegates and harm-causing charlatans within the community.

## Titus

A third profile is provided by Titus. The positive instruction concerning order in the household and God's civilizing grace (2:1–3:8) is framed by instructions concerning opponents. They contradict sound teaching, are "insubordinate" and are "empty talkers and deceivers," who are from "the circumcision," hold to "Jewish myths," and teach what they should not for profit, upsetting entire households (1:9–16). They engage in "stupid controversies, genealogies, dissensions, and quarrels over the law" (3:9), specifically, it appears, discussions concerning purity (1:15). It is probable that these members of the "circumcision party" (*hoi ek tēs peritomēs*, 1:10) are also members of the community: the leaders appointed by Titus should be able to confute those who contradict sound teaching (1:9). Generally, Paul wants them silenced (1:11) because of the harm they pose to households; he wants Titus to rebuke them sharply so that they might be sound in the faith (1:13). The fractious person (*hairetikon anthrōpon*) should be admonished twice and then shunned (3:10–11). The only substantive correction offered by Paul is that "to the pure all things are pure, but to the corrupt and unfaithful nothing is pure; their very minds and consciences are corrupted" (1:15, adapted).

*Summary of Evidence*

What does this survey of the evidence concerning opposition to Paul yield?

1. In terms of overt efforts to stop his mission, both Acts and the letters point to the Jews.[61]
2. Paul's communities experience opposition, perhaps even persecution, from persons of unknown identity (2 Thess 1:5; Phil 1:28).
3. Some of Paul's letters have no significant reference to active opposition (Philemon, Ephesians, 1 Corinthians, and, with the exceptions noted, Romans and 1 Thessalonians).
4. Only in 2 Corinthians and the three letters to Paul's delegates do we find teachers or preachers within the larger Christian movement who can be called rivals to Paul; even if they do not actively "oppose" Paul, they claim authority over other believers.
5. Even though Paul himself uses the language of "a different gospel" (Gal 1:6–7; 2 Cor 11:4), little by way of what we would call doctrinal difference is identified, in clear contrast to the explicitness of the Johannine letters:[62] the claim of a "realized resurrection" is explicitly held

61. See Acts 9:23–24, 29; 13:45, 50; 14:2–5, 19; 17:5, 13; 18:6; 21:11, 27–31; 22:22; 23:12–15; 24:9; 25:2; Rom 15:31; 2 Cor 11:24, 26; 1 Thess 2:15.
62. See 1 John 2:22; 4:3; 2 John 7.

by the charlatans in 2 Tim 2:18 and may be implicit in the attitudes of some Paul addresses in 1 Corinthians,[63] but the challenge to Paul does not otherwise seem to be based on the basic elements of the kerygma.

6. Whether stimulated by contact with outsiders, or aroused by exposure to Paul himself, or simply generated by ancient religious competitiveness, some within Paul's communities sought something beyond what Paul offered: the (apparent) security of Torah-observance (Galatians, Colossians, 1 Timothy, Titus), with practices of asceticism (Colossians, 1 Timothy), mysticism (2 Corinthians, Colossians), or even extraordinary spiritual charisms (1 Corinthians). Such ambition does not seem to be connected either to a desire to reject Paul or to a distinctive ideology.

7. Paul's concern in all his letters is not the destruction of opponents, despite the harsh language he employs in the manner of ancient rhetoric, but the building up of his readers. He does not want them defrauded or deceived; he does not want them to be tearing each other apart. He does not want them judging, condemning, or disqualifying each other.

In sum, the topic of Paul's opponents does not, as the Tübingen school supposed, provide a key to the historical development of earliest Christianity along the lines of a sustained conflict between Pauline and Jewish parties.[64] The topic does, however, indicate how attractive Judaism was for some of Paul's gentile converts, and how powerfully the psychology of religious perfectionism manifested itself in his communities.

## A Pauline School

A standard way to treat the supposed inauthentic letters of Paul is to attribute them to some sort of school, which produced them after the apostle's death. As you will have realized from my earlier discussion of the Pauline correspondence, I find the hypothesis unsustainable for at least three reasons.

First, as I have already shown, the grounds for dismissing some of the canonical collection as pseudonymous are weak: the criteria generally applied

---

63. See Horsley, "Spiritual Elitism in Corinth."

64. It is worth repeating that in the single letter that portrays rivals as (at least claiming) equal authority to Paul (2 Corinthians), the observance of the law plays no role; in 1 Timothy and Titus, those advocating the law are represented, not as representatives of a sustained movement, but as local agitators with intellectual pretensions.

are both formally and materially inadequate, and the premise of a "Pauline standard" by which other letters can be judged glosses over the presence of stylistically and substantively distinct clusters within the correspondence.[65]

Second, there exists no positive evidence for a social context or structural framework within which such literary production might have been carried out. Indeed, so different are Colossians and Ephesians from the letters to Paul's delegates, and so different are these from 2 Thessalonians, that it is difficult to construct a coherent portrayal of a school that might have produced them.[66] The only real support for the hypothesis is the existence of letters that scholars have chosen to regard as pseudepigraphical. Indeed, the more we try to make the production of the letters concrete and specific, the more implausible the scenarios appear.[67]

Third, although it is true that pseudonymous literature was produced in both Jewish and Greco-Roman contexts,[68] the fit of the category to Paul's disputed letters is inexact. Here we are not talking about schoolroom exercises (as in Greco-Roman literary mimesis)[69] or a claim to the authority of a long-ago hero (as in Jewish apocalyptic).[70] Here we have letters seeking to pass as Paul's own within decades of his death, while his other letters are still in circulation. They do not represent a transparent and harmless fiction; they seek to deceive the reader. A more appropriate term would therefore be "forgery."[71]

There is, however, another way in which the existence of a Pauline "school" in the decades after his death might be thought of—namely, as those disciples/learners who regarded Paul as teacher and made significant use of

---

65. See the discussion in chap. 3, "Clusters of Letters and an Adequate Model of Authorship."

66. Eduard Lohse on Colossians is vague enough: "Col presupposes a Pauline school tradition. It is likely that this school tradition was based in Ephesus as the center of the Pauline mission in Asia Minor, and that it was cultivated and further developed in the circle of the Apostle's students" (*Colossians and Philemon*, 181). Earl J. Richard sees 2 Thessalonians as a pseudonymous composition countering apocalypticism: "To counter such apocalyptic fervor, an unknown author, following current practice, employs Paul's authority by composing a shrewd letter in his name" (*First and Second Thessalonians*, 32).

67. The hypothesis advanced by Goodspeed, *Meaning of Ephesians*, that Ephesians was written as a Pauline homage on the basis of Colossians by the freed slave Onesimus, has the great appeal of specificity but requires too many dots to be connected. It was enthusiastically taken up by Mitton, *Pauline Corpus*.

68. See the classic essay by Aland, "Problem of Anonymity."

69. See Fiore, *Function of Personal Example*, 108–13.

70. See Russell, *Jewish Apocalyptic*; J. Collins, *Apocalyptic Imagination*.

71. Metzger, "Literary Forgeries."

his writings.[72] In chapter 1, I provided a quick survey of such use of Paul's letters in Clement of Rome, Ignatius of Antioch, and Polycarp of Smyrna. Here I return to Polycarp for a fuller discussion, because Polycarp's *Letter to the Philippians*, written after the death of Ignatius (ca. 110) and his own martyrdom (155), is a key and disputed witness. On one side, the heavy use of Paul's letters, including 1 and 2 Timothy, can be taken as evidence for the existence and influence of a large part of the Pauline collection (as well as 1 Peter, the Johannine letters, and Luke-Acts). On the other side, it has been argued that Polycarp himself is the author of the Pastoral Letters, and makes allusions to them in his letter to the Philippians, to help secure their authority as "Pauline."[73]

Polycarp is writing to the Philippian church, we remember, because they had requested from him a collection of Ignatius's letters (Ign. *Phil.* 13.2), and he takes the opportunity to send along a compendium of moral exhortation, which is also a virtual florilegium of passages from the New Testament.[74] The difficulty of detecting citations and allusions when formulas of citation are lacking is clear. Should we take Polycarp's reference in 1.2 to Jesus's death and resurrection, "whom God raised up, having loosed the bonds of Hades" (*hon ēgeiren ho theos, lysas tas ōdinas tou hadou*), as a deliberate allusion to Acts 2:24, whose diction it matches exactly? Or when in 1.3 he continues, "in whom, though you did not see him, you believed in unspeakable and glorified joy" (*eis hon ouk idontes pisteuete chara aneklalētō kai dedoxasmenē*), should we see an allusion to 1 Pet 1:8, whose language it echoes (*hon ouk idontes agapate, eis hon arti mē horōntes pisteuontes de agalliasthe chara aneklalētō kai dedoxasmenē*)? In both of these instances, the language is so distinctive that allusions are virtually certain, suggesting Polycarp's knowledge of both Acts and 1 Peter.[75]

Polycarp does not rely entirely on allusion. In 2.3 he introduces an out-of-sequence catena of gospel texts (Matt 7:1–2; Luke 6:36–38; 6:20; Matt 5:3, 10) with "remembering what the Lord taught when he said" (Lake's translation).

72. See esp. Rensberger, "As the Apostle Teaches."
73. Most notably Campenhausen, *Polykarp von Smyrna*. For my argument against Campenhausen, see L. Johnson, *First and Second Letters to Timothy*, 291–300; see also Rensberger, "As the Apostle Teaches," 170–174. Richard Pervo considers the Pastorals to be inauthentic and dates them ca. 125, but he recognizes that Polycarp makes use of them, dating *Philippians* ca. 130–35; see Pervo, *Pastorals and Polycarp*, 14, 85.
74. I am using the translation of Lake, *Apostolic Fathers*.
75. The language of 1 Pet 1:13 and 2:22 is echoed also by *Phil* 7.1 and 8.1. First John 4:2, 8 is clearly echoed by *Phil* 7.1

Similarly, he attaches "as the Lord said" to another set of gospel sayings (Matt 26:41; Mark 14:38) in 7.3. And in 11.2 he quotes 1 Cor 6:2, "do we not know that the saints shall judge the world," adding, "as Paul teaches." Most impressively, Polycarp tells the Philippians, "These things, brethren, I write to you concerning righteousness, not at my own instance, but because you first invited me. For neither am I, nor is any other like me, able to follow the wisdom of the blessed and glorious Paul *who when he was among you in the presence of the men of that time taught accurately and steadfastly the word of truth.* And also when he was absent sent letters to you *from the study of which you will be able to build yourself up into the faith given to you*" (3.1-2, emphasis added). This introductory statement both locates Paul in a previous generation and prepares the reader to regard the following instructions as drawn largely from Paul's letters. Leaving aside more problematic cases, Polycarp's language clearly alludes to Gal 4:26 (3.3); 6:7 (5.1); 5:17 (5.3); to Rom 14:10 (6.2); to 1 Cor 6:2 (11.2); 6:9-10 (5.3); 15:58 (10.1); to Phil 2:16 (9.2); 3:18 (12.3); 2:10 (1.3); to Eph 2:8-9 (1.3); 4:26 (12.1); to 1 Tim 2:1 (12.3); 5:5 (4.3); 6:7, 10 (4.1); and to 2 Tim 2:12 (5.2); 2:25 (11.4); 4:10 (9.2). The allusions to the two letters to Paul's delegates do not stand out in any way, nor are they more frequent than the echoes of other Pauline letters. What is abundantly clear is that Polycarp, at least, viewed 1 and 2 Timothy (he does not allude to Titus) *and* Ephesians as being as thoroughly Pauline as Romans, Galatians, and 1 Corinthians.

Polycarp presents us with a stark choice. If we think he wrote the Pastorals and then seeded them into his letter to the Philippians in order to help them "pass" as Pauline, the bishop and martyr was a forger and deceiver. But if, as I have tried to show, he knew and used Ephesians and 1 and 2 Timothy as he knew and used other Pauline letters (Galatians, Romans, 1 Corinthians, Philippians), then we must conclude that, at least for this student of Paul, those letters were part of the authentic Pauline collection. By no means does the latter conclusion demonstrate the actual authenticity of those three disputed letters, but it does argue against dating them in the mid-second-century. Together with Clement and Ignatius, Polycarp shows us how disciples of Paul knew and used his letters in the first half of the second century.

## Conclusion

This chapter has examined three ways of approaching the question of Paul's place in earliest Christianity. We saw first that, despite his unquestioned creativity, Paul cannot be considered the true founder of Christianity. His letters show how he drew from both Hellenistic and Palestinian forms of Christianity existing before him; other early Christian writings, such as James, Hebrews, and Revelation, confirm that Paul did not invent but rather stood within a wider stream of tradition. Second, a close analysis of the kinds of opposition Paul faced in his ministry revealed a complex set of issues in his communities, some of which may have been generated by outside agitators, but others which may have been stimulated by a spirit of competition from within. In any case, we saw that it is impossible to construct a single movement (such as Jewish or gnostic Christianity) that stood in opposition to the apostle. Third, consonant with the position taken earlier concerning the composition of Paul's letters—namely, that something like a "school" was at work in all his correspondence—we have entertained the idea that the best way to think about a "Pauline school" after his death is in terms of such avowed readers and students as Clement of Rome, Ignatius of Antioch, and, above all, Polycarp of Smyrna.

*Part 2*

# THE MATERIALS

*Chapter 5*

# What Kind of Jew Is Paul?

I use the term "symbolic world" for the complex combination of social structures, dynamics, and ideas, within which any individual and group, ancient or modern, lives and seeks meaning. Material processes—social structures and dynamics—stand in a reciprocal relationship with symbols, both expressing and reinforcing a certain construal of reality.[1] In the largest sense, Paul's symbolic world consisted of all the complex elements of the first-century Mediterranean, involving Roman rule, Hellenistic culture, and, most critically, his Jewish heritage. These elements, in turn, were catalyzed by Paul's experience of and convictions concerning the death and resurrection of Jesus, and were given new shape by his own creative thought. I turn now to examine some of the aspects of the symbolic world (or worlds) within which Paul worked and wrote. In the next part of the book, I touch on some of Paul's distinctive reworkings of that world.

The most important and certainly the most intimate dimension of Paul's identity is his Jewishness. The question of Paul's Jewish identity is far more likely to arouse strong responses today among both Jews and Christians than the question of the Jewishness of Jesus.[2] But we can ask the question today more precisely and dispassionately than was sometimes possible in the past, when some Christian scholars regarded Paul as the one who liberated

---

1. For language about "symbolic worlds," see L. Johnson, *Writings of the New Testament*, 1–15.

2. The Jewishness of Jesus is one of the staples of contemporary historical Jesus research, although assessments of his Jewish character vary considerably; for a sense of the range, see Falk, *Jesus the Pharisee*; Vermes, *Jesus the Jew*; E. Sanders, *Jesus and Judaism*; Crossan, *Historical Jesus*; Meier, *Marginal Jew*.

Jesus from Jewish "particularity,"[3] and when some Jewish scholars saw him as the inventor of a romantic religion completely alien to classical Judaism.[4]

We can ask the question more precisely today because the past hundred years have taught us so much more about Judaism in the first century of the Common Era,[5] and so much more about Paul's social world and correspondence.[6] We can ask the question more dispassionately today because the study of Paul is a more genuinely ecumenical enterprise. Both Jewish and Christian scholars alike now engage Paul to better understand the past that continues to shape both Christian and Jewish communities, without the bias and even rancor that at times marked earlier exchanges.[7]

New attitudes and new knowledge certainly help in one way, but in another way they make it harder. When we could assume that the rabbinic version of Judaism was "normative" already in the first century, it was fairly easy to show how Paul did or did not fit within that frame.[8] Likewise, it was

3. See, e.g., the passages discussed in the previous chapter from works by F. C. Baur and Adolf Von Harnack, found in Meeks and Fitzgerald, *Writings of St. Paul*, 399–408, 419–24.

4. As in the classic 1938 essay by Leo Baeck that appears as "Paul's Romanticism" in the first (but not second) edition of Meeks, *Writings of St. Paul*, 334–39.

5. Compare, e.g., the knowledge of "Jewish eschatology" based on a handful of writings in Schweitzer, *Mysticism of Paul the Apostle*, 52–104, to the nuanced treatments in Charlesworth, *Old Testament Pseudepigrapha*; it is hard to believe that only fifty-two years separate these publications. In the same period, Gershom Scholem opened up the world of Jewish esotericism in the rabbinic tradition; see *Major Trends in Jewish Mysticism* and *Jewish Gnosticism*. Pioneering work was done on the interconnections of the rabbinic tradition and Greco-Roman culture by Lieberman, *Greek in Jewish Palestine*, and Fischel, *Talmudic Literature* and *Rabbinic Literature*. Simultaneously, Jacob Neusner was applying historical-critical methods to the internal development of the rabbinic movement, as in *From Politics to Piety* and "Formation of Rabbinic Judaism." Similarly, the historian Josephus has been subjected to close scrutiny; see Rajak, *Josephus*; Pastor, Stern, and Mor, *Flavius Josephus*. All this, plus the epochal discovery in 1947 of the Dead Sea Scrolls at Qumran and the excavations at Dura-Europos in the 1930s, each of which opened up unexpected perspectives on the complexities of Judaism both in Palestine and in the diaspora; for Qumran, see Cross, *Ancient Library at Qumran*, and Flint and VanderKam, *Dead Sea Scrolls*; for the impact of Dura, see Goodenough, *Jewish Symbols*.

6. For the complexities of Paul's correspondence, see chap. 3 above; for Paul's social world, see esp. Meeks, *First Urban Christians*; Holmberg, *Paul and Power*; Judge, "Early Christians."

7. Notable Jewish scholars contributing to the study of Paul include Sandmel, *Genius of Paul*; Segal, *Paul the Convert*; Boyarin, *Radical Jew*; Nanos, *Mystery of Romans*; Levine, *Jewish Annotated New Testament* and *Feminist Companion to Paul*; Fredriksen, *Paul*; and Eisenbaum, *Paul Was Not a Christian*.

8. The term "normative Judaism" assumes that the rabbinic tradition was in full flower

easier when it was assumed that Galatians and Romans were the only letters of Paul worth examining, and that they gave direct access to his identity.

But once we have learned to read his letters not as windows into his soul but as rhetorical constructions that seek to persuade, once we grasp that Paul practiced the ancient rhetorical ideal of writing in character,[9] we are less confident about being able to draw deductions about who he was from what he wrote. The same realization helps us appreciate the full diversity of the Pauline collection, which shows us a variety of "Pauls" addressing a variety of distinct rhetorical situations.[10] Caution about concluding too quickly and directly from a Pauline letter to the person "Paul" is sharpened by the realization that something like a school was at work already in his correspondence, which produced a number of distinct Pauline epistolary "clusters."[11]

The rhetorically diverse and occasional character of Paul's correspondence, in turn, gives a sharper edge to the truism that Paul is not a systematic thinker but a pastoral theologian, whose thought is directed not to the adjudication of religious systems but to the survival and integrity of fragile intentional communities under stress. We are better readers when we appreciate that Paul was not in a position to assess "Judaism" as a religion any more than he was to define "Christianity" as a religion.[12] He was, rather, caught up in a complicated negotiation demanded by his commitment to a crucified and raised Messiah, a negotiation that involved rereading everything in his past in light of his present. Such negotiation Paul carried out, not in an isolated study, but with his fellow workers and delegates who struggled with him to shape communities capable of existing in the same state of liminality.[13]

---

even before Yavneh, and that other Jewish manifestations of the first century were somehow "marginal." See esp. G. Moore, *Judaism in the First Centuries*, as well as Schechter, *Aspects of Rabbinic Theology*, and Urbach, *Sages*. A classic work on Paul that accepts the basic premise of normative Judaism is W. D. Davies, *Paul and Rabbinic Judaism*.

9. See Stowers, "Romans 7:7–25."

10. The elusiveness of Paul even in the undisputed letters was the basis for the classic essay by Meeks, "The Christian Proteus," in Meeks and Fitzgerald, *Writings of St. Paul*, 689–94.

11. As described in chap. 3, I argue for five distinct clusters, which are stylistically and substantively distinct within the canonical collection: (1) 1 and 2 Thessalonians; (2) Galatians and Romans; (3) 1 and 2 Corinthians; (4) Colossians and Ephesians; (5) Titus, 1 and 2 Timothy, with Philippians and Philemon as outliers.

12. Leave aside the difficulties of defining "religion" in the first place; for recent struggles, see Schewel, *Seven Ways*.

13. For my use of the term "liminality," see L. Johnson, "Ritual Imprinting," 94–97.

## The Complexities of the Question

There are at least four cautionary corollaries to this realization. First, as I noted earlier, we are not able fully to reconstruct any of the situations Paul addresses, and must deal always and only with Paul's perception and presentation of his interlocutors' positions. Second, we have available no overarching grid to help us reconcile the apparent inconsistencies in Paul's statements, as for example when he says in 1 Cor 7:19 (RSV), "Neither circumcision counts for anything nor uncircumcision, but keeping the commandments of God," while also saying in Gal 6:15 (RSV), "Neither circumcision counts for anything, nor uncircumcision, but a new creation."[14] Third, we cannot assume that Paul is more Jewish when he is talking about the law and less Jewish when he does not mention the law. Paul is surely no less or more Jewish in 1 and 2 Thessalonians than he is in Galatians and Romans. Fourth, we must recognize that Paul is a writer capable of playing with words even when he is making his most serious points.

The single word *nomos*, for example, can mean several things even within the same sentence, as Paul plays the scales of polyvalence: Does he mean in this case law or scripture or principle or norm?[15] Likewise, the term *erga* ("deeds" or "works") can be used negatively when joined to *nomos* ("works of law") and positively when joined to *pistis* ("works of faith").[16] Similarly, the combination *pistis Christou* is capable of being read in quite different directions as meaning the believers' faith in Jesus or Jesus's faith in God.[17]

---

14. Unless otherwise indicated, Scripture quotations in this chapter are from the NRSV.

15. A classic example is Rom 3:27-28: "Then what becomes of our boasting? It is excluded. On what principle [*nomos*]? Of works [*erga*]? No, but on the principle of faith [*nomos tēs pisteōs*], for we hold that a person is justified by faith [*pistis*] apart from the works of the law [*erga nomou*]" (RSV, adapted). Again, in Rom 7:21-23: "So I find it to be a law [*nomos*] that when I want to do right, evil lies close at hand. For I delight in the law of God [*nomos tou theou*], in my inmost self, but I see in my members another law [*heteron nomon*] at war with the law of my mind [*nomos tou noos mou*] and making me captive to the law of sin [*nomos tēs hamartias*] which dwells in my members" (RSV).

16. The usage "works of the law" appears exclusively in Romans (3:20, 28; 4:2, 6; 9:11, 32; 11:6), Galatians (2:16; 3:2, 5, 10, 19), and Ephesians (2:9), and "work of faith" in 1 Thess 1:3 and 2 Thess 1:11. Mostly, Paul uses "works" in the neutral sense of "deeds" (Rom 2:6, 7, 15; 13:3, 12; 14:20; 1 Cor 3:13-15; 5:2; 9:1; 15:58; 16:10; 2 Cor 9:8; 10:11; 11:15; Gal 6:4; Eph 2:10; 4:12; 5:11; Phil 1:6, 22; 2:30; Col 1:10, 21; 3:17; 1 Thess 5:13; 2 Thess 2:17; 1 Tim 2:10; 3:1; 5:10, 25; 6:18; 2 Tim 1:9; 2:21; 3:17; 4:5, 14, 18; Titus 1:16; 2:7, 14; 3:1, 5, 8, 14).

17. For the exegetical issues, see L. Johnson, "Rom 3:21-26."

In short, for those who read him most closely and responsibly, Paul is not a constant but a variable. But so was Judaism in the first century. This is a conclusion to which all scholars now subscribe, though they less often follow through on the implications.[18] Jews were certainly distinct in the first-century Mediterranean world because of their convictions and practices.[19] But internally, Jews were not only diverse in their expressions of such convictions and practices; they were often also in sharp disagreement.[20]

Although Jews in the diaspora and in Palestine had to work out the tension between assimilation and separation within distinctly different social realities,[21] we can no longer simply equate diaspora Judaism with "Hellenistic Judaism," for Greek language and perceptions were found as frequently within Palestine as outside it.[22] For that matter, the diaspora Jew Philo of Alexandria was by no means unique in his fusion of Greek and Jewish perceptions, but rather stands within a remarkably prolific Jewish literature based on the Septuagint and engaged with Greek culture.[23] Philo was joined by others in regarding Judaism as a form of mystery religion with multiple initiations.[24] And some Jews who shared Philo's philosophical readings of

18. See, e.g., Wright, *New Testament*, where, despite recognizing the diversity in first-century Judaism in the abstract, he mostly ignores the diaspora in favor of Palestine and speaks of "mainline Jews" (286).

19. The shared convictions included belief in one God who elected a single people as his own and made a covenant with them whose obligations were articulated by commandments that were at once an obligation and the source of wisdom. Practices included circumcision and Sabbath observance; see J. Smith, "Fences and Neighbors."

20. For a fuller treatment of the succinct comments here, see L. Johnson, "Ways of Being Jewish."

21. Whereas Jews in the diaspora, while vulnerable to local anti-Semitic activity, were able to practice their religion freely and legally within a pluralistic context, those living in Palestine inevitably had to negotiate the specific social realities of the land and the temple in a context of repression from the side of Greek culture and Roman rule. It was unproblematic for Philo to attend the gymnasium as well as the synagogue, to read Homer as well as Torah, but the same activities were fraught with political implications for Pharisees or Essenes in Eretz Israel.

22. According to the legend of the translation of the Septuagint under Ptolemy II (285–247 BCE) in the *Letter of Aristeas*, it was Greek- and Hebrew-speaking scholars from Palestine who came to Egypt and carried out the translation. For Hellenistic culture in Palestine, see Hengel, *Judaism and Hellenism*; Goldstein, "Jewish Acceptance."

23. See Tcherikover, *Hellenistic Civilization*; Holladay, "Jewish Responses," and "Paul and His Predecessors."

24. See, e.g., Goodenough, *By Light, Light*; Cerfaux, "Influence des Mystères"; L. Johnson, *Religious Experience*, 89–99.

Scripture concluded that they could indeed still call themselves Jews without practicing circumcision.[25]

The production of apocalyptic literature is, in turn, associated with Eretz Israel, even though its imaginative construction of a reality counter to the one appearing on the surface cannot be attached with confidence to any particular group.[26] And the Dead Sea Scrolls have shown us that Josephus's neat division of elite schools—Pharisees, Sadducees, Essenes, and Zealots[27]—captures only some of the multiple permutations of Jewish practice and conviction in a land where religious symbols were inextricably connected to specific social and political institutions.[28] At Qumran we find Jews who were simultaneously scrupulously legal in observance, devoted to wisdom, fond of mysticism, passionately apocalyptic, morally and ritually dualistic, and complexly messianic, while also conceiving of themselves as the embodiment of a new covenant and a living temple.[29] The sectarians at Qumran were not the only Jews who could combine elements we once thought separate; we have come to recognize the practice of Merkabah mysticism among the earliest and greatest of the Pharisaic teachers who gave shape to the rabbinic tradition.[30]

We can add to our catalogue those claimants to the heritage of Israel who also occupied Eretz Israel and were deeply conservative in their keeping of Torah—calling themselves *ha shomrim* ("the preservers")—whose significance we tend to dismiss, as did their Judean rivals, as "the Samaritans."[31] And these versions are only the varieties that rise to our attention because they were elite and literate—or came to the attention of those who were elite and literate. How many other combinations of piety and politics might we discover among the many folk who thronged to Jerusalem for the great festivals, if their passions and longings also had been committed to writing?

25. A position Philo himself emphatically rejects; see *On the Migration of Abraham* 89–93; *Embassy to Gaius* 209–12; see also Josephus, *Against Apion* 1.42–43.

26. For an orientation, see J. Collins, *Apocalyptic Imagination*; Sacchi, *Jewish Apocalyptic*.

27. Josephus, *Jewish War* 2.119–66; *Antiquities of the Jews* 18.11–25; on the sects, see also Saldarini and VanderKam, *Pharisees, Scribes, and Sadducees*; E. Sanders, *Judaism*.

28. See, e.g., Horsley with Hanson, *Bandits, Prophets, and Messiahs*.

29. See, e.g., Boccaccini, *Beyond the Essene Hypothesis*; García Martinez and Barrera, *People of the Dead Sea Scrolls*; Schiffman, *Reclaiming the Dead Sea Scrolls*; Ulrich and Vander-Kam, *Community of the Renewed Covenant*.

30. See, e.g., Gershom Scholem, *The Varieties of Jewish Mysticism*, and *Jewish Gnosticism, Merkabah Mysticism and Talmudic Tradition*.

31. See Coggins, *Samaritans and Jews*; Mor and Reiterer, *Samaritans*.

Not only were Jews diverse, they were also divided. Their elite sects represented ideological and political responses to Hellenistic culture and Roman rule, and, as so often happens in such situations, the hostility they turned on each other sometimes exceeded what they directed to the external enemy. Our extant literature has so much invective directed by Judeans against Samaritans, by Pharisees against *am-ha-aretz*, by House of Hillel against House of Shammai, by Josephus against a range of enemies, and by the sectarians at Qumran against everyone else who was not a covenanter, that we might reasonably conclude that a good definition of a Jew in the first century is someone willing to fight about the meaning and social implications of Torah.[32]

Now, if Paul's letters are more various than we sometimes have regarded them, and if first-century Judaism is far more various than we sometimes have thought, what are the implications for asking what kind of Jew Paul was?

## Paul's Jewish Identity

Perhaps surprisingly, one effect is that the claims made for Paul's Jewishness by the New Testament appear more plausible. Leaving aside the portrait in Acts,[33] and taking into account only Paul's letters,[34] we have no reason to doubt, in light of all the diversity we have observed, the accuracy of Paul's claim to be a Hebrew, and an Israelite, and a descendent of Abraham (2 Cor 11:22). Nor do we have any grounds to think impossible his boast in Phil 3:5-6, "I have been circumcised on the eighth day, a member of the people of Israel, of the tribe of Benjamin, a Hebrew born of Hebrews, as to the law, a Pharisee, as to zeal, a persecutor of the church, as to righteousness under the law blameless."

Similarly, we can grant the veracity of Paul's characterization of his earlier days as being "advanced in Judaism beyond many among my people of the same age, for I was far more zealous for the traditions of my ancestors"

32. For textual examples of each sort of invective, see L. Johnson, "New Testament's Anti-Jewish Slander."

33. A powerful case for Paul's positive portrayal vis-à-vis Judaism in Acts is made by Jervell, *Luke and the People of God*, and Jervell, *Unknown Paul*.

34. As with other topics, the selection of letters here is dependent entirely on whether they contain evidence pertinent to the subject, without regard to their being "undisputed" or "disputed."

(Gal 1:14). Paul, after all, is the very first person from antiquity whom we know as identifying himself as a Pharisee. Rather than dismiss the claim, we ought rather to consider its implication, not alone for understanding Paul, but also for understanding the range of possibilities for Pharisaism in the mid-first century.[35]

In the same way, there is no need to doubt the sincerity of Paul's claim to be "speaking the truth in Christ" when he declares, "I have great sorrow and unceasing anguish in my heart, for I would wish that I myself were accursed and cut off from Christ for the sake of my own people, my kindred according to the flesh. They are the Israelites; and to them belong the adoption, the glory, the covenants, the giving of the law, the worship, and the promises; to them belong the patriarchs and from them, according to human descent, comes the messiah" (Rom 9:1-5, author's translation), or that his "desire and prayer to God for them is that they be saved" (Rom 10:1, author's translation).[36]

That his sense of anguish concerning his kinsmen is real is made more plausible by the course of his argument through Rom 9-11, which reaches its climax in his expectation that "all Israel will be saved" (11:26), and his bold assertion concerning his fellow Jews, "As regards the gospel they are enemies of God for your sake; but as regards election they are beloved, for the sake of their ancestors; for the gifts and the calling of God are irrevocable. Just as you were once disobedient to God but have now received mercy because of their disobedience, so they have now been disobedient in order that, by the mercy shown to you, they too may now receive mercy. For God has imprisoned all in disobedience so that he may be merciful to all" (11:28-32).

Paul's explicit statements concerning Torah, moreover, support his claim to be a *Ioudaios* not simply by birth but by religious allegiance.[37] The Jews have been given "the oracles of God" (*ta logia tou theou*, Rom 3:2). The law is spiritual (Rom 7:14); "the law is holy, and the commandment is holy and just and good" (Rom 7:12). Doers of the law are righteous in God's eyes (Rom 2:13, 25). Not circumcision but keeping the commandments of God matters (1 Cor 7:19). Paul declares in 1 Tim 1:8 that "the law

---

35. Paul not only carries the title proudly into his diaspora and gentile communities, but assumes that his readers would be aware of what being a Pharisee meant, since in his letters he never explains the term. While taking Paul's background as a Pharisee seriously, Neyrey tends to collapse Paul into the frame thus established, making him a "typical" Pharisee rather than an exceptional one; see *Paul in Other Words*.

36. See Dahl, "Future of Israel."

37. See Tomson, *Paul and the Jewish Law*.

is good, if any one uses it lawfully" (RSV), and in 2 Tim 3:16 he states that "all scripture is inspired by God and profitable for teaching, for reproof, for correction, and for training in righteousness" (RSV), just as in Rom 15:4 he says, "whatever was written in former days was written for our instruction, that by steadfastness and by the encouragement of the scriptures we might have hope" (RSV). Finally, in Rom 2:17-20 he speaks to one carrying the name of a Jew as one who can "rely on the law, and boast of your relation to God, and know his will, and approve of what is excellent, because you are instructed in the law, and . . . you are a guide to the blind, a light to those in darkness, a corrector of the foolish, a teacher of children, having in the law the embodiment of knowledge and truth" (RSV, adapted). Even though it has been surpassed by the new covenant in the Spirit, the revelation of God's law on Sinai through Moses nevertheless had "glory"—that is, it manifested the presence and power of God (2 Cor 3:7-11).

Paul's negative statements on the law derive not from his personal difficulties in keeping it[38] but from his experience of the crucified and exalted Lord Jesus, which showed him the dangers of an absolute reading of Torah and the falsity of the claims made for it.[39] Taking Torah as absolute means eliminating Jesus as Messiah, for Deut 21:23 declares the man who hangs upon a tree as cursed—in all probability a text that Paul himself threw against believers when he was persecuting them (Gal 3:13; see 1 Cor 12:3). It is in light of this application that Paul can speak of a "ministry of death" and a "letter [that] kills" (2 Cor 3:6-7 NRSV).

The written law, moreover, can indicate God's will, but it cannot supply the power to do it (Rom 3:20; 7:7). In this sense, the law can be "the power of sin" (1 Cor 15:56), because it turns transgression into rebellion and disobedience (Rom 7:7-23). The law promises to give life to those who observe it (Gal 3:12; Lev 18:5), but a written code cannot enliven, cannot empower; only God's Spirit can do that: "If a law had been given which could make alive, then righteousness would indeed be by the law" (Gal 3:21 RSV). Only because Christ, "the life-giving Spirit" (1 Cor 15:45 RSV), has by the gift of the Spirit (Rom 5:5) set believers free from "the law of sin and death" (Rom 8:2), can "the just requirement of the law might be fulfilled in us, who walk not according to the flesh but according to the Spirit" (Rom 8:3-4; cf. Eph 2:15; Col 2:14).

---

38. On this point, see above all Stendahl, "Apostle Paul."

39. This is a fundamental contribution of E. P. Sanders, who memorably stated it as "the solution preceding the problem." *Paul and Palestinian Judaism*, 442.

There is, furthermore, no reason to question Paul's allegiance to his Jewish identity because of the polemic he occasionally uses for fellow Jews[40]—and it is occasional, since Paul saves his best shots not for his fellow Jews but for gentiles[41] and those who want gentiles to act like Jews.[42] When Paul says of actual Jews that they are blinded (2 Cor 4:4), or are veiled and have their hearts hardened (2 Cor 3:14-15), or are ignorant (Rom 10:3) and enemies of God (Rom 11:28) who have stumbled (Rom 11:11), his rhetoric is mild by the standards of the day, positively anemic compared to the full-blooded curses by the Jews at Qumran leveled against all Jews not members of their community. Such evidence of internal rivalry and hostility never leads us to question whether the members of the new covenant at Qumran were truly Jews! Nor should it in the case of Paul. His hope for the salvation of all Israel, furthermore, represents an embrace of the people as a whole that is the exact opposite of Qumran's ready assignment to the everlasting pit of those not among its members.[43]

Although we have determined that Paul really was a Jew, that he was, so far as we can tell, a sincere Jew, and that he hoped for the salvation of his fellow Jews, we have not yet really answered the question, "What kind of Jew was Paul?" For the question involves more than being a good or bad Jew, a sincere or treacherous Jew; it pushes us to try to locate Paul and his thought within the complex Jewish world of the first century of the Common Era.

## Paul's Place in the Jewish World

My examination works exclusively with the letters, taking with full seriousness both their complexity and the complexity of first-century Judaism as we have come to know it, and searches for connections that arise inductively. So I shift the question just slightly: "What kind of Jew do Paul's letters show him to be?" And I move from what is most external and obvious to what is more internal and obscure.

Most external and obvious are Paul's language and the language of the Scripture that he cites. Paul's letters evince a vivid and somewhat idiosyn-

40. See Boyarin, "Is Paul an 'Anti-Semite'?"

41. Most impressively in Rom 1:18-32, but see also 1 Thess 1:9; 4:5, 13; Gal 4:8-9; 5:20-21; Eph 2:2-3, 12; 1 Cor 5:1; 10:22; 12:1; 2 Cor 6:14-18.

42. See Gal 3:1; 4:17, 30; 5:4, 12; 6:12-13; Col 2:16-19, 23; 1 Tim 1:6-7; 6:9-10, 20; Titus 1:10-16; 3:9-10.

43. E.g., Cairo Genizah copy of the Damascus Document (CD) 6.14-7.6; Rule of the Community (1QS) 2.4-10; 4.9-14; War Scroll (1QM) 1.2.

cratic form of Koine Greek,[44] and he quotes Scripture from the Septuagint.[45] On this basis, our first instinct would be to identify Paul immediately as a Hellenistic Jew of the diaspora. Some have done so, and then drawn conclusions about what Paul must or must not have thereby thought, for example, about the law.[46] But we must be careful. We remember first that Greek was widely used by Jews in Palestine, and that Jewish literature originating in Palestine also used the Septuagint.[47] Then, when we compare Paul to our other best-known Hellenistic Jew of the diaspora, Philo of Alexandria, the differences are greater than the similarities.

In contrast to Philo's tendency, for example, Paul indulges in an allegorical interpretation of Scripture only once, and then awkwardly (Gal 4:21–31).[48] More significant, he lacks entirely the Platonic worldview that we find everywhere structuring and directing Philo's reading of Scripture.[49] Paul is no Platonist.[50] The contrast between Paul and Philo is more obvious when we see how another New Testament composition, the Letter to the Hebrews, does share precisely Philo's Platonic framework for reading Scripture, and in that degree can be seen as non-Pauline, despite its many superficial resemblances to Paul's letters.[51] By no means does this suggest that Paul is not engaged with Greek culture; subsequent chapters will show how Greco-Roman philosophy, rhetoric, religion, and politics assist in understanding his letters. But it does mean that Paul aligns awkwardly with such representatives of "Hellenistic Judaism" as Philo and Aristobolos.

The letters do not tell us where Paul was born or spent his youth, but

44. We must keep in mind, on this point, the considerable range in Greek style displayed in the canonical collection, supporting the suggestion made in chap. 3 that several hands were at work in the composition of Paul's letters.

45. The designation "Septuagint" (LXX) camouflages a range of complex issues concerning the actual shape of the Greek text; see, e.g., Peters, "Septuagint"; Jobes and Silva, *Invitation to the Septuagint*; Jellicoe, *Studies in the Septuagint*.

46. See Schoeps, *Paul*.

47. Of first importance here is the evidence pulled together by Holladay, *Fragments*, and Hengel, *Judaism and Hellenism*.

48. In contrast, see Philo virtually everywhere, as in *Post.* 1–2; *Planting* 163–67; *Abr.* 275–76; *Migr.* 130; *Decal.* 20–31.

49. Philo finds a basis for the cosmological distinction between the material and the ideal in the two creation accounts of Genesis (*Alleg. Interp.* 1.31; *QG* 1.4) and in the LXX's rendering of Exod 25:40 as *kata ton typon*, the ideal heavenly temple of which the earthly one is an imitation (*QE* 82; *Alleg. Interp.* 3.102).

50. *Pace* Boyarin, *Radical Jew*, 57–85; see 2 Cor 5:1–5 for a passage in Paul where Platonic language is most noteworthy. See Dupont, *ΣΥΝ ΧΡΙΣΤΟΙ*.

51. See J. W. Thompson, *Beginnings of Christian Philosophy*; L. Johnson, *Hebrews*.

they do support the proposition that Paul was at home in the diaspora, most of all because of his obvious comfort with the urban context of the empire,[52] his avoidance of identifying religious commitments with sociopolitical structures,[53] and his sensitivity to the problems of assimilation and separation facing intentional communities in a pluralistic culture.[54] Such reflexes, even more than Paul's language and use of the LXX, suggest that he was a diaspora Jew.

On the other side, we can note the strong claim that Jerusalem and Judea had on him. Although he states that at the time he first went to Jerusalem after his call to be an apostle, "I was still unknown by sight to the churches of Judea that are in Christ; they only heard it said, 'The one who was formerly persecuting us is now proclaiming the faith he once tried to destroy'" (Gal 1:22), Jerusalem holds a central spot in Paul's symbolic universe.[55] It was not, to be sure, the temple or its cult that attracts his loyalty. Like the sectarians at Qumran, Paul transposed the language of temple and cult to his diaspora communities. They were the house of God in which the Spirit dwelt (1 Cor 3:16-17; Eph 2:11-22). They offered spiritual sacrifices (Rom 12:1-2).[56] In contrast, Paul regards "the present Jerusalem" as a place of slavery (Gal 4:25).

It was, rather, the city of Jerusalem as the place where Jesus was killed and where the first community was gathered that commanded his attention and his loyalty (1 Thess 2:14-16). It is in Zion, Paul says in Rom 9:33 (quoting Isa 28), that God laid a stone that made people stumble, and likewise Paul

---

52. Paul is clearly more comfortable thinking in terms of houses (1 Tim 3:12-15; 2 Tim 2:20-21), temples (1 Cor 3:16-17; 2 Cor 6:16; Eph 2:14-22; 2 Tim 2:19), and the games (1 Cor 9:24-27; Phil 3:13-14; 2 Tim 2:5) than he is in terms of fields (1 Cor 3:6-9) and plants (Rom 11:17-24). And no reader of Rom 13:1-7 can doubt that Paul was positively disposed toward the imperial order, a fact that flies in the face of all "postcolonial" readings of the apostle.

53. Paul does not envisage communities that "go out of the world" (1 Cor 5:10), but communities that participate in the structures of the world—marriage, property, household—"as though not" (1 Cor 7:29-31); for him, all social arrangements, whether circumcision/uncircumcision, marriage/singleness, or slavery/freedom, are *adiaphora*, as are the observance of days and the eating of certain foods (1 Cor 7:1-8:13; Rom 14:1-23): the rule of God does not consist in such arrangements (Rom 14:17) but in obedience to God's call in every circumstance (1 Cor 7:19-24).

54. 1 Cor 6-14, Rom 14, and 1 Tim 5 are strikingly realistic about the difficult choices facing believers and how different practices could generate conflict.

55. Thus, he speaks of his mission as extending "from Jerusalem and as far around as Illyricum" (Rom 15:19) at the very moment he is planning to bring the collection "for the saints in Jerusalem" (15:26) before using Rome as his base for a mission to Spain (15:28).

56. See Gärtner, *Temple*.

says in Rom 11:26 (quoting Isa 59), "Out of Zion shall come the deliverer; he will banish ungodliness from Jacob" (adapted). The greatest and most difficult enterprise of Paul's ministry, we remember, was his effort to organize a collection from among his gentile communities for the saints in Jerusalem, not only to provide financial aid, but above all to signify fellowship between gentile and Jewish believers (Gal 2:10; 1 Cor 16:1–4; 2 Cor 8–9; Rom 15:25–32).[57]

Now we can ask how Paul fits within the varieties of Judaism in ancient Palestine. By the simple process of elimination, we find that Paul best matches the group within Judaism with which he explicitly aligns himself—namely, the Pharisees. Nobody can read Rom 13 and suspect Paul of being a Zealot,[58] and the little we know about the Sadducees conflicts directly with Paul's most central convictions; they did not believe in resurrection,[59] and for Paul everything starts with the resurrection of Jesus (1 Cor 15:1–11) and ends with the resurrection of believers (15:20–28).

In contrast, elements in Paul's letters line up impressively with both Qumran and Pharisaism, though here also we must be cautious because of the state of our sources and the impossibility of ascribing phenomena exclusively to one group or another. First, the sources: in the case of Qumran, we have evidence exactly contemporary to Paul; the community was destroyed in the war with Rome (67–70 CE);[60] in the case of the Pharisees, we are forced to rely on elements that can reasonably be inferred from post–200 CE evidence where it converges with information given by the Gospels and Acts.[61] Second, the phenomena: both Essenes and Pharisees read Torah in Hebrew with great precision and also great freedom; both had messianic expectations expressed through apocalyptic symbolism; both had hope for the future life; both reveal tendencies toward mysticism; both were committed to purity of life and required degrees of separation from the unclean.

Situating Paul with respect to these two versions of Palestinian Judaism is like locating a moving dot between two uncertain points. We can see that, like the sectarians at Qumran (and perhaps also some Pharisees), Paul had an apocalyptic view of history;[62] but unlike them, he saw the climactic mo-

---

57. Nickle, *Collection*.
58. For the Zealots, see Hengel, *Zealots*.
59. Josephus, *Jewish Antiquities* 18.11–17; Acts 23:8; see Meier, *Marginal Jew*, 3:389–487.
60. Magness, *Archaeology of Qumran*.
61. See Neusner, *Rabbinic Traditions*.
62. For Qumran, see J. Collins, *Apocalypticism*. There are four main elements in Paul's apocalypticism: (1) he speaks explicitly of new revelations of what had been hidden (Rom

ment of history as already happening in Jesus's exaltation. Like the writers of the Dead Sea Scrolls, Paul spoke of his community as a living house for the Spirit, God's temple, but unlike them, he established no priestly leadership in his communities.[63] Like them, he read Scripture as being fulfilled in the messianic community, but unlike them, Paul considered the Messiah already present at his community's meals rather than simply anticipated by them.[64]

We can also see that although Paul shared hermeneutical premises with the Qumranites—specifically, that Scripture found its authentic voice when heard as addressing the present community[65]—his actual interpretive practice more frequently resembles the midrash we find among the rabbis.[66] Like the Pharisees as well, Paul looked for the resurrection of the dead,[67] but unlike them, he regarded the resurrection of Jesus as the firstfruits of those who would rise to new life (1 Cor 15:20). Like both the Pharisees and Qumranites, Paul wanted his communities to be holy—that is, different from the profane world.[68] But unlike the Qumran community, Paul considered it

---

1:17–18; 3:21–26; 16:25–26; 1 Cor 15:51; Eph 1:9; 3:9–10; Col 2:2–3; 2 Tim 1:9–10; (2) he uses language (as with reference to the parousia) that is saturated with symbolism found in apocalyptic writings (1 Thess 4:13–5:3; 2 Thess 1:6–10; 2:1–12; 1 Cor 15:51–57; Phil 3:20–21) (3) he envisages human characters as engaged with cosmic powers (1 Cor 5:5; 2 Cor 10:3–6; Gal 4:8–11; Eph 2:1–2; 6:10–15; 1 Thess 3:5; 2 Thess 2:8–12; 1 Tim 4:1; 5:15); (4) he speaks of God's decisive intervention in behalf of humans (Rom 3:21–26; 5:6–11; 8:1–4; 1 Cor 1:26–31; 15:3–11; 2 Cor 1:18–22; 4:13–14; 5:14–15, 18–21; 8:9; 13:4; Gal 1:3–4; 2:20; 4:4–7; Eph 2:13–18; Phil 2:5–11; Col 1:13–22; 1 Thess 4:14; 5:10; 1 Tim 1:12–17; 2:5; 2 Tim 1:10; 2:8–13; Titus 2:11–14; 3:4–7.

63. The point deserves emphasis. In contrast to Qumran (on one side) and Ignatius of Antioch (on the other), both of which not only prescribe hierarchical ranks but legitimize them theologically, Paul's scattered references to local leadership (1 Thess 5:12; 1 Cor 12:29; 16:15–18; Rom 12:6–8; Phil 1:1; Eph 4:11; 1 Tim 3:1–13; 5:17) focus on function and lack any cultic connotations.

64. 1 Cor 10:16–23; 11:23–32; for Qumran, see Zimmermann, *Messianische Texte aus Qumran.*

65. For *pesher*, see Dimant, *History*; for Paul, see Rom 15:4–5; 1 Cor 10:10–11; 2 Tim 3:14–17.

66. See, e.g., Paul's use of the *middah* known as *gezerah sevah* in Gal 3:10–14 (as discussed by Dahl, "Contradictions in Scripture") and his exploitation of the singular/collective *sperma* (in Callan, "Pauline Midrash"). See also the use of *qal va-chomer* argument in Rom 5:12–21.

67. See Levenson, *Resurrection.*

68. Thus Paul's use of "saints" (*hagioi*) for members of the assembly (Rom 1:7; 8:27; 12:13; 15:25–26, 31; 16:2; 1 Cor 1:2; 6:1–2; 14:33; 16:1, 15; 2 Cor 1:1; 8:4; 9:1, 12; 13:13; Eph 1:1, 15, 18; 2:19; 3:18; 4:12; 5:3; 6:18; Phil 1:1; 4:21–22; Col 1:2, 4, 12, 26; 1 Thess 3:13; 2 Thess 1:10; 1 Tim 5:10; Phlm 5,7), and of "sanctify" (*hagiazein*) and "sanctification" (*hagiosynē*)

unthinkable to physically remove members of the community from all association with the unclean (1 Cor 5:19). And unlike the Pharisees, with whom he agreed on the need to stay in contact with the rest of humanity, Paul did not construct rules of ritual purification for reentry into the community,[69] but sought instead to define holiness in moral rather than in ritual terms.[70] Finally, like certain adepts both at Qumran and among the rabbis, Paul also, on the evidence of 2 Cor 12:1–5, was a practitioner of Merkabah mysticism.[71]

This process of comparison and contrast could extend itself indefinitely, but the complexity of comparison and the cautions required for every judgment lead to two overall conclusions. The first is that Paul's convictions and practices are totally at home in Palestinian Judaism. The second is that Paul's convictions and practices cannot be reduced to those of the two groups of Palestinian Jews he most closely resembles. We can add a third: all of this mysticism, scriptural interpretation, holiness, apocalypticism, and messianism in Paul is carried out in the Greek language rather than in Hebrew, and on the basis of the Septuagint rather than the Hebrew Bible. It remains a startling fact that three New Testament writers—Paul, James, and Luke—share the distinction of interpreting the Greek Bible using the methods and sharing the symbolic world of Palestinian Jews who interpreted the Hebrew Bible.[72]

## A Prophetic Jew

Even when carried out carefully, however, this process of locating Paul among other Jews of the first century leaves us frustrated, not only because it reminds us of how much we still do not know about those other Jews, but even more because it still does not get to the heart of the question of what kind of Jew Paul was. To get to this central question, we must move beyond a description of convictions and practices and inquire into the character of Paul's self-understanding as it is indirectly revealed in his letters.

No one, I think, would today argue with the proposition that Paul

as community ideals (Rom 6:19, 22; 15:16; 1 Cor 1:30; 6:11; 1 Thess 4:3; 5:23; 2 Thess 2:13; Eph 5:26).

69. As codified in Mishnah Toharot; see Kazen, *Issues of Impurity*.

70. This is perhaps most striking in 1 Thess 4:1–12 and Rom 6:1–23.

71. For the Pharisees, see M. Smith, "Observations on Hekaloth Rabbati"; for Qumran, see P. Alexander, *Mystical Texts*; for Paul, see Wallace, *Snatched into Paradise*.

72. See L. Johnson, *Septuagintal Midrash*.

was a *Homo religiosus*, and this to a remarkable degree.[73] Paul was neither a marginal nor a minimal Jew. Concerning his earlier life, when he was a persecutor of the church, Paul says that he was blameless with regard to righteousness under the law and zealous for his ancestral traditions (Phil 3:6; Gal 1:14).[74] Precisely his commitment to the entirety of Torah and his zeal for God's honor revealed in Torah, in fact, best explain why he persecuted the followers of Jesus. Paul's self-characterization as a blasphemer, persecutor, and arrogant man, the first among sinners (1 Tim 1:12–15), is a retrospective perspective. He had acted, he says, "unknowingly in faithlessness" (1 Tim 1:13, author's translation). In a word, he was then where he sees his fellow Jews now: "I bear witness concerning them that they have zeal for God but not according to recognition" (Rom 10:2, author's translation).[75]

We learn much more about Paul's religious character after his own moment of "recognition," when, as he says, God "reveal[ed] his Son in [or to] me" (Gal 1:16, author's translation). This was not a recognition Paul reached by logical deduction or scriptural analysis. It was a matter of a gift (grace) and mercy shown him by God (1 Cor 15:10; Gal 1:15; 2:8; 1 Tim 1:14–15). Nor was it a purely cognitive or emotional experience. It was an encounter with God through the resurrected Jesus. Paul says, "Last of all . . . he appeared also to me" (1 Cor 15:8). He says, "Have I not seen Jesus our Lord?" (1 Cor 9:1 NRSV). And he declares, "It is the God who said, 'Let light shine out of darkness,' who has shone in our hearts to give the light of the knowledge of the glory of God in the face of Jesus Christ" (2 Cor 4:6). The experience, moreover, was one that filled Paul with power (Eph 3:7) and gave him a specific mission to "proclaim the good news to the nations" (Gal 1:16). As Peter had been empowered as an apostle to the circumcised, so was Paul entrusted with the good news to the uncircumcised (Gal 2:8; Eph 3:7).

Paul's empowerment manifests itself in a panoply of religious expres-

---

73. Recognized by Reitzenstein, *Hellenistic Mystery-Religions*, 426–500, and Gunkel, *Influence of the Holy Spirit*, 77, 170–178.

74. So, correctly, Stendahl, "Apostle Paul."

75. The argument in Galatians, in fact, can be seen in just such experiential terms: the gentile converts enamored of Paul's Jewish privilege and seeking it for themselves and others, fail to grasp the point of Paul's own story: it was as a Jew "righteous under law" that he persecuted the church—just as he sees them doing to their fellow believers (6:12–13). They want to be as he was then; he wants them to be as he is now, glorying only in "the cross of our Lord Jesus Christ" (6:14).

sions.[76] He has visions that direct his life (Gal 2:2) and reveal to him things he cannot describe (2 Cor 12:1–5). He works signs and wonders (2 Cor 12:12; Rom 15:19). He speaks in tongues (1 Cor 14:18). Most striking are Paul's characterizations of his activity and speech. He has the Spirit of God (1 Cor 7:40). He preaches by "the power of the Spirit of God" (Rom 15:19). He tells the Thessalonians that "the gospel came to you not in word only, but also in power and in the Holy Spirit and with full conviction" (1 Thess 1:5), and "when you received the word of God that you heard from us, you accepted it not as a human word but as what it really is, God's word, which is also at work in you believers" (1 Thess 2:13).

Now, within the symbolic world of Torah, language about working signs and wonders, about speaking in the Spirit, and about speaking God's word all points to a single image, that of the prophet.[77] We are justified, therefore, in reading Paul's self-designation of *apostolos* (one sent out on a commission to represent the sender)[78] as another way of describing his self-understanding as God's prophet (*prophētēs*) and, more, the prophet of the Messiah.[79]

This is a designation considerably more exalted than that ascribed to teachers (even the teacher of righteousness) and scholars within other Palestinian Jewish groups. But that Paul sees himself as a prophet is strongly supported by the way he clothes his own calling with imagery drawn from his prophetic predecessors. When Paul speaks of being set apart by God "from my mother's womb," and being called by grace to proclaim good news to the nations (Gal 1:15–16), his language strongly echoes two prophetic texts.

The first prophetic precedent comes from Isa 49:1, "The LORD called me before I was born, / while I was in my mother's womb he named me," and, a little later, "I will give you as a light to the nations / so that my salvation may reach the end of the earth" (Isa 49:6, adapted). Given the impressively thor-

---

76. On the range of religious experience shared by Paul and his converts, see Wallace, *Snatched into Paradise.*

77. For this combination of characteristics, see L. Johnson, *Prophetic Jesus, Prophetic Church.*

78. See Rom 1:1; 11:13; 16:7; 1 Cor 1:1; 9:1; 15:9; 2 Cor 1:1; 12:12; Gal 1:1; Eph 1:1; Col 1:1; 1 Thess 2:6; 1 Tim 1:1; 2:7; 2 Tim 1:1, 11; Titus 1:1.

79. To be clear, I am not suggesting that Paul himself equates the terms. He never uses *prophētēs* of himself and, in fact, distinguishes apostles and prophets in the local church (1 Cor 12:28–29; Eph 2:20; 4:11). Rather, Paul uses "apostle" in a manner equivalent to the biblical understanding of the prophet. Note that he sees apostles and prophets alike as recipients of God's revelation (Eph 3:5).

ough reading and use Paul makes of Second Isaiah elsewhere,[80] we might even ask whether his question in 1 Cor 9:1, "Have I not seen Jesus our Lord?" also might, consciously or unconsciously, echo the story of Isaiah's calling, "I saw the Lord" (Isa 6:1).[81]

Paul's statement concerning his call in Gal 1:15 makes an even stronger allusion, however, to the call of the prophet Jeremiah: "Before I formed you in the womb I knew you / and before you were born I consecrated you; / I appointed you a prophet to the nations" (Jer 1:5). The Jeremiah passage continues, "See, today I appoint you over nations and kingdoms, / to pluck up and pull down, / to destroy and to overthrow, / to build and to plant" (Jer 1:10). Paul is fond of using planting and building imagery for his apostolic labors (see Rom 15:20; 1 Cor 3:5-15; 9:11), and in Gal 2:18 he speaks of building up again that which he had torn down.

But it is in his second letter to the Corinthians that the Jeremiah passage most clearly colors his language about his pastoral practice. In 2 Cor 10:8 he speaks of the authority that the Lord gave him for their building up rather than their tearing down, and at the end of the composition he declares, "I write these things while I am away from you, so that when I come, I may not have to be severe in using the authority that the Lord has given me for building up and not for tearing down" (2 Cor 13:10). The language Paul chooses to use suggests that he regarded his apostolic authority as a prophetic authority like that given to Jeremiah.

And as Jeremiah spoke long ago of a new covenant that God would make with his people, not like the covenant made when they came out of Egypt, the covenant that they broke, but a covenant that would be written on human hearts, so that all would know the Lord (Jer 31:31-34), so Paul sees himself as the *diakonos* ("administrator") of a "new covenant," one that is not written on stone tablets but is written by the Holy Spirit on the human hearts of his Corinthian community (2 Cor 3:2-6). Because of this prophetic role, Paul can confidently compare himself to the first and greatest of Israel's prophets, Moses (see Deut 34:10).

In the extraordinarily dense passage of 2 Cor 3:4-17, Paul contrasts the fading glory on the face of Moses with the enduring power and glory of this new covenant, which comes from the Lord who is Spirit, and which is transforming those gazing on the image of the Lord from one degree of glory

---

80. L. Johnson, "Isaiah the Evangelist."
81. That such an allusion is not impossible is demonstrated by John 12:41.

to another.[82] Perhaps even more daringly, in Rom 9:3 Paul mimics Moses's gesture of self-renunciation for the sake of the people in Exod 32:31–32, when he declares, "I could wish that I myself were accursed and cut off from Christ for the sake of my own people, my kinsmen according to the flesh."[83]

I propose, in short, that Paul's choice of language about himself and his role indicates that he considers himself a prophetic Jew. I don't think this is simply a literary conceit, still less that it was a manipulative effort to clothe himself with impressive precedents. I think, rather, that Paul searched for and found in Scripture such texts precisely because he needed to find words and images that fit the nature of his encounter with the risen Jesus and his sense of call that arose from that unexpected and transformative encounter.

Nor do I think we go nearly far enough when we say that Paul, like all other early Christians—and, for that matter, like the sectarians at Qumran— read Scripture "prophetically," in the sense that the prophecies spoken of old found their true meaning, their "fulfillment" in the present age, though this is certainly also true.[84] On this point, in fact, we can note that although the Qumran sectarians did read the prophets in that fashion, they did so within the framework of a consistently literal, even rigid, appropriation of the legal texts of Torah as well, whereas in Paul the balance shifts dramatically to the prophetic voice within Scripture, to the point of reading even the narrative portions of Scripture in prophetic terms.[85]

Calling Paul a prophetic Jew means more than that he cites the prophetic texts of the past as applied to the present. It means, as I have tried to show, that Paul considers the spirit of prophecy to be active and powerful in himself and in others because of the resurrection of Jesus. For Paul, Jesus was the *eschatos Adam*, who became by virtue of his exaltation the "life-giving Spirit" who was even now transforming the hearts of believers, showing that the living God was doing a new thing that could not be regarded as historical, as was the giving of the law on Sinai, but could only be called eschatological.

Indeed, the only appropriate analogy for Paul is God's creation of the world. The God who raised Jesus is the God who "gives life to the dead and

---

82. See Van Unnik, "'With Unveiled Faces'"; Marks, "Pauline Typology"; Hafemann, *History of Israel*.

83. The RSV translation of Exod 32:31–32 is: "Alas, this people has sinned a great sin; they have made for themselves gods of gold. But now, if thou wilt forgive their sin—and if not, blot me, I pray thee, out of thy book which thou hast written." For discussion, see Jewett, *Romans*, 560–61.

84. See, e.g., Juel, *Messianic Exegesis*.

85. This aspect of things will be developed in a subsequent chapter.

calls into being that which does not exist" (Rom 4:17), who "calls into being the things that are not in order to reduce to nothing the things that are" (1 Cor 1:28, author's translation). "It is the God who said, 'Let light shine out of darkness,'" Paul tells the Corinthians, "who has shone in our hearts to give the light of the glory of God in the face of Jesus Christ" (2 Cor 4:6). In Christ, says Paul, "there is a new creation. Behold, the old things have passed away, everything is new" (2 Cor 5:17, author's translation; see Gal 6:15).

Jesus, therefore, is the true Adam, the image of God in which a new humanity can be shaped (1 Cor 15:44–45; Rom 5:12–21; Col 1:15; 3:10–11). This is why, for Paul, the Jesus who interpreted his blood that he shared with his followers as the blood of a new covenant (1 Cor 11:25) cannot be compared to Moses. It is Paul who is the prophet/apostle of this new covenant/new creation, who appropriately sees himself as a new Moses.

Finally, Paul's apprehension of this new covenant/new creation/new age and new humanity, and of himself as the prophet who was to announce and enact this good news to the nations, is at one and the same time the most radical element of discontinuity distinguishing Paul from other Jews of the first century, whether in diaspora or in Eretz Israel—Qumran's claims for itself and for its teacher of righteousness pale by comparison—and also, remarkably, the most impressive evidence for Paul's continuity with the tradition of Israel.

Although they are refocused and reshaped by the experience of a crucified and resurrected Messiah, none of the symbols used by Paul to express this new reality come from elsewhere than Torah. Indeed, Paul taps directly into one of the deepest and most powerful themes of the Jewish tradition: that the living God moves ahead of the people in new and surprising ways, and calls them to an ever-renewed obedience.

*Chapter 6*

# Paul and Scripture

In the last chapter, I advanced a number of points concerning Paul's Jewishness that are pertinent to the subject of Paul and Scripture. I restate them here as briefly as possible before moving to a more substantive discussion. First, Paul is not a Jew in a marginal or merely formal sense, but a Jew who is deeply committed to the world shaped by Torah. Second, his pronouncements on Torah are far more positive than negative: the law is holy and spiritual and good; it reveals God's will for humans, and it instructs in wisdom. Third, Paul's negative stance toward the law is by way of resisting false claims concerning the power of the law—it cannot give life, it cannot empower full obedience to God—and resisting efforts to impose the law on gentiles who are Christ-believers; in short, Paul's difficulties with the law do not precede his experience of the risen Lord but follow from it. Fourth, Paul focuses particularly on the prophetic character of all of Scripture: it finds its full meaning as it is actualized in present-day experience; indeed, Paul sees himself as standing in the line of Jeremiah and Isaiah, as one called by God to bring good news to the nations.

These basic points can, I hope, be assumed as I turn in the present chapter to a fuller examination of Paul's engagement with and employment of Scripture. In recent decades the topic of Paul and Scripture has been well trammeled, both in general[1] and with reference to specific texts.[2] Enough

---

1. Among others, see Ellis, *Paul's Use of the Old Testament*; Ellis, *Old Testament in Early Christianity*; Koch, *Die Schrift als Zeuge des Evangelium*; Evans and Sanders, *Paul and the Scriptures of Israel*; Moyise, *Paul and Scripture*; Porter and Stanley, *As It Is Written*; C. Stanley, *Paul and Scripture*; Gench, *Encountering God in Tyrannical Texts*; Hays, *Conversion of the Imagination*.

2. E.g., Rosner, *Paul, Scripture, and Ethics*; McAuley, *Paul's Covert Use of Scripture*;

work has been done to stimulate a worry about overkill.[3] But such, alas, is the nature of biblical scholarship: the field is both small and overrun with workers. I begin by noting briefly some of the more technical aspects that have been thoroughly worked over by other scholars before turning to an approach that proves more fruitful.

It is clear, first of all, that Paul read and made use of the Old Testament in Greek, the translation of Scripture from Hebrew that, according to tradition, took place ca. 250 BCE in Egypt and is for convenience' sake termed the Septuagint (LXX).[4] I say "for convenience' sake" because the study of the Septuagint itself gives rise to any number of complex issues.[5] Thus, when Paul tells the Corinthians that when they partake of idol worship, they sit at the table of demons (1 Cor 10:19–22), his identification of idols with demons clearly depends on the LXX of Ps 96:5, "the gods of the heathen are demons," rather than the MT's "the gods of the heathen are idols."

As for Paul's usage of texts, it is mixed. In some cases, as in Rom 3:4, for example, he quotes verbatim from the LXX Ps. 50:6, and in 4:7 from the LXX Ps 31:1. In contrast, the start of the scriptural catena in Rom 3:10–12 is very loosely drawn from LXX Ps 14:1–3, with some apparent influence of LXX Ps 53:2–4. Similarly, at a critical point in Paul's argument in Rom 9:33, he cites as "standing written" (*gegraptai*) a mixed citation from Isa 28:16 and 8:14, with touches of his own.

But there are a few cases in which the Hebrew (MT) appears to be the basis for Paul's "citation" in Greek. One of the most significant of these is Paul's citation from Hab 2:4 in his thesis statement of Rom 1:17. Paul agrees with the MT with his *ho de dikaios ek pisteōs zēsetai* ("But the righteous one will live by faith/faithfulness"). The LXX has something quite different. The manuscripts designated S and W have "the righteous one will live by my faithfulness," referring to the fidelity to God, while manuscripts A and C have "my righteous one will live by faith" (a version found also in Heb

---

Han, *Swimming in the Sea of Scripture*; Swinson, *What Is Scripture?*; Wakefield, *Where to Live*.

3. See Watson, "Scripture in Pauline Theology."

4. The Jewish tradition is laid out most extensively by the *Letter of Aristeas*; for discussion of the complexities of the designation, see, e.g., Peters, "Septuagint."

5. See, e.g., Jootsen and Thomson, *Voces Biblicae*; McLay, *Use of the Septuagint*; de Vries and Karrer, *Textual History*; Clines and Exum, *Reception of the Hebrew Bible*; Wilk, "Letters of Paul"; Rüsen-Weinhold, *Der Septuagintapsalter*; Porter and Pitts, *Language of the New Testament*; Karrer, Kreuzer, and Sigismund, *Von der Septuaginta zum Neuen Testament*; Wagner, *Reading the Sealed Book*.

10:38), which has God designating the righteous one as his own. The complexity of these textual issues is suggested by the fact that one major New Testament manuscript "corrects" Paul's citation in the direction of LXX manuscripts A and C.[6]

Significant attention has also been paid to Paul's modes of introducing scriptural citations.[7] Most familiar is the introduction *kathōs gegraptai*— the perfect tense connotes what has been written in the past and remains written.[8] But Paul also uses a variety of other introductory formulas, some involving writing,[9] more involving variants of speech, giving Scripture a personal voice.[10] As my references show, however, Paul's explicit citations from Scripture are concentrated in a handful of letters: Romans and Galatians above all, and to a much lesser extent 1 and 2 Corinthians. In contrast, Ephesians, 1 Timothy, and 2 Timothy each have only one scriptural citation.[11] More startling, Philippians, Philemon, Titus, 1 Thessalonians, Colossians, and 2 Thessalonians (six of the thirteen letters in the canonical collection) all lack either explicit scriptural citation or introductory formula. Was Paul less influenced by Scripture in these compositions? If we had only those six letters in our possession, would we conclude that Paul was not, after all, much of a "scriptural Jew"? And if we noted in addition the isolated character of the single citations in Ephesians, 1 Timothy, and 2 Timothy, we might conclude that the "Torah-defined Paul" was present in only four of his thirteen letters.

Partly in light of this realization, other scholars have approached the topic of Scripture in Paul, not through explicit citations, but through scriptural allusions or echoes, where Paul does not make explicit citations but

---

6. See the discussion in Jewett, *Romans*, 144–47.

7. See Ellis, *Paul's Use of the Old Testament*; Hanson, *Paul's Technique and Theology*; and esp. C. Stanley, *Paul and the Language of Scripture*.

8. Paul uses the introduction sixteen times in Romans, nine times in 1 Corinthians, two times in 2 Corinthians, and four times in Galatians; the construction occurs also in Matthew (ten times), Mark (four times), and Luke-Acts (thirteen times), and once each in 1 Peter and Hebrews.

9. "Moses writes" (Rom 10:5), "word that was written" (1 Cor 15:54), "according to what was written (2 Cor 4:13).

10. "Scripture says" (Rom 4:3; 9:17; 10:11; 11:2, 4; 15:10, 12; Gal 4:30; 1 Tim 5:18); "Scripture promised ahead of time" (Gal 3:18); "God says" (Rom 9:15; 2 Cor 6:17; Eph 4:18); "it says" (Rom 9:25; 2 Cor 6:2 adapted); "Isaiah says" (Rom 10:16, 20–21); "the law says" (Rom 7:7).

11. Eph 4:8 cites Ps 68:19 (18); 1 Tim 5:18 cites Deut 25:4 (as does 1 Cor 9:9); and 2 Tim 2:19 has a pastiche from Num 16:5; Sir 17:26; and Isa 26:13.

rather evokes scriptural texts and themes.[12] The language of allusion and echo recognizes the profoundly intertextual character of the New Testament.[13] The basic issue in all such analysis is determining just how significant the citation, allusion, or echo might be in a particular instance. Does a citation, for example, serve simply to give authority to a fairly straightforward point, as when Paul quotes Deut 25:4 ("You shall not muzzle an ox while it is treading out the grain") with reference to the financial support of apostles (1 Cor 9:8–12)?[14] Or does it carry with it nuances of meaning found in the original context of the cited text, as when Paul cites Ps 69:9 with reference to mutual service among the Roman believers (Rom 15:3)?[15] To what extent, in other words, do such citations, allusions, and echoes represent not merely the appropriation of diction but also the transposition of meaning?

I propose approaching the question of Paul and Scripture from another angle entirely, one that enables us to interrogate letters that lack explicit scriptural markers as well as those that do. I propose asking to what extent Paul inhabits a scripturally defined world. Does he view reality from within the symbols given by Scripture, or does he view the symbols of Scripture from another conception of reality? Does he see himself as tasked with explaining Scripture or as embodying Scripture? This is not an obvious or easy approach, but it is one that enables us to move beyond the counting of citations and detecting of allusions to appreciating that Paul is as "scriptural" a Jew when those are absent as when they are present.

## A Scripture-Defined World

Paul's distinctive way of viewing reality from within scriptural symbols can be demonstrated first by means of comparison. I mentioned in the previous chapter that Paul stood within a large cohort of Jews who produced literature based on the Septuagint. Yet, when compared to the most prolific and well-known of those authors—namely, Josephus and Philo—the distance from Paul is considerable.

---

12. The most influential figure here is Hays, *Echoes of Scripture*; see, e.g., Wagner, *Heralds of the Good News*; Beetham, *Echoes of Scripture*; Campbell, "Echo of Scripture."

13. See, e.g., Evans and Zacharias, *Early Christian Literature and Intertextuality*; Scott, *Hermeneutics*; Witherington, *Isaiah Old and New*.

14. Unless otherwise indicated, Scripture quotations in this chapter are from the NRSV.

15. See Hays, "Christ Prays the Psalms."

Although in his *Antiquities of the Jews* Josephus basically rewrites large portions of the biblical accounts,[16] he truly does *rewrite* from top to bottom: his language maintains a deliberate distance from both the contents (especially miracles) and the diction of his Greek source.[17] His stance is that of the apologist who seeks to make the strange ways of his people as intelligible and acceptable as possible to those who view the world differently than they do. To that extent, he stands outside biblical symbolism as an explainer of it (see esp. the prologue, 1–4). Nowhere in this massive work do we have the sense that Josephus regards the words of Scripture as *logia tou theou* in the manner of Paul, or that they speak prophetically to present circumstances. Josephus makes the LXX the source for his version of Jewish apologetic history.[18]

Likewise, although no one could doubt the piety of Philo of Alexandria, neither could one be confused about the philosophical perspective of Platonism from which he consistently interprets the text of the Septuagint. Thus, in his *On the Creation*, Philo reads the creation account in Gen 1 as the divine vision of the ideal order of creation, parallel to Plato's world of ideas. Like Josephus, he comments on the LXX's use of *hēmera mia* ("one day") rather than "first," but does so approvingly, since it represents the perfect number "one" that encompasses the entire realm of ideas (*Creation* 15). Thinking of the creation account as an "exordium" (*archē*) for the laws by Moses the philosopher, he states, "It consists of an account of the creation of the world, implying that the world is in harmony with the law, and the law with the world, and that the man who observes the law is constituted thereby a loyal citizen of the world [*kosmopolitou*], regulating his doings by the purpose and will of nature [*to boulēma tēs physeōs*], in accordance with which the entire world itself is also administered" (1).[19] Not only is Philo's diction philosophical; his entire construal of Moses's project is fitted to his

---

16. He states, "Well-nigh everything herein related is dependent on the wisdom of our lawgiver Moses," and praises him generously, declaring that he could not have written the way he did if he had not ordered his own life correctly, before turning to contemplation of God's work: "For neither could the lawgiver himself, without this vision, ever attain to a right mind, nor would anything that he should write in regard to virtue avail with his readers." Josephus, *Antiquities of the Jews* 1.4 (Thackeray, LCL).

17. For his slighting of miracles, see, e.g., *Antiquities of the Jews* 1.108, 2.348, 3.25, 3.81. Beginning with a direct citation from a version of the LXX, *en archē epoiēsen ho theos ton ouranon kai tēn gēn* (Gen 1:1), he moves forward without employing the diction of the LXX. Indeed, he finds it necessary to comment (in 1.27) on the oddity of the usage "day one" (*hēmera mia*), which, he says, should properly have been "the first day" (*protē hēmera*).

18. See Sterling, *Historiography and Self-Definition*.

19. English translations by Colson and Whitaker, LCL.

Platonic outlook: "Moses, because he had attained the very summit of philosophy, and because he had been divinely instructed in the greater and most essential part of nature's lore [*tōn tēs physeōs anadidachtheis*], could not fail to recognize that the universal must consist of two parts, one part active cause and the other passive object" (11).

Compare this sort of diction to Paul's own use of the creation account: "For it is the God who said, 'Let light shine out of darkness,' who has shone in our hearts to give the light of the knowledge of the glory of God in the face of Jesus Christ" (2 Cor 4:6). Here there is no talk of Moses as legislator, still less as philosopher. The words of Genesis are, for Paul, God's living word. Even more, that word continues to be expressed: the same God who spoke then has shone the light on the face of Christ in the hearts of believers. There is distinction here, to be sure: Paul's "angle of perception" is the crucified and exalted Lord Jesus; but there is no distance. Paul is not explaining the text or rendering it in another mode. He sees it as directly speaking to present experience.

A good test case for my thesis that Paul's diction is Scripture-shaped is his first letter to the Thessalonians. Everybody agrees that it is genuinely Pauline. Yet it has no explicit citations from Scripture. It contains, moreover, more than a few traces of popular philosophical language. When Paul in 4:11 tells the Thessalonians to "live quietly and mind [their] own affairs" (*hēsychazein kai prassein ta idia*), some have seen an echo of the Epicurean ethos.[20] And in Paul's extended discussion of his first visit among them (2:1–12), it is possible to detect several topoi of popular moral teachers like Dio Chrysostom (see esp. *Oration* 32 and 77/78).[21] Finally, some of the letter's language is dictated by such quotidian matters as travel and the sending of delegates (3:6–10), and common Pauline turns: "you yourselves know, brothers" (2:1); "for the rest, brothers, we implore and exhort you" (4:1, author's translation); "we do not want you to be ignorant" (4:13, author's translation). Given these factors, the degree to which Paul's diction (and outlook) in this letter can be called scriptural is impressive.

The difficult part is knowing what to choose. We can start with the basic framework Paul shares with the Septuagint. In contrast to the idols worshiped by the nations,[22] Paul and his readers serve (*douleuein*) the "living God" (*theos*

20. As in DeWitt, *St. Paul and Epicurus*.

21. See esp. Malherbe, *Paul and the Thessalonians*; Malherbe, *Letters to the Thessalonians*.

22. For *eidola* in 1:9, see Wis 14:1, 12, 30; Ps 113:12; Isa 57:5; for *ethnē* in 2:16 and 4:5 (where they "do not know God"), see Deut 2:25; 4:6; 29:24; Ps 21:27; 65:7; 85:9 (all psalm numberings are according to the LXX); Wis 14:11; 15:15.

*zōn*), whose proper name is "the Lord" (*kyrios*, now applied to the risen Jesus in 1 Thess 1:1; 2:15; 4:1).[23] As gentile readers, indeed, they have "turned" (*epistrephein*) from idolatry to the living God (1:9).[24] The living God is able to "save" (*sōzein*, 2:16; 5:9) or "rescue" (*rhyein*, 1:10) them from persecution (*diōkein*, 2:15), which is an expression of God's "wrath" (*orgē*, 1:10; 2:16; 5:9) and parallels the "tribulation" (*thlipsis*) now being experienced by believers (3:3).[25] This living God is able to "test the hearts" (*dokimazein tas kardias*, 2:4) and stand as "witness" (*martys*, 2:5), as believers are "tested" (*peirazein*, 3:5) by Satan (2:18) and by every guise of evil (*eidous ponērou*, 5:22).[26]

By implication, Paul includes himself among the "prophets" (*prophētai*, 1 Thess 2:15) who, like the Lord Jesus, have been killed or, like Paul, have been persecuted (2:14–15), for he "proclaims" (*kēryssein*, 2:9) the "good news from God" (*euangelion tou theou*, 2:8; cf. 1:5) to the Thessalonians, which is the "word of the Lord" (*logos tou kyriou*, 1:8; 4:15), which he also terms "the word of God" (*logos theou*, 2:13).[27] Believers seek to do God's will (*thelēma tou theou*, 4:3), to please God (*areskein theō*, 4:1), by walking worthily of God (*peripatein axiōs tou theou*, 2:12; 4:1), who has called them (*kalein*, 2:12; 4:7) into his kingdom (*basileia*, 2:12) and glory (*doxa*, 2:12) as beloved (*ēgapēmenoi*, 1:4) and his elect (*eklogē*, 1:4),[28] and has gifted them with his

23. For "serving God," see 1 Sam 7:3–4; Ps 2:11; 99:2; 101:22; Sir 2:1; Isa 65:13; for "living God," see Num 14:21, 28; Deut 4:33; 5:26; Josh 3:10; Ps 17:46; 83:2; Hos 1:10; Isa 37:4; for "Lord," see Exod 3:2, 16.

24. For *epistrephein* in the sense of turning or returning to God, see Deut 4:30; 30:2; Hos 3:5; 5:4; 6:1; Amos 4:6; Joel 2:13; Zech 1:3.

25. For "save," see Deut 33:29; Judg 2:16; 3:9; Ps 7:10; 16:7; for "rescue," see Exod 5:23; 6:6; 14:30; Josh 22:31; Judg 6:9; Ps 96:10; 105:43; 106:6; for "persecuting," see Lev 26:7, 17; Judg 4:22; 9:40; Job 19:22; for "wrath," see Exod 4:14; 15:7; 32:12; Num 11:10; 25:4; Deut 11:17; 29:14; Ps 7:6; 26:9; 36:8; 77:31; Isa 5:25; 13:9; for "tribulation," see Gen 35:3; Exod 4:31; Deut 4:29; Ps 19:1.

26. For "testing the heart," see Jer 12:13; Ps 16:17; 25:2; 65:10; 94:9; 138:23; Wis 1:3; 2:19; for God as "witness," see Gen 31:44, 50; 1 Sam 12:5, 6; 20:23; Ps 88:37; Wis 1:16; Jer 36:23; for "testing," see Exod 17:2; Judg 2:22; Ps 34:6; 77:41; Wis 2:17; 12:26; for "guise/appearance," see Gen 29:17; Exod 24:17; Prov 7:10; for "evil (one)," see Ps 34:12; 40:1; 139:1. The LXX does not use "Satan" as Paul does for the tester of God's people.

27. For "prophet," see Deut 18:18–22; 1 Sam 19:20, 24; 2 Kgs 2:3; for "proclaim," see Isa 61:1; Joel 1:14; the LXX does not have the noun form but does have the verb form for "proclaiming good news," as in Ps 39:9; 67:11; Isa 40:9; 60:6; for "word of the Lord," see Judg 2:17; 1 Sam 15:24; 2 Sam 24:11; Mic 4:2; Isa 1:10; Jer 7:2; for "word of God," see Judg 3:20; 1 Chr 15:15; 25:5; Isa 1:10; Jer 1:2.

28. For "God's will," see Ps 1:2; 27:7; 39:8; Sir 8:15; 16:3; Isa 44:28; for "pleasing God," see Num 23:27; Ps 68:31; for "walking" in the sense of behavior, see Prov 8:20; Qoh 11:9; for

Holy Spirit (*pneuma hagion*, 1:5; 4:8; 5:19).²⁹ God will "speed their way" (*kateuthynai ton hodon*, 3:11)³⁰ so that the ones testing them will not succeed. But God wants the Thessalonians above all to be holy (*hagiosynē, hagioi*, 3:13) before God (*emprosthēn tou theou*, 3:13); their sanctification (*hagiasmos*, 4:3, 4) is indeed God's will for them, and God will in fact sanctify (*hagiazein*, 5:23) them completely.³¹ This means that believers must avoid all forms of sexual immorality (*porneia*, 4:3), so associated with idolatry, because God is the punisher (*ekdikos*, 4:6) of this sort of uncleanness (*akatharsia*, 4:7).³²

The letter contains many other terms and expressions that have Septuagintal precedent, such as "returning thanksgiving" (*eucharistian apodounai*, 1 Thess 1:2; 3:9), "prayer" (*proseuchē*, 1:2), "remembering" (*mnēmoneuein*, 1:3), "faith/having faith" (*pistis/pisteuein*, 1:3, 8; 3:2, 5, 6, 7, 10; 5:8 / 1:7; 2:4, 10, 13; 4:14), "endurance" (*hypomonē*, 1:3), "hope" (*elpis*, 1:3; 2:19; 4:13), "joy" (*chara*, 1:6; 2:19, 20; 3:9), and "love" (*agapē*, 1:3; 3:12), specifically toward each other (4:9).³³ Such terms occur in the larger koine, but their close clustering, together with the expressions already identified, helps locate Paul's language as Septuagintal, as does his referring to "sins" (*hamartiai*, 2:16), his command not to despise or reject prophecy (*exouthenein prophēteian*, 5:20), his taking of an oath (*enorkizein*, 5:27), and even his greeting the community with "grace" (*charis*) and "peace" (*eirēnē*, 1:1).³⁴

---

"worthily," see Wis 1:16; 3:5; 9:12; 12:7, 26; for "calling," see Exod 3:4; Isa 4:1; 43:22; 48:12; 62:2; for God's "kingdom," see Wis 6:4, 20; 10:10; for "glory," see Exod 16:7, 10; 24:16; 40:35; Lev 9:6; Deut 5:24; Ps 18:1; Isa 6:1; for "beloved," see Gen 22:2; Deut 21:15; for "elect," see Ps 86:4; 77:68; 104:26.

29. For "holy spirit," see Wis 1:5; 9:17; Isa 11:2; 61:1; 63:10–11.

30. The expression occurs in Jdt 12:8 and Ps 5:8.

31. For "holiness," see Ps 29:4; 95:6; 96:12; Sir 7:13; Ezek 45:4; also Exod 25:7; Isa 8:14; Ezek 11:16; for "holy ones," see Ps 21:3; 33:9; 73:3; 88:5; 150:1; for "sanctify," see Exod 13:2; 29:1; Lev 8:11; Num 5:9. The language of holiness totally pervades the book of Leviticus, and the section of the letter where Paul uses this language is sometimes thought of as a holiness code like that in Leviticus.

32. For sexual immorality, see Gen 38:24; Wis 14:12 (which especially links it to idolatry); Sir 41:17; for the Lord as punisher, see Exod 12:12; Wis 12:12; for "uncleanness," see Lev 5:3; 7:20; 19:23; Wis 2:16.

33. For the phrase "returning thanks," see Jdt 8:25, while "thanksgiving" appears in Wis 16:28; 2 Macc 2:27; 20:7; 3 Macc 7:16; for "prayer," see Ps 4:1; 6:9; 38:12; for "remembering," see Ps 6:5; 62:6; Wis 2:4; Isa 43:18; for "faith," see Hab 2:4; Jer 9:3; Wis 37:26; for "having faith," see Exod 4:1–30; Ps 77:22, 32; Wis 12:2; 16:26; for "endurance," see Ps 19:8; 38:7; 70:5; for "hope," see Ps 13:6; 15:9; 21:9; for "joy," see Ps 20:6; 29:11; 125:2; Wis 8:16; Sir 1:12; for "love," see Wis 3:9; 6:18; Sir 48:11; for loving each other, see Lev 19:18, 34; Deut 10:18; Tob 4:13.

34. For "sins," see Deut 5:9; 9:18; Ps 31:1; 50:2–9; for "prophecy," see Num 11:26–29;

For Paul, the point of discontinuity with Scripture is not derived from historiography or philosophy but from the experience of the death and resurrection of Jesus (1 Thess 1:10; 4:14; 5:10). But especially when speaking of Jesus's future work, Paul employs Septuagintal diction. Jesus will rescue believers from God's wrath "from out of the heavens" (*ek tōn ouranōn*, 1:10) at his royal arrival (*parousia*, 2:19; 3;13; 4:15; 5:23).[35] Paul's description of the parousia makes use of such Septuagintal locutions as "the trumpet of God" (*salpingi theou*, 4:16), "in the clouds" (*en nephelais*, 4:17), and "the day of the Lord" (*hēmera kyriou*, 5:2).[36] Just when people declare that all is "peaceful and safe" (*eirenē kai asphaleia*), then the "destroyer" (*olethros*) will strike, and pains like those of childbirth will ensue (*odin en tē gastri*, 5:3).[37] Believers are, therefore, to be on watch (*grēgorein*, 5:6), wearing the breastplate of faith and love (*thōraka pisteōs kai agapēs*) and the helmet that is the hope of salvation (*perikephalaion elpida sōtērias*, 5:8),[38] for the obtaining of their salvation (*peripoiēsin sōtērias*, 5:9) through the Lord Jesus Christ.[39]

Significant in this analysis is not only the large number of Septuagintal terms—and the list could be extended—but the complete lack of any other perspective but the scriptural. Paul appropriates and actualizes the language of the psalms and the prophets because they alone are adequate to express his view of the world, even when the disruptive experience of the dying and rising Messiah—who will come again on "the day of the Lord"—stretches even that language. And if 1 Thessalonians can be read as saturated by scriptural language, how much more might that be the case in the places where Paul explicitly cites and implicitly alludes to the texts that shape his world?

---

2 Chr 15:8; Sir 24:33; 36:20; for the phrase "rejecting prophecy," see 1 Sam 10:19; for "taking an oath," see Gen 24:37; 50:5; Neh 13:25; Num 5:21; for "grace," see Gen 6:8; Exod 3:21; 12:36; Ruth 2:10; Wis 3:9; 4:15; for "peace," see Judg 6:23; 18:6; 19:20; 1 Sam 1:17; 2 Kgs 5:19.

35. For "out of the heavens," see Deut 3:24; 4:39; Ps 2:4; 10:5; 13:2; 17:13; 19:6; for "royal arrival," see Neh 2:6; Jdt 10:18.

36. For the "trumpet of God, see Ps 46:5; Zech 9:14; for "in the clouds," see Gen 9:13; Exod 19:9; Num 9:15; Ps 96:2; 98:7; Dan 7:13; for "day of the Lord," see Amos 5:18, 20; Zech 1:7; 14:1; Joel 1:15; 3:14; Isa 2:12; 34:8.

37. For "peaceful and safe" (that is, "safe"), see Ps 123:5; Lev 26:5; for "destroyer," see Wis 17:4; 18:13; Isa 13:8; for "labor pains," see Ps 47 (48):6; Hos 13:13.

38. "Breastplate" does not occur in the LXX, but we have seen the Septuagintal precedents for faith and love; for "helmet of salvation," see Isa 59:17; for "keeping watch," see Neh 7:3; Jer 38:28.

39. For "obtaining," see Hag 2:10; for "salvation," see Wis 18:7; Isa 45:17; 52:7, 10.

## Scripture as Implied Premise

Without question, the prophet Isaiah, together with the Psalms, provided the earliest believers their richest scriptural resource for interpreting the shocking experience of a crucified and raised messiah. Isaiah, indeed, deserves the title of the "fifth evangelist."[40] Three aspects of the prophet in particular would have invited believers to see him as the one who, more than any other, spoke of Jesus: (1) the prophet's use of the term "proclaiming the good news" for the very voice of prophecy; (2) the prophet's initial vision and commission in Isa 6:1–13; and (3) the script for the suffering messiah provided by the servant song in Isa 52:13–53:12. The combination of these elements, rather than any one of them alone, made Isaiah the definitive messianic prophet for Christians.[41]

First, the LXX of Isaiah uses the verb *euangelizasthai* ("proclaim good news") seven times in four passages. In three instances, the LXX straightforwardly translates the Hebrew *basar*: "Let the one who proclaims good news in Zion be raised up. Lift up in strength your voice, the one who proclaims good news to Jerusalem" (40:9); "How beautiful on the mountains are the feet of the one proclaiming good news, proclaiming good news of peace, the one who proclaims the good news of peace" (52:7); "The spirit of the Lord is upon me because the Lord has sent me to proclaim good news to the poor" (61:1). The fourth instance is an addition to the Hebrew that is found in some manuscripts of the LXX: after the Hebrew text of Isa 60:6, "they shall bring gold and frankincense and proclaim the praise of the Lord," these manuscripts add, "the salvation of the Lord is being proclaimed as good news." Isaiah's striking repetition of the phrase is more notable for the relatively sparse use of the term elsewhere.[42]

Second, for those convinced that Jesus is now the exalted Lord (*kyrios*),[43] Isaiah's declaration that "I saw the Lord [*kyrios*] high and lifted up" (6:1) could easily be taken as a vision of the resurrected Jesus, especially since the vision includes the failure to hear the prophet, as the Gospel of John forthrightly asserts:

40. See Sawyer, *Fifth Gospel*; Sawyer's title derives from Saint Jerome's introduction to the prophet in the Vulgate (see *Praefatio Hieronymi in Librum Isaiam*, PL 28:825).

41. In this section I use material developed in my article "Isaiah the Evangelist."

42. Outside Isaiah, the verb *euangelizasthai* is found three times in the Psalms (LXX 39:9; 67:11; 95:2), once in Joel 2:32, and once in Nah 1:15 (a parallel to Isa 52:7), and once in Jer 20:15.

43. See 1 Cor 12:3; Phil 2:11; Rom 10:9.

Though he had done so many signs before them, yet they did not believe in him; it was that the word spoken by the prophet Isaiah might be fulfilled,

"Lord, who has believed our report,
and to whom has the arm of the Lord been revealed?" [Isa 53:1]

Therefore they could not believe, for Isaiah said again,

"He has blinded their eyes and hardened their hearts,
lest they should see with their eyes and perceive with their heart,
and turn for me to heal them." [Isa 6:10]

Isaiah said this because he saw his glory [Isa 6:1] and spoke of him.
(John 12:37–41 RSV)

Third, in the prophet's narrative account of the servant whose appearance was shocking and without comeliness (Isa 52:13–53:12), Christians could and did find the script followed in the suffering and death of the one they now confessed as Messiah and Lord (Acts 2:36). The servant who was "exalted and lifted up" (Isa 52:13) had first been humbled, with "no form or majesty" that demanded attention (Isa 53:2). His appearance was off-putting, without comeliness (52:14). He was despised and rejected by others, a man of sorrows, not esteemed (53:3). He was numbered among transgressors (53:12). He bore the infirmities and diseases of others (53:4) and was smitten by God for the sins of others (53:6). Although he committed no violence or deceit (53:9), he was oppressed and afflicted (53:7), suffering as silently as an animal led to slaughter (53:7). As a consequence, he will see long life (53:10) and through him many will be made righteous (53:11). In this lengthy account, Christians could easily see the story of Jesus, who suffered innocently for others before he himself was exalted and lifted up.

The suffering servant song is obviously applied to Jesus in two New Testament passages. In Acts 8:26–40, Luke has Philip encounter the Ethiopian court official of Queen Candace who is reading this passage from Isa 53:7–8:

"As a sheep is led to a slaughter
or a lamb before its shearer is dumb,
so he opens not his mouth.
In his humiliation justice was denied him.
Who can describe his generation?
For his life is taken up from the earth." (Acts 8:32–33 RSV)

When asked to whom this passage refers, "Philip opened his mouth, and beginning with this scripture he told him the good news of Jesus [*euange-lisato autō ton Iēsoun*]" (Acts 8:35). In 1 Pet 2:21–25 the passage is not cited and then applied to Jesus. Instead, the words of Isaiah are appropriated for the suffering of Jesus. "Christ also suffered for you," Peter declares, in order to leave them an example so that they can walk in his footsteps (2:21), and continues, "who did no sin, nor was any deceit found in his mouth" (a direct citation of Isa 53:9, author's translation). Each of the next three verses reworks the words of Isaiah. "When he was abused he did not return abuse; when he suffered, he did not threaten" in 2:23 echoes Isa 53:7, "he was oppressed, and he was afflicted, yet he did not open his mouth." The words "he himself bore our sins in his body on the cross" in 2:24 reworks Isa 53:4, "he has borne our infirmities and carried our diseases." The words "by his wounds you have been healed" in 2:24 are clearly drawn from Isa 53:5, "by his bruises we are healed." And the final verse, "for you were going astray like sheep," echoes Isa 53:6, "All we like sheep have gone astray." For 1 Peter the prophet Isaiah simply spoke what happened in Jesus.

The question arises as to how Paul might also have made use of the suffering servant song from Isaiah, even if implicitly, and how it might have functioned within his letter to the Romans. Before pursuing that question, I note that Richard Hays has argued effectively that Paul, even in discursive passages, can allude to an implicit story concerning Jesus,[44] and that, even when not quoting directly, Paul's language can deliberately echo the words of Scripture.[45] In his analysis of Rom 15:3, in fact, Hays shows how Paul's citation of LXX Ps 68:9 represents an early stage of the interpretation of Jesus's story in light of Scripture, and of "finding" the suffering messiah in prophetic texts.[46] So instructed, we can approach Romans to see whether a passage from Isaiah might be present, and even represent a key element of Paul's argument, even if not explicitly cited.

We can observe, first, that Paul makes particularly vigorous use of the prophet Isaiah throughout Romans. Using the indicators provided by the Nestle-Aland 28th Critical Edition, there are allusions to Isa 5:21 in Rom 12:16, Isa 8:14 in Rom 9:32, and Isa 29:16 in Rom 9:20. But it is above all

---

44. Hays, *Faith of Jesus Christ*. Hays's insight is developed further by Grieb, *Story of Romans*; by L. Johnson, *Reading Romans*; and most effectively by Nicolet-Anderson, *Constructing the Self*.

45. Hays, *Echoes of Scripture*.

46. Hays, "Christ Prays the Psalms."

the part of Isaiah containing the Servant Songs (Isa 40–59) that Paul employs most, with sixteen citations or allusions coming from this section of the prophet. Following the sequence of the prophetic composition, we find verbal echoes, allusions, or citations of Isa 49:18 (Rom 14:11); 50:8 (Rom 8:33); 51:5 (Rom 1:17); 51:7 (Rom 2:15); 51:8 (Rom 1:17); 52:5 (Rom 10:5); 52:15 (Rom 15:21); 53:1 (Rom 10:16); 53:5 (Rom 15:21); 53:11 (Rom 5:19); 53:12 (Rom 4:24); 54:16 (Rom 9:22); 59:7 (Rom 3:15–17); 59:20 (Rom 11:26). Two immediate conclusions are warranted: (1) Paul made use of the LXX of Isa 40–60—whether from memory or, as is more likely, a scroll—in the composition of Romans; (2) so frequent are his allusions that the argument in Romans appears to be in conscious conversation with that part of the prophet containing the songs of the servant of the Lord.

These observations, in turn, press the question of why Paul did not actually make use of the part of the song describing the afflictions of the suffering servant in Isa 52:13–53:12. He certainly does not make explicit reference to it in the overt manner of Acts or 1 Peter. Is it, then, missing altogether? Or is it perhaps the implicit scriptural premise underlying all the other uses of Isaiah in the letter, a premise so obvious to Paul and his readers that, like the story of the faith of Jesus, it did not require explicit narration?

Entertaining this possibility enables us to make better sense of a section of Romans that otherwise seems, to many readers, to be obscure. I refer to the dense section of Paul's midrashic argument in Rom 9–11, in which he seeks to interpret God's dialectical plan of salvation for both Jews and gentiles. In the first part of this argument (9:1–29), Paul declares his allegiance to his fellow Jews, while also demonstrating from Scripture how Israel according to the Spirit depends on God's choice and is both smaller and larger than historical Judaism: some gentiles have been called in, and some Jews have turned away, leaving only a faithful remnant among contemporary Jews.

In 9:30–10:21 Paul reflects scripturally on this remarkable development, by which Jews who sought righteousness have fallen short, because they sought righteousness through works (*erga*) rather than faith (*pistis*), while gentiles have attained the righteousness that is out of faith (*ek pisteōs*, 9:30–32). In speaking here of faith and works, however, Paul is not referring to opposing religious systems.[47] He is speaking about a specific sort of recognition of a specific person—namely, Jesus.

Paul had already argued in 3:21–5:21 that all humans are put in right relationship with God, not through their own doing, but through the gift that

---

47. On this point, E. Sanders, *Paul and Palestinian Judaism*, is certainly correct.

was the faithful obedience of the human person Jesus. To "have faith in Jesus," then, means to accept the gift that God gave humans through the faithful obedience of Jesus himself. Paul makes this clear through his explicit citation of LXX Isa 28:16: Jesus is the stone of stumbling (*skandalon*) that God placed in Zion (Rom 9:33). As Paul states in 1 Cor 1:23, it is specifically the cross of Jesus—that is, the manner of his death—that is a *skandalon* to Paul's fellow Jews, the offense that blocks their acceptance of Jesus as their messiah.

Now, in Rom 10:1–3 Paul again affirms his devotion to his own people and his prayer that they be saved—that is, brought within the people God is forming from Jews and gentiles alike.[48] He bears witness that they have zeal for God, but this zeal is not "according to recognition" (*zēlon theou echousin all' ou kat' epignōsin*). The issue, then, is not whether they love God, but whether they have "recognized" the way that God has now worked among them. By stumbling over the crucified Jesus, they have shown themselves "ignorant of the righteousness that comes from God," and can be accused of "seeking to establish their own [righteousness]," for they have not "submitted to the righteousness that comes from God" (*tē dikaiosynē tou theou ouch hypetagēsan*, 10:3). The note here of "recognition" is critical to the entire argument, for it echoes the charge made at the beginning of the letter concerning the idolatrous gentiles, that "they did not see fit to acknowledge God" (*ton theon echein en epignōsei*, 1:28; see also 3:20), and it throws light on the entire passage that follows. What should Paul's fellow Jews have "recognized" when they saw the suffering of Jesus? Why, by implication, are they "without excuse" (see 1:20)?

Paul now proceeds to show this, beginning with the flat statement, "Christ is the goal (*telos*) of the law [*nomos*] unto righteousness for everyone who has faith" (10:4, author's translation). If one has followed Paul's argument thus far, the correct understanding of the classic crux is fairly obvious. Paul is not declaring an "end" to the law as prescription[49]—in Rom 8:4 he had said that the just requirement of the law was being brought to fulfillment among those who walk in the Spirit and not in the flesh—but is rather making a point about Scripture. The goal or the point of *nomos* considered as Scripture (cf. Gal 3:21–22) is the Messiah Jesus, who reveals that righteousness is out of faith.[50] Paul's argument in 9:30–10:21, in short,

---

48. See L. Johnson, "Social Dimensions of Sōtēria."

49. For the argument that Paul means "the end" of the law, see Fitzmyer, *Romans*, 584–85.

50. For the understanding of *telos* as "goal" or "culmination," see, e.g., Byrne, *Romans*,

is hermeneutical rather than soteriological. He seeks to show how, if Scripture is read properly—with the right messianic lens—Jesus should have been recognized, acknowledged, as the Messiah.

The first stage of Paul's demonstration is 10:5–13, where he boldly re-reads Deut 9:4 and 30:12–14 in the light of the crucified and raised Messiah Jesus. Actually, much more than "in the light of": as in 1 Cor 10:3, Paul collapses the distance between Torah and gospel. When Deuteronomy speaks of "the word," Paul identifies it as Christ (Rom 10:6–7). When Deuteronomy says, "Your word is near, in your mouth and in your heart," Paul declares, "*This* is the word concerning faith, which we are proclaiming" (10:8, author's translation). To nail down the point about faith, Paul returns to Isa 28:16, "the one having faith in him will not be put to shame," and uses Joel 2:32 to secure the point that such faith pertains to gentiles as well as Jews: "All who call on the name of the Lord will be saved" (Rom 10:11–13, author's translation). To what did these prophets refer? "If you confess with your lips that Jesus is Lord and have faith in your heart that God raised him from the dead, you shall be saved" (Rom 10:9, author's translation).

The next part of Paul's argument is more difficult, and it brings us back to the prophet Isaiah as evangelist. This is sometimes missed by commentators, who assume that 10:14–15 refers to Paul's own day, and that Paul uses the citation of Isa 52:7, "how beautiful are the feet of those proclaiming good news" (RSV adapted), as adornment, as though the issue were simply the ability of Jews in Paul's own day to hear the gospel preached by Christian missionaries.[51] But we ought to read this section exactly the way we read 10:5–13—that is, with Paul assuming that Christ is already present in Torah. And when we do, we notice immediately that Paul quotes three passages of Isaiah in quick order. He begins in 10:15, we have seen, with Isa 52:7. Then, in 10:16 he quotes the plaintive question from Isa 53:1, "Lord, who has heard our report?" (author's translation). Finally, in 10:20–21, to conclude this section of his argument, he quotes in a split citation Isa 65:1, "I have been found by those who did not seek me; I have shown myself to those who did not ask for me," and Isa 65:2, "All the day long I hold out my hands to a disbelieving people" (author's translation). The text not cited is Isa 52:13–53:12 (with the exception of 53:1 as a kind of hint), which describes the suffering servant.

---

315; Moo, *Epistle to the Romans*, 638–43; Jewett, *Romans*, 619–20. For full treatment, see Badenas, *Christ, the End of the Law*.

51. This standard view can be found in discussions of Rom 10:14–21 in Fitzmyer, *Romans*, 594–601; Moo, *Romans*, 661–69; Byrne, *Romans*, 320–28; Jewett, *Romans*, 642–44.

Given Paul's concentrated use of the rest of Isa 52–53 in the rest of Romans, the omission must be seen as deliberate. In good midrashic fashion, Paul leaves unspoken the most critical part of the prophetic text for his argument, the description of the one rejected by humans but vindicated by God, and thereby making others righteous. He does not include it because he does not need to include it. For his readers as for himself, I suggest, the figure about whom Isaiah spoke was obvious.

And this is precisely Paul's point. His fellow Jews should also have recognized the crucified Jesus as the Messiah. If they had recognized that the telos of the law was the Messiah (10:4), and if their zeal for God had been "according to recognition" (10:2, author's translation), they would have seen in Jesus the figure of the suffering Messiah already "proclaimed" by Isaiah. They had, in short, already "heard the good news" if they had properly read the prophet Isaiah, who was certainly one of those stated by Paul in the opening of this letter as among the sacred writings who pre-promised the good news from God (Rom 1:1–2; see also 16:26). When, therefore, Paul asks in 10:18, "But I ask, have they not heard?" he is able to answer his own question: "indeed they have," for the word was given to Israel through the Psalms, the Law, and the Prophets (10:18–21).[52]

## Conclusion

Paul's view of Scripture as a whole is stated most formally in 2 Tim 3:16.[53] He tells his delegate, "Every scripture is God-inspired and useful for teaching, reproving, correcting, toward an education in righteousness, in order that the man of God might be fit, prepared for every good work."[54] The statement might well have been made before Paul's conversion. We have seen in this chapter that, even when he does not quote Scripture directly, it always shapes his view of the world. He does not so much "approach" Scripture as "inhabit" it. Yet his relationship to Scripture is dialectical, because of the experience of the cross and resurrection of Christ. If Scripture is to be read

---

52. Although he does not note the specific use of Isaiah that I have tried to trace, Moo catches the point of part of Paul's argument: "From their own scriptures, then, Israel should have recognized that God is at work in the gospel." *Romans*, 668.

53. As throughout this book, I take the letters to Paul's delegates (the Pastorals) to represent Paul's own views.

54. Translation and comment can be found in L. Johnson, *First and Second Letters to Timothy*, 416–26.

correctly, it must be read as prophetic concerning the experience of God now being revealed through the Holy Spirit given by the risen Christ. Thus, the statement in 2 Tim 3:16 just cited is preceded by this one in 3:15: "You have known the sacred writings since you were a child. They are capable of making you wise concerning salvation through the faith that is in Christ Jesus" (author's translation).

*Chapter 7*

# Paul and Greco-Roman Culture

Asa Jew who was born in the emphatically Hellenistic city of Tarsus in Cilicia, who was plausibly a Roman citizen, and who preached the good news to both Jews and gentiles in major cities of the Roman Empire in the middle decades of the first century CE, Paul inevitably knew and interacted with significant aspects of Greco-Roman culture.[1] He was not an Essene sectarian who withdrew from all contact with gentiles and those who associated with them.[2] Even if he was, as Luke proposes, educated as a Pharisee in Jerusalem, he would not, even there, escape the influence of Greek culture and Roman rule.[3] Paul and Barnabas, moreover, were sent on mission not by Jerusalem but by the church in Antioch, another city with strong Hellenistic character,[4] and Paul pastored churches in cities (Corinth,

---

1. For these assertions, see chap. 2; for the Hellenistic character of Tarsus, see Van Unnik, *Tarsus or Jerusalem*; for the issue of Paul's Roman citizenship, which is repeatedly stated by Acts (in 16:37–39; 22:25–28; 23:27), see Sherwin-White, *Roman Society*, 48–70.

2. Qumran's ideal of separation from the larger society is found in 1QS 5.1–3, 7.24–25, 8.13–16, 8.22–24. Although 2 Cor 6:14–7:1 calls clearly for separation between believers and nonbelievers, 1 Cor 5:9–10 mitigates that position (perhaps a fragment from Paul's original letter to the Corinthian church) by insisting only that they do not associate with the immoral in the world; they are not to leave society entirely.

3. For the presence of Roman troops, see Josephus, *Jewish War*, and for the role of centurions as intermediaries between army and populace, see Kyrychenko, *Roman Army*; see also N. Pollard, *Soldiers, Cities, and Civilians*. The degree of Hellenization with Palestine is well summarized by Hengel, *Judaism and Hellenism*. The Hellenization of Galilee is shown above all by archaeological research; see Strange and Longstaff, *Excavations at Sepphoris*; Fiensy and Strange, *Galilee*.

4. See Strabo, *Geography* 16.2.5–7; Josephus calls Antioch "third among the cities of the Roman world" (*Jewish War* 3.29); see also Downey, *Ancient Antioch*; De Giorgi, *Ancient Antioch*; Kondoleon, *Antioch*.

Thessalonika, Philippi, Ephesus) in which the overwhelming presence of Roman rule and Greek culture were unavoidable.[5] The major question for scholarship today is the character, range, and depth of such influence.[6] The most reasonable positions avoid the extremes of denying any real Hellenistic influence on Paul (because, like Jesus, he is a Jew who thinks poetically rather than logically)[7] or insisting that Paul is essentially defined by Greco-Roman culture (as he sets about shaping the "Christ cult" he inherited from the gentile church in Antioch).[8]

In this chapter, I provide the essential framework for reading an author of the first century who writes in Greek and works within a political context that was dominated by the Roman imperium. I take up the three aspects of Paul's Greco-Roman environment concerning which some degree of knowledge is critical to the responsible reading of his correspondence: rhetoric, philosophy, and religion. But before taking up those topics, three preliminary questions require some attention: (1) How valid is the current tendency to read Paul within a "postcolonialist" framework, or, to put it another way, how important was Rome's power and ideology for Paul, positively or negatively? (2) Is the use of the shorthand term "Greco-Roman" by New Testament scholars historically accurate or just sloppy characterization? (3) What do the letters suggest concerning the sort of education—specifically education in *paideia* (Greek culture)—that the diaspora Jew Paul might have had?

## Preliminary Questions

### Postcolonial Interpretation

The term "postcolonial" arose from the twentieth-century collapse of European empires that had, beginning with European world exploration in the sixteenth century, exercised sovereignty in one fashion or another around

---

5. The fact that Philippi and Corinth were Roman colonies adds another level of complexity to their cultural mix; see Sweetman, *Roman Colonies*. For Corinth, see Lang, *Cure and Cult*; Friesen, Schowalter, and Walters, *Corinth in Context*; Schowalter and Friesen, *Urban Religion in Roman Corinth*; Murphy-O'Connor, *St. Paul's Corinth*; for Thessalonica, see Lane Fox, *Ancient Macedon*; Nasrallah, Bakirtzis, and Friesen, *From Roman to Early Christian Thessalonikē*; for Philippi, see J. Wilson, *Rediscovering Caesarea Philippi*; for Ephesus, see Koester, *Ephesos*.

6. For a useful set of essays, see Sampley, *Paul in the Greco-Roman World*.

7. As in Hatch, *Influence of Greek Ideas*.

8. As in Bousset, *Kyrios Christos*.

the globe, most notably in Africa, the Middle East, India, and Latin America. The most far-reaching and powerful of these colonial powers was the British Empire, whose production of literature concerning its "subject peoples" is, in hindsight, perceived as deeply biased, especially by the emerging class of scholars from among such former colonies.[9] European scholars projected Western and specifically Christian categories on, for example, Islam and Indian religion.[10] In its proper form, then, postcolonial literature and scholarship is a double-edged sword. It seeks to reclaim indigenous symbols, categories, and modes of thought, which are not derived from the Greco-Roman/Christian-based Western scholarship, and from that basis challenges "Western" symbols, categories, and modes of thought as "provincial" in character and far from the standard by which other cultures ought to be understood or judged. An example of such a faulty "Western" bias is, indeed, its fondness for empire. Postcolonialism is intrinsically anti-imperial, for it is empires that establish colonies and hegemonic modes of discourse.[11] So far, so good. It makes all the sense in the world for those formerly dominated by foreign powers to assert their own view of the world, supplementing political liberation with cultural independence.

In an odd bit of cultural misappropriation, however, "postcolonialism"—as so many other ideological criticisms that had their origin in real life—has found its way into the halls of academe inhabited by people who have never lived under any imperial power greater than the university tenure process, or any ideological tyranny other than the ones they have eagerly embraced. And, as happens with equal frequency, biblical scholarship comes late to the game, training young scholars to view their own and the ancient world with eyes that see only what "postcolonialism" allows them to see.[12] In the case of New Testament scholarship, the first-century Roman Empire is understood in terms of the nineteenth- and twentieth-century British Empire at its worst,[13] and the animus toward Rome found among some (by no

---

9. See esp. Said, *Orientalism*; V. Kennedy, *Edward Said*; Afzal-Khan and Seshadri-Crooks, *Pre-occupation of Postcolonial Studies*; Desai and Nair, *Postcolonialisms*; Harlow and Carter, *Imperialism and Orientalism*. A quick overview is provided by R. Young, *Postcolonialism*.

10. See, e.g., Kalmar, *Early Orientalism*; Reinders, *Borrowed Gods and Foreign Bodies*; Schopen, *Bones, Stones, and Buddhist Monks*.

11. Deeply influential in shaping this perspective are the foundational works by Fanon, *Wretched of the Earth*, and Freire, *Pedagogy of the Oppressed*.

12. See, e.g., S. Moore and Segovia, *Postcolonial Biblical Criticism*; Dube and Wafula, *Postcoloniality*; Lee and Yoo, *Mapping and Engaging*.

13. In *Jesus: A Revolutionary Biography*, John Dominic Crossan makes explicit his pro-

means all) first-century Jews[14] provides a basis for reading Paul within an anti-imperial framework.[15] The triumph of the postcolonial perspective can be seen clearly in the recent massive commentary on Romans that minimizes the contrary evidence of 13:1–7 and holds that Paul's entire argument has Roman imperial ideology and Roman *machismo* as its target.[16]

Such a postcolonialist approach to Paul is problematic in two major ways. First, one cannot simply map the eighteenth- and nineteenth-century experience of empire and colonialism on the ancient Mediterranean world.[17] There are, to be sure, analogies to be drawn. On one side, Rome made every effort to impose and maintain its rule over peoples, whose economic well-being was subordinated to that of Rome; the presence of Roman military was a visible sign of foreign domination; taxation on provinces was onerous; Rome had a huge slave population, and slaves were legally defined as property so long as they were in bondage.[18] Imperial propaganda masked the face of raw power through a portrayal of the emperor as a paterfamilias overseeing a vast and variegated household (*oikoumenē*).[19] On the other side, the Roman rule of law—and the cult of the imperial family—was welcomed by many and even invited;[20] Rome was remarkably accepting of native religions and cultural practices;[21] the ancient structure of the *polis* (city-state)

---

jection of British imperial policies and practices in Ireland onto the Roman Empire of the first century.

14. For a survey of the political realities in Palestine, see Cohen, *From the Maccabees to the Mishnah*; Schürer, *History of the Jewish People.*

15. See, e.g., Horsley, *Paul and Empire*; Crossan and Reed, *In Search of Paul*; C. Stanley, *Colonized Apostle*; Punt, *Postcolonial Biblical Interpretation*; George, *Paul's Identity in Galatians*; Kamudzandu, *Abraham Our Father*; Marchal, *Politics of Heaven*; J. Harrison, "Apostle Paul." For the anti-imperial inferences that might be drawn from the letters, see Wright, "Paul and Empire."

16. Jewett, *Romans*, 78–803; see also N. Elliott, *Arrogance of Nations.*

17. For orientation, see Garnsey and Saller, *Roman Empire*; MacMullen, *Roman Social Relations*; Veyne, *History of Private Life*, vol. 1; a valuable collection of primary texts is Lewis and Reinhold, *Roman Civilization.*

18. See, e.g., Salmon, *Roman Colonization*; Millar, *Roman Empire*; Bradley and Wilson, *Greek and Roman Colonization*; Voss and Casella, *Archaeology of Colonialism.*

19. The role of Augustus was decisive in shaping this "familial" construal of the *oikoumenē*; see Mellor, *Augustus*, and Isaac, *Empire and Ideology*. The "paranoid style" in Roman imperialism is masterfully described by MacMullen, *Enemies of the Roman Order.*

20. See Friesen, *Twice Neokoros.*

21. See Livy, *History of Rome* 29.10.24, for the reception of the Asian mother goddess in Rome; in contrast, see the suppression of the Isis cult because it was regarded as subversive of the Roman order, in *History of Rome* 39.8.19; see also Ogilvie, *Romans and Their Gods.*

remained intact, along with forms of local and regional authority (Rome had the last word but did not insist on having every word);[22] while slavery was harsh and demeaning, it was not racially based, and held the possibility of manumission;[23] and while some slaves labored and died in the mines, or organized themselves into a revolt,[24] others served peacefully within wealthy Roman households as teachers.[25]

Indeed, the violent resistance of Israel first to Greek and then to Roman empires is unique in its ferocity and sustained character. From the Maccabean revolt in the second century BCE to the final crushing of the Bar Kokhba revolt in 135 CE, a significant portion of the Jews in Palestine resisted empire, even at the cost of martyrdom and ruinous war.[26] But not all Jews even within Eretz Israel shared the same animus.[27] And if Josephus and Philo are allowed to speak for the majority of Jews—those in the diaspora[28]—Greek culture and Roman rule were regarded more as a blessing than a curse.[29] In addition, rather than allowing themselves to be subject to foreign ideology, Jewish apologists used the cultural forms of Hellenism to assert the superiority of the Jewish law and way of life. In fact, what was

22. The speeches of Paul's younger contemporary Dio Chrysostom (40–115 CE) provide a good sense of the significance of the emperor (see *Orations* 1–4, 56, 62), as well as the continuing role of individual cities; notable are his addresses to Nicaea and Nicomedia (*Orations* 38–39) and those to Prusa and Apameia (*Orations* 40–41).

23. See Urbainczyk, *Roman Slavery*; Patterson, *Slavery and Social Death*.

24. Three so-called Servile Wars erupted under the republic, the first two in Sicily (135–132 and 104–100 BCE), and the third in Italy, led by the gladiator-general Spartacus (73–71 BCE); see Schiavone, *Spartacus*.

25. Even within the imperial household; see Marcus Aurelius, *Meditations*, book 1. For a sense of the complex and sometimes multivalent aspects of slavery in Paul's time, see D. Martin, *Slavery as Salvation*.

26. In addition to 1–4 Maccabees and Josephus's *Jewish War*, see Rhoads, *Israel in Revolution*; Hayes and Mandell, *Jewish People*; Horsley with Hanson, *Bandits, Prophets and Messiahs*; Hengel, *Zealots*; Yadin, *Masada*.

27. A difference of perspectives regarding Hellenistic culture and Roman rule is certainly one of the factors in the development of sects; see Stemberger, *Jewish Contemporaries of Jesus*; Goldstein, "Jewish Acceptance"; Neusner, *From Politics to Piety*.

28. By far the greatest number of first-century Jews lived in the diaspora; see Tcherikover, *Hellenistic Civilization*; Smallwood, *Jews under Roman Rule*; Barclay, *Jews in the Mediterranean Diaspora*.

29. Josephus wrote *The Jewish War*, we remember, at least in part to persuade his fellow Jews not to further resist Roman rule, on whose side he considered the God of the Jews to be (see 5.396–412), and Philo of Alexandria's *Embassy to Gaius* appealed to the emperor in the time of Caligula.

good in Greek culture, some of them asserted, actually came from Moses.[30] In short, there is scant evidence that the sort of cultural hegemony and political oppression posited by postcolonialists on the basis of later European imperialism characterized the empire during Paul's ministry in the diaspora.

A second and even more important reason for rejecting a postcolonial reading of Paul's letters is that they offer no real evidence to support such an interpretation. That there are utopian and countercultural elements in Paul's letters cannot be disputed. Within the *ekklēsia*, Paul relativized the ethnic, gender, and class distinctions that governed life outside the church (Gal 3:28; 1 Cor 12:13; Col 3:11). His concern for the weak in the community (Rom 15:1-2; 1 Cor 8:7-13; 12:22-26; 1 Tim 5:3-16), his call for lowly mindedness and mutual service (Rom 12:16-21; 14:15-19; 1 Cor 8:1-3; Phil 2:1-4; Eph 4:25, 32; 5:21), his recognition of women in public roles within the mission (Phil 4:2-3; Rom 16:1-3, 6-7, 12; 1 Cor 1:11; 7:34-35; 16:19)—these all certainly challenge the stereotypical notes of masculinity and nobility associated with the Roman Empire. But such male-defined ideals were well in place before the Roman imperium, and even the Greek empire that preceded it; they are clearly enunciated in classical Athens and embodied in the city-state of Sparta.[31] Indeed, *andreia* as the measure for humanity is a standard feature of ancient Near Eastern cultures (Babylonian, Assyrian, Persian, Parthian, Egyptian) and is only given a distinctive guise when clothed as *Romanitas*.

Even more to the point, although Paul advocates countercultural ideals and dispositions within the community of believers, he does not—indeed, could not—challenge the societal order as such. Paul tends toward a conservative posture concerning the traditional patriarchal household, for example, mitigating its hierarchical structure through attitudinal adjustments, but leaving in place the structure itself (Rom 7:1-3; 1 Cor 11:2-16; 14:33-36; 16:15-18; Col 3:18-4:1; Eph 5:22-6:9; 1 Thess 1:4-6; 1 Tim 2:11-15; 3:4-5, 12; 5:4-8; 2 Tim 3:6; Titus 1:11; 2:2-6).[32] Thus, women are free to remain single

---

30. In addition to the supreme self-confidence revealed in all of Philo's many works, see also the remarkable testimonies found in the fragments of other Hellenistic Jewish authors by Eusebius; Holladay, *Fragments*.

31. See, e.g., Nortwick, *Imagining Men*; Rosen and Sluiter, *Andreia*; C. Williams, *Roman Homosexuality*.

32. Scholars who are uncomfortable with this often appeal to a difference supposedly found between the "authentic" letters and the "inauthentic" letters on points such as these; see, e.g., Scroggs, "Paul." But apart from the general weakness of that argument (see chap. 3, "Clusters of Letters and an Adequate Model of Authorship"), a glance at these passages shows that they are found across the canonical compositions. The embarrassment of having

and work for the Lord (1 Cor 7:25-35), but if they marry, they are to be submissive to their husbands (Col 3:18-19; Eph 5:22-24). Paul's greatest difficulties concerning gender roles, indeed, come in those places where ecclesial attitudes and practice (the utopian ideal) are in tension with the conventions of the patriarchal household (1 Cor 11:2-16; 14:33-36; 1 Tim 2:11-15; 5:3-16).

Similarly, Paul never challenges the institution of slavery: he calls for slaves to be submissive to masters (Col 3:22-24; Eph 6:5-9; 1 Tim 6:1-2) and returns the slave Onesimus to his master Philemon as the law required in cases of runaways (Phlm 8-18). Paul recognizes the tension that can arise when both masters and slaves are believers (1 Tim 6:1-2). But even when slaves have the opportunity to become freedmen, Paul's advice is at best equivocal (1 Cor 7:21-24).[33] Finally, Paul does not either directly or indirectly question the larger political structure.[34] As for others of his generation (and many, many more after), the Roman Empire was a fact of life that had to be negotiated but was not likely to disappear. Thus, Paul's statements in Rom 13:1-7 portray the power of the state as benign, and even as an instrument of God.[35] Just as believers were to play their appropriate roles in the household, then, so were they to be good citizens (Titus 3:1-2) and, in the manner of diaspora Jews, show their nonrevolutionary disposition by offering prayers for kings and rulers (1 Tim 2:1-2).[36] In sum, the evidence of Paul's letters simply cannot be fitted to a view of him as a social revolutionary beyond the confines of the *ekklēsia*.

Precisely this conservative posture toward the larger social order, to be sure, can fuel a postcolonial interpretation of Paul that is not laudatory

---

the "authentic Paul" conservative on household structure and dynamics leads to the alternative strategy of claiming that such passages are interpolations. Thus, e.g., Murphy-O'Connor, "Non-Pauline Character."

33. See Bartchy, *Mallon chrēsai*; Braxton, *Tyranny of Resolution*.

34. I leave aside the portrayal of Paul in Acts, which not only has Paul exploit his status as a Roman citizen but is in general entirely positive toward the empire; see the overdone but nevertheless intriguing case made by Walaskay (*"And So We Came to Rome"*) that Acts can be read as an apologia for the empire in the manner of Josephus.

35. For discussion of Rom 13:1-7, see Käsemann, "Principles of Interpretation." If Paul's reference to "the restrainer" (*to katechōn*) in 2 Thess 2:7 refers to the Roman Empire, as ancient tradition thought (see Tertullian, *The Resurrection of the Flesh* 24; John Chrysostom, *Homily on 2 Thess.* 4), this would be consistent with Rom 13 in seeing the empire as having a providential role; see discussion in Richard, *First and Second Thessalonians*, 337-40; Malherbe, *Letters to the Thessalonians*, 432-33.

36. For the Jewish practice, see Ezra 6:10; *Letter of Aristeas* 45; 1 Macc 7:33; Josephus, *Jewish War* 2.197, 2.409-410; Philo, *Embassy* 157, 317; *Pirke Avot* 3.2.

but condemnatory. In this reading, Paul, in contrast to the Jesus who proclaimed a "brokerless kingdom,"[37] or the James who rejected every form of "friendship with the world,"[38] accommodated himself and the good news to an oppressive social order, even in his undisputed letters, thus setting a precedent for later betrayals of the radical gospel through various compromises with the world.[39] But whatever view is taken of Paul's statements regarding the social and political institutions of his day, it is clear enough that Paul does not challenge the structure of the household, or slavery, or the empire. Do his confessions of the lordship of Jesus (Phil 2:5-11; Rom 10:9; 1 Cor 8:4-6; 12:3) bear within them the potential to subvert the absolute claims of any political order? Indeed they do, just as his utopian vision of the *ekklēsia* can fund a subversion of social structures and dynamics. But as we shall see in a later chapter, Paul by no means makes such subversion the point of his teaching. His understanding of liberation and salvation is more radical still than that espoused by contemporary liberation theologies.[40]

### The Term "Greco-Roman"

The characterization "Greco-Roman" (or "Graeco-Roman")[41] is widely used to describe the peculiar cultural mix that dominated the Mediterranean world—infecting even so resistant a body as Judaism—from considerably before Paul's time, and extended itself in Byzantium for another 1,500 years after Paul. To be sure, the elements of "Greek" and "Roman" themselves built on earlier cultural patterns distinctive to the Mediterranean: an economy based primarily on agriculture, a taste for trade and warfare, a love of display and a delight in language, a craving for honor and a fear of shame. This was a world of large households run by patriarchs, with slaves and owners. Disparities in wealth and status were alleviated through a complex system of patronage: benefactors helped clients, who reciprocated with praise, while the

---

37. See esp. Crossan, *Historical Jesus.*
38. See L. Johnson, "Friendship with the World."
39. For those regarding the letters to Paul's delegates as inauthentic, the evil progression toward compromise with the world starts with them; see Schleiermacher, *Über den sogenannten Ersten Brief des Paulos,* 58-59, 78, 125, 160; Campenhausen, *Ecclesiastical Authority,* 107-20.
40. See chap. 11.
41. According to the *Oxford English Dictionary,* the earliest use of the term for literature and not wrestling was in Edwin Johnson's 1888 study of Christian Origins, *Antiqua Mater.*

exchange of quid pro quo was mollified by ideals of friendship and harmony. These cultural patterns corresponded to the realm of the divine, where many gods and goddesses—like an unruly household—carried out intrigues and fratricidal jealousy. The power of the gods was pervasive and was distributed among a collection of personalities as varied and vivid as those of the humans within whom they frequently commingled.[42]

When Alexander the Great set out to conquer Persia in 334 BCE, he was engaged in a cultural as well as a military mission. He sought to shape the entire known world according to the ideals of classical Athens. Himself a student of Aristotle, he brought with him scientists, poets, and philosophers as agents of cultural transformation. The instruments of Hellenization were (a) the *polis*, or city-state, with its distinctive cultural institutions (such as the *gymnasion*), which for Greeks was the source of identity; (b) the Greek language, which became the common language (*koinē*) of the empire; (c) intermarriage between Hellenes and non-Hellenes, in the service of creating a single Panhellenic world; and (d) religious syncretism, which enabled distinct polytheistic systems to merge and create a single religious umbrella for a new Hellenistic world.[43] The world of the Greek empire was not, in fact, much like ancient Athens. The fact of empire itself reduced the importance of local identity; language and literature were transformed as new peoples grappled with Greek ideals. Nevertheless, Greek *paideia*—the word means both "education" and "culture"—represented the ideal expression of civilization even for the Roman conquerors, whose empire retained and cultivated this Hellenistic heritage.[44]

When the Romans established their control over the Mediterranean, maintaining it for centuries through force of arms and the rule of law, the influence of Greek culture remained strong. Koine Greek continued to be spoken and written, even in the "Latin West," for centuries,[45] and remained the language of the Eastern empire until its fall in 1453. Roman thinkers and writers actively engaged—and sometimes imitated—Greek models in poetry, rhetoric, philosophy, and religion. The term "Greco-Roman," then, points to this complex cultural reality. Nobody wrote purer Latin than Ci-

---

42. See L. Johnson, *Among the Gentiles*, 32–49.

43. For an overview of the Hellenistic project, see Hadas, *Hellenistic Culture*; Tarn, *Hellenistic Civilization*; P. Green, *Alexander to Actium*.

44. See above all the pioneering work of Jaeger, *Paideia*, and for the perdurance of the ideal, see Borg, *Paideia*.

45. Suetonius speaks of the emperor Claudius (41–54 CE) referring to "our two languages" (*Life of Claudius* 42).

cero, yet his education in Athens revealed itself in his dialogues, his treatises on rhetoric, and his political writings.[46] Nobody wrote a crisper or more masculine Latin than Seneca, yet he is clearly familiar with Greek writings and finds much to please him in the philosophy of Epicurus.[47] Musonius Rufus and Epictetus are also notable Stoic philosophers, yet each taught their students in Greek. The emperor Marcus Aurelius (161–80 CE) composed his *Meditations* in Greek. In the second century CE, an even more enthusiastic celebration of Greek culture is found in the writings of Aelius Aristides and Lucian of Samosata—Lucian imagined that even the dead in the underworld spoke in Greek![48] Perhaps the best example of all is Plutarch, who wrote in Greek and was a priest at the shrine at Delphi, yet who also took his place within the Roman order, filling the role of magistrate. Plutarch gathered sayings (*apophthegmata/sententiae*) from both Greek and Roman sources, and devoted himself to the compiling the *Parallel Lives* of great Greek and Roman figures.[49]

As we saw in earlier chapters, Jewish thinkers and writers, both within Palestine and in the diaspora, also added to the cultural mix through their embrace of the Greek language (as in the Septuagint), Greek literature, and Greek philosophy. The writings of Saint Paul, like the other writings of the New Testament and the major portion of early Christian literature, draw from and add to this rich cultural stew. The issue is not whether Judaism and earliest Christianity were affected by Greco-Roman culture but how much and how significantly they were affected. This is an issue that cannot be settled by a priori judgments; it can be resolved only by the patient and careful analysis of each ancient writing.

## Paul and *Paideia*

As already stated, the term *paideia* connoted both education and culture; the double meaning suggests the importance of education within Greco-Roman society as well as the aim of study—namely, to learn, embody, and eventually transmit the best ideals of Greek civilization. The young

46. See D. Bailey, *Cicero*; Dorey, *Cicero*; Lacey, *Cicero*.
47. See, e.g., *On the Happy Life* 12–14; on Seneca, see Fitch, *Seneca*.
48. Lucian, *Dialogues of the Dead* 25; on Lucian, see Branham, *Unruly Eloquence*. On the Second Sophistic of the second century CE, see Philostratus, *Lives of the Sophists*, and G. Anderson, *Second Sophistic*.
49. See C. Jones, *Plutarch and Rome*; Mossman, *Plutarch and His Intellectual World*.

man (and sometimes also woman)[50] typically passed through a number
of educational stages, beginning with basic moral education carried out
at home under the supervision of the paterfamilias, which also included
basic instruction[51] in reading, writing, and arithmetic. Such instruction
and moral supervision were sometimes carried out by a trusted slave, who
was called a *paidagōgos*. As the child progressed, the memorization and
imitation of literary texts would increase, as well as participation in the
*gymnasion*, where both mental and physical excellence were cultivated. At
the age of twelve, a *grammateus* advanced the skills of reading and writing,
introducing students to the close analysis of poetry. Only more gifted (and
wealthy) students would move on to the formal study of rhetoric, the essential preparation for a career in law and politics. Some students would also
add instruction in philosophy. This progression, begun in classical Athens,
persisted throughout the Roman period.[52]

Such was the formal system. In how much of it could a diaspora Jew
hope to participate? The evidence of some Hellenistic Jewish writers, above
all Philo of Alexandria, points to a thorough immersion in Greek *paideia*.[53]
What about Paul? According to a speech attributed to him by Acts, he was
born in Tarsus of Cilicia, raised in Jerusalem, and "educated [*pepaideumenos*]
at the feet of Gamaliel according to the strict dictates of ancestral law" (Acts
22:3, author's translation). This would suggest that Paul's "higher education"
was not in Greek literature, rhetoric, and philosophy but in the study of
Torah according to Pharisaic principles. But it is entirely possible, indeed
probable, that the earlier stages of his education would follow the basic lines
of the Greek cursus, although in his case the poetry and history memorized
or imitated might be that found in the Septuagint.

We must also remember, however, that a smattering of learning in rhetoric and philosophy was available to any inhabitant of an ancient polis, just as

50. See Musonius Rufus, *Fragment 3: That Women, Too, Should Study Philosophy*, in
Lutz, *Musonius, "The Roman Socrates."*
51. See Cribiore, *Writing, Teachers, and Students*.
52. For the educational *cursus*, see the classic work by Marrou, *History of Education in
Antiquity*, and S. Bonner, *Education in Ancient Rome*. For an ancient discussion that focuses
especially on the formation of character, see Plutarch, *On the Education of Children*.
53. In addition to the obvious case of Philo, the effects of classical education are found
as well in Ezekiel the Tragedian, Pseudo-Orpheus, and *The Sentences of Pseudo-Phocylides*,
the latter of which was determined to be from a Jewish author only after the research of
Jakob Bernays in 1856; for the history of research, see van der Horst, *Sentences of Pseudo-
Phocylides*, 66.

a smattering of knowledge about Freudian psychology, Marxist philosophy, and Eastern religions is available to the contemporary citizen of New York City, through simple attention to the speech of others. Such a combination of early basic education in the Greek mode, later technical study in the texts of Judaism, and a layperson's casual acquaintance with Greek higher learning fits what the letters suggest about Paul's education.

The Greek style in Paul's letters is various, as we have seen, but nowhere does it approach the sort of higher koine that characterizes Jewish authors like Philo and Josephus—or, for that matter, the Letter to the Hebrews. If there is an influence on Paul's diction, it is, as I showed in the previous chapter, the diction of the Septuagint.[54] It is also clear that Paul is not steeped in Greek literature. In Acts, Luke has Paul cite Aratus's *Phaenomena* 5 ("in him we live and move and have our being") while addressing the philosophers in Athens (Acts 17:28), identifying the line as one declared by "some of your poets." In the defense speech before Agrippa, Paul's quotation from the risen Jesus, "it is hard for you to kick against the goad" (Acts 26:14, author's translation), echoes Euripides's *Bacchae* 795. Each of these reflects the sort of "knowledge" of the poets as could be picked up in common discourse: they represent sentiments abstracted from literature and circulated as bits of wisdom, rather than the close reading of literature.[55]

The same is true of the two passages in his letters where references to classical authors can be detected. In 1 Cor 15:33, "wicked conversations destroy good character" (*phtheirousin ēthē chrēsta homiliai kakai*, author's translation) seems to derive from the *Thais* of Menander (fourth century BCE), a poet whose work survives almost entirely in fragments.[56] This is again the sort of *apophthegma* that would be widely circulated outside its original literary context, eventually to be collected by anthologists like Stobaeus.[57] The same is undoubtedly true of the line quoted by Paul in Titus 1:12, "Cretans are always liars, wicked beasts, empty bellies" (author's translation), which since the time of Clement of Alexandria has been attributed to

---

54. See chap. 6, "A Scripture-Defined World." Please remember that when I speak of "Paul," I am speaking of the self-presentation in the canonical letters. What pertains to the individual Paul in this analysis, then, pertains as well to the colleagues that made up his school and helped produce his letters.

55. "Kicking against the goad," in fact, is cited by Julian, *Oration* 8.426B as a "proverb" (*paroimia*).

56. For similar statements, see also Aeschylus, *Seven Wise Men of Thebes* 605, and Diodorus Siculus, *Roman History* 16.54.

57. Wachsmuth, Hense, and Stobaeus, *Ioannis Stobaei Anthologium*.

the sixth-century BCE Cretan poet and seer Epimenides.[58] Paul introduces it this way: "A certain prophet from among them himself said" (Titus 1:12, author's translation).[59] The fact that the letters cite Greek authors only twice, and then only in the manner of commonplaces, supports the position that Paul did not advance to the higher stages of Greco-Roman education represented by the formal study of rhetoric and philosophy, and when a comparison is made between these few citations and the depth of Paul's immersion in Scripture, the statement of Acts that Paul was "educated . . . according to the strict dictates of ancestral law" (Acts 22:3) is plausible.

Such an educational background also makes sense of Paul's disparaging remarks concerning "higher education" in rhetoric and philosophy. He declares defensively in 2 Cor 11:5-6 (NRSV), "I think that I am not in the least inferior to these super-apostles [*tōn hyperlian apostolōn*]. I may be untrained in speech [*idiōtēs tō logō*], but not in knowledge [*gnōsei*]; certainly in every way and in all things we have made this evident to you." The term *idiōtēs* connotes a nonprofessional, someone who has not received technical training.[60] Paul therefore claims sufficient knowledge, even if he has not been educated at the highest levels.

Paul's animus toward the higher reaches of rhetoric and philosophy is clearest in 1 Corinthians and Colossians. In 1 Cor 1:17 he contrasts "eloquent wisdom" (*sophia logou*) to the power of the gospel proclamation, and follows with a series of antitheses in 2:1-5: he did not come "in lofty words of wisdom" (*ou kath' hyperochēn logou ē sophias*, 2:1), or "plausible words of wisdom" (*ouk en peithois sophias logois*, 2:4), so that faith would rest on the power of God, not "human wisdom" (NRSV; *mē en sophia anthrōpōn*, 2:5). He asks, in light of the cross and resurrection, "Where is the one who is wise? Where is the scribe? Where is the debater of this age?" (NRSV; *pou sophos, pou grammateus, pou syzētētēs tou aiōnos toutou*, 1:20). When he turns to disclose the wisdom (*sophia*) that is given to the mature (2:1), he again asserts that this mystery owes nothing to human rhetoric or philosophy: "we speak

---

58. Clement, *Stromateis* 1.59.2. The citation is discussed in Kidd, "Titus as Apologist," and Thiselton, "Liar Paradox."

59. In a series of articles in the *Expositor* (1906, pp. 305-17; 1907, pp. 331-37; 1912, pp. 348-53), James Rendel Harris back-translated the ninth-century Syriac commentary on the Acts of the Apostles by Isho'dad of Merv, which contains a passage purportedly from Epimenides's *Kretika* that had "all Cretans are liars" in the second line and "in you we live and move and are" in the fourth line. If this attribution were correct, two of the "Pauline" citations of Greek literature would come from the same four lines of poetry.

60. For a precise analysis, see Munoz, "How Not to Go Out of the World."

of these things in words not taught by human wisdom but taught by the Spirit" (NRSV; *ha kai laloumen ouk en didaktois anthrōpinēs sophias logois all' en didaktois pneumatos*, 2:13). The cross appears as foolishness (*mōria*) to the educated of the world, but it is the measure of wisdom (*sophia*) for believers (1:21-27). A similar disjunction occurs in Col 2:8: "See to it that no one takes you captive through philosophy and empty deceit, according to human tradition . . . and not according to Christ" (NRSV; *dia tēs philosophias kai kenēs apatēs kata tēn paradosin tōn anthrōpōn . . . kai ou kata Christon*); in Col 2:2-3 Paul states that "all the treasures of wisdom and knowledge are in the mystery that is Christ" (author's translation), and adds in 2:4, "I am saying this so that no one may deceive you with plausible arguments" (*hina mēdeis hymas paralogizētai en pithanologia*, author's translation).

Finally, we can note that Paul's explicit references to education tend to focus on the elementary rather than higher stages of *paideia*. Thus such educational commonplaces as we find in 1 Corinthians: they may have many pedagogues, but Paul is their only father, who has the responsibility to instruct them in morals (4:15);[61] he threatens to come to them with a staff for punishment (4:21); he is incapable of giving them meat and can give them only milk, because they act like children (3:1-2); the Corinthians are not to go "beyond what is written" (*mē hyper ha gegraptai*, 4:6).[62] In Paul's most daring appropriation of the language of Greco-Roman education, he declares in Titus 2:11-12, "For the grace of the savior God has appeared to all humans (*epephanē gar hē charis tou theou sōtērios pasin anthrōpois*) in order to educate us (*paideuousa hēmas*), so that by rejecting impiety and worldly passions, we might live in this age soberly, righteously, and piously."[63] Here, God's gift in Christ is itself the instrument of transforming humans from savage to civilized.

If Paul was not professionally trained in rhetoric or philosophy, it by no means follows that he was completely ignorant with respect to either. Both rhetoric and philosophy in Paul's day were "in the air" culturally in a manner difficult to imagine in an age when higher learning tends to hide itself in academic institutions. Sophists (professional rhetoricians) gave public

61. For *paidagogos*, see also Gal 3:24; for "guardians and trustees" of children, see Gal 4:2; for Paul as "father" of the community to which he writes, see 1 Thess 2:11.

62. On these commonplaces, see now D. White, *Teacher of the Nations*, and Hauge and Pitts, *Ancient Education and Early Christianity*.

63. My translation. I take the participle *paideuousa* as expressing purpose, giving it the full value of its ancient educational resonances, which go far beyond "training." For discussion, see L. Johnson, *Letters to Paul's Delegates*, 236-41.

declamations, often in the presence of considerable crowds; plaintiffs and defendants argued their cases in public trials; even some popular philosophers taught in the open air. We should not be surprised, then, to find the diaspora Jew Paul, despite having his own "higher education" in Jewish law, able to make use of the sort of rhetorical and philosophical conventions that were so readily available, even to those who were, in terms of higher education, *idiōtai*.

## Rhetoric[64]

From beginning to end, Greco-Roman culture had a highly rhetorical character, as the speeches in ancient epics and dramas already show.[65] Speaking well in public carried over into writing well: oral and literary expression were intricately intertwined, since writing was dictated and literature was read aloud.[66] Letter writing is the perfect illustration: many ancient letters were dictated to a secretary (*amanuensis*)—actual *writing* in the physical sense tended to be regarded as menial labor—and, when delivered to a recipient, were read aloud rather than silently. Many letters thus had a semipublic character simply through the process of their production.[67]

Sophists or orators in the Greco-Roman world enjoyed considerable public esteem, whether their skill was displayed in the law court in behalf of a client, or at a festival as part of the celebration, or as a spokesman seeking to mediate between cities. Plutarch's *Parallel Lives* singles out Demosthenes among the Greeks and Cicero among the Romans as preeminent in the art of public speaking, but they stood among many others who spoke for pay, and aspects of rhetorical art certainly permeated the wider culture.[68] Plato considered rhetoric to be so powerful—and dangerous—that he devoted three dialogues to it (*Protagoras, Gorgias, Phaedrus*). Aristotle, in turn, gave such close attention to the goals and means of rhetoric (*Rhetoric*)[69] that

64. For an overview, see G. Kennedy, *Classical Rhetoric*; Gunderson, *Ancient Rhetoric*; Habinek, *Ancient Rhetoric and Oratory*.

65. See Knudsen, *Homeric Speech*; Woodruff, "Rhetoric and Tragedy."

66. See Robbins, *Tapestry of Early Christian Discourse*.

67. Cicero's letters provide the outstanding example (e.g., *Letters to Atticus* 7.13, 8.13, 10.3, 11.24, 13.25); see Blumell, "Scribes and Ancient Letters"; see also Stowers, *Letter Writing*.

68. For a sense, see the two works by Philostratus, *Lives of the Sophists* and *Apollonius of Tyana*.

69. See Gross and Walzer, *Rereading Aristotle's Rhetoric*.

his systematic analysis needed only to be elaborated and modified by later theoreticians like Cicero (*On Invention, Brutus, On Oratory, The Orator*).[70]

Rhetoric was essentially about persuasion: a speaker sought a response from listeners. In forensic speech, a decision of guilt or innocence was sought concerning past actions. In epideictic speech, praise or blame was sought for present circumstances. Deliberative rhetoric sought a decision concerning future action. Forensic attacked or defended a client; epideictic praised or derided a person or populace or monument or practice; deliberative pushed for good or bad action. The production of an effective speech involved five stages: invention (the finding or crafting of proofs/evidence); arrangement (putting the argument into proper form); style (using the language appropriate to speaker, occasion, and audience); memorization (important for oral presentation); and delivery (in a voice strong enough to reach the back rows).

Although the last four elements most affected the experience of the hearers, the real meat of good rhetoric was invention. Here Aristotle speaks of three kinds of argument: those based on logic and analysis (*logos*), those based on the character of the speaker (*ēthos*), and those based on an appeal to feeling (*pathos*). Here again, *ēthos* and *pathos* arguments probably were most effective in the actual delivery of speeches, while *logos* arguments (where the proofs/evidence are worked out) make the most direct impact on the reader of a speech that has been committed to writing.

Greco-Roman rhetorical handbooks went into considerable detail on all these aspects and laid out an ideal arrangement or structure for the various types of rhetoric, with each section of the speech identified and described.[71] But real life does not usually follow the prescriptions of textbooks, and in the actual speeches of orators like Cicero and Aelius Aristides, one can find the various *elements* identified by the handbooks, but seldom if ever in the sort of mechanical *arrangement* they recommend. The same can be said of the handbooks that identified and described various letter types: the friendly letter, the advisory letter, the letter of rebuke.[72] Epistolary conventions reflected

70. The work *To Herennius* is usually regarded as spurious. See May, *Brill's Companion to Cicero*, and for Roman oratory as a whole, see Dominik and Hall, *Companion to Roman Rhetoric*.

71. Above all in the twelve-volume *Institutes of Oratory* by Quintilian (35–100 CE); it is, in truth, a treatise on education from childhood to full participation in the life of the state; see Smail, *Quintilian on Education*.

72. See Malherbe, *Ancient Epistolary Theorists*; there is an analogy to types of letters formerly learned by grade-school children: the business letter, the letter of congratulation, the condolence letter.

and reinscribed social relationships between correspondents—a friendship letter, for example, could be written between social equals but not between unequals, like parents and children.[73] But again, real-life letters did not always follow such conventions, or followed them only partially.

The realization that Paul wrote his letters within such a tradition of Greco-Roman rhetoric was a significant awakening among contemporary scholars to an awareness that was not altogether lacking among earlier interpreters (such as John Calvin). As with other such "new" discoveries, certain scholars have allowed their enthusiasm to outrun the evidence, leading to efforts to systematically apply handbook recommendations for arrangement to Paul's arguments.[74] Such efforts sometimes hit the mark, but often did not, forcing Paul's arguments into handbook-derived procrustean beds. Far more important is the now common—and correct—perception that Paul's letters are, in fact, *rhetorical instruments*—that is, they are written not as immediate or impulsive outpourings that disclose his personality but as carefully crafted arguments that seek to persuade his audience (readers). This is, indeed, a major accomplishment, one that puts the interpretation of his letters on a proper footing.

Taken as a whole, then, Paul's letters are all examples of deliberative rhetoric. The dominant interest in each of them is persuading readers not about the rightness or wrongness of the past, not about the praise- or blameworthy character of the present, but about making right decisions concerning the future. Paul seeks to change the direction his readers are taking (or to reinforce the correct dispositions most of them already have): even a superficial reading makes clear that this is the case in 1 and 2 Corinthians, 1 and 2 Thessalonians, Philemon, Philippians, Colossians, 1 Timothy, 2 Timothy, Titus). Ephesians and Romans are less taken up with local circumstances, and therefore less easy to categorize, though both surely fit more easily into the category of deliberative rhetoric than forensic or epideictic. Galatians has been read as forensic rhetoric—with Paul's "self-defense" the salient factor[75]—but it also is more deliberative than forensic: Paul seeks, after all, to convince his readers in the Galatian churches to live in peace and cease agitating for circumcision. This does not mean that one type of

---

73. Stowers, "Social Typification."

74. An influential example is Betz, *Galatians*; less impact has been made by the series of "socio-rhetorical" commentaries by Ben Witherington III, including *1 and 2 Thessalonians* and *Paul's Letter to the Philippians*.

75. As in Betz, *Galatians*.

oratory cannot contain elements of other types: Paul's remarks about himself in Gal 1-2 and 2 Cor 10-12 certainly have the feel of an apologia, and parts of Romans (notably chaps. 5 and 8) and Ephesians (especially chap. 1) could be excerpted and read as epideictic.

In terms of invention, Paul's letters display abundant appeals to *logos* argumentation. Most obvious here are the first eleven chapters of Romans, which—apart from its epistolary elements—resembles the scholastic diatribe,[76] with its thesis (1:16-17), antithesis (1:18-3:20), restatement of thesis (3:21-31), exemplum (4:1-25), demonstration (5:1-21), and response to objections (6:1-11:36). Such a formal mode of argumentation, together with the stylistic elements associated in the Greco-Roman world with diatribal discourse and the intense midrashic engagement with Scripture, makes Romans the clearest evidence for my position that a Pauline school was at work in the production of his correspondence even during his lifetime. Other examples of strong *logos* argumentation are Gal 3-4 and 1 Cor 12-15. Appeals to the character of the speaker (*ēthos* argumentation) are found in 1 Thess 1-3, Gal 1-2, and throughout 2 Corinthians, which is best read as a species of *ēthos* argument.[77] Paul also makes appeal to the feelings of his readers through *pathos* arguments, as in Gal 4 and 2 Tim 4.[78]

As I have suggested, trying to fit Paul's letters into the forms of arrangement recommended by ancient rhetorical handbooks is a hazardous undertaking. Certainly Romans, distinctive in this as in almost every other respect within the corpus, comes closest to the sort of formal arrangement advanced by such authorities as Quintilian. In contrast, several of Paul's letters convincingly correspond to the conventions of letter types prescribed by epistolary handbooks. While never using the word *philia* ("friendship"), for example, Philippians evokes all the associations with friendship common in the culture and can be regarded as a "friendly letter."[79] Philemon (and Rom 16) has the elements of ancient commendatory letters (or letters of recommendation).[80] Second Timothy is the most perfect example from antiquity of a personal paraenetic letter,[81] while 1 Timothy and Titus can be read as examples of *mandata principis* letters—letters from superiors to delegates.[82]

---

76. Stowers, *Diatribe*; L. Johnson, *Reading Romans*.

77. See Stegman, *Character of Jesus*.

78. See Kraftchick, "Ethos and Pathos Arguments."

79. See several of the essays in Fitzgerald, *Friendship*.

80. Stowers, *Letter Writing*.

81. L. Johnson, *First and Second Letters to Timothy*, 320-24.

82. Fiore, *Function of Personal Example*; Wolter, *Pastoralbriefe als Paulustradition*, 137-41.

Here, as in other cases, we find that statements applying to some set of Paul's letters do not necessarily apply to others.[83] First and Second Corinthians, Galatians, Colossians, Ephesians, 1 and 2 Thessalonians do not display in any clear fashion a correspondence to ancient letter types.

In short, we find in Paul's letters precisely the sort of rhetorical influences we might expect in a diaspora Jew who had only a limited higher education on the Greek side despite serious technical study in Scripture. Paul expresses disdain for the pretensions and arrogance of the *sophoi*, and employs only so much of their art as would be readily available to one who had moved through the earlier stages of education, and who was alert to the public life that surrounded him.

## Philosophy[84]

What I have sketched concerning rhetoric applies substantially to philosophy as well, which Paul explicitly warns the Colossians against (Col 2:18), and which would surely be included in his contempt for the "wisdom of this age," which God made foolish through the proclamation of the cross of Christ (1 Cor 1:20–21). As in the case of rhetoric as well, Paul's dismissal of philosophy, and his status as an *idiōtēs* (2 Cor 11:6) without formal training in philosophy, does not mean that he was unaffected, even if indirectly, by so conspicuous a feature of first-century Mediterranean culture.

In the early empire, the four great schools of philosophy continued to gather students and teach according to the traditions of their founders: the Academy of Plato, the Lyceum of Aristotle, the Garden of Epicurus, and the Porch of Zeno. Indeed, in a wonderful example of what we mean by "Greco-Roman," the philosopher-emperor Marcus Aurelius, a devotee of the Greek Stoic philosopher Epictetus, in 176 CE gave Roman funding for the four chairs of philosophy in Athens. Adherents of these schools engaged in vigorous polemic across ideological lines.[85] But the ancient schools were vari-

83. Some letters evade easy categorization: Malherbe (*Letters to the Thessalonians*) judges that 1 Thessalonians is a pastoral paraenetic letter, but Abraham Smith (*Comfort One Another*) regards it as a letter of consolation.

84. For overviews, see Copleston, *History of Philosophy*, vol. 1; Long, *Hellenistic Philosophy*; Long and Sedley, *Hellenistic Philosophers*; Reale, *History of Ancient Philosophy*; Nussbaum, *Therapy of Desire*; Sharples, *Stoics, Epicureans and Skeptics*.

85. Sometimes the attacks were substantive, as in Plutarch's *Against Colotes* and *On*

ously influenced by Pythagoreanism, Skepticism, and Cynicism, as well as by other factors, so that even formal philosophy had a more eclectic character after the passage of centuries: the "middle Platonism" that we find in Philo and Plutarch, for example, is some distance from the dialogues of Plato himself,[86] and in the early empire, Stoicism was infected by Cynicism, so that the descriptor of "Cynic-Stoic" is often applied to a teacher like Epictetus.[87] The one school that was genially despised by all the others was Epicureanism, yet despite professional scorn, it too had its adherents and found admirers (like the Stoic Seneca) in unexpected quarters.[88] It is a tedious business to sort out all the possible antecedents to a philosopher's statements in the period between Cicero and Marcus Aurelius, for theoretical purity or consistency was not really the point of the philosophers' task in the early Roman Empire.

The fact of empire—beginning already with the Hellenistic empire—affected philosophy in profound ways. Whereas thinkers like Plato or Aristotle, living in the city-state of Athens, could compose treatises on the ideal state[89] and engage in theoretical disquisitions on the nature of reality,[90] conditions of life in the empire encouraged a turn to the question of how to be a good person in an alienating and often frightening environment; philosophy made a turn from theory to therapy. The philosopher's concern became the shaping of good character within the household and within the individual person. Thus, the analysis of virtue and vice became central, with the object of moral discourse being persons' leaving a life of vice and turning to a life of virtue. Because of this focus, the acute dissection of these characterological habits by Aristotle—especially in the *Nicomachean Ethics*—was widely deployed.[91]

---

*Stoic Self-Contradictions*; other times, simple slander was employed; see L. Johnson, "New Testament's Anti-Jewish Slander."

86. See Berchman, *From Philo to Origen*; Boys-Stones, *Platonist Philosophy*; Wolfson, *Philo*; Dillon, *Middle Platonists*.

87. For the Cynics, see Branham and Goulet-Cazé, *Cynics*; for Epictetus, see Hersbell, "Stoicism of Epictetus."

88. The poet Lucretius (90–55 BCE) wrote his influential *De rerum natura* as an exposition and praise of Epicurus's teaching, and in the eighteenth century, some thirty-six treatises of the Epicurean philosopher Philodemus of Gadara (ca. 110–40 BCE) were discovered in the ruins of Herculaneum, some in multiple copies. Herculaneum was destroyed with Pompeii when Mount Vesuvius erupted in 79 CE.

89. As in Plato's *Republic* and *Laws*; as in Aristotle's *Politics*.

90. As in Plato's *Phaedo, Timaeus*, and *Theaetetus*; as in Aristotle's *On Generation and Corruption, Physics*, and *Metaphysics*.

91. E.g., in the *Moralia* of Plutarch: see *On Virtue and Vice, On Envy and Hate, On Brotherly Love*.

Philosophy at the time of Paul, in fact, bore a strong resemblance to present-day cognitive psychology. Right ideas led to right affections and right actions; bad ideas led to distorted affections and destructive behavior. Certain metaphors were regularly employed: one was educational, emphasizing the aspect of training and discipline inherent in *paideia*; a second was athletic, emphasizing again training and hard labor in preparation for the Olympic contest that was life; the third—and perhaps most dominant—was medical, in which virtue was health and vice was sickness, the philosophical school was a hospital, and the philosopher was a doctor who diagnosed sickness and showed the way to health.

Paul's letters provide no evidence that he was any more educated formally in philosophy than he was in rhetoric. They do not exhibit conformity to a single philosophical school, in this quite unlike the consistently Platonic worldview—modified by Semitic cosmology—found in Philo of Alexandria and the Letter to the Hebrews. Platonism was the default philosophical framework of early Christianity, but while Paul's letters here and there might exhibit some tinges of Platonism—think of his tripartite psychology in 1 Thess 5:23, or his language concerning being out of the body and with Christ in 2 Cor 5:1–5—they remain only faint allusions rather than a consistent framework for interpreting the world. The reason why Platonism served ancient Jews and Christians so well was its ability to translate the biblical cosmology of "heaven and earth" into a contrast between "spiritual and material." Certainly, later Christian interpreters often read Paul through such a lens, making sense of a passage like that concerning Paul's ascent into the third heaven (2 Cor 12:1–10) within a more pronounced Platonic framework than one employed by Paul himself.[92]

Most decisively, Paul's anthropological language does not agree with the Platonic dualism of body and soul (above all in the *Phaedo*), which sees the body as a shell from which the soul seeks escape.[93] When Paul speaks of the flesh and spirit, he does not mean parts of a human composite, but rather a mode of behavior measured simply in human terms, and a mode of life measured by the reality of God's Spirit (Gal 5:16–26; 1 Cor 15:50; Rom 7:14–8:26; Eph 4:17–32; Col 2:16–23). And the body is not to be shed in the resurrection, but is to be transformed (1 Cor 15:35–49).

Traces of Epicureanism or Aristotelianism are even less in evidence. Paul's advice to the Thessalonians to "live quietly and to mind your own affairs" (1 Thess 4:11, adapted) might be taken, as I have observed earlier, as

92. See Wallace, *Snatched into Paradise*.
93. See *Phaedo* 62B, 64E, 67A–B; also *Gorgias* 493C; *Cratylus* 400C.

an echo of the Epicurean slogan,[94] but note that it is followed by the instruction "to work with your hands," which not only is a Pharisaic ideal[95] but also would be unthinkable to the aristocratic members of the Garden.[96] Similarly, the sort of abstinence from the politics of the larger world found in Paul's letters could be seen as expressing an Epicurean posture, but it equally could be understood as the natural instinct of a sect in its first stages of existence. As for Aristotelianism, Paul's letters reflect the widespread employment of the great philosopher's analysis of emotions and moral habits. Thus, the friendship diction of Philippians and the fellowship diction of 1 Corinthians find a basis in books 8 and 9 of the *Nicomachean Ethics*, just as Paul's understanding of rivalry and envy as corrosive of friendship and fellowship can be found in the *Rhetoric* (1387B). But Paul shows no signs of having derived them from reading the works of Aristotle. It is far more likely that he made such connections through contact with the ambient moral discourse of the age.

A long-standing and recently renewed argument has been made for the influence of Stoic philosophy on Paul. Once more, however, the evidence consists mainly in a number of phrases in some of Paul's letters and in the (rather remarkable) resemblance in sensibility between some parts of Paul and the *Discourses* of the Cynic-Stoic teacher Epictetus. Thus, in several of his letters, Paul uses the term *syneidēsis* ("conscience") for the human capacity for internal discernment (see Rom 2:15; 9:1; 13:5; 1 Cor 8:7, 10, 12; 10:25, 27, 28, 29; 2 Cor 1:12; 4:2; 5:11; 1 Tim 1:5, 19; 3:9; 4:2; 2 Tim 1:3; Titus 1:15), employing it as roughly equivalent to the scriptural term *kardia* ("heart"; see Rom 1:21, 24; 2:15, 29; 1 Cor 7:37; 2 Cor 9:7; 1 Tim 1:5). Similarly, in chapters 1–2 of Romans, Paul uses "nature" (*physis*) in a manner that echoes the Stoic slogan for moral behavior "according to nature" (*kata physin*; Rom 1:26; 2:14, 27; see also 1 Cor 11:14), while also employing the terms *para physin* and *kata physin* in a nonmoral sense in Rom 11:21 and 11:24.[97] The argument that Paul's

---

94. Epicurus's *Sovereign Maxims* 14 reads, "When tolerable security against our fellow men is attained, then on a basis of power sufficient to afford support and material prosperity arises in most genuine form the security of a quiet private life withdrawn from the multitude." Translation by R. D. Hicks in Diogenes Laertius, *Lives of Eminent Philosophers*, LCL 185 (Cambridge: Harvard University Press, 1979). See DeWitt, *St. Paul and Epicurus*.

95. Pharisees and some Greco-Roman teachers advocated manual labor as an appropriate setting for moral teaching; see Hock, *Social Context*.

96. Not to mention that a chapter later (1 Thess 5:23) Paul speaks of the Thessalonians' "body, soul, and spirit," which the materialist Epicureans never would.

97. The uses of *physis* in Gal 2:15; 4:8; and Eph 2:3 have no discernible resemblance to Stoicism.

term for "spirit" (*pneuma*) resembles Stoicism because it is not, for him, an entirely nonmaterial reality fails to convince both because everything else in Paul's cosmology (and eschatology!) is so at odds with the doctrines of the Stoic school, and because the more obvious source for Paul's language is the Septuagint.[98] For the doctrines of Stoicism, as for those of the other Greek philosophical schools, the best that can be said is that Paul picked and chose what was useful, or, perhaps better, made use of what he had picked up here and there. In this sense, when it comes to philosophy, the characterization of Paul at the Areopagus in Athens by the Stoics and Epicureans—according to Acts 17:18—as *spermologos* ("someone who has picked up bits of knowledge") is not entirely unfair.

In another way, however, Paul can justly be placed among the philosophers of the early empire, but not because he adhered to—or even had much real knowledge of—the doctrines of the various schools, for his "doctrines" were entirely derived from the world of Torah reshaped by the experience of the crucified and raised Messiah Jesus. Paul can be considered a philosopher because he shared the sense of mission, the passion, and the intense focus on forming moral character among his readers. It is precisely here that we find the truly remarkable resemblance between Paul and the Cynic-Stoic philosopher Epictetus, not in doctrine, but in sensibility.

A reader coming to Epictetus from the reading of Paul is startled by the ways in which his "homilies" to the students of his philosophical school resemble stylistically the elements that have been identified as "diatribal" in some of Paul's letters: the development of a thesis, the use of personification, speaking to an imagined interlocutor, asking rhetorical questions, using hyperbole, answering objections, employing vivid examples from life and from classic texts. Even more, the reader is impressed by the passion to teach, indeed to transform, his audience, so that the discourses are far from dry disquisitions: they are filled with urgency, for Epictetus makes clear that the very health of his hearers is at stake.

It is above all in Epictetus's *Discourse* 3.22, "On the Ideal Cynic," that the resemblance to Paul is greatest.[99] Epictetus did not expect all his students to meet the ideal he sketches; indeed, he considers the true philosopher to be a rare phenomenon. It is not a matter of wearing a long beard and distinctive

98. Engberg-Pedersen, *Cosmology and Self*.
99. For other representations of the true philosopher, see Dio Chrysostom, *Oration* 77/78; Julian, *Oration* 6 and 7; and Lucian's *Demonax* and *Nigrinus*.

gear (staff and wallet), or of simply being unpleasant to passers-by. The true Cynic is called by God to be a scout or messenger to the people, with purity of intention (without unworthy motives) and with a thorough preparation of body and mind. The philosopher is himself a person of virtue and offers himself as an example of virtue, free of the love of pleasure (*philēdonē*), love of possessions (*philargyria*), and love of human praise (*philodoxia*). He lives a life of freedom (*eleutheria*) and free speech (*parrhēsia*) answerable only to his own conscience and unafraid of human opinion.

The ideal philosopher serves humanity by showing it the path to health and virtue, turning it away from vice and sickness. He speaks candidly, sometimes with gentleness, sometimes with harshness, according to circumstance, but always with the intention to save those plunging to their own self-destruction through ignorance and vice. Such an "open air" life, such availability, demands of the Cynic that he live without spouse or children, in order to be available to all. It also means that the philosopher can expect rejection and suffering at the hands of those who do not appreciate being spoken to so frankly. And, in fact, exile was a common lot for these moralistic philosophers: Cicero, Seneca, Musonius Rufus, Epictetus, and Dio Chrysostom all experienced exile ordered by the emperor. Preaching freedom and free speech made each of them, at least for a time, "enemies of the Roman Order."[100]

Paul recounts his first visit among the Thessalonians by emphasizing the ways in which he did not come with deceit, impure motives, and trickery; did not seek to please humans but sought to please only God; did not come with flattery; did not seek wealth or praise (1 Thess 2:1–6). He says he was gentle among them like a nurse tenderly caring for her children (2:7) and was among them like a father with his children (2:11). Each is a note that could be—and was—struck by the popular philosophers.[101] Likewise, Paul's claim to have contentment (*autarkeia*, "self-control") in Phil 4:11 and his instructions on the same topic in 1 Tim 6:6–10 are immediately familiar to those who have studied the Greco-Roman moral philosophers.[102] Above all, when Paul is read as a moral teacher who sought to form right thinking and right behavior among his readers, he is read in the way the popular philosophers of the early empire should be read.

100. See MacMullen, *Enemies of the Roman Order*.
101. See Malherbe, *Paul and the Thessalonians*.
102. L. Johnson, *Letters to Timothy*.

## Religion[103]

The Paul of the letter displays none of the irenic disposition toward gentile religiosity suggested by the Areopagus speech in Acts 17:22–31. For Paul as a diaspora Jew, all gentile forms of religion are idolatry, which derives from a fundamental rejection of God's claim on human existence and the darkening of the mind that leads humans to shape gods according to their desires; such idolatry is the basis of every form of vice (Rom 1:18–32).[104] Idolatry must be left behind if believers are to "serve the living and true God" (1 Thess 1:9 NABRE); they must abandon the passions of lust that characterize the "heathens who do not know God" (1 Thess 4:5) and are without hope in the face of death (1 Thess 4:13). He tells his gentile converts in the churches of Galatia, "Formerly, when you did not know God, you were in bondage to beings who by nature are not gods . . . weak and elemental spirits" (Gal 4:8–9, adapted), and lists "idolatry" as one of the "works of the flesh" (Gal 5:19–20). In Ephesians, Paul sketches the readers' gentile past as one of following "the price of the power of the air, the spirit who is now at work among the sons of disobedience," which involved them in unruly passions and desires (2:2–3, adapted); they were like people with "no hope and without God in the world" (Eph 2:12). In Col 2:20 he reminds his readers that with their baptism they have "died to the elemental spirits" and are called to live according to this new identity rather than according to the vices "in [which] you once walked" in idolatry (Col 3:5–7).

Paul's disdain for gentile religion and morals is patent in the Corinthian correspondence. He rebukes readers for tolerating a form of sexual immorality "of a sort not heard of even among Gentiles" (1 Cor 5:1, author's translation). He acknowledges that there may be "so-called gods in heaven or on earth—as indeed there are many gods and lords—yet for us there is one God" (1 Cor 8:5–6, adapted). Clearly under the influence of the LXX translation of Ps 96:5 ("the gods of the nations are demons"), Paul warns against participating in meals at pagan shrines: "What do I imply then? That food offered to idols is anything, or that an idol is anything? No, I imply that what pagans sacrifice they offer to demons and not to God. I do not want you to be partakers with demons. You cannot drink the cup of the Lord and the cup of demons. You cannot partake of the table of the Lord and the table of

---

103. For an overview, see L. Johnson, *Among the Gentiles*, 1–6, 158–64.

104. The passage resembles the attack on idolatry in Wis 14:1–28 but is even more scathing: they are "without excuse."

demons" (1 Cor 10:19–21, RSV adapted). And in 2 Cor 6:14–18 he calls for an absolute rejection of everything associated with idolatry. It is not clear how much Paul actually knew about gentile religion, but it is certain that he did not in the least like what he did know.

But is it possible that Paul was, consciously or unconsciously, influenced by the Greek and Roman mysteries, which formed a significant element in the religious environment in Antioch and the other cities in which he worked, especially in his ideas about the death and resurrection of Jesus, and in the practice of baptism and the Lord's Supper? A long tradition of Protestant anti-Catholic polemic, which Jonathan Z. Smith calls "Pagano-Papism," regarded early Christianity as corrupted by such Greco-Roman influences, beginning already with Paul.[105] More sober historical research, however, calls into question any such influence or dependence.[106] The same can be said for theories that Paul employed an existent proto-gnostic "myth of the redeemed redeemer" as the pattern for his Christology.[107] We have seen earlier that Paul "invents" neither the belief in the resurrection nor the sacraments; both were elements of the Christian tradition before him, not only in Antioch, but in Palestine as well.[108] And the recent effort to align the Lord's Supper with Greco-Roman meals for the dead fails as miserably as did older attempts to connect baptism to the Mithras cult.[109]

In another way, however, Paul can be seen to exemplify a certain kind of religious sensibility, which is also attested among gentiles. Leaving aside those in the Greco-Roman world who were simply profane and unconcerned about religion,[110] or who rejected religion altogether,[111] or who manipulated the religion of others as charlatans,[112] or mocked excessive religiosity,[113] we can identify four basic types of religiosity (or religious temperament) among

105. J. Smith, *Drudgery Divine*, 1–35, 114–15.
106. See esp. L. Johnson, *Among the Gentiles*.
107. E.g., Yamauchi, *Pre-Christian Gnosticism*.
108. See the discussion in chap. 4, under "Paul as Founder of Christianity."
109. See my response to Jonathan Z. Smith in L. Johnson "Meals Are Where the Magic Is."
110. Such are the thoroughly profane characters Encolpius and Giton in Petronius's *Satyrika* (see 75, 79, 83–85, 95, 96, 100, 101, 128), and the language of the mysteries for a sexual orgy (16–18).
111. This, notoriously, was the reputation of Epicurus, celebrated as well by his admirer, the poet Lucretius.
112. We are grateful that the second-century satirist Lucian of Samosata turned his brilliance toward such cases in *The Passing of Peregrinus* and *The False Prophet*.
113. The portrait of the "Superstitious Man" by Aristotle's contemporary Theophrastus in his *Characters* is exquisite.

Paul's non-Jewish neighbors, depending on how they perceived of divine power and its purpose.[114]

By far the greatest number of religious gentiles fell into a category I term "participation in divine benefits": the constant round of festivals and feasts, of sacrifices and prayers, of temples and shrines, of miracles and prophecies, were based on the conviction that the divine power (distributed among any number of divine beings) was accessible through such means and led to safety and success in life. This type of religiosity was not restricted to the uneducated or unsophisticated; one of the most learned and accomplished rhetoricians of the second century CE, Aelius Aristides, fits into this category perfectly.[115]

A second sort of religiosity is affirming of participation in benefits but does not place its emphasis on their enjoyment. It perceives the divine power as immanent within humans, leading them to change themselves and the world. I designate this type as "religion as moral transformation." The supreme example is Paul's contemporary Epictetus, who affirmed and celebrated the entire round of religious participation but insisted on the necessity for moral change.[116]

Another ancient stream of religiosity, with roots in Pythagorean and Orphic traditions, dismissed everything based in material reality and saw value in the cultivation and ultimately the liberation of the soul. This third type I call "religion as transcending the world," and it manifested itself above all in the Hermetic literature.[117]

A fourth sort of religious disposition, which I designate as "stabilizing the world," is found mostly among those representing the "supply side" of the first type: these are the people who are the benefactors of religious festivals, who function as priests and keepers of temples. They tend to regard religion as a matter of civic duty, of maintaining the "city of gods and men" that constituted Greco-Roman civilization. Plutarch of Chaeronea, who was priest of the temple of Apollo at Delphi, is the perfect spokesperson for this sensibility.

It is noteworthy that all these "ways of being religious" are attested as well in Paul's Jewish world—indeed, the four types may be found even more widely in later Christianity and in other religious traditions as well.[118] And if

114. See L. Johnson, *Among the Gentiles*, 32–49.
115. See L. Johnson, *Among the Gentiles*, 50–63.
116. See L. Johnson, *Among the Gentiles*, 64–78.
117. See L. Johnson, *Among the Gentiles*, 79–92.
118. See L. Johnson, *Among the Gentiles*, 111–75.

Paul is placed within this typology, he clearly fits within "religion as moral transformation." He not only is positive toward all the ways in which the divine power is at work in the empirical world, and makes startling claims to the experience of such power both for himself and for his readers (more on that in the next chapter). But he ultimately regards such power not merely as the means to salvation but above all as the impetus to a profound moral transformation for individuals and communities as a whole. In this respect as well, Paul's resemblance to the religious fervor and moral passion of Epictetus is most striking.

## Conclusion

As a diaspora Jew who wrote in Greek and read Scripture in Greek, and who proclaimed Jesus in thoroughly Hellenized cities, Paul can legitimately be called a Hellenistic Jew. But in contrast to Philo, Josephus, and other Hellenized Jews, the designation must be heavily qualified in Paul's case. His letters show at best a conventional attitude toward imperial power. They disclose that he knew only a few taglines from Greek literature. He had a rudimentary knowledge of Greek education, rhetoric, philosophy, and religion. Concerning rhetoric, philosophy, and religion, moreover, his disdain is explicit. He shows himself to be what he claims to be, a nonprofessional (*idiōtēs*) in these elements of Greco-Roman culture. His knowledge and deployment of rhetorical and philosophical commonplaces are precisely of the sort that we would expect of a person exposed to the larger culture, even in many ways immersed in it, but nevertheless far from explicitly embracing any dimension of it. But although Paul was neither a lover of Greco-Roman culture nor a professional practitioner within it, the pervasiveness and power of that culture is evident everywhere in his letters to those who have taken the time to study this aspect of Paul's world.

*Part 3*

# THE ELEMENTS

*Chapter 8*

# The Claims of Experience

Considered as ancient religious literature, the canonical letters of Paul are distinctive—as a collection, perhaps even unique—in the role played in them by experience, both individual and communal, both ordinary and extraordinary. What Paul himself and what his communities have experienced and are experiencing at the time of his writing is a constant and dominant feature of his correspondence. Even Epictetus, who we have seen resembles Paul in remarkable ways, only provides passing glimpses of his own life.[1] And while Plato's dialogues show the many sides of Socrates's wit and wisdom, only his trial and death form the substance of Plato's philosophical reflections,[2] and of Plato's own experience we learn virtually nothing.[3]

Similarly, among Paul's Jewish contemporaries, we find nothing like the experiential element in Paul's letters. Philo provides only some tantalizing suggestions about his religious experience, but with no indication that or how it affected his thought.[4] Josephus provides readers quite a lot of information about his life, but apart from his changed perspective on the

---

1. See, e.g., *Discourses* 1.16.15–20, 3.5.7–11.

2. The difficulties of disentangling the "historical Socrates" from the contemporary attack by Aristophanes (*The Clouds*), the admiring but not entirely harmonious writings of his students Xenophon and Plato, and the half-legendary biography of Diogenes Laertius, are notorious. See, e.g., Stone, *Trial of Socrates*.

3. Plato's thirteen letters, the authenticity of which have had as long a history of debate as disputes about Paul's letters, offer considerable biographical information, especially concerning relations with political leaders. Aristotle notoriously eliminates anything about his own experience from his writings. As for Epicurus, his *Sovereign Maxims*, at least, appears as a prophylactic against troubling experiences. While the letters of Cicero and Seneca tell us a considerable amount about their personal experience, their reports are largely pedestrian in character and have little connection to their philosophical positions.

4. See, e.g., *On the Creation of the World* 71 and *On the Cherubim* 48.

Jewish War, his experiences do not deeply affect his account. At Qumran, the *hodayoth* arise from and reflect on the singer's relationship with God,[5] but there is little else of an experiential dimension in the writings of the sectarians.[6] The contrast to Paul's letters is sharp; in them, the experiential pervades everything.

I suggested in chapter 5 that Paul is best considered as a prophetic Jew, and the prophets of Israel—above all Hosea and Jeremiah and Ezekiel, all of whom mined their own experience as witness to God's work in the world—provide the best comparison to Paul.[7] There are dissimilarities: Paul writes in Greek rather than Hebrew; he writes letters in prose rather than reciting poetic oracles; unlike Isaiah and Jeremiah and Ezekiel, he does not, with the singular exception of 2 Cor 12:1–5, describe an ecstatic state. But he is very much like the ancient prophets in his perception of the living God at work here and now in his own life and in the lives of his congregants, and in his use of his own and their experience to bear witness to God and to elucidate God's will in the world.

Together with the occasional and circumstantial character of Paul's correspondence, this constant engagement with experience, past, present, and anticipated in the future, gives his letters their intensely dynamic energy and defies any pretense of treating Paul as though he were a systematic theologian whose letters were only the opportunity to work out some further wrinkle in an elaborate and fully formulated (in his mind at least) body of doctrine. Paul is instead an existential thinker, who is driven by powerful experiences of, well, power, to interpret and reinterpret his symbolic world—above all the world imagined by Scripture. To miss the dialectical character of his thought is to miss Paul altogether. He does not move deductively from the premises of Scripture to an application to Jesus as an expected Messiah. Rather, the shattering experience of the crucified and exalted Jesus—an experience mediated to believers through the power of the Holy Spirit—demands that everything in Scripture be read anew, in light of this "new creation" (2 Cor 5:17; Gal 6:15).[8]

I am convinced that it is impossible to engage Paul's letters adequately without dealing with this dimension, which is both multifaceted and com-

5. See, e.g., Thanksgiving Hymns (1QH) 2.7–35, 3.7–29, 4.33–38, 5.12–36, 7.1–27.

6. Except to the degree that the sectarian spirit of the community may have roots in the experience of despoliation at the hands of the "wicked Priest" in Jerusalem (see, e.g., Pesher Habakkuk [1QpHab] 8.8–12, 11.1–6, 12.9–12).

7. For a discussion of the religious experiences of the prophets, see L. Johnson, *Miracles*.

8. Unless otherwise indicated, Scripture quotations in this chapter are from the NABRE.

plex. In this chapter I try to provide some sense of what the claims of experience are in his correspondence. But first I must deal at least briefly with the persistent (if irritating) objections that are sometimes made to even taking this element into account.

## Objections to the Experiential

Biblical scholars and theologians tend to grow nervous when the topic of experience arises, especially when the term "religious experience" enters the conversation. In part, such restlessness may be ascribed to their inhabiting the flattened universe of the Enlightenment, which views all individual and particular instances—as opposed to general laws and principles—with suspicion; "experience" seems to them to be too slippery for analysis, too subjective.[9] But in equal part, their discomfort is based on the simple fact that they are scholars and theologians, who much prefer the *logos* to be displayed neatly and unequivocally, without being confused by the messy stuff of embodied existence. This bias helps account for the way in which "Pauline theology" tends to be based on Romans, not only because of its length, but above all for its apparent systematic character[10]—ignoring the facts that the letter is generated by the desire to raise travel funds for a mission to Spain (Rom 1:13–15; 15:23–16:2) and is based on Paul's recent experience founding churches in the East and the collection he took up for the saints in Jerusalem (15:15–22: his personal experience), and that the argument of the letter hinges on his readers' experience of the Holy Spirit active among them (5:5; 6:1–11; 8:9–17, 26–27).

I have tried in a number of other publications to define and defend the notion of religious experience.[11] It needs definition and defense because it is not an easy topic, for the very reasons I have already stated: scholars inherit a worldview in which experience is assigned little cognitive significance,

---

9. It is difficult to overemphasize the influence of David Hume's essay "On Miracles" in *An Inquiry Concerning Human Understanding* (1748), in which he excludes from consideration any claim to individual experience that "violates" the "laws of nature," which are, in effect, the ordinary experiences of the majority of people the majority of the time.

10. Cf., e.g., Bultmann, *Theology of the New Testament*; Beker, *Paul the Apostle*; Dunn, *Theology of Paul the Apostle*; Campbell, *Deliverance of God*; Wright, *Paul and the Faithfulness of God*; Barclay, *Paul and the Gift*.

11. See the discussions in L. Johnson, *Faith's Freedom*, 30–59; *Religious Experience*, esp. 39–68; *Among the Gentiles*, 15–26.

and their ordinary practice makes them prefer concepts to embodied states and feelings. Outside the precincts of philosophers and scholars, however, the importance of personal experience—and its cognitive significance—is almost universally acknowledged.

Only a little reflection is required for the ordinary person to see that we usually speak of an "event" as something that is public and visible and potentially verifiable (or at least disconfirmable) through empirical testing. The Normandy Invasion in 1944 was such an event, as was the destruction of the Jerusalem temple in 70 CE. And we ordinarily speak of an "experience" as something that an individual (and sometimes a group, though always in distinct degree and manner) senses, perceives, or feels in the body. I can read about the Normandy Invasion, but this is something very different than having experienced the brutal violence and fear of those awful hours. Those who did experience it could never have the same detached view of the "event" as those who had only read about it in books. The "event" we call the Holocaust or Shoah is both the same as and distinguishable from the "experience" of it by millions of Jews, and as witnessed to by survivors like Elie Wiesel and Primo Levi.

And only the most stubborn among rationalists would deny the reality and significance of such ordinary life experiences as becoming adolescent, falling in love, birthing a child, becoming addicted, failing at our life's work, being depressed, losing a loved one; we all know how our lives can be shaken, shattered, reshaped, even by experiences that are common to all humans. Each of these life experiences, moreover, affect not only ourselves but also those around us; they have a "share" in our experience as we are altered by it: parents who endure a child's adolescence; friends who sense the change in us as we find "the one"; family and friends who celebrate with us the birth of a child; colleagues who suffer our addiction or failure as we do; family who grieve together at the death of my spouse, their mother or father.

Even individual experiences of the most normal and mundane character have a social impact and effect. Those affected by our individual experience could write a story as well as we could about how their and our lives were changed as a result of what we (and they) experienced. Such is the stuff of biography and sometimes even of history. General Grant getting drunk when lonely for his wife was not an experience without effect on others; General Patton's impulsive rage at a soldier reverberated through all the complex webs of Allied command in World War II.

The epistemological significance of experience, moreover, has in recent decades been widely asserted by those who insist that some aspect of their lives fundamentally shaped them, so much so that to ignore that aspect would be to deny it in a fundamental way. The distinctive experiences of growing up in contemporary America as black or female or gay or abused are regularly advanced—and accepted!—as a privileged and unassailable cognitive perspective on reality, so much so that the older notion of a detached and "objective" stance on any subject is now often regarded as risible, the manifestation of still another experiential "bias" based on the experience of "white supremacy" or "male dominance" or "heterosexualism." At an extreme, such claims themselves become ludicrous, when those holding them insist that "you can't possibly understand me at all because I am X or Y." But they are helpful when they remind us that life experiences truly do make a difference in how one views the world, and that the deeper and more powerful the experience, the more profoundly the view of the world can be affected.

The explicit recovery of the experiential is the basis for a new appreciation for personal narratives as a mode of expressing truth.[12] Even when such narratives are expressed fragmentarily, or remain implicit, we have come to understand their importance for appreciating the perspective of another and, for that matter, of ourselves as well. Simultaneously, we now grasp how the truths expressed through narrative are not less valid than scientific propositions, although they require a different sort of hearing and testing. At the very least, even those fonder of ratiocination than of personal witness can appreciate that it takes a special sort of stupidity to insist on the basis of tone-deafness that music is just a lot of bunk, or on the basis of color-blindness that fine art is hokum.

If the experience of beauty in music or literature or art is granted a distinctive value—one that is not necessarily available to all, and requiring certain qualities of receptivity—how much more ought we to recognize the distinctive value of religious experience, even if we ourselves have not had the equivalent in our own lives. Fakery, manipulation, and neurosis can all figure in the claims to religious experience. But in the case of an Isaiah, or Jesus, or Paul, or Siddhartha, or Muhammad, to deny or ignore even the claims to such experience made by them, or on behalf of them by others, is to reduce them beyond recognition and miss completely the importance of

---

12. Among early works, see Stroup, *Promise of Narrative Theology*; Hauerwas, *Community of Character*; Hauerwas and Jones, *Why Narrative?*; L. Johnson, *Scripture and Discernment*. The flow has become a flood: among many others, see Sauter and Barton, *Revelation and Story*; Lucie-Smith, *Narrative Theology*; Ganzevoort, de Haardt, and Scherer-Rath, *Religious Stories We Live By*.

what they said and did. And, at the risk of repeating myself, to miss the experiential in Paul's letters, and to read them only at the level of the conceptual, is to miss their significance altogether.

## The Resurrection Experience[13]

By far the most important of the experiences that shape the view of the world in Paul's letters is the resurrection.[14] Immediately, readers uncomfortable with the term "experience" will bristle even more at my using it for the resurrection: Is it better called an event? Does not speaking of it as an "experience" detract from its ontological or (for some) historical reality concerning Christ? Are we not on the slippery slope to subjectivism and relativity? Does not the psychological reductionism of a Renan or Loisy or Spong lurk just around the corner once we use this sort of language?[15]

Paul's language about the resurrection is, in fact, extraordinarily complex, and some patience is required if it is to be properly assessed. We can distinguish four ways in which Paul speaks of the resurrection. First, he can speak of the resurrection or, better, the exaltation of Jesus as an event brought about by God; second, he can speak of this event as a reality that

13. Among recent works on the resurrection in Paul, see R. Meyer, *La Vie après la Mort*; Mason, *Resurrection According to Paul*; R. Longenecker, *Life in the Face of Death*; Dyer and Neville, *Resurrection and Responsibility*; Scott, *Trouble with Resurrection*; Paul Brown, *Bodily Resurrection and Ethics*; Tappenden, *Resurrection in Paul*.

14. The basic lines of my argument here are anticipated in L. Johnson, *Writings of the New Testament*. My insistence on the reality of the resurrection stands in marked contrast to scholarly "explanations" that ultimately deny that reality; see, e.g., Strauss, *Life of Jesus Critically Examined*, 735–44, or Weiss, *Earliest Christianity*, 1:14–44. Similarly, my position on the reality of the resurrection rejects the view that such a conviction was distinctive only to Pauline Christianity, with other streams of "early Christianity" unaware of any such claim; see, e.g., Mack, *Who Wrote the New Testament?*, and J. Smith, *Drudgery Divine*.

15. Ernst Renan ascribed belief in the resurrection to the delusionary infatuation of Mary Magdalene; see *Life of Jesus*, 357. Alfred Loisy held that Easter meant the rising of faith rather than Jesus; see *Birth of the Christian Religion*, 97–98. Bishop John Shelby Spong considered the resurrection to be the result of a cognitive adjustment in the mind of Peter; see *Resurrection*. At a scholarly level, the tradition of Renan lives on in such works as Lüdemann, *Resurrection of Jesus*, and Marxsen, *Resurrection of Jesus of Nazareth*. The tradition of Loisy continues in studies that ascribe resurrection belief to the resolution of cognitive dissonance among the disciples; see, e.g., Jackson, "Resurrection Belief"; Wernik, "Frustrated Beliefs." The resurrection faith can even be construed as a disease of language; see Devenish, "So-Called Resurrection."

affects others; third, he can speak of the resurrection as a reality in which others participate. Although logically distinct, these first three modes of discourse tend to intersect and commingle. Fourth, while not necessarily using the terms for resurrection, Paul's use of the title "Lord" for Jesus, and his statements concerning the power of the Holy Spirit present among believers are also part of his resurrection discourse. In brief, the resurrection is an event inasmuch as God exalted Jesus to his status as Lord after his death and burial (the last "historical" moments of Jesus as a particular human person). But it is also an experience inasmuch as his becoming Lord and life-giving Spirit" (1 Cor 15:45) establishes a "new creation" which, through the power of the Holy Spirit, transforms other humans. It may be helpful to look more closely at each of the four kinds of statements I have identified, bearing in mind that they often lie side by side or in combination.

## *The Resurrection of Jesus*

Paul opens his letter to the Romans by declaring that Jesus was "established as Son of God in power according to the spirit of holiness through resurrection from the dead, Jesus Christ our Lord" (1:4). He says that righteousness will be credited to those who believe "in the one who raised Jesus our Lord from the dead" (4:24), and that those who "confess with [their] mouth that Jesus is Lord and believe in [their] heart that God raised him from the dead" will be saved (10:9). In 1 Corinthians, Paul states as the heart of the good news that "he was raised on the third day in accordance with the scriptures" (15:4), certifies the "event" character of the resurrection by listing the witnesses to his appearances (15:5–11), and states, "Christ has been raised from the dead, the firstfruits of those who have fallen asleep" (15:20). In 2 Cor 4:14 Paul speaks of God as the one who "raised Jesus," and says in 13:4, "He was crucified out of weakness, but lives by the power of God." In the greeting to his letter to the Galatians, Paul declares that he is an apostle through Jesus Christ "and God the Father who raised him from the dead" (1:1).

Eph 1:20–21 asserts that God raised him from the dead to sit at God's right hand, and in 4:8–10 speaks of Christ as having both descended and ascended. In Phil 2:9–11 Paul celebrates the vindication of Christ after his death as a servant: "God greatly exalted him . . . that at the name of Jesus . . . every tongue [should] confess that Jesus Christ is Lord, to the glory of the Father." Colossians calls Christ "the firstborn of the dead" (1:18) and states that he is "seated at the right hand of God" (3:1). In 1 Thess 1:10, Paul declares that God raised Jesus "from the dead." First Timothy 3:16 hymns Jesus as one who was "taken up in glory." Second Timothy 1:10 (RSV) asserts that Christ "abolished death and brought life and immortality to light," and in 2:8 (RSV) Paul tells Timothy to "remember Jesus Christ, risen from the dead."

Now, while this is an impressive set of statements, and leaves us in no doubt concerning Paul's conviction that the resurrection of Jesus from the dead and his exaltation to the right hand of God were "events" that happened in the past, they are relatively rare (even absent from 2 Thessalonians, Titus, and Philemon) and are far less frequent than the statements that we consider next, which connect the resurrection to the state/condition/experience of humans other than Jesus.

### The Resurrection as Affecting Others

In Rom 4:24–25 Paul specifies the belief "in the one who raised Jesus our Lord from the dead" with the statement "who was handed over for our transgressions and raised for our justification." The resurrection is not simply what happened to Jesus in the past; its effect continues in the present for believers. Similarly, in Rom 8:34 Paul states that "Christ who died, rather, was raised, who also is at the right hand of God, who indeed intercedes for us"; the living Jesus acts now in behalf of others. Once more in Romans, Paul makes the resurrection of Jesus proleptic of believers' future: "If the Spirit of the one who raised Jesus from the dead dwells in you, the one who raised Christ from the dead will give life to your mortal bodies also, through his Spirit that dwells in you" (8:11).

In 1 Cor 15:5–11 Paul's recitation of eyewitnesses to Christ's appearance clearly falls into this category: his resurrection was a reality that they experienced through their senses; in the case of Paul, we have a firsthand witness to the reality of the resurrection (15:8). As he says in 1 Cor 9:1, "Have I not seen Jesus our Lord?" Similarly, in Gal 1:12 Paul speaks of the good news he preaches as originating not in humans but "through a revelation of Jesus Christ." And in 1:16 he clearly refers to an experience of the resurrected Jesus, "when God . . . was pleased to reveal his Son to me."

The entire passage of 1 Cor 15:12–19 likewise links the resurrection of Jesus to others: if he is not raised, then the dead are not raised, and if he is not raised, then their faith is in vain, they are still in their sins, and Paul is a false witness. In the same fashion, Christ's resurrection as "the firstfruits of those who have fallen asleep" is proleptic of the resurrection of others: "For just as in Adam all die, so too in Christ shall all be brought to life" (1 Cor 15:20–22).

Three passages in 2 Corinthians link Jesus's resurrection to its effect on believers. In 4:14 Paul says he knows "that the one who raised the Lord Jesus will raise us also with Jesus and place us with you in his presence." Similarly, in 5:15 he says, "He indeed died for all, so that those who live might no longer live for themselves but for him who for their sake died and was raised." And in 13:4, after stating, "He was crucified out of weakness, but he lives by the power of God," Paul adds, "So also we are weak in him, but toward you we shall live with him by the power of God." Similarly, after stating that God raised Jesus and seated him at his right hand, Paul adds in Eph 1:22–23 that "he put all things beneath his feet and gave him as head over all things to the church, which is his body, the fullness of the one who fills all things in every way." In 1 Thess 5:9–10 Paul declares that they are destined "to gain salvation through our Lord Jesus Christ [see 1:10], who died for us, so that whether we are awake or asleep we may live together with him."

*Participation in the Resurrection*

A third set of statements in Paul's letters point to a human participation in Christ's resurrection, either now or in the future—usually mediated by the Spirit (see also the next category). Thus, in speaking of the experience of baptism among the Roman believers, Paul says, "We were indeed buried with him through baptism into death, so that, just as Christ was raised from the dead by the glory of the Father, we too might live in newness of life. For if we have grown into union with him through a death like his, we shall also be united with him in the resurrection" (Rom 6:4–5), and he continues, "If, then, we have died with Christ, we believe that we shall also live with him. . . . Consequently, you too must think of yourselves as being dead to sin and living for God in Christ Jesus" (6:8–11). And later still, "If the Spirit of the one who raised Jesus from the dead dwells in you, the one who raised Christ from the dead will give life to your mortal bodies also, through His Spirit that dwells in you" (8:11).

In 1 Cor 6:13–17 Paul links the present condition of the Corinthians with respect to the Spirit and their bodies to the resurrection: "The body . . . is not for immorality, but for the Lord, and the Lord is for the body; God raised the Lord and will also raise us by his power. . . . Whoever is joined to the Lord becomes one spirit with him." We note here the confluence of language about resurrection, lordship, spirit, power, and human bodies. The same linkage is made in his discussion of the resurrection in 1 Cor 15:45–49: "'The first man, Adam, became a living being,' the last Adam a life-giving spirit. . . . The first man was from the earth, earthly; the second man, from heaven. . . . Just as we have borne the image of the earthly one, we shall also bear the image of the heavenly one." The intense present participation of believers in the death and resurrection is expressed by Paul in 2 Corinthians when he speaks of himself and his fellows "carrying about in the body the dying of Jesus, so that the life of Jesus may be manifested in our body. For we who live are constantly being given up to death for the sake of Jesus, so that the life of Jesus may be manifested in our mortal flesh" (4:10–11).

In Gal 2:19–20 Paul states of himself, "I have been crucified with Christ; yet I live, no longer I, but Christ lives in me; insofar as I now live in the flesh, I live by faith in [or of] the Son of God who has loved me and given himself up for me." Similarly, in Phil 1:20–21 Paul declares that "my eager expectation and hope is that . . . Christ will be magnified in my body, whether by life or by death. For to me life is Christ, and death is gain." Later in this letter, Paul says of himself that he lives by the righteousness that comes from faith, "to know [Christ] and the power of his resurrection and the sharing of his sufferings by being conformed to his death, if somehow I may attain the resurrection of the dead" (3:10–11). And still later, "Our citizenship is in heaven, and from it we also await a Savior, the Lord Jesus Christ. He will change our lowly body to conform with his glorified body by the power that enables him also to bring all things into subjection to himself" (3:20–21). This hope of a future resurrection based on what has already been given is found also in 1 Thess 4:14, "For if we believe that Jesus died and rose, so too will God, through Jesus, bring with him those who have fallen asleep," and 2 Tim 2:11, "If we have died with him, we shall also live with him."

The resurrection life as defining the present of all believers is found also in Eph 2:5–6: "[God] brought us to life with Christ (by grace you have been saved), raised us up with him, and seated us with him in the heavens in Christ Jesus." It is emphasized especially by Colossians, where Paul declares, "You were buried with him in baptism, in which you were also raised with him through faith in the power of God, who raised him from the dead" (2:12), and, "If then you were raised with Christ, seek what is above, where Christ is seated at the right hand of God. . . . For you have died, and your life is hidden with Christ in God. When Christ your life appears, then you too will appear with him in glory" (3:1–4).

Even though there is far from a uniformity of expression in all the passages I have cited, it is abundantly clear that although the resurrection of

Jesus is for Paul an event of the past, it is even more an existential reality in the present—defining the condition of believers—and that present power of the resurrection provides the hope for a future participation in the glory of God, which can even now be seen shining on the face of Christ (2 Cor 4:6). But in order to fully appreciate the way in which Paul sees the resurrection as a present experience, we need to examine his language about the lordship of Jesus and the power of the Spirit.

## Jesus Is Lord / The Power of the Spirit

For Paul, Jesus's resurrection is not a resuscitation, a coming back to mortal life, but is his exaltation to a status as "Lord," sitting at the "right hand of the Father," participating fully in God's presence and power, exercising cosmic rule. The connection between his exaltation and status as Lord is clearly stated by two passages containing what is probably the earliest Christian confession: "Jesus is Lord."[16] In Phil 2:11 Paul says that, as a consequence of Jesus's exaltation by God, "every tongue [should] confess that Jesus Christ is Lord, to the glory of God the Father." In Rom 10:9, likewise, Paul declares that "if you confess with your mouth that Jesus is Lord and believe in your heart that God raised him from the dead, you will be saved." When Paul therefore sends greetings to his churches from God the Father and "our Lord Jesus Christ" (Rom 1:4; 1 Cor 1:2; 2 Cor 1:2; Gal 1:3; Eph 1:2; Phil 1:2; 1 Thess 1:1; 2 Thess 1:2; 1 Tim 1:2; 2 Tim 1:2; Phlm 3), he sends them as one sent on a commission as an apostle by a living and powerful presence.

The medium of Christ's presence as Lord is the Holy Spirit. We remember that Christ's exaltation as the final Adam meant he became "life-giving spirit" (*pneuma zōopoioun*); he is not only living but life-giving in the way that only God can be.[17] And as Lord, he bestows the Spirit on those who call on his name (1 Cor 12:4–5; Gal 3:1–5); the fundamental gift is God's love poured into human hearts through the Holy Spirit (Rom 5:5). The Spirit is the means of transformation into the image of Christ; with astonishingly

16. Its antiquity is attested not only by the confessional character of these passages but by Paul's use of *maranatha* in 1 Cor 16:22.

17. The use of *zōopoioun* in Scripture is reserved to God: in the LXX, see 2 Kgs 5:7; Neh 9:6; Job 36:6; Ps 70:20; in the New Testament, see John 5:21; 6:63; Rom 4:17; 8:11; 1 Cor 15:22, 36, 45; 2 Cor 3:6; Gal 3:21; 1 Pet 3:18.

dense language, Paul states in 2 Cor 3:17–18, "Now the Lord is the Spirit, and where the Spirit of the Lord is, there is freedom. All of us, gazing with unveiled faces on the glory of the Lord, are being transformed into the same image from glory to glory, as from the Lord who is Spirit." The possession of the Holy Spirit, indeed, is the experiential correlative to their confession of Jesus as Lord. Paul declares emphatically in 1 Cor 12:3, "No one can say, 'Jesus is Lord,' except by the Holy Spirit" (adapted).

The power of the resurrection in the experience of believers is therefore the power of the Holy Spirit at work among them (Phil 1:19; Gal 3:5). Thus, when Paul tells the Corinthians, "In the name of our Lord Jesus: when you have gathered together and I am with you in spirit with the power of the Lord Jesus" (1 Cor 5:4), the Spirit he means is the Holy Spirit, which dwells within the community (see 1 Cor 3:16–17; 6:19–20). It is the Spirit that enables believers to live with new dispositions in the world: "Whoever does not have the Spirit of Christ does not belong to him. But if Christ is in you, although the body is dead because of sin, the spirit is alive because of righteousness. If the Spirit of the one who raised Jesus from the dead dwells in you, the one who raised Christ from the dead will give life to your mortal bodies also, through his Spirit that dwells in you" (Rom 8:9–11).

Such passages can be multiplied,[18] but the essential point is that through the power of the Holy Spirit, the resurrected presence of Christ is the essential element in the experience of Paul and his churches, and the supreme premise of all that he writes. Note how Paul's language about *power* intersects frequently with language about the resurrection and the Spirit.[19] He can speak of the Spirit of God and the Spirit of Christ as "dwelling in them" (Rom 8:9; 1 Cor 3:16) or "in them" (Rom 8:11), as well as of them being "in Christ" or "in" the Spirit. Because of this, Paul can use the phrase "in the Lord,"[20] "in Christ,"[21]

---

18. See Rom 15:13–19; 1 Cor 2:4–14; 12:3–13; 2 Cor 3:3–18; 12:18; Gal 5:5–25; Eph 2:18–22; 4:3–4; Col 1:8; 1 Thess 1:5–6; 4:8; 5:19; 2 Thess 2;13; 2 Tim 1:7, 14; Titus 3:6.

19. See Rom 1:4, 16; 8;7; 15:13, 19; 1 Cor 1:24; 2:4–5, 14; 4:19–20; 5:4; 6:14; 12:3, 6, 11; 15:43; 2 Cor 4:7; 6:7; 12:9, 12; 13:4; Gal 3:5; 5:6; Eph 1:11, 19, 20; 3:7, 16, 20; 6:10; Phil 2:13; 3;10, 21; Col 1:11, 29; 1 Thess 1:5; 2:13; 2 Tim 1:7.

20. See Rom 6:23; 8:39; 15:30; 1 Cor 1:31; 4:17; 7:22, 39; 9:1–2; 11:11; 2 Cor 2:12; Gal 5:10; Eph 1:15; 2:21; 3:11; 4:1; 5:8; 6:1, 10; Phil 1:14; 2:19, 24, 29; 3:1; 4:1, 2, 4, 10; Col 3:18, 20; 4:17; 1 Thess 3:8; 4:1; 5:12; 2 Thess 3:12.

21. See Rom 6:11, 23; 8:1, 2, 39; 9:1; 12:5; 15:17; 16:3, 7, 9, 10; 1 Cor 1:24, 30; 3:1; 4:10, 15, 17; 15:18, 19, 31; 16:24; 2 Cor 2:17; 3:14; 5:17–19; 12:2; Gal 2:4, 17; 3:26, 28; Eph 1:1, 10, 12, 20; 2:6, 7, 10, 13; 3:6, 11, 21; Phil 1:1, 13, 26; 2:1, 5; 3:14; 4:7, 19, 21; Col 1:2, 28; 1 Thess 2:14; 5:18; 2 Thess 1:1; 3:12; 1 Tim 1:14; 3:13; 2 Tim 1:1, 9, 13; 2:1, 10; 3:12, 15; Phlm 8, 20, 23.

and "in the Spirit"[22] virtually synonymously as shorthand for the new reality within which they live, and which enables them to regard themselves as a new creation (2 Cor 5:17; Gal 6:15).

## The Texture of Experience in the Letters

The experience of the resurrection—that is, the experience of the power of the Holy Spirit understood as coming from the exalted Lord Jesus—is most fundamental, the basis and substance of the good news that Paul proclaims to his churches (1 Cor 15:1–4), and the premise for the life and activity of believers. But a broad range of other human experience appears in Paul's letters, stimulating and in part shaping his thought.

Some of Paul's experiences are of the most quotidian character: visiting churches, sending delegates, writing letters, collecting money. In the same way, we see his communities in the round of normal human activity: receiving and sending delegates, engaging in ritual behavior, and negotiating the problems involved in such everyday activities as eating and drinking, going to court, having licit and illicit sex, and entering into dispute over nearly all of these, since there as yet existed no guidebook for how the confession of Jesus as Lord and the experience of the Holy Spirit's power should be translated into worldly behavior. But along with such ordinary-appearing experiences, Paul speaks also of his own extraordinary religious experiences as one who "[has] the Spirit of God" (1 Cor 7:40)—experiences of visions (1 Cor 9:1; 15:8; Gal 1:11; 2 Cor 12:1–5), auditions (1 Cor 11:23; 2 Cor 12:8–9), speaking in tongues (1 Cor 14:18), performing signs and wonders (Rom 15:19; 2 Cor 12:12), and undergoing suffering for the sake of Christ (Rom 8:18–25; 1 Cor 4:9–13; 2 Cor 1:8–11; 4:8–15; 11:23–29; Eph 3:1; 6:20; Phil 1:17–29; 3:10; Col 1:24–29; 2 Tim 3:10–12). He speaks as well of the extraordinary religious experiences of believers, who in a variety of ways are touched by and express the powerful presence of the Spirit (1 Cor 12–14; 2 Cor 12:12; Gal 3:1–5); they also share in affliction and persecution for their faith (Rom 8:18–25; 2 Cor 1:3–7; Gal 6:12; 1 Thess 1:6; 4:13; 2 Thess 1:4–10; 2 Tim 4:4–5).

I call the present discussion the "texture of experience" in Paul's letters because of the way in which the ordinary and extraordinary are woven

---

22. See Rom 7:6; 8:9; 9:1; 15:13, 19; 1 Cor 2:4; 6:11, 19; 12:3, 9, 11, 13; 2 Cor 6:6; 12:18; Gal 6:1; Eph 2:18, 22; 3:5; 5:18; 6:18; Phil 1:27; Col 1:8; 1 Thess 1:5; 1 Tim 3:16.

together, so that something as normal as returning a runaway slave can be the occasion for fellowship in the Spirit and an expression of grace (Philemon), and something so spectacular as speaking in tongues can be regulated by a concern for the stability and growth of the community (1 Cor 14). This interweaving of ordinary and extraordinary (religious) experience—and the way in which together they provide the occasion and the specific shape of Paul's discourse in each letter—makes his canonical letters truly distinctive.[23]

The best way of appreciating this characteristic of the canonical letters is to consider them individually under the rubric of experience. In this discussion, I do not take up again Paul's language concerning the experience of the resurrection, since I have already provided that evidence.

*Romans*

In the case of Paul's longest and most systematically organized letter, we catch only glimpses of the readers' worldly or religious activities, and these are the matter of some dispute.[24] Paul refers to their baptism (Rom 6:1–11) and the exercise of spiritual ministries (12:5–8). If 14:1–23 is not merely hypothetical, then they may have disputed over dietary matters and the observance of special days. Otherwise, these gentile believers (1:5; 11:13) remain mostly unknown to us, although Paul clearly considered them sufficiently stable and prosperous to provide funding for his new mission to Spain (15:22–16:2). As for Paul, he is clear that his intended visit to Rome has practical ends: he seeks support from them, having completed his preaching endeavors in the East, from Jerusalem to Illyricum (15:19–21). Although he is under obligation to both Greeks and non-Greeks, his missionary experience in the East, above all the gentile acceptance of the gospel and the Jewish rejection of it (9:30–10:4), undoubtedly helped shape the argument of the letter. Since Paul did not establish the church at Rome, yet expects from it practical support for his ministry, his fund-raising letter—in addition to providing a substantial list of persons who can vouch for him (16:3–16)—must present his understanding of the good news that he asks them to support.

23. I avoid the word "unique" because something of the same texture is found as well in 1 Peter, Hebrews, and James—all writings that have either been associated with Paul (Hebrews, 1 Peter) or taken as a polemic against Paul (James).

24. See Donfried, *Romans Debate.*

As a result, Paul's reflection on his ministry becomes a magisterial argument concerning the righteousness of God's working in the world.[25]

What about the experience of the Roman Christians themselves? Paul makes mention only of their experience of baptism (6:1–11), but it is far from a mere mention, and baptism is far from a rote ritual. For Paul, baptism is the point where believers enter into participation with the death and resurrection of Jesus; it is the place where God's saving work through the faithful/obedient death of Jesus and his exaltation becomes their own experience. The love of God is poured into their hearts through the Holy Spirit (5:5), enabling them to live "in newness of life" (6:4), with the ability to discern "according to the Spirit" (8:5–13). This change in them is not formal or theoretical; it is experiential and practical. As Paul states in 8:14–17: "Those who are led by the Spirit of God are children of God. For you did not receive a spirit of slavery to fall back into fear, but you received a spirit of adoption, through which we cry, '*Abba*, Father!' The Spirit itself bears witness with our spirit that we are children of God, and if children, then heirs, heirs of God and joint heirs with Christ, if only we suffer with him so that we may also be glorified with him." It is because believers experience the power of the Spirit given them by the risen Christ—a power that affects their bodies (6:13; 8:11), their emotions (8:15), their cognition (8:5–6), and their will (8:7–8)—that they can, in their moral life, seek to realize this new identity according to the image of the one whom God made the "firstborn among many brothers" (8:29), and "put on the Lord Jesus Christ, and make no provision for the desires of the flesh" (13:14).[26]

## First Corinthians

Paul's First Letter to the Corinthians is far and away the most obviously circumstantial of his letters. Without it, we would be severely impoverished in our knowledge of earliest Christianity.[27] It should take no elaborate argument to confirm that in this instance, at least, Paul's thought was stimulated and shaped by his own and his community's experience. Paul refers

---

25. On this, see Dahl, "Missionary Theology"; L. Johnson, *Reading Romans*.

26. For the story character of Romans, see L. Johnson, *Reading Romans*; Grieb, *Story of Romans*; Nicolet-Anderson, *Constructing the Self*.

27. It is noteworthy how much Meeks's classic study, *First Urban Christians*, depended on the data offered by 1 Corinthians.

explicitly to oral reports he has received from Chloe's household concerning the Corinthians' behavior in his absence (1:11–12), to a misunderstanding of an earlier letter he had written them (5:9–10), and he sets out to answer a series of questions put to him by members of that church (7:1). We are nevertheless struck by the sheer amount of information this letter contains about experience and the degree to which experience helps give shape to Paul's thought.[28]

We learn first a great deal about Paul's perception of his past experience with them, as in his manner of first coming among them and preaching (1:17–2:5), his inability to speak to them as mature (3:1–4), his work as the founder of their community (3:5–10), his apostolic sufferings (4:8–13), his refusal to exploit his right to travel with a wife or receive financial support (9:3–15), his being in danger and fighting the beasts at Ephesus (15:30–32). He speaks of his now sending his delegate Timothy (4:17) before his own visit (4:19–21). He looks forward to having the collection gathered before he visits and sends on a delegation with the collection to Jerusalem (16:1–8). Paul also lays claim to extraordinary religious experiences: his call to be an apostle (1:1) that impels him to preach and pastor churches; his encounter with the risen Lord Jesus (9:1; 15:8); his having the Spirit of God (7:40); his receiving words from the Lord (11:23); his speaking in tongues (14:18).

We learn from this letter as well about the experiences of the Corinthian community—remembering that we are dependent on Paul's perception and expression of them. Thus, Paul celebrates their call by God (1:2) and the abundance of grace that enriches them "in every way, with all discourse and all knowledge" (1:4–5), a recognition that is expanded in Paul's discussion of the spiritual gifts in chapters 12–14: some among them speak in tongues, interpret tongues, teach, prophesy, and receive revelations, while others work wonders and heal (12:4–26; 12:27–30; 14:1–32). We learn as well that the Corinthians have, like the Roman believers, experienced baptism, now described as a washing and sanctification (6:11), and an incorporation into one body, and a drinking of the Holy Spirit (12:13). They also share a sacred meal called "the Lord's supper" (11:20), at which the words of Jesus over the bread and wine before his death are shared in memory of that death (11:23–32), and as a participation in the body and blood of Christ (10:15–21).

Paul enables us to see the Corinthians engaging in a variety of secular activities: they engage in sex, both licit and illicit (5:1–13; 6:12–20; 7:1–40);

28. For a thorough examination of the issues at Corinth and Paul's rhetorical response to them, see Mitchell, *Paul and the Rhetoric of Reconciliation*.

they sue each other in small claims court (6:1–8); they purchase and consume meats that have been offered in sacrifice (8:1–13); they eat meals at temples dedicated to the gods (10:23–30). Above all, they are contentious, dividing among themselves and entering into disputes concerning which leaders are fit to teach them (1:10–16; 3:1–4) and concerning all these sexual, dietary, and ritual behaviors, including the ones (such as ecstatic utterance and the Lord's Supper) that are intended to build up the community.

In 1 Corinthians we see the apostle thinking on his feet as he is presented with these contested issues, whether by oral report or by letter. In two places Paul appears to be making use of "set pieces" that may have been worked out earlier—namely, his reflection on Wisdom and the Spirit (2:6–16), and his argument concerning the resurrection (15:1–58), but even these are responses to Paul's perception of the Corinthians as arrogant in their dispositions (1:11–13, 26–31; 2:4; 4:18; 5:2) and as in some fashion denying the reality of the resurrection of the dead (15:12, 33–35). Otherwise, Paul's arguments appear as ad hoc responses to the behaviors and experiences of the Corinthians as they have been reported to him.

## Second Corinthians

The composition of 2 Corinthians arises directly out of the painful experience of alienation between Paul and the Corinthian church. It is written, indeed, in the midst of an ongoing effort on Paul's part to reconcile himself to a community that appears to prefer other apostles to him.[29] The difficulties of reconstructing the specific events leading to this relationship crisis are notorious—such as the sequence of Paul's visits and the sending of delegates—and one of the reasons why 2 Corinthians is often regarded as a series of notes that have been joined together. But some elements are discernible: a painful visit by Paul to the church (2:2); a letter "written in tears" that caused grief in the community (2:4–11); the suspicious sending of delegates to take up a collection (11:11; 12:16–18) after Paul had declared in his first letter to them that he did not seek their support (1 Cor 9:12–18); the appearance within the community of those Paul calls "super-apostles" whose written credentials (3:1), Jewish antecedents (11:22), rhetoric (10:10; 11:6), wonder-working (12:11–12), and endurance of afflictions (11:23–28) make them appear to the Corinthians as desirable apostolic alternatives to Paul.

29. For a sober assessment of the issues, see Sumney, *Identifying Paul's Opponents*.

Much of the letter is taken up by Paul's responses to these individual irritants, taking up in turn his own experience and his perception of the Corinthians' experience. In asserting his authority over against the claims of the super-apostles, Paul recites his own catalogue of sufferings for Christ (11:23–29), and in renewing his plea for the collection, he clarifies his own position through recounting his past and present experience with regard to fund-raising and support (9:3–5; 11:7–11). But he also appeals to their fellowship in mutual suffering and consolation as the basis for a reconciled relationship (1:3–7), building on his own experience of affliction in Asia, which seemed like a sentence of death and made him "despair of life" (1:8–11).

And, in one of his most brilliant leaps from experience to theology, he makes the suffering that he and his associates are experiencing (not least from the Corinthians themselves!) an essential component in his ministry of reconciliation in the world, which in turn embodies the reconciling ministry of Christ, who through his death brought life to others (4:7–15; 5:11–15), who by becoming sin made others righteous (5:21), who by becoming poor made others rich (8:9), and who by dying in weakness empowered new life in others (13:3–4). This pattern of life for others, of suffering even death so that others might live, effects a marriage between the work of the Holy Spirit in Paul's own life and the work of God in Christ bringing about a new creation.

Thus, Paul follows his boldest claim to religious experience, his being snatched into the third heaven and hearing "ineffable things" (12:1–5), with a report about his being afflicted with a "stake in the flesh" (author's translation) that kept him from becoming too inflated, and deducing from the words of Jesus spoken to him that "I will rather boast most gladly of my weaknesses, in order that the power of Christ may dwell with me" (12:7–10). In 2 Corinthians, Paul works with the drama of his own conflicted relationship with his most refractory church to shape his most profound theological reflection on Jesus's work and on the apostle's ministry.

## Galatians

Experience plays an absolutely critical role in Paul's letter to the churches in Galatia, where agitators are advocating the practice of circumcision on the basis that the Galatians' first ritual of initiation, baptism, was inadequate, and that to be fully members of God's people, they must also observe the law of Moses.[30] Paul seeks to convince his readers to stand within what they have already received, because in this instance to add more means cutting themselves off from the gift they have already received (Gal 5:1–6). The heart of his argument is an appeal to their experience and his own.

In 3:1–5 Paul asks rhetorically of the "stupid Galatians" whether they had received the Spirit through the observance of the law or through hearing the good news with faith. If they had not, in fact, received the Spirit and had it confirmed by "mighty works," Paul's argument would fail utterly: his interpretation of Torah in light of faith (3:6–22) would be empty. Notice also that Paul concludes this midrashic exposition with another appeal to their experience—namely, their reception of the Spirit at baptism (3:27–29): "As proof that you are children, God sent the spirit of his Son into our hearts, crying out, '*Abba*, Father!' So you are no longer a slave but a child, and if a child then also an heir, through God" (4:6–7). Paul reminds them also of the inconsistency of their present behavior toward him: they now treat him as an enemy, whereas when he brought them the good news, they received him "as a messenger from God, as Christ Jesus" (4:14, author's translation).

In chapters 1 and 2, Paul recounts at considerable length his own story of turning from a fanatic adherent of the law—to the degree that he persecuted the church—to becoming an apostle to the gentiles after receiving the revelation of the risen Christ (1:11–14). Paul himself "died to the law, that I might live for God. I have been crucified with Christ; yet I live, no longer I, but Christ lives in me; insofar as I now live in the flesh, I live by faith in [or of] the Son of God who has loved me and given himself up for me" (2:19–20). Paul sees that the circumcising Galatians want to move to a place that Paul himself abandoned, and in contrast to his refusal to "nullify the gift of God" (v. 21, adapted) run the risk of cutting themselves off from the gift (5:2–4). He wants them likewise to remain within the gift that has given them life, and not seek to be incorporated into the law, for the law cannot give life (3:21).

But there is more to Paul's account of his experience, which he recounts not as a form of defense for his apostleship but rather as an example that his readers might follow. Paul shows how he did not give in to pressure from those believers who followed the law. He consulted with Peter and James three years after his call (1:18–24), but when he went again to Jerusalem after fourteen years, it was in response to a revelation; he disclosed to the pillars of

---

30. For the situation in Galatia, see L. Johnson, *Writings of the New Testament*, 289–301; my reading is influenced above all by Munck, "Judaizing Gentile Christians." For the importance of the gift of the Spirit for Paul's argument, see Lull, *Spirit in Galatia*.

the church the good news as he proclaimed it, but did not require his gentile delegate Titus to be circumcised, and he resisted the "false brothers" who tried to take away the "freedom that we have in Christ Jesus," so that "the truth of the gospel might remain intact for you" (2:1–5). Paul also resisted the pressure put by "some people from James" on the believers in Antioch to abandon their mixed table fellowship, pressure to which even Barnabas succumbed. When Peter appeared to give way as well, Paul accosted him in public, defending the freedom of gentile believers (2:11–18). Paul similarly wants the gentile Galatians to resist efforts to impose circumcision and the law. They have been called to freedom; they should not submit again to the yoke of slavery (5:1). Paul's experience stands as the model for their own.

In my discussion of the resurrection experience above, I noted the intensity of Paul's own sense of conformity to the risen Christ in Galatians: "I live, no longer I, but Christ lives in me" (2:20). In the same way, he wishes for the Galatians that "Christ be formed in you" (4:19). They live now according to the measure of the Spirit: "If we live in the Spirit, let us also follow the Spirit" (5:25), and "if you are guided by the Spirit, you are not under the law" (5:18). The Holy Spirit working within them enables them to live with a power that makes external markings irrelevant: "For in Christ Jesus, neither circumcision nor uncircumcision counts for anything, but only faith working through love" (5:6), or, as Paul states at the end, "Neither does circumcision mean anything, nor does uncircumcision, but only a new creation" (6:15).

*Ephesians*

In sharp contrast to the letters Paul wrote to the Corinthians and Galatians, the Letter to the Ephesians reveals nothing of any on-the-ground experience of Paul's readers.[31] Probably written as a circular letter to be read to a number of communities, Ephesians most resembles Romans—written by Paul to a church he had never met—but is even more detached from the specific circumstances of its composition. Paul says that he is a prisoner (3:1; 4:1; 6:20), and that he experiences sufferings "for them" (3:13), but he gives no detail. The only specific biographical detail is Paul's sending of Tychicus to tell them all the news concerning Paul (6:21), so that "you may know about us and he may encourage your hearts" (6:22). Otherwise, Paul speaks of the

31. For a classic statement of the challenge posed to readers by Ephesians, see Cadbury, "Dilemma of Ephesians 1."

mystery that was given to him by revelation for their benefit—namely, "that the Gentiles are coheirs, members of the same body, and copartners[32] in the promise in Christ Jesus through the gospel," and that Paul was made a minister of this revelation "by the gift of God's grace that was granted me in accord with the exercise of his power" (3:3–7). As we have seen in an earlier chapter, Paul warns his readers from being deceived by empty arguments, but without any indication that this is a present danger among his readers (4:14; 5:6–7). Paul speaks in general terms about their past experience as gentiles (2:1–3; 4:1–24; 5:8, 17), and in equally general terms about their being baptized, receiving the Spirit, and exercising the spiritual gifts as members of the same body (4:3–16). In the case of Ephesians, then, neither Paul's personal experience nor the specific quotidian experiences of his readers stimulate and shape his thought.

Yet the entire first part of the letter is taken up with celebrating the gift that God had given his readers, a gift that they experienced in their own lives. God had blessed them (1:3), chosen them (1:4), destined them (1:5), adopted them (1:5), redeemed them (1:7), forgiven them (1:7), revealed his will to them (1:9), and given an inheritance to them (1:11). And the experiential dimension? God had sealed them with the seal of the Holy Spirit (1:13; see 4:30). Although as gentiles they had once been given over to ignorance and vice (2:1–3; 4:1–24; 5:8, 17), they had been raised up with Christ (2:6), saved by grace (2:8), and brought near in reconciliation (2:13), built up as a living temple as a dwelling place of the Spirit (2:18–22). This overwhelming gift of God has been made actual in their lives through baptism and the outpouring of the Spirit (4:1–13), which enables them to achieve full maturity in Christ (4:13) and build Christ's body in love (4:16). Paul's moral exhortations in Ephesians (4:23–6:20) have this experiential base: his readers are called to put aside their former way of life and "be renewed in the spirit of your minds, and put on the new self, created in God's way in righteousness and holiness of truth" (4:22–24).

## Philippians

Here we again find the sort of lively exchange between Paul and his community that characterized the Corinthian correspondence.[33] We learn that

---

32. With Jewish believers; see Eph 2:1–22.

33. For the circumstances and overall shape of the composition, see L. Johnson, *Writings of the New Testament*, 325–36.

Paul is in prison (Phil. 1:7, 13), that he sends Timothy to them as his delegate (2:19) and returns to them Epaphroditus ("your messenger and minister in my need," 2:25), and that he receives gratefully the financial gift from them (4:10–13), a gift consistent with their support of him from "the beginning of the gospel" (4:15–19). Paul acknowledges a fellowship with the Philippians in suffering for the good news (1:29). He also shows himself aware—perhaps through the report of Epaphroditus?—of certain problems in this community. Some are preaching the good news "from envy and rivalry" rather than good will (1:15). It is probable that Paul's exhortation to Euodia and Syntyche to "come to a mutual understanding in the Lord" (4:2–3) is connected to this competitive spirit. Less certain is the presence of agitators for the law (3:2–4, 18–19)—Paul's rhetoric in 3:2–21 serves protreptic purposes more clearly than it does polemic ones.

What is most striking in Philippians is the way in which the entire shape of Paul's letter responds to his perception of the experience of rivalry and envy. As noted earlier, Philippians is a splendid example of a "friendship letter."[34] It employs all the stereotypical motifs associated with *philia* in antiquity: fellowship, being of one mind, being in agreement, being "together" (*syn-*) in every sort of endeavor. In ancient moral discourse, friendship was the opposite of envy. Envy sought the good of the individual in competition with others. Friendship sought the good of the community in cooperation with others.[35] The shape of Paul's argument in Philippians responds precisely to (in this case a negative) experience. A key factor in that argument, furthermore, is Paul's presenting positive examples of behavior/experience that display looking to the interests of others rather than only one's own interest (2:4).

The supreme example, to be sure, is Jesus, who "did not regard equality with God something to be grasped," and emptied himself out, taking the form of a slave—by definition, in service to others (2:4–7). Paul's delegate Timothy, too, sought their interests rather than his own (2:20); their colleague Epaphroditus risked his life "to make up for those services to me that you could not perform" (2:30). Finally, Paul presents the sketch of his own life, as he did in Galatians, not in self-defense, but to provide an example from his own experience that they might imitate. Although Paul had every reason to have confidence in the flesh, he emptied himself out

---

34. See the essays in Fitzgerald, *Friendship*.

35. See the development of this opposition in L. Johnson, "Friendship with the World," 202–20.

to gain a fellowship with Christ: "to know him and the power of his resurrection and the sharing of his sufferings by being conformed to his death, if somehow I may attain the resurrection from the dead" (3:10-11). Paul is "poured out as a libation upon the sacrificial service of your faith" (2:17). That Paul intends these experiences/behaviors to instruct the Philippians and help turn them from a spirit of rivalry and self-seeking is clear from his conclusion to this series of examples: "Join with others in being imitators of me, and observe those who conduct themselves according to the model you have in us" (3:17).

## Colossians

Paul did not personally found the church in Colossae, and his knowledge concerning his readers relies on the information provided by his fellow prisoner Epaphras, who did establish this community—and probably those in Laodicea and Hierapolis—as part of Paul's network of coworkers (Col. 1:7; 2:1; 4:12-13). Paul writes to them from prison (4:3, 10) at the same time he returns the runaway slave Onesimus to the household of Philemon (4:9) through his delegate Tychicus (4:7-8).[36] From the greetings at the end of the letter, we get some notion of the extent of Paul's network (4:7-17). But of Paul's own experience we have nothing beyond short references to the mystery with which he has been entrusted, and to his imprisonment and suffering for the sake of the gospel (2:1-3; 4:2-4): "For this I labor and struggle, in accord with the exercise of his power working within me" (1:29).

Paul's argument in Colossians addresses a situation similar to that in Galatians. In this case, though, he writes to a church he did not found—and thus cannot speak of his direct experience with them—and to which he himself did not display a knowledge of Torah. The issue involves the adequacy of their religious experience: When they were baptized, did they experience the fullness of the mystery of God in Christ, or—as some in the community seemed to be insisting—were additional levels of initiation necessary for them to become "perfect" or "mature"? Did those who adopted circumcision (2:11), or practiced asceticism (2:20-23), or had prayer experiences like those of Merkabah practitioners (2:18), have the right to "pass judgment on" (2:16) or "disqualify" believers who had only baptism (2:18)?[37]

---

36. For the connections here, see L. Johnson, *Writings of the New Testament*, 337-71.
37. L. Johnson, "Ritual Imprinting," 69-103.

Paul's resounding "no" to such questions is based entirely on the Colossians' experience of baptism. In it they experienced the power of God that was revealed in the death and resurrection of Jesus (1:15–20), and which "qualified" them "to share in the inheritance of the holy ones in light" (1:12): "For in him dwells the fullness of the deity bodily, and you share in this fullness in him, who is the head of every principality and power. In him you were also circumcised with a circumcision not administered by hand, by stripping off the carnal body, with the circumcision of Christ. You were buried with him in baptism, in which you were also raised with him through faith in the power of God, who raised him from the dead" (2:9–12). True maturity (4:12) is not a matter of adding new practices but a matter of gaining ever new insight into what they have already experienced (1:6–8, 23; 2:2; 3:2).

*First Thessalonians*

In what is probably Paul's earliest extant letter, his personal experience surfaces in two ways.[38] First, he is at pains to remind his gentile readers of the circumstances of his initial visit to them, when he came "not in word alone, but also in power and in the Holy Spirit and in much conviction" (1 Thess. 1:5, author's translation). After experiencing affliction in Philippi (2:2), Paul brought the good news to them with sincerity, as the best of moral teachers (2:3–6), gentle as a nurse (2:7), like a father with his children (2:11), working with his own hands as an example to them (2:9; see 4:11). The Thessalonians, in turn, "receiv[ed] the word in great affliction, with joy from the Holy Spirit," becoming imitators of Paul and the Lord (1:6); they received it, not as a human word, "but, as it truly is, the word of God, which is now at work in you who believe" (2:13). Paul's past experience, in short, was also the Thessalonians' past experience.

Second, the more recent experience that leads Paul to write the letter consists of frustration at not being able to visit them (2:17–20), and being forced to send Timothy as a delegate to discover whether and to what degree the Thessalonians were "disturbed in these afflictions" (3:3), or whether "the tempter had put you to the test and our toil might come to nothing" (3:5). He has noted, after all, that "you suffer the same things from your compatriots as they [the churches in Judea] did from the Jews" (2:14). Timothy's return with news of the community reassured Paul as to their faith and love and their

38. See esp. Malherbe, *Paul and the Thessalonians*.

affection for him (3:6). Significantly, Paul here omits a third term, "hope," that he had earlier in the letter ascribed to them: "calling to mind your work of faith and labor of love and endurance of hope" (1:3).

Paul tells the Thessalonians that their faith is widely known (1:8), assuring them that on the subject of love they have no need of instruction (4:9–10). But Paul sees them as deficient in the hope that is necessary for endurance through affliction (1:3). The Thessalonians have apparently, through means natural or not, lost loved ones through death, and that experience has made them waver concerning their loved ones' sharing in the triumph of God. Paul begins his discussion of the parousia of Jesus with the telling words, "We do not want you to be unaware, brothers, about those who have fallen asleep, so that you may not grieve like the rest, who have no hope" (4:13). Paul addresses their grief and despair through assurances concerning the future triumph of God, in which those who have fallen asleep will very much participate (4:14–5:3). But the real key to hope is the fundamental experience of the resurrection that the Thessalonians accepted when they turned from idols to the living God (1:9). So Paul reminds them, "If we believe that Jesus died and rose, so too will God, through Jesus, bring with him those who have fallen asleep" (4:14).

Their lives, therefore, should be daytime lives, sober, alert, watchful, wearing "the breastplate of faith and love and the helmet that is hope for salvation" (5:8), and Paul reminds them of the basis for this stance: "For God did not destine us for wrath, but to gain salvation through our Lord Jesus Christ, who died for us, so that whether we are awake or asleep we may live together with him" (5:9–10).

As in Philippians, a letter written to another beloved Macedonian community, Paul in 1 Thessalonians shapes his entire argument to address a specific, and highly experiential, issue among his readers.

## Second Thessalonians

This short letter from Paul, Silvanus, and Timothy (2 Thess. 1:1), the same senders of 1 Thessalonians, is best understood as a response to a situation that had developed in the Thessalonian community after Paul's first letter to them, composed soon after the previous letter.[39] Such a context helps make sense of three features of the letter: (a) the scant information about Paul,

---

39. L. Johnson, *Writings of the New Testament*, 249–60.

beyond a short reminder of how he had enjoined working with the hands (3:7–10; see 1 Thess 2:9; 4:11); (b) the urgent tone of the letter and its sharper directions concerning behavior (3:14–15); (c) the nature of the experience that necessitated the letter.

Paul makes clear that the community is in a state of panic with regard to the parousia of the Lord, concluding on the basis of some sort of experience in the prayer assembly that the day of the Lord was at hand: Paul asks that they "not . . . be shaken out of your minds suddenly, or . . . be alarmed either by a 'spirit,' or by an oral statement, or by a letter allegedly from us to the effect that the day of the Lord is at hand" (2:1–2). Whatever the precise character of their revelatory experience, it has caused them—in a classic example of millenarian excitement—to stop attending to their daily responsibilities, such as working (3:10–13). Paul's sense of urgency is stimulated by their experience and subsequent behavior.

The causes of their panic seem clear enough. First, the "affliction" they had suffered at the time of Paul's first letter has escalated (1:6–7), now involving active persecution (*diōgmos*, 1:4). Second, Paul's use of traditional eschatological language in 1 Thess 4:13–5:3 encouraged a preoccupation with the intensity of the "afflictions"—when would they become the "birth pangs"? Third, Paul's earnest exhortation to be "watchful" as children of the day—"let us not sleep as the rest do, but let us stay alert and sober" (1 Thess 5:5–6)—could easily be understood, not as an exhortation to be attentive to quotidian affairs, as he intended, but precisely as a call to knife-edge hyper-alertness. The tinderbox of apocalyptic panic was ready to be lighted by a charismatic experience in worship.

Paul's response seeks to restore some order to the community through a reminder of his commands to them, and the encouragement of basic social pressure (2 Thess 3:11–15), and through showing the Thessalonians that there is a great difference between local experience and cosmic event. The parousia, when it comes, will be marked by definite signs and will be unmistakable (2:3–12). Their experience of affliction and persecution is real and important, but it is not the birth pangs of the end time. They need to relax a bit and pay attention to the work God is already doing among them: "your faith flourishes ever more, and the love for every one of you for one another grows ever greater" (1:3).

The experience that necessitates the writing of 2 Thessalonians is, in Paul's view, more negative than positive, but it nevertheless is the key to understanding what he wrote. In this letter above all, the reader cannot miss how both secular experience (persecution) and religious experience (auditions, spirit letters) stimulate and shape both the Thessalonian panic and Paul's response to it.

## First Timothy

For a letter so dominated by practical instructions for his delegate Timothy to carry out in the church at Ephesus (1 Tim 3:1; 4:6, 11), 1 Timothy touches on the experiential in perhaps a surprising number of ways.[40] As in 1 Corinthians, we can surmise certain experiences and behaviors that give rise to Paul's directives: assertive teachers advancing a "gnosis" that somehow involves the law (1:3–7; 4:1–4, 7–8; 6:20–21); gender tensions in worship and in the household (2:8–15; 5:1–15); the support and failures of elders (5:17–25); the arrogance of the wealthy (2:9–10; 6:3–10, 17–19). But this is mainly a matter of guesswork. Paul tells us more explicitly about his own and his delegate's experience.

Concerning Timothy, Paul three times makes mention of his experience of prophetic call. In 1:18, "I entrust this charge to you, Timothy, my child, in accordance with the prophetic words once spoken about you," and in 4:14, "Do not neglect the gift you have, which was conferred on you through the imposition of hands of the presbyterate," and in 6:12, "Lay hold of eternal life, to which you were called when you made the noble confession in the presence of many witnesses."

But crucial to Paul's argument in chapter 1 against those would-be teachers of the law, advancing a heteronomous norm for Christian life rather than "love from a pure heart, a good conscience, and a sincere faith" (1:5), is his account of his own call in 1:12–17, which he designates as an "empowerment" (*endynamoō* in 1:12). Paul asserts that as a persecutor he had the same negative dispositions as those he lists in 1:8–10, and that he was changed, not by the law, but by God's display of mercy toward him: "I have been mercifully treated because I acted out of ignorance in my unbelief. Indeed, the grace of our Lord has been abundant, along with the faith and love that are in Christ Jesus" (1:13–14). God's gift enabled him to have "faith and love" (see 1:5!) in displacement of his previous arrogance. Paul insists that his own experience of transformation is paradigmatic for others: "For that reason I was mercifully treated, so that in me, as the foremost, Christ Jesus may

---

40. For the situation of the three letters to Paul's delegates and his response to each situation, see esp. L. Johnson, *Letters to Paul's Delegates*.

display all his patience as an example for those who would come to believe in him for everlasting life" (1:16). In its basic structure, Paul's experience-based argument against advocates of the law is deeply similar to the one he makes in Galatians.

### Second Timothy

As would be expected in a personal paraenetic letter, 2 Timothy is rich in references to the experience of Paul and his delegate. Paul remembers Timothy and his faith (and tears) in his prayer (1:3–5). He speaks of his being a prisoner (1:8) and of suffering for the sake of the good news (1:12; 2:9). He recalls being abandoned because of his chains by everyone in Asia except Onesiphorus, who searched for Paul in Rome and found him (1:15–16). He reminds his delegate of the persecutions and sufferings he had endured in Antioch, Iconium, and Lystra, from which the Lord delivered him (3:10–11). He sees himself as one who has finished his race and is now being poured out as a libation (4:6–7). In the final part of the letter, he repeats the theme of abandonment, together with the confidence that the Lord will rescue him and "bring me safe to his heavenly kingdom" (4:9–18).

The note of Timothy's "tears" in 1:4 is not irrelevant, for Paul sees Timothy as vulnerable to discouragement and even fear, because of the trials faced by Paul, and because of his own sufferings caused not least by the inroads made by false and disruptive teachers (2:14–19; 3:1–9). Thus, Paul seeks to "stir into flame the gift of God that you have through the imposition of my hands. For God did not give us a spirit of cowardice but rather of power and love and self-control" (1:6–7). Paul's speaking of his own endurance in suffering, then, has the precise purpose of presenting Timothy with a model to imitate in his own hard experiences. Paul is "confident that [Christ] is able to guard what has been entrusted to me until that day" (1:12), and he wants his delegate to share the same confidence: "Take as your norm the sound words that you heard from me, in the faith and love that are in Christ Jesus. Guard this rich trust with the help of the Holy Spirit that dwells within us" (1:13–14).

In addition to remembering how Paul endured his afflictions (1:9; 3:10–11), Timothy is to remember the experience of growing up in the faith of his grandmother and mother (1:5; 3:14) and the Scripture he has known from his youth (3:15–17), which has equipped him "for every good work." Paul wants his delegate to "bear [his] share of hardship along with me like a good soldier of Christ Jesus" (2:3), mindful that a soldier, an athlete, and a farmer must all endure struggle in order to have a reward (2:4–6). Above all, he is to "remember Jesus Christ, raised from the dead" (2:8), understanding that the saying is reliable, that "if we have died with him we shall also live with him; if we persevere we shall also reign with him" (2:11–12). As in Paul's masterful argument in 2 Corinthians, the experience of imprisonment, suffering, and rejection of the apostle and his delegate is daringly made by Paul the continuation of the salvific suffering and death of Jesus and the basis of his boast: "On this account I am suffering these things; but I am not ashamed" (1:12; see 1:8).

## *Titus*

This short *mandata principis* letter written to Paul's delegate in Crete tells us little about Paul himself, apart from some brief travel plans (Titus 3:12–14), or Titus, apart from his appointment by Paul to "set right what remains to be done and appoint presbyters in every town" (1:5). Like 1 Timothy, the letter is dominated by practical directives, with the difference that it focuses more on the household than on the church. Titus's task is not an easy one, since Paul portrays the Cretan population as raw and crude, and certain law-observant teachers are upsetting households by their insistence on a form of purity based on the law (1:10–12). As in 1 Timothy, Paul sees the contest as one between heteronomous norms (deriving from laws) and autonomous ones (deriving from character). Titus is to emphasize, then, good character in the choice of elders/supervisors (1:6–9) and good character in household relations (2:1–10).

But how does character change from bad to good? Here is where the experience of God's grace (or gift) is pivotal. In two passages that are sometimes thought of as intrusive bits of doctrine, Paul asserts the experiential basis for human change. In 2:11–14 he declares, "For the grace of God has appeared, saving all and training us [*paideuousa* = "educating us"] to reject godless ways and worldly desires and to live temperately, justly, and devoutly in this age, as we await the blessed hope, the appearance of the glory of the great God and of our Savior Jesus Christ, who gave himself for us to deliver us from all lawlessness and to cleanse for himself a people as his own, eager to do what is good." Not laws of purity but the purification (cleansing) of people themselves is the key to righteous lives, and this cleansing comes about by the experience of grace, which itself has an educational character.

No less than in Rom 6–8, Paul here affirms the transformative power of the experience of grace.

The second passage, 3:3–7, makes the change in believers' character even clearer, and connects it to the experience of baptism: "For we ourselves were once foolish, disobedient, deluded, slaves to various desires and pleasures, living in malice and envy, hateful ourselves and hating one another. But when the kindness and generous love of God our savior appeared, not because of any righteous deeds we had done but because of his mercy, he saved us through the bath of rebirth and renewal by the Holy Spirit, whom he richly poured out on us through Jesus Christ our Savior, so that we might be justified by his grace and become heirs in hope of eternal life."

### Philemon

This shortest extant letter from Paul to a slave-owning householder and leader of the church named Philemon is a letter of commendation accompanying the return of the runaway slave Onesimus, whom Paul met while in prison and became his "father" by making him "useful" (*euchrēstos* = "good Christian," 10–11).[41] Although Paul is legally obligated to return him, he seeks two things from Philemon, who has been a benefactor of the saints (7), but who must regard Paul as his own benefactor, since Paul also converted him ("you owe me your very self," 19). First, Paul desires that Onesimus be received not as a slave but as beloved brother; Paul asks that Philemon welcome him the same way he would Paul (16–17); second, Paul wants Philemon to release Onesimus and send him back to Paul to assist him (13, 21).

The letter is entirely experientially based and motivated: the imprisoned state of Paul, the running away of Onesimus, his meeting and being converted by Paul, his being returned to his owner, that owner's past financial support of the church and personal obligation to Paul to whom he owes his very life. Not doctrine or polemic, but the intricacies of ancient notions concerning patronage, and the real-life adventures of three individuals who have been caught up in the good news from God yet must live out the new creation within the fabric of the existing social order, give the letter its particular poignancy.

---

41. See Petersen, *Rediscovering Paul.*

## Conclusion

I fully understand the impatience a reader may feel when being subjected to such a long catalogue as this one, but I truly do not know of any way to make the critical point about the role of experience in Paul's letters other than showing its presence in each individual letter. In this matter, as in so many others, abstraction or abbreviation actually distorts.

When we appreciate the way in which the fundamental reality of the resurrection serves as an experiential foundation for all of Paul's teaching, and weave that experience into the texture of other ordinary and extraordinary experiences of Paul and his readers to which all the canonical letters bear witness, we come closer to grasping the reason why Paul's letters appear so filled with energy and tension, and why they remain so compelling and challenging even to readers today. His letters are, in the end, not the repositories of dull dogma but instruments of human transformation, conveying to those who read them now a sense of God's presence and power in the fabric of human freedom.

*Chapter 9*

# Convictions, Myths, Symbols, and Metaphors

In this chapter, I consider the complex interactions among experience, convictions, myths, symbols, and metaphors in the canonical Pauline collection. The basis for such an examination is the recognition of the preeminent role of experience in stimulating and shaping each of Paul's letters. As we have seen, Paul is far from a deductive or systematic thinker. He responds rather to what is happening in his own life and what he perceives as happening in the lives of believers. Specifically, his concern is always with what God is doing now in real human lives. If we miss this, I have suggested, we miss everything.

In an earlier chapter, I answered the question of what kind of Jew Paul was by identifying him as a prophet who saw himself as called by God (through an encounter with the risen Lord Jesus) and sent to proclaim as God's word the good news from and about God embedded in the experience of a crucified and raised Messiah (Gal 1:15-17). As it was for the prophets, for Paul the Spirit of God was alive, present, and powerfully active, both in himself and in the lives of others. In my earlier discussion of Paul and Scripture, I also argued that, even when he was not explicitly citing the sacred writings, he lived within, and perceived reality from within, the perspective of Scripture.

Informed by these considerations, we are prepared to enter more fully into Paul's language by suggesting that his central convictions, myths, symbols, and metaphors are all enlivened and complicated by the experience of God's presence and power in the world. I treat more briefly his convictions and symbols, because these are generally better known and appreciated, and spend more time looking at Paul's myths and metaphors, in part because they are such an important dimension of his language, and in part because they are far less appreciated or understood.

## Convictions

By "convictions" I mean fundamental beliefs concerning God and the world. Another term for convictions might be "premises." Expressed in the form of propositions, they constitute a kind of creed or, perhaps better, a construction of reality at the most basic level.[1] But they do not need to be expressed in propositions, or even made explicit, in order to govern perception and thought. Epicurus, for example, had the conviction that "natural science" (in Democritian physics) freed humans from superstition (religion). Sigmund Freud had the conviction that unconscious human drives (having to do with sexuality and death) accounted for individual human behavior. Karl Marx had the conviction that economic conflict between classes accounted for the progress of history. Paul's convictions, in contrast, were entirely religious in character and were derived mainly from the Scriptures that were so critical to the shaping of his Jewish identity.

The list of such truly fundamental convictions that can be stated in the form of straightforward propositions is less lengthy than might be supposed. It starts with the belief that there is but one God (Rom 3:30; 1 Cor 8:6; Gal 3:20; Eph 4:6; 1 Tim 2:5)—the "living and true God" in contrast to idols (1 Thess 1:9)—who is the source and goal of all that is (Rom 11:36; 1 Cor 8:6), a God who creates the world (Rom 4:17; 9:19–24; 1 Cor 1:28; 8:6; 1 Tim 4:4) and whose presence and power can be discerned from the shape of creation itself (Rom 1:19–20).[2] This one God is sovereign over all creatures (Rom 9:19–24) but has chosen Israel to be his special people in the world (Rom 9:1–13; 11:1–36) and revealed his will to them through the prophets and the writings (Rom 1:2; 3:1–2; 9:25–10:21; 1 Cor 7:19; 10:1–13; 14:20–25; 2 Cor 3:7–18; Gal 3:7–29; 4:21–31; Eph 1:4, 11; 2 Tim 3:15–16).[3] Paul believes that this God has what Gianbattista Vico called "maker's knowledge" of creatures,[4] able to see the minds and hearts of humans with impartiality (Rom 2:5–16; 1 Cor 8:3; Gal 4:9) and rewarding or punishing humans justly according to their deeds (Rom 2:6; 2 Tim 4:8, 14). He holds that the living God does not stand aloof from humans but enters into relations with them

---

1. For the ways in which creeds construct worlds, see L. Johnson, *Creed*.

2. Unless otherwise indicated, Scripture quotations in this chapter are from the NRSV.

3. It is worth repeating the observation that this element of the canonical letters is concentrated in the six letters cited (above all Romans and Galatians!), and scarcely appears in 1 and 2 Thessalonians, Colossians, Philippians, Titus, 1 Timothy, or Philemon.

4. Giambattista Vico's (1668–1744) great work is the *Scienza Nuova* (1725). The idea of maker's knowledge can be found in paragraph 331.

through covenant (Rom 9:4; 11:27; 1 Cor 11:25; 2 Cor 3:6, 14; Gal 3:17; 4:24; Eph 2:12) and rescues them from affliction (Rom 9:27; 10:13; 11:14, 26; 1 Cor 1:18, 21; 15:2; 2 Cor 2:15; Gal 1:4; Eph 2:5, 8; 2 Thess 2:10; 1 Tim 2:4; 2 Tim 1:9; Titus 3:5). Paul holds that God alone is the giver of life who raises the dead (Rom 4:15; 8:11; 1 Cor 15:45; 2 Cor 3:6; Gal 3:21). If the positive experience of God in this life is a matter of gracious gift and mercy (Rom 9:23; 11:31; 15:9; Eph 2:4; 1 Tim 1:2; 2 Tim 1:2, 18; Titus 3:5), the negative experience is a matter of wrath and destruction (Rom 1:18; 2:5, 8; 3:5; 9:22; Eph 2:3; 5:6; Col 3:6; 1 Thess 1:10; 2:16; 5:9). All these convictions are bedrock for a first-century Torah-observant Jew like Paul. What gives them a distinctive color, as we have seen, is the experientially based conviction that God's agent of intervention in the present is the crucified and exalted Lord Jesus, whose Spirit is powerfully present among those who profess their faith in him.

Less firmly grounded in Scripture is the conviction expressed widely throughout Paul's letters that opposition to God's will (God's kingdom) is greater than individual human rebelliousness. Resistance to God's sovereignty takes on a cosmic force, whether personified as Satan—who briefly appears in Scripture (1 Chr 21:1; Job 1:6–12; 2:1–7; Zech 3:1–2) but now serves as an agent who hinders Paul's mission and the integrity of his communities (Rom 16:20; 1 Cor 5:5; 7:5; 2 Cor 2:11; 11:14; 12:7; 1 Thess 2:18; 2 Thess 2:9; 1 Tim 1:20; 5:15), or as demons who sponsor idolatrous cults and false teaching (1 Cor 10:20–21; 1 Tim 4:1), or more elaborately as "powers and principalities" (Rom 8:38; 1 Cor 15:24; Eph 1:21; 3:10; 6:12; Col 1:16; 2:10, 15) and "elements of the universe," who hold humans in thrall and whose power must be overcome (Gal 4:3, 9; Col 2:8, 20).[5] Similarly, "death," "sin," and "flesh" are negatively personified by Paul as inhibitors of human freedom and therefore as inimical to God's sovereignty, to a degree not anticipated by Scripture (see esp. Rom 5:14–21; 6:9; 7:5, 13, 25; 8:6, 38; 1 Cor 15:26–56; Gal 5:13, 17; 2 Tim 1:10). Are such constructions of cosmic opposition to God derived from contemporary Jewish literature?[6] Surely, in part. Are they given their distinctive emphasis by Paul's own experience? In part, almost certainly.

The interactions of such convictions and experience are multiple within the canonical letters. To begin with, experience can be a *confirmation* of convictions. Paul's experience of God's power at work in Christ's resurrection and exaltation, for example, massively confirms the conviction that God

---

5. See Schlier, *Powers and Principalities*; G. Williams, *Spirit World*.
6. See Münderlein, "Die Überwindung der Mächte."

creates from nothing and gives life to the dead (Rom 4:17). The presence of the Holy Spirit acting and speaking within Paul and his communities emphatically confirms the conviction that what the prophets foretold is actual in the present experience of the church (Rom 1:2; 1 Cor 11:3-16; 14:1-40).

But experience can also be a *challenge* to a former understanding of fundamental convictions. Thus, God raising to new life one who according to Scripture was cursed by God (Deut 21:23; Gal 3:13) challenges both Scripture's adequacy to comprehend God's work and the notion that the resurrection is only future and only for those considered righteous under the law. Similarly, God's raising a people out of nothing from among the gentiles (1 Cor 1:26-31; Rom 9:6-33; Gal 2:8; 1 Thess 2:16; Eph 2:11-22; Col 1:27) challenges the understanding of election as pertaining only to the biological descendants of Abraham (Rom 3:26-31; 9:6-11:36; Gal 4:21-31).

Such challenges, in turn, can lead to the *modification* of convictions. Thus, the experience of new life from the risen Christ shows that life does not come from observance of the law but from the power of the Holy Spirit (Rom 8:1-17; Gal 3:10-14); similarly, although righteousness—in the sense of being rightly related to God—remains a fundamental conviction, it is modified: it is enacted not by observance of the law but by faithful obedience to the living God (Rom 3:21-26; 5:18-21; Gal 2:16-21).

It was not the reading of new writings, or conversations with different teachers, or a process of logical deduction, that led Paul to find his basic beliefs at once confirmed, challenged, and modified. It was precisely the powerful experiences of God's power in his own life and in his communities that strengthened, tested, and altered the beliefs that were his as a pious Jew.

His experience could even lead to the *expansion* of an inherited conviction. Such is the case with Paul's understanding of God's action on behalf of humans through Jesus as gift (*charis, dosis, dōrea*). Certainly, Scripture already stressed the fact that God's call of Israel and God's mercy toward his people were not earned but the result of God's gracious free choice. Indeed, the choice of Israel appeared even to the Israelites themselves as paradoxical, impossible to account for in terms of normal human calculation (see Deut 4:32-40). But in Paul's experience and that of his churches, the gift character of God's action here and now—the surprising and even startling way God worked through a crucified and raised Messiah and was calling the gentiles to a share in his life—makes even clearer that what is being experienced is not a human accomplishment but a pure gift from the Creator. It is by gift that humans are saved (Eph 2:5), that God's love is poured into their hearts through the Holy Spirit (Eph 5:6, 15), that a persecutor of the church has become an apostle (1 Cor 15:10), that the church as God's assembly exists at all (Eph 2:5; Titus 2:11). Paul's letters are steeped in the language of gift, precisely because that is the dimension of God's sovereignty he and his readers experience most directly.[7]

Such an expanded conviction occurs on the opposite side as well. Corresponding to the overwhelming experience of God's power that comes by gift is the contrary experience of rejection of the gift, not only among the Jews who ought to have recognized this new manifestation of God's graciousness (1 Thess 2:13–16; 1 Cor 2:8; 9:30–10:31), but also among those who in various ways distort the gift that has been given (2 Cor 11:4–6; Gal 1:6–7; Col 2:16–23; 1 Tim 1:7–20). Above all, it is the experience of persecution that convinces Paul of a more cosmic resistance to God's will than can be attributed to mere human frailty (Rom 8:38–39; 16:17–20; 2 Cor 1:3–11; 10:1–6; Col 1:24–25; 1 Thess 2:18; 2 Thess 1:3–10; 2:3–12; 2 Tim 3:1–14)—thus the expanded sense of the demonic, the satanic, and the rule of personified forces. It is not as though, for Paul, God's power is matched by such powers of resistance: the death and resurrection of Jesus have fundamentally destroyed their reign over humans (Rom 5:12–21; 1 Cor 15:24–25; Phil 2:9–11; Col 2:14–15; Eph 1:20–23). But the total elimination of such resistance lies still in the future, when "God will be all things in all things" (*panta en pasin*, 1 Cor 15:28). To use a military analogy, although the Vicksburg Campaign and Sherman's March to the Sea ensured that the South could not win the Civil War, Confederate resistance did not utterly disappear, and soldiers continued to fight and die in battle. For Paul, similarly, believers in Christ must continue to do battle against the forces that continue to resist the gift of God's freedom (Rom 6:13–14; 1 Cor 10:20–22; 2 Cor 10:2–4; Eph 6:10–17).

Finally, Paul's experience, and that of his churches, *complicated* the most fundamental conviction of all derived from his Jewish heritage, the oneness of God. In 1 Cor 8:5–6 (NABRE) he declares: "Even though there are so-called gods in heaven and on earth (there are, to be sure, many 'gods' and 'lords'), yet for us there is one God, the Father, from whom are all things and for whom we exist, and one Lord, Jesus Christ, through whom all things are and through whom we exist."[8]

---

7. For *charis*, see Rom 1:5; 3:24; 4:4, 16; 5:2, 15, 17, 20, 21; 6:1, 14, 15; 11:5–6; 1 Cor 1:4; 3:10; 2 Cor 1:12; 4:15; 8:1; 12:9; Gal 2:21; 5:4; Eph 1:6–7; 2:7–8; 3:2, 8; 4:7; Phil 1:7; Col 1:6; 3:16; 2 Thess 1:12; 2:16; 1 Tim 1:12, 14; 2 Tim 1:9; 2:1; Titus 3:7; for *dosis*, see Phil 4:15; 2 Cor 9:7; for *dōrea, dōrean, dōrema, dōron*, see Rom 3:24; 5:15, 16, 17; 2 Cor 9:15; 11:7; Eph 2:8; 3:7; 4:7. This aspect of Paul's letters has been examined by Barclay, *Paul and the Gift*.

8. Cf. 1 Tim 2:5–6: "For there is one God, and one mediator between God and the

## Myth and Symbol

It is important to state at once that, for Paul, all these convictions or beliefs point to realities that are experientially based and tested. God's creation of the world is not a cipher for some other truth; it is literally true: God brings into being that which did not exist; God is the single and sovereign power to which all creatures are ordered. Paul insists that this truth is accessible to the human heart and mind that is not blinded or disordered (Rom 1:19–23). Similarly, as I have already shown, the resurrection of Jesus is not an allegory for a universal truth; it is a real event concerning a real person and a real experience for those touched by the power unleashed by that event (1 Cor 15:3–8). The one who became "life-giving Spirit" is the source of the power manifested within and among believers (1 Cor 15:45; 12:13). The changes among them and within them caused by the experience of this power, changes inexplicable in terms of ordinary human transactions, constitute the empirical evidence for the reality of the event itself: "No one can say 'Jesus is Lord' except in the Holy Spirit" (1 Cor 12:3, adapted). Conversely, resistance to God's rule is also real, and its power shows itself empirically in oppression and persecution (1 Thess 2:15–16). At their core, Paul's letters are neither embroidered tales about the past nor fanciful visions for the future; they deal with what he experienced as real, indeed as most real, in the present.

Readers have little difficulty in taking Paul's language as literal when he speaks of his visits, or sending delegates, or taking up a collection. His language in such cases has empirical reference to actual persons and places. He could just as easily be speaking of pots and pans and preparing supper, or, for that matter, be speaking of Jesus's death on the cross, or the persecution he and his colleagues endure. But when Paul seeks to express the *causes* of the present experience of power, or tries to state its *meaning* or *significance*, his language necessarily requires other registers, for in these cases truth cannot be stated with the same flat, empirically referential language used for events, persons, places, and interactions that are either completely quotidian (pots and pans) or historically disconfirmable (death on the cross, persecution). In such cases, truth must be expressed through mythic, symbolic, or metaphorical language. I consider the first two briefly before considering metaphor in greater detail, recognizing that the three kinds of language often intermingle.

human race, Christ Jesus, himself human, who gave himself as a ransom for all" (author's translation).

## Myth

Just as the canonical letters dismiss rhetoric and philosophy, yet, as we have seen, make use of both in a nonprofessional manner, so also do the canonical letters reject "myths and genealogies" (1 Tim 1:4; 4:7; 2 Tim 4:4) and "Jewish myths" (Titus 1:14), because Paul regards them as leading to useless speculation and debate rather than attention to God's way of ordering the world.[9] Yet, in the anthropological sense of the term, Paul clearly himself uses mythic language when he tries to express the cause of the present power and presence experienced by himself and his communities. Language is mythic when—usually but not always in the form of a story or a story fragment—supernatural beings or powers (by definition nonempirical realities) are said to intersect the empirical plane, interacting with or affecting empirical things and persons.[10] The case of miraculous discourse is classic: something happens on the empirical level (a sickness is suddenly healed), and the cause of that effect is ascribed to a nonvisible supernatural cause (God).[11]

I cite only two classic examples within the canonical letters. In 2 Cor 5:19 Paul states that "God was in Christ reconciling the world to himself."[12] The sentence is perfectly lucid in lexical, grammatical, and syntactical terms. Linguistically, it is as simple as "Mother is in the kitchen boiling potatoes for supper." But in Paul's simple sentence, there is only one implied empirical subject—namely, Jesus—and even he is characterized in terms of a religious/political title, "the Anointed One."[13] Otherwise, "God," "the world," and "reconciling" lack any real definition (or verifiability). Despite that, the subject "God" is said to effect a result ("reconciliation") with another subject ("world") through or in a third subject ("Christ"), and this in the form of a past activity (using a periphrastic imperfect). We have, in other words, a highly nonspecific characterization of the effect of Jesus's ministry, life, and death, or even his very existence—an effect caused by the invisible subject "God" on a completely generalized object, "world."

9. See Colson, "Myths and Genealogies"; L. Johnson, "1 Timothy 1:1–20."

10. For a sense of how mythic language is approached by various fields, see Sebeok, *Myth*; Von Hendy, *Modern Construction of Myth*; Strenski, *Four Theories of Myth*.

11. See L. Johnson, *Miracles*, 68–75.

12. Author's translation of *Hoti theos ēn en Christo kosmon katallassōn heautō*. The mythic character of the statement is unaffected by the choice to read *en Christo* instrumentally ("through/in Christ") or locatively/ontologically ("God was *in* Christ").

13. The nuance is emphasized by the consistent translation of *ho Christos* as "the Anointed" in Hart, *New Testament*.

This is the language of myth. Nothing in the statement is even potentially verifiable through any epistemology calibrated to historical or scientific subjects. Yet, for Paul (and for us, his readers), it is a statement that is profoundly true, because it rightly identifies that our experience of reconciliation has its ultimate source not in ourselves but in God; has come to us not through our own efforts but through the gift that is the Messiah Jesus; that has significance not only for us but for all creation.[14]

Because the language of myth has had such a troubled existence, it is necessary to state once more exactly what I mean when I use the term. I do not align myself with the rationalistic tradition extending from David Hume to Rudolf Bultmann that demands of the biblical language that it be tested for "truth" by the criteria of natural science, and designated as "false" when it does not conform to the linguistic standards regarded as appropriate to science or philosophy in the critic's own age.[15] I am not in the least suggesting that Paul's language needs "demythologization" so that a kernel of existential truth (about the human condition today) might be salvaged from a language that fundamentally misleads about reality (that is, God and the world). Just the opposite: I hold that the language of myth should enthusiastically be embraced by believers, because such discourse can express truth in a manner that other language cannot.

A second example. In Gal 4:4–5 (NABRE) Paul states, "When the fullness of time came, God sent his Son, born of a woman, born under the law, to ransom those under the law, so that we might receive the adoption [as sons]."[16] Once more, the story fragment[17] concerns the human being Jesus, not in his ministry, death, and resurrection, but in his birth. And Paul supplies the empirical details: he was "born of a woman" like other humans, and "born under the law" like other Jews. But the framing of these empirical facts concerning Jesus can only be called mythic in the sense I have defined. Paul's gentile readers are said in Gal 4:3 to have been "enslaved to elements of the world"

---

14. For a fuller discussion, see L. Johnson, "God Was in Christ."

15. The epistemological reduction carried out by David Hume in *An Inquiry Concerning Human Understanding* (1748) and systematically applied by Strauss in *Life of Jesus Critically Examined* forms the premise for Bultmann's "New Testament and Mythology."

16. *Hote de ēlthen to plērōma tou chronou, exapesteilen ho theos ton huion autou, genomenon ek gynaikos, genomenon hypo nomon, hina tous hypo nomon exagorasē, hina tēn huiothesian apolabōmen.* Once more, the mythic character of the statement is not affected by the exegetical problem posed by the two successive *hina* clauses, which lead us to ask about the reference of each.

17. See Hays, *Faith of Jesus Christ.*

(author's translation).[18] Jesus is "God's Son"; he is "sent by God"; his task was to "ransom" those under the law, so that "we might receive the adoption [as sons]"—that is, as sons of God. This framework and statement of purpose is decidedly nonempirical. Neither the elemental forces nor God, nor God's Son, nor the act of ransoming, nor adoption by God, is locatable within the discourse used to describe ordinary human events or natural occurrences. It is true that the term "sent" could refer to an assigned mission or task, and that is part of its sense here. But in this place, it also suggests being "sent" from one place (where the Son was with God) to another place (where the Son was with humans, working to rescue and elevate them). As with 2 Cor 5:19, Paul's mythic language in Gal 4:3–5 is employed to express this truth: God's power and presence were at work in Jesus, and that truth has as its support the experience among his readers of that same power and presence (Gal 3:1–5).

In both of these examples, Paul is not spinning a tale about divine figures of the distant past. He is speaking about the higher significance of a man who was crucified only twenty-odd years earlier. The language of myth enables Paul to cast the story of that man within a cosmic drama that, even though it cannot be seen or touched, measured or counted, is nevertheless real. It is language that is required if first-order speech about "God" as a subject is to be possible. Precisely the premise that "God" and "world" can be subject and predicate in the same sentence elicits the use of mythic discourse.

These two examples of mythic discourse also show the intermixture of metaphor and myth. As I will show, when Paul speaks of "reconciliation" in 2 Cor 5:19, he uses metaphorical language drawn from the realm of ancient diplomacy. Likewise, in Gal 4:3–5 he uses metaphors drawn from ancient economics (slavery/ransom) and kinship (children/adoption). More on this after we look briefly at Paul's use of symbols.

*Symbol*

Symbols are words or gestures (signs) that point beyond themselves to some deeper reality, but do so in a nonarbitrary fashion, because they also participate in that reality.[19] Traffic signs have no depth of meaning, because

18. *Houtōs kai hēmeis, hote ēmen nēpioi, hypo ta stoicheia tou kosmou ēmetha dedoulōmenoi.*

19. For perspectives, see Douglas, *Natural Symbols*; Whitehead, *Symbolism*; Urban, *Language and Reality*; Olson, *Myth, Symbol, and Reality*; Dupré, *Symbols of the Sacred*.

they not only could take any shape or color but also signify only one thing (stop or go or yield). Bread, in contrast, is a natural symbol for human life, because eating bread actually supports the life of the body. Eating bread together is consequently also a natural symbol for community, because when people eat together, they are, at least for that moment, in communion as a social "body." Similarly, wine is a natural symbol of life and pleasure. Like bread (made of wheat), it consists in elements of God's creation (grapes) that have been transformed by human craft. Drinking wine together is, like sharing bread, a symbol for community. Blood also is a natural symbol for life. Within the body, it can be regarded as the life force; draining blood from the body is draining life from the body (see Gen 9:4-6; Lev 17:11). It is a short step to seeing the pouring out of wine as a libation as a symbol of the offering of blood, or the drinking of wine together as a sharing in a common lifeblood.

### Bread/Wine, Body/Blood

Like other ancient associations and cults, Christ-believers ate bread and drank wine together as a religious ritual.[20] But as we see in 1 Corinthians, the natural symbols of bread and wine become symbols for the death and resurrection of Jesus and his continuing presence. In 11:23-25 Paul cites the words spoken by Jesus on the night he was arrested: "Taking bread and giving thanks, he broke it and said, 'This is my body which is for you. Do this in my memory.' In like manner he took the cup after the meal, saying, 'This is the cup of the new covenant which is in my blood. Do this in my memory'" (author's translation). Bread and wine become signs of the death of Jesus: his body is given for them; his blood is drained for them. Bread and wine do not signify life in any simple or straightforward fashion: the bread gives life to the Corinthian "body" because Jesus gave his body "for them"; the wine gives life to the Corinthian community because Jesus spilled his blood as a "new covenant" for them. Their life, in short, comes at the cost of his life as a human person. So they eat and drink, Paul says, to "proclaim the Lord's death until he comes" (11:26).

But Christ is not absent from this community meal. Christ not only still lives, but he shares in the life and power of God as "life-giving Spirit," so that the Corinthians who participate in his meal have a real share in his

---

20. See L. Johnson, "Meals Are Where the Magic Is."

resurrected life.[21] The bread and wine now point both to the continuing powerful presence of the Lord among them (see 1 Cor 5:1–5) and to the sacrificial death that was the passage to his exaltation as Lord. Thus, Paul asks his readers who want to share in the Lord's supper while continuing to participate in other religious cults:

> The cup of blessing that we bless, is it not a participation [*koinōnia*] in the blood of Christ? The bread that we break, is it not a participation [*koinōnia*] in the body of Christ? Because there is one loaf of bread, we many are one body, because we all share [*metechomen*] in the one loaf of bread. . . . You cannot drink the cup of the Lord and the cup of demons; you are not able to share in the table of the Lord and the table of demons. Or, are we testing the Lord? Surely we are not more powerful than He! (1 Cor 10:16–17, 21–22 NAB adapted)

Here once more, in the realm of symbols, we see how the experience of Paul and his communities, above all the experience of the death and resurrection of Jesus, gives new shape to ancient terms and gestures.

## Cross

Although he uses the explicit language in only six of his letters,[22] the cross is another term Paul uses both literally and symbolically. As an instrument of Roman execution that was employed mainly for slaves and those the Romans wanted to portray as slaves, crucifixion already bore with it resonances of shame, suffering, and poverty, on top of the obvious experience of (yes) excruciating pain and death.[23] Paul uses *stauros* and *stauroun* literally with reference to Jesus's death: he was crucified by "the rulers of this world" (see 1 Cor 1:13, 23; 2:2, 8; Col 1:20; 2:14; Eph 2:16; Phil 2:8), a manner of death that was a "stumbling block" to faith especially for Jews (1 Cor 1:23; Gal 5:11; see also Rom 9:32), since, according to Torah, "hanging upon a tree" meant that one was cursed by God (Deut 21:23; Gal 3:13).

---

21. My position is directly opposite that of J. Smith, *Drudgery Divine*, 116–43.

22. The noun *stauros* ("cross") appears in 1 Cor 1:17, 18; Gal 5:11; 6:12, 14; Eph 2:16; Phil 2:8; 3:18; Col 1:20; 2:14, and the verb *stauroun* ("to crucify") occurs in 1 Cor 1:13, 23; 2:2, 8; 2 Cor 13:4; Gal 3:1; 5:24; 6:14.

23. See Hengel, *Crucifixion in the Ancient World*.

But as Paul insists to the Galatians, it was when they responded with faith to Paul's "displaying before [their] eyes Jesus Christ as crucified" (3:1, author's translation) that they received the Holy Spirit and had powerful deeds worked among them (3:1-5).[24] Paul likewise tells the Corinthians that the "word of the cross" (*logos tou staurou*, 1 Cor 1:18 RSV), which is foolishness to Greeks and a stumbling block to Jews, is, for those called, "Christ, the power of God, the wisdom of God" (*Christon theou dynamin kai theou sophian*, 1:24, author's translation), the occasion for the "demonstration [among them] of the Spirit and Power [or: spiritual power, or powerful spirit]" (2:4), so that their faith is not in human wisdom but "in the power of God" (2:5). The cross thus becomes for Paul more than a fact about Jesus's death. It becomes a symbol of the paradoxical way in which God's wisdom and power are manifested in his experience and that of his readers. It becomes so, to be sure, because Paul and his readers in fact experienced the power of the Spirit in connection with the proclamation of "the word of the cross."

The cross also becomes the symbol for the life of obedient faith lived in accord with that same pattern of power-in-weakness for the sake of others. Paul sees himself and his colleagues as "carrying in the body the death of Jesus, so that the life of Jesus may also be made visible in our bodies. . . . So death is at work in us, but life in you" (2 Cor 4:10-12). This death-for-life existence replicates the pattern of the cross: "He was crucified in weakness, but lives by the power of God. For we are weak in him, but in dealing with you we will live with him by the power of God" (2 Cor 13:4).

The *manner* in which Jesus underwent his suffering and death is also paradigmatic. Although in the form of God, he emptied himself and took the form of a slave, "and being found in human form, he humbled himself and became obedient to the point of death—even death on a cross" (Phil 2:8). Such a disposition of humility is one Paul enjoins on the Philippians: they are to seek not only their own interest but also that of others (2:3-4), thus being of the same mind as Christ (2:5). Paul's own self-emptying of privilege (3:2-11) and the way in which Timothy and Epaphroditus sought the interests of the Philippians rather than their own (2:19-30) are living exemplars of this pattern of life: "Brothers and sisters, join in imitating me, and observe those who live according to the example you have in us" (3:17). In contrast, Paul declares, those who seek their own benefit "live as enemies of the cross" (3:18).

Similarly, Paul regards those pressuring others in Galatia to be circumcised as seeking to "boast about your flesh," and not be persecuted for the

---

24. Unless noted otherwise, Scripture translations in this paragraph are mine.

cross of Christ (Gal 6:12–13). But Paul says of himself, "May I never boast of anything except the cross of our Lord Jesus Christ, by which the world has been crucified to me and I to the world" (6:14; cf. 2:19). And he wants the Galatian believers to follow the same pattern: "Those who belong to Christ Jesus have crucified the flesh with its passions and desires. If we live by the Spirit, let us also be guided by the Spirit" (5:24–25). Because of the death and resurrection of Jesus, the cross, formerly a symbol only of human cruelty and degradation, has been transmuted into a symbol for the paradoxical way in which God exercises power, and the pattern of humble obedience and service among believers.

### Spirit

As the quotation from Gal 5:24–25 indicates, "Spirit" is another powerful and even more pervasive symbol for Paul.[25] He uses *pneuma* conventionally with reference to human psychology, where the term *pneuma* points to a dimension of the self, especially to human interiority and intentionality (see, e.g., Rom 1:9; 2:29; 1 Cor 2:11; 5:4; 7:34; 14:15; 16:18; 2 Cor 2:13; 7:1, 13; 12:18; Gal 6:1, 18; Phil 4:23; Col 2:5; 1 Thess 5:23; 2 Tim 4:22; Phlm 25). He uses *pneumata* as well for (especially inimical) cosmic forces (see 1 Cor 12:1; Eph 2:2; 1 Tim 4:1). But he uses the term *pneuma* most often as a symbol for God's presence and power active among humans, whether *pneuma* occurs by itself or is qualified as "the Holy Spirit" (*to hagion pneuma, to pneuma to hagion*).

The element of *power* appears frequently where the (Holy) Spirit is used instrumentally, as an enabling energy connected to the resurrection of Jesus (Rom 1:4; 8:11; 15:19; 1 Tim 3:16), or to the energizing of believers generally (Rom 15:13; Eph 3:16; 1 Thess 1:5–6; 2 Thess 2:8; 2 Tim 1:7), or with more specificity: with the outpouring of God's love (Rom 5:5); with newness of life (Rom 7:6; 8:10; 2 Cor 3:3–8; Gal 5:25; Eph 4:23; Titus 3:5); with holiness (2 Thess 2:13); with liberation (Rom 8:2); with guidance (Rom 8:14; Gal 5:18); with adoption by God (Rom 8:15); with God's rule (Rom 14:17); with prophecy (1 Cor 7:40; 12:10; 14:32); with revelation (1 Cor 2:10, 12; Eph 3:5); with gifts of prayer and utterance (1 Cor 13:2; 14:2); with wonders (Gal 3:2–5); with the promise of God to Abraham (Gal 3:14); with access to God (Eph 2:18); with the capacity to proclaim Jesus as Lord (1 Cor 12:3).

25. See Fee, *God's Empowering Presence.*

The element of *presence* dominates in passages that speak of the Spirit as "dwelling" in believers (Rom 8:9, 11; 1 Cor 3:16; 6:19; Eph 2:22; 2 Tim 1:14); as that "in which" believers are baptized, or which they drink (1 Cor 12:13); as a pledge (2 Cor 1:22; 5:5) or seal (Eph 1:13, 17); as that with which believers are "filled" (Eph 5:18) or united (Phil 2:1); or as the gift given by God (Rom 5:5; 1 Thess 4:8; 2 Tim 1:7).

Paul personalizes the *pneuma* in passages that speak of the Spirit of God not just as power or presence but as a subject who acts. The Spirit testifies (Rom 8:16), comes to the assistance of believers (Rom 8:26), moans (Rom 8:26), has a *phronēma* (Rom 8:27), bears witness (Rom 9:1), searches all things (1 Cor 2:10–11), enables and distributes all gifts of speech (1 Cor 12:11), can be grieved (Eph 4:30) or spurned (1 Thess 5:19), supplies (Phil 1:19), and speaks (1 Tim 4:1). The Spirit even appears as a subject identified with the risen Christ, who, as 1 Cor 15:45 states, had become "life-giving spirit." Thus, Rom 8:9 speaks synonymously of the Spirit dwelling in believers and Christ dwelling in them. Thus, Gal 4:6 speaks of God sending the Spirit of his Son. Thus, Paul states flatly in 2 Cor 3:17, "The Lord is the Spirit," and concludes his second letter to the Corinthians with language that unmistakably links the Spirit to both God and Jesus in a fashion that can later support the development of trinitarian thought: "The grace of the Lord Jesus Christ, the love of God, and the communion of the Holy Spirit be with all of you" (2 Cor 13:13).

## Metaphor

Paul's language is richly metaphorical. By "metaphor" I do not mean the casual figures of speech common to all, as when Paul refers to a "door [*thyra*] opening" for his mission, with the obvious sense of "an opportunity" (1 Cor 16:9; 2 Cor 2:12; Col 4:3). I mean rather the sort of speech by which Paul, drawing on diverse and culturally well-embedded linguistic fields, seeks to express the mystery of God's working among humans through the crucified and raised Messiah Jesus.[26] Paul's most important metaphorical constructions have to do with the reality of salvation and the character of the church.

26. For the cognitive dimensions of metaphor, see M. Johnson, *Philosophical Perspectives on Metaphor*; M. Johnson, *Moral Imagination*; Lakoff and Johnson, *Metaphors We Live By*; Lakoff, *Women, Fire, and Dangerous Things*; Wheelwright, *Metaphor and Reality*.

*Metaphors for Salvation*[27]

When it comes to the activity of God in behalf of humans, to be sure, even the language of "salvation" is metaphorical. In ordinary usage, "saving" means getting someone or something out of a negative condition (peril, poverty, slavery) through an act of rescue and placing them in a positive condition (safety, prosperity, freedom). In his reading of the LXX, Paul would have found salvation language used for the many interventions of God on behalf of his people Israel: the Lord saved them (*sōzein*; see Deut 33:29; Judg 2:16; 3:9; 6:14; 1 Sam 4:3; Ps 7:10; 16:7; Isa 63:9), establishing them in a place of safety or salvation (*sōtēria*; see Deut 32:15; 1 Chr 16:35; Ps 23:5; 24:5; 26:1; Isa 12:2; 25:9), so that he could properly be designated as savior (*sōtēr*; see Exod 14:13; 1 Sam 11:13; 2 Sam 10:11; 2 Kgs 13:5; Ps 37:32; 87:1). Paul can therefore speak of God's intervention through the death and resurrection of Jesus, and his future intervention at the parousia, in terms of salvation: God saves (Rom 5:10; 11:28), delivers (1 Thess 1:10; 2 Tim 3:11; 4:8), rescues (Gal 1:4); believers are "those being saved" (Rom 10:13; 11:11; 1 Cor 1:18; 15:2; Eph 2:5; 2 Tim 1:9; Titus 2:11, 13–14; 3:5), who already have or are anticipating the "day of salvation" (2 Cor 6:2; see also Phil 1:19, 28; 2:12; 1 Thess 1:10; 2 Thess 2:13; 2 Tim 2:10) and can call both the Father and Christ their "Savior" (Phil 3:20; Eph 5:23; 1 Tim 1:1, 15; 2:3–4, 15; 2 Tim 1:10; Titus 1:4; 3:4).

If the language of salvation expresses in broadest terms the changed reality (the new creation) effected by God through Christ, other, more specific metaphorical fields are also used by Paul as pointers to a truth that is incapable of being stated adequately through any set of propositions or metaphors. Each has its own logic and distinctive language.

*Political/Diplomatic/Military* Paul does not advance a political agenda in the normal sense of that term: he does not establish a state that encompasses a single population or occupies a single place. But building once more on the precedent of Scripture, political language serves as an overarching metaphor for his speech about God's work in the world. Here we find his

---

27. This section expands on the insight of Boring, "Language of Universal Salvation." I treat here only major metaphors. Paul uses a variety of other metaphors that are less dominant or coherently developed, such as the metaphor of mirror/image/illumination (Rom 8:29; 1 Cor 13:12; 15:49; 2 Cor 3:17–18; 4:4–6; Eph 1:18; 3:9; 5:14), stages of human growth (1 Cor 3:1–3; 14:10–12, 20), athletics (1 Cor 9:24–27; 15:32; Gal 2:2; 5:7; Phil 1:27, 30; 2:16; 3:14; 4:1, 3; Col 1:29; 2:18; 1 Thess 2:19; 4:7–10), medicine (1 Thess 2:7; 2 Tim 2:16–17), clothing (1 Cor 15:53–54; 2 Cor 3:14; 4:3; 5:3–4; Gal 3:27; Eph 4:24; Col 3:12), and education (1 Cor 4:6, 15, 21; Gal 3:24–25; Eph 4:20–21; Phil 4:9; Titus 2:12).

use of "kingdom/rule of God" (1 Cor 6:9–10; 15:24; Rom 14:6–9; Eph 5:5; Col 1:13; 4:11; 1 Thess 2:12; 2 Thess 1:5; 2 Tim 4:18), of the lordship of God and Jesus (1 Cor 1:2; 8:4–6; Rom 10:9; Eph 4:6; Phil 1:2, 14; 2:11; 3:8; Phlm 3, 16; 2 Thess 2:1; 1 Tim 1:17; 6:15), and of the rule exercised by death (Rom 5:14–21), sin (Rom 5:21; 6:12–14), God (Rom 1:9; 14:9), and Christ (Eph 1:21)—including the suppression of powers and principalities (Eph 3:10; Col 1:16; 2:10). Indeed, the title *Christos* ("anointed one") finds it place within this register, as in the frequent designation "Jesus Christ our Lord" (Rom 1:4, 7; 5:1, 11, 21; 6:23; 7:25; 8:39; 13:14; 15:6; 16:20; 1 Cor 1:2, 3, 7, 8, 9, 10; 6:11; 8:6; 15:31, 57; 16:23; 2 Cor 1:2, 3; 13:13; Gal 1:3; 6:18; Eph 1:2, 3, 17; 3:11; 5:20; 6:23, 24; Phil 1:2; 2:11; 3:20; 4:23; Col 1:3; 2:6; 3:24; 1 Thess 1:1, 3; 5:9, 23, 28; 2 Thess 1:1, 2, 12; 2:1, 14, 16; 3:6, 12, 18; 1 Tim 1:2, 12; 6:3, 14; 2 Tim 1:2; Phlm 3, 25) as well as in the "anointing" or "sealing" of believers (2 Cor 1:22). Within this metaphorical framework, the term "covenant" (2 Cor 3:6; Gal 4:24; Eph 2:12) finds its place, as does the promulgation of law through a mediator (Gal 3:19–20), the "arrival" (*parousia*) of a ruler (Phil 3:12; 1 Thess 3:13; 2 Thess 2:1) or a ruler's "appearance" (*epiphaneia*, 1 Tim 6:14; 2 Tim 1:10; Titus 2:13), a form of triumph announced by the blowing of a trumpet (1 Cor 14:8; 15:52; 1 Thess 4:16).

The term *ekklēsia* certainly has political associations (1 Cor 6:4; 10:32; 11:18), as does language designating aliens, strangers, and citizens (Eph 2:19; Phil 1:27; 3:20). Although they can also appear in cultic discourse, "bending the knee" (Eph 3:14) and "having boldness" (*parrhēsia*, 2 Cor 3:12; Eph 3:12; Col 2:15) and "access" (*prosagōgē*, Rom 5:2; Eph 2:18; 3:12) also have political resonances. Besides providing the broad framework for the metaphors of diplomacy and warfare for salvation, the metaphor of politics most directly expresses the experience of God's present activity through speaking of the exaltation of the crucified Jesus to "the right hand of God" (Col 3:1; Eph 1:20) and his being given the name over every other name, "Lord," so that all creatures must bend the knee before him (Phil 2:11) and all of God's enemies will be put under his feet (1 Cor 15:27–28; Eph 1:22).

The language of diplomacy is a subset of the political, and Paul uses it as a metaphor for God's saving action. Here the human condition of distance from God is expressed as alienation (Rom 5:10–11; 11:28; 2 Cor 5:18–20; Eph 2:12, 16). God acts to effect reconciliation (Rom 5:10–11; 11:15; 2 Cor 5:18–20; Col 1:20; Eph 2:16). Christ is an ambassador (Rom 5:11; 2 Cor 5:18) or mediator (1 Tim 2:5) who effects peace between God and humans (Rom 5:1; 1 Cor 7:15; Eph 2:14–17; Phil 1:7, 9; Col 1:20; 3:15; 2 Thess 3:16; 2 Tim 1:2). To this metaphorical field belongs the sending of representatives (apostles and del-

egates; Gal 1:1; 4:4; Titus 1:1; 2 Cor 5:18–20; 9:3, 11–12; Phil 2:25) and heralds
(1 Tim 2:7; 2 Tim 1:11) to proclaim (Rom 10:8, 14; 1 Cor 1:23; 9:27; 15:11–12;
2 Cor 1:9; 4:5; 11:4; Gal 2:2; 5:11; Phil 1:15; Col 1:23; 1 Thess 2:9; 1 Tim 3:16;
2 Tim 4:2) the good news from God (Rom 1:1, 16; 2:16; 10:16; 11:28; 15:16,
19; 1 Cor 4:15; 9:12, 14, 18, 23; 15:1; 2 Cor 2:12; 4:3–4; 8:18; 9:13; 10:14; 11:4,
7; Gal 1:6, 7, 11; 2:2, 5, 7, 14; Eph 1:13; 3:6; 6:15, 19; Phil 1:5, 7, 12, 16, 27; 2:22;
4:3, 15; Col 1:5, 23; 1 Thess 1:5; 2:2, 4, 8, 9; 3:2; 2 Thess 1:8; 2:14; 1 Tim 1:11;
2 Tim 1:8, 10; 2:8; Phlm 13). From this diplomatic realm derives the language
concerning letters of commendation (2 Cor 3:1; 10:11–12), of "qualification"
(2 Cor 3:4–5; Col 1:12), of "seal" (Eph 1:13; 4:30), and of "pledge" (Eph 1:14).

Less frequently employed is military imagery, another subset of the
political metaphor. Thus God conquers all enemies (Rom 8:37) and will
win the final victory (1 Cor 15:57) by destroying death (1 Cor 15:26; 2 Tim
1:10), displaying the victory won through the death and resurrection of Jesus
through a triumphal march (1 Cor 4:9–13; 2 Cor 2:14–16; Col 2:17). Since the
final victory has not yet been accomplished, believers are to serve as God's
soldiers (1 Cor 9:7; Phil 2:22; 2 Tim 2:3–4; Phlm 2), wearing the armor of
righteous lives as they do battle against cosmic forces (2 Cor 10:3–6; Rom
13:12; Eph 6:10–17; 1 Thess 5:8), making their members the weapons of righteousness (Rom 6:13).

*Economic* In economic diction, the condition of distance between God
and humans is expressed in terms of slavery (Rom 6:6, 17; 8:21; Gal 4:1,
8–9; Titus 2:9). God's action is expressed as a redemption (Rom 3:24; 8:21;
1 Cor 1:30; Gal 3:13; Eph 1:7; Col 1:14; 1 Tim 2:6). Christ's death is a ransom
(Gal 4:5; 1 Tim 2:6) that "purchases" humans (1 Cor 6:20; 7:23) and thereby
"frees" them (Rom 7:6; 8:2; 1 Cor 7:21–23; Gal 4:22–23). The positive result
is a condition of freedom (Rom 6:18; 8:21; 2 Cor 3:17; Gal 5:1, 13), which
finds expression in believers being "slaves" of the Lord (Phil 1:1; 2 Tim 2:24;
Titus 1:1).

*Cultic* In the language of the cult, the human condition of separation
from God is expressed by sin (Rom 3:9; 5:12; 1 Cor 15:56; Gal 3:22; Eph 2:1;
Col 1:14; 1 Thess 2:16; 1 Tim 5:24; 2 Tim 3:6). The work of Christ is a sacrificial death for sins as the Passover lamb (1 Cor 5:6–8) and a covenant in
his blood (Rom 3:21–25; 8:32; 1 Cor 10:18, 28; 11:25; 15:3; 2 Cor 5:21; Gal 1:4;
Eph 1:7; 2:13; 5:2; Col 1:14, 20), which accomplishes atonement and human
"access" to God (Rom 3:25; 5:2; Eph 2:18; 3:12). Humans are thereby "made
holy" or "sanctified" (Rom 6:19, 22; 15:16; 1 Cor 1:2, 30; 6:11; Eph 1:4; 5:26;
Col 1:22; 1 Thess 4:3, 7; 5:23; 2 Thess 2:13; 1 Tim 2:15; 2 Tim 1:9; 2:21). They

are "the holy ones" (Rom 1:7; 1 Cor 6:1–2; Eph 1:1, 4; Phil 1:1; Col 1:2, 4, 12; 1 Thess 3:13; 1 Tim 5:10; Phlm 5).

*Kinship* God is the father (2 Cor 6:18; Eph 2:18; 3:14–15; 4:6), who is head of the household and directs its management (Eph 1:10; 3:2, 9; 1 Tim 1:4). Humans are potential heirs of God (Rom 4:13–14; 8:17; 1 Cor 6:9–10; 15:50; Gal 3:18, 29; 4:1, 7, 30; 5:21; Eph 1:14, 18; 5:5), according to his will (Rom 9:4; 11:27; Gal 3:15, 17; Eph 2:12) and promise (Rom 4:13, 14, 16, 20; 9:4, 8, 9; 15:8; 2 Cor 1:20; 7:1; Gal 3:14–18, 21–22, 29; 4:23, 28; Eph 1:14, 18; 2:12; 3:6; 1 Tim 4:8; 2 Tim 1:1). But while they are still children, they are no better than slaves (Gal 3:15–29; 4:1–3). Before Christ they have not received what has been promised. Christ is God's own Son, whom God sends to ransom/liberate humans (Gal 4:4–5). Through the Holy Spirit, God makes them his adopted children (Rom 8:15, 23; 9:6–13; Gal 4:5–6; Eph 1:5), who will be conformed to the image of the Son, so that he is the "first-born of many children" (Rom 8:29; Eph 5:1, 8; see Col 1:15, 18), and they can receive the inheritance that is theirs as children of God (Eph 1:11, 14, 18; 3:6; 5:5; Col 1:12; 3:24; Titus 3:7).

*Forensic* The metaphor of the law court is used with great fluency by Paul. God is judge over all things (1 Cor 4:2–15; 5:13; 1 Thess 2:4; 2 Tim 4:1); he is righteous (Rom 1:17; 3:5, 21, 22, 25, 26; 10:3; 2 Tim 4:8) and renders judgment on the deeds of humans (Rom 2:2; 3:6) without partiality (Rom 2:11; 3:22; Eph 6:9; Col 3:25), responding to wrongdoing with condemnation (Rom 5:18; 8:1, 3; 2 Thess 1:8) or wrath (Rom 1:18; 2:5, 8; 4:15) and responding to righteous deeds with mercy (Rom 9:23; 11:31; Gal 6:16; 1 Tim 1:16–18), writing the names of the righteous in the book of life (Phil 4:3), by "reckoning" who is righteous and who is not (Rom 4:10, 11; 4:22, 23; 5:13; 8:8; Gal 3:6; Phil 3:7, 13, 18). At the heart of this metaphorical field is the law revealed by God (Rom 3:31; 4:13, 14; 5:13; 6:14; 7:1–23; 8:2, 3, 7; 9:31; 10:5; Gal 2:19; 3:11–13, 18–19, 21, 24; 4:21; 6:2; 1 Tim 1:8–9) with its commandments (Rom 7:8, 10, 13) that God wishes to be obeyed. These, globally, are "the works of the law" (Rom 3:28; 4:2; 9:31; Gal 2:17; 3:5, 6, 10), by the performance of which humans—according to the law itself—would be reckoned righteous and "live" (Gal 3:10–12).

Within the forensic framework, the human peril before God can be called "sin" (Rom 3:9, 12, 13, 16, 21; 2 Cor 5:21; Gal 1:4; 2:15), "unrighteousness" (Rom 1:18, 29; 6:13; 2 Thess 2:10; 2 Tim 2:19), "lawlessness" (Rom 6:19; 2 Cor 6:14; 2 Thess 2:7; 1 Tim 1:9; Titus 2:14), "transgression" (Rom 2:23; 5:14; Gal 2:18; 3:19; Eph 2:1; Col 2:13; 1 Tim 2:14), "faithlessness" (Rom 3:3; 11:20; 1 Tim 1:13), or "disobedience" (Rom 11:30–32; Eph 2:2;

5:6; Col 3:6). Christ in this framework is the "righteous one" (1 Cor 1:30) who, through his faithful obedience (Rom 1:17; 3:22–25; 5:12–21; Gal 2:16, 20; 3:11, 16, 23; Phil 2:5–11; 2 Cor 1:19–21) to God and apart from "the law" (Rom 3:21), was the means by which God "made righteous" others (Rom 3:26; 4:5, 24)—that is, established the possibility of human righteousness through faith, or being in right relationship with God and the world (Rom 3:24, 28; 4:3; 5:1, 16–19; 9:30–31; 10:10; 1 Cor 1:3; 6:11; 2 Cor 5:21; 11:15; Gal 2:16–17, 21; Eph 6:1–2; Phil 1:11; 3:6, 9; 2 Tim 3:5, 7–9). Indeed, although Christ himself shares in the judging role of God (2 Cor 5:10), he also serves as an advocate for believers (Rom 8:33–34).

Before turning to Paul's major metaphors for the church, a few comments on these discrete Pauline metaphors for "salvation" are appropriate. First, the evidence makes clear that there is no single metaphor that dominates or controls the others. The forensic metaphor is often taken to be such, at least in part because Romans is taken to be the center of "Paul's thought." But it is striking that forensic language scarcely appears in the Corinthian or Thessalonian correspondence. Second, each metaphor has its own logic and distinctive diction. Grasping how each works brings a better understanding of Paul's language. Third, Paul sometimes mixes his metaphors. Thus, in Rom 3:21–26 the cultic language of sacrifice and expiation appears within a passage that otherwise is thoroughly forensic in character. Such mixing does not indicate a theologically motivated interpolation, but only a fairly frequent Pauline practice. Fourth, the fact that Paul uses so many distinct dictions and mixes them so freely argues that the reality toward which he points is incapable of being captured by any single set of propositions or any single metaphor or set of metaphors. He seeks to speak of an experience of God's presence and power that can be experienced but cannot adequately be stated. All images are welcome. But none of them, alone or together, can capture the reality that has captured Paul and his readers.

*Metaphors for the Church*

As with "salvation," it is easy to forget that the word translated as "church" or "assembly" or "congregation" (*ekklēsia*) itself has a certain metaphorical quality, drawn first from the political assemblies of the Greco-Roman world and then applied to voluntary associations and cults.[28] Paul uses the term

28. See K. Schmidt, "ἐκκλησία"; Harland, *Associations, Synagogues, and Congregations.*

straightforwardly for the assemblies that he addresses in his letters, making clear, however, that these are not simply associations formed through the choice of their members but assemblies "called" into existence by God (*kalein*, Rom 8:30; 9:24–26; 1 Cor 1:9; Eph 4:4; 1 Thess 2:12; 4:7) as was the *qahal* of Israel in the wilderness (see Exod 16:3; Num 14:5; Deut 31:30). It is, therefore, "God's assembly" (1 Cor 1:2; 10:32; 15:9; 2 Cor 1:1; Gal 1:13; 1 Thess 2:14; 2 Thess 1:4; 1 Tim 3:5, 15) or the "assembly of Christ" (Rom 16:16), a gathering that ideally is enlivened by the Holy Spirit and directed by God's will, rather than by mere human enthusiasm or political debate.[29]

### God's Plantation

Paul only calls the congregation "God's field/planting" (*geōrgion*) in one passage (1 Cor 3:6–9): Paul planted, Apollos watered, but God gives the growth. The same image is implicit when he speaks of a vineyard in 1 Cor 9:7 and refers to "reaping and sowing" in Gal 6:8–9 and to "harvesting" in 1 Cor 9:9–11 and Rom 1:13. His use of agricultural imagery elsewhere (Rom 6:5; 7:4; 11:16–24; 1 Cor 15:20, 23, 37, 42; 2 Cor 9:6, 10; Eph 3:17; 5:9, 11; Phil 1:11, 22; Col 1:6, 10, 25; 2:2; 1 Tim 5:18; 2 Tim 2:6), however, is too random to support anything but the notion that "God's plantation" was for Paul only a minor metaphor.[30]

### God's House

Much more significant is the second metaphor enunciated in 1 Cor 3:9–15: Paul laid the foundation that is Christ, Apollos built on that foundation, and the community is "God's house" (*theou oikodomē*; see also 1 Tim 3:15; 2 Tim 2:19; Eph 2:22; Col 1:23). The metaphor is at work whenever Paul speaks of "building up" (*oikodomein*) the community (1 Cor 8:1; 14:3–5, 17, 26; 2 Cor 10:8; 13:10; Col 2:7; Rom 14:19; 1 Thess 5:11). The metaphor develops in two directions. The first employs household and kinship language for members

---

29. A good example of the extension of a major metaphor for salvation (in this case the diplomatic) to the church is Paul's calling the congregation in Corinth "a letter written by the Spirit in hearts" that can (and should) serve as a recommendation for Paul's apostleship (2 Cor 3:2–3).

30. For the combination of "plantation" and "house" at Qumran, see Gaertner, *The Temple and the Community*, 28.

of the community: Paul and Apollos are "household managers" (*oikonomoi*) of God's mysteries (1 Cor 4:1); believers are "household members" (Eph 2:19; Gal 6:10) or even household "vessels" (2 Cor 4:7; Rom 9:22–23; 2 Tim 2:20–21). Paul is the "father" of believers (1 Cor 4:15; Phlm 10, 16; 1 Thess 2:11; see 2 Cor 12:14), and Timothy is his genuine (if fictive) "son" (1 Cor 4:17; Phil 2:22; 1 Tim 1:2; 2 Tim 1:2).

The second development is to speak of "God's house" (the community) explicitly as a temple because it is the dwelling place of the Holy Spirit: "Do you not know that you are the temple of God [*naos theou*], and that the Spirit of God dwells in [or among] you?" (1 Cor 3:16 NABRE). Paul continues, "If anyone destroys God's temple, that one God will destroy. For the temple of God is holy, and such are you" (*hoitines este hymeis*, 1 Cor 3:17, author's translation). The understanding of the community as the temple raises the stakes concerning the acts of "building up" and "tearing down."[31]

Paul pushes the metaphor even further in 1 Cor 6:19, combining the image of the temple with that of the body, with the link being the presence of the Holy Spirit among believers: "Or do you not know that your [plural] body [*sōma*] is the temple of the Holy Spirit among you [*en hymin*], which you have from God—and you do not belong to yourselves?" (author's translation). The church as temple appears also in 2 Cor 6:16–17; Eph 2:21; 1 Tim 3:15; 2 Tim 2:19. In 1 and 2 Timothy the image of the household and temple merge. In Ephesians the magnificent extended metaphor of the temple begun in 2:11 reaches its climax in this splendid merging of metaphors: "Through him [Christ] we both have access [*prosagōgē*] to the Father in one Spirit. You are therefore no longer strangers and aliens, but are fellow-citizens of the saints and household members of God. You have been built up on the foundation of the apostles and prophets, whose cornerstone is Christ Jesus, in whom the whole building, being knit together, grows into a holy temple in the Lord, in whom you also have been built up to become the dwelling place [*katoikētērion*] of God in the Spirit" (Eph 2:18–22, author's translation).

*Body of Christ* The body is a fairly obvious metaphor for society and is found in Greco-Roman moral writings, with a dual emphasis on harmony among members and the proper ranking of the members that assures such harmony.[32] And if the understanding of the church as the "body of Christ"

31. See now Suh, "Power and Peril in Corinth."
32. See Schweizer, "σῶμα"; for discussion of Paul's use against the Greco-Roman background, see Mitchell, *Paul and the Rhetoric of Reconciliation*, 157–64; D. Martin, *Corinthian Body*, 3–66; Neyrey, *Paul in Other Words*, 102–46.

is not the most frequent designation for the church, it is one of Paul's most vivid and memorable. In four passages Paul speaks of the community as the *sōma Christou*, with a similar focus on unity but also with an emphasis on the diversity and reciprocity of members' gifts (Rom 12:4–5; 1 Cor 12:12–31; Col 1:24; Eph 3:6). In three places Paul puts particular emphasis on the presence of the Spirit as the life force of this body (1 Cor 6:19; 12:13; Eph 4:4). In 1 Cor 15:44–45 we find Christ as "life-giving spirit" (*pneuma zōopoioun*) and also as a "spiritual body" (*sōma pneumatikon*), who will put all God's enemies beneath his feet at his parousia (1 Cor 15:23–25). The exalted Christ, it follows, is precisely the source of the Spirit that enlivens the church as his body (1 Cor 12:4) and exercises lordship over it (1 Cor 12:3).

That Christ is "head" (*kephalē*) of the church that is his body in virtue of his exaltation is made explicit by Ephesians, which speaks of the great power among believers, "which [God] has activated in Christ by raising him from the dead and seating him at his right hand in the heavens, above every rule and authority and power and lordship and above every name that is named not only in this age but also in the age to come, and has put all things under his feet and has made him head over all the church, which is his body, the fullness of the one who fills all things in all things" (1:20–23, author's translation). Paul speaks of Christ again as "the head of the body of the church" (author's translation) in Col 1:18, and in Eph 5:23–24, after telling women to be submissive to their own husbands as to the Lord, adds, "For the man is the head of the woman just as also Christ is the head of the church, himself the Savior of his body; but as the church is submissive to Christ, so the women to husbands in every respect" (author's translation).[33] Conversely, he exhorts men to "love their wives as their own bodies . . . as Christ did the church, for we are members of his body" (Eph 5:28–30, adapted).

Just as Ephesians provided a complex merging of the metaphors of building and temple with that of the body in 2:18–22, so we also find this elaboration of the body metaphor in terms of growth toward adulthood/ perfection and the head who is Christ. In this rendering, the headship of Christ is not simply authority but the source of life and nourishment, as well as the goal toward which the community strives. Speaking of the gifts of the Spirit (4:7–11), Paul says that they have been given

to equip the holy ones for all the work of ministry, for building up the body

---

33. Compare Paul's stating in 1 Cor 11:3 that Christ is "the head of every man," God is "the head of Christ," and the man is "the head of the woman."

of Christ, until we all attain to the unity of faith and knowledge of the Son of God, to mature manhood, to the extent of the full stature of Christ, so that we may no longer be infants, tossed by waves and swept along by every wind of teaching arising from human trickery, from their cunning in the interests of deceitful scheming. Rather, living the truth in love, we should grow in every way into him who is the head, Christ, from whom the whole body, joined and held together by every supporting ligament, with the proper functioning of each part, brings about the body's growth and builds itself up in love. (Eph 4:12–16 NABRE)

## Conclusion

Examining several aspects of the language in Paul's canonical letters immediately after considering the claims of experience in those same compositions helps clarify a number of things. First, it reveals how central those experiential claims are, and how consistently they span the canonical compositions. Second, the ways in which those experiential claims intersect Paul's central convictions concerning God, humanity, and the world similarly demonstrate that it is impossible to grasp Paul's letters without acknowledging their fundamentally existential and responsive character. Third, when Paul seeks to express "the event" underlying that experience, he necessarily uses mythic discourse, for there is no other medium available for speaking of divine agency in the empirical realm. Fourth, elements of the experiential claims, such as "the cross" or "the Spirit," acquire complex levels of meaning within his correspondence. Fifth, Paul employs a variety of metaphorical fields to speak of the mystery of salvation and the nature of the church. If there is a single lesson to be derived from these observations, it is that the biggest mistake one can make in interpreting Paul is to reduce this complexity to a false simplicity, by choosing to consider only certain letters as pertinent, for example, or by reifying certain symbols and metaphors and literalizing them into a systematic body of propositions that are then taken to be "Paul." The careful reading of the canonical letters reveals constantly shifting levels of language that ought to challenge such artificial structures and encourage the reader to humbly and patiently engage each particular feature.

# Chapter 10

# Paul's Voice—Philemon

Given the complexity of the compositions ascribed to Paul in the canonical collection, the question naturally arises of where to find the best point of entry into the world those compositions help construct. The default choice for many interpreters, especially those who like to consider Paul first of all as a theologian, is the Letter to the Romans. The reasons are obvious. It is the longest of Paul's letters, it is written under his name alone (without cosponsors),[1] it is the most systematic in its argument, and it appears—at least on the surface—to be the least motivated by quotidian concerns.[2] But in just these ways Romans is also the least typical of Paul's letters. Apart from Romans and Ephesians, indeed, the canonical letters seem more generally concerned with issues in local churches and the matters of everyday life. Perhaps an equally valid entry into Paul's world is provided by one of the letters that shows Paul's pastoral self, the apostle whose thought, as we have seen, is shaped by the experiences and problems of his communities.

If we approach from this direction, then the Letter to Philemon is an excellent port of entry. It is the shortest of Paul's letters. Although it is cosponsored by Timothy, the note is highly personal in character, with Paul even adding lines in his own hand to what he has dictated, and Philemon being addressed in the second-person singular throughout. The Letter to Philemon deals, moreover, with an issue that is at once highly personal and practical: the letter accompanies Paul's return of the slave Onesimus to his owner Philemon. Despite its limited scope, Philemon provides a small but valuable window on the character of Paul's ministry and correspondence.

---

1. In Rom 16:22 (RSV) we find, "I Tertius, the writer of this letter, greet you in the Lord," but the scribe's possible contribution to the composition is impossible to ascertain.
2. Among many others, see Campbell, "Christ and the Church."

I am not by any means the first to suggest that Philemon provides a fine vantage point for viewing Paul. Two predecessors, in particular, are worth noting. In 1985 Norman A. Petersen's *Rediscovering Paul: Philemon and the Sociology of Paul's Narrative World* advanced the then novel proposition that epistles revealed narrative contexts, and that such narrative contexts, in turn, disclosed "symbolic worlds," so that careful attention to Philemon could lead as well to a sense of how Paul's view of the world conformed to and clashed with that of the larger society.[3] Almost thirty years later, N. T. Wright began his massive work on Paul with an extended treatment of Philemon.[4] There are, in fact, striking similarities between the two treatments. Each author begins with a short letter dealing with slavery from a pagan author as a point of reference,[5] each pays attention to the literary dimensions—not so much the rhetorical aspects—of the composition, and each moves from implied narrative world to symbolic world,[6] in order to show how Paul subverts the social order and its attendant ideological supports.

Neither Petersen nor Wright, however, deals with the complexities attaching to Philemon as a canonical letter. They share the conventional view, for example, that Philemon is an "authentic" Pauline letter according to the usual criteria. But they make no positive case for that authenticity; they simply accept the default position. Nor do they offer any discussion concerning Philemon's inclusion in the Pauline collection; if it is authentic, they seem to imply, then its place in the canon follows naturally. They spend no time puzzling over the odd fact that such a short note, written to an obscure personage in an uncertain location, should have been preserved at all, much less included in the Pauline corpus with letters like Romans and Galatians.

Finally, they take no real account of the canonical connections that Philemon has to Colossians and Ephesians.[7] Petersen is content to declare

3. Petersen is otherwise best known for his work *Literary Criticism for New Testament Critics*. His language concerning "symbolic world" was drawn, as is mine, from the groundbreaking work of Berger and Luckmann, *Social Construction of Reality*.

4. Wright, *Paul and the Faithfulness of God*, 3–74.

5. Petersen cites a letter from Mysterion, ca. 50 CE; Wright quotes Pliny the Younger's *Epistle* 9.21 to Sobranius.

6. Consistent with his usage throughout his work, Wright uses the term "worldview" rather than "symbolic world," but he means pretty much the same thing.

7. That such connections between Philemon and Colossians exist is implicitly acknowledged by the habit of commentary series treating the two (or three) letters together; see, e.g., Dunn, *Epistles to the Colossians and to Philemon*; Lohse, *Colossians and Philemon*; O'Brien, *Colossians–Philemon*; Moule, *Epistles of Paul the Apostle to the Colossians and to Philemon*; Moulton, *Colossians, Philemon, and Ephesians*; M. MacDonald, *Colossians and*

that Colossians is inauthentic and therefore should not enter into the discussion on Philemon,[8] and to note that Philemon's position on slavery does not conform to the household instruction in Col 4:1.[9] In a late footnote, he categorizes Ephesians as "Deutero-Pauline," and otherwise refers to it only for a lexical comparison.[10] In his discussion of the sources to be used for the study of Paul, Wright states that he thinks both Colossians and Ephesians should be regarded as authentic.[11] In his analysis of Philemon, however, he only suggests that Onesimus's trip back to his master may correspond to that reported of Tychicus in Col 4:7–9,[12] and finds a parallel between the language of Phlm 4–5 and Eph 4:12–15.[13] Neither scholar engages in a sustained examination of the literary and thematic links between Philemon and the other two letters, the distinctive rhetorical functions of the respective letters, or the fairly obvious possibility that such links account for the canonization of Philemon itself.

In contrast, I argue here that the connections among the three letters are precisely the reason why such an obscure personal note should have been canonized, and that the same connections suggest how this short note worked rhetorically. For me to make that argument, some patience is required of the reader, because the connections are ones that are too seldom taken seriously.

## Connections

Each of the three letters is written from captivity (Phlm 1; Col 4:10, 18; Eph 3:1; 4:1; 6:20). It is not of great moment to determine the place of Paul's imprisonment. More to the point is that—together with Philippians and 2 Timothy—this handful of letters makes up Paul's captivity correspondence. As for ascribed authorship, Ephesians joins Romans as the only Pauline letters claiming to come from Paul alone without other sponsors/cowriters. In contrast, both Philemon and Colossians reveal a more common Pauline

---

*Ephesians*; Talbert, *Ephesians and Colossians*; R. Martin, *Colossians, Philemon, Ephesians*; Witherington, *Letters to Philemon, the Colossians, and the Ephesians*.

8. Petersen, *Rediscovering Paul*, 32.
9. Petersen, *Rediscovering Paul*, 87–88.
10. Petersen, *Rediscovering Paul*, 190, 289.
11. Wright, *Paul and the Faithfulness of God*, 60–61.
12. Wright, *Paul and the Faithfulness of God*, 14.
13. Wright, *Paul and the Faithfulness of God*, 17–18.

pattern: Philemon is cosponsored by Paul's chief delegate, Timothy (1), and Paul writes at least part of the letter in his own hand (19). Colossians likewise comes from Paul and Timothy (1:1), with Paul adding at least the final greeting (4:18).

A considerable and compelling overlapping of personal names occurs in this cluster of letters. According to Philemon, Paul has with him in prison his "fellow prisoner" Epaphras, as well as Mark, Aristarchus, Demas, and Luke (23–24). Paul is sending the slave, Onesimus, back to Philemon, his owner (10). In the assembly meeting in Philemon's household, Paul greets his "sister" Apphia and his "fellow soldier" Archippus (2). We meet some of the same cast of characters in Colossians, plus others. Paul says he is sending Tychicus (Col 4:7–9) and Onesimus to report to the community concerning him, calling Onesimus "the faithful and beloved brother, who is from among you" (4:9, author's translation).[14]

In Colossians, Paul names as fellow prisoners Aristarchus, Mark, Jesus Justus (4:10–11), Luke, Demas (4:14), and Epaphras, "one of yourselves" (4:12 RSV). With the exception of Tychicus and Jesus Justus, the names match those in Philemon completely. Among those in the church at Colossae, moreover, Paul sends a message specifically to Archippus (named also in Phlm 2): "See that you fulfil the ministry that you have received in the Lord" (4:17 RSV). In this letter, Paul also greets the Christians in Laodicea, including "Nympha and the church at her house" (4:15 RSV, adapted). He furthermore wants the Colossians and Laodiceans to exchange letters (4:16), supporting the conclusion that Paul saw the churches of Hierapolis, Colossae, and Laodiaea as part of a circuit of churches bound by mutual communication (4:13).

On the face of it, such a concentration of identical names would seem to suggest that Philemon and Colossians were written at the same time from the same place by the same person. In sharp contrast, Ephesians lacks any personal references, apart from 6:21–22 (RSV): "Now that you may know how I am and what I am doing, Tychicus the beloved brother and faithful minister in the Lord will tell you everything. I have sent him to you for this very purpose, that you may know how we are, and that he may encourage your hearts." As the deliverer of information about Paul, the figure of Tychicus links Ephesians and Colossians, and as also the companion of Onesimus, he links Colossians and Philemon.

---

14. Unless otherwise indicated, Scripture quotations in this chapter are from the NABRE.

The network of names is not exclusive to this cluster of letters. If this Mark is the cousin of Barnabas, we know that he was a travel companion of Paul for a time (Acts 15:37–39), and his presence is requested by Paul in 2 Tim 4:11. Tychicus, in turn, appears as an important figure among Paul's delegates also in Acts 20:4; 2 Tim 4:12; Titus 3:12. Aristarchus was similarly a fellow worker (Acts 19:29; 27:2), as were also Luke (2 Tim 4:11) and Demas (2 Tim 4:10). In contrast, the local personalities Epaphras and Onesimus are attested only in Colossians and Philemon. Paul's companion Jesus Justus is mentioned only in Colossians, and Philemon appears only in the letter written to him.

What about style and theme? Once more, the evidence is asymmetric. Colossians and Ephesians share much common vocabulary, have many similar sentence structures, and have some common themes (the death and exaltation of Jesus, conquest of cosmic powers, baptism, moral transformation, household ethics). The similarities can be overdrawn. Each letter has emphases not found in the other, and the shared language often occurs in distinct contexts and with different nuances.[15] But if we view the compositions side by side, it is easy to assume some sort of literary relationship, even if not necessarily one of direct dependence. In contrast, Philemon is so short that stylistic comparison to the other letters is difficult. It is clear, however, that the writer, perhaps Paul writing in his own hand (Phlm 19), is capable of graceful and even subtle prose. As for theme, Philemon is dominated by the effort to secure a happy reconciliation of slave and master, a topic which occurs in Colossians and Ephesians only in the tables of household ethics (Col 3:22–4:1; Eph 6:5–9).

The three letters differ most in their implied audiences and rhetorical functions. Philemon, as I have observed, is basically a personal note, which greets members of the church, but is written throughout in the second-person singular; the householder (and slave owner) Philemon himself is the intended reader. The letter also has a practical purpose. Paul wants Philemon to welcome back his slave Onesimus, who had joined Paul (and apparently joined in his ministry).[16] The exhortation "receive him as you would receive me" (Phlm 17 RSV) makes the note, in effect, a letter of recommendation:

15. See the careful analysis of Lau, *Politics of Peace*.

16. Paul's statements in Phlm 18–19 suggest that Onesimus's presence with Paul involved a material loss to Philemon, either through his running away or through his stealing something, or both: "If he has done you any injustice or owes you anything, charge it to me. I, Paul, write this in my own hand: I will pay" (NAB).

Onesimus is no longer to be regarded as property; he is a brother in the faith and should be received as such.[17]

Colossians, in contrast, is written not to an individual (though it names many) but to a community that has been founded, not by Paul himself, but by his fellow prisoner, Epaphras (1:7). In it Paul responds to a local crisis arising from some members insisting on post-baptism "add-ons" (circumcision, asceticism, mysticism) and disqualifying others as insufficiently "mature" on that basis.[18] In effect, the issues resemble those in the Galatian churches, except that the details here are less clear, and Paul is forced to instruct a church that is within the range of his ministry but that he has never met personally.[19] Nor has this church been exposed to Paul himself and his tension-filled relationship to Torah, as were the Galatian churches; here, therefore, Paul's argument does not involve the reinterpretation of Torah but shared traditions concerning baptism.

Ephesians is the hardest letter to locate. Partially, this is due to the letter's impersonal character. The delegate Tychicus alone is named. But the Ephesian church was, according to Acts 19:1–40, one that Paul knew intimately. How could he write without mentioning any names of the believers there, when he was able to greet many in churches he had never met in both Rome and Colossae? Ephesians presents other problems. As noted earlier, its style is much closer to Colossians than to some other Pauline letters, although a case can be made that some of its lines come close to parallels in Romans and 2 Corinthians.[20] The argument is often made that the thought in Ephesians is too mystical, perhaps even too gnostic, to be "authentically" Pauline, although it is recognized that the letter also contains distinctively Pauline emphases, such as the death and exaltation of Jesus, the church as the body of Christ, transformation through the Holy Spirit, and salvation through faith, not human works. Two aspects of the letter particularly seem to represent a time later than Paul's own lifetime: the picture of the recon-

---

17. See Stowers, *Letter Writing*. That Paul is fully aware of the conventions attending such letters of commendation is clear from 2 Cor 3:1–6; 4:1–6. Rom 16:1–2 can be read as a commendation of Phoebe, Paul's patroness and road manager. Third John is a straightforward recommendation, written by the Elder on behalf of Demetrius, who is being sent as a delegate to Gaius.

18. See L. Johnson, "Religious Imprinting."

19. That he should nevertheless be able to greet individuals in the community by name presents no more of a problem than in the case of Rom 16, even less, since in this case Paul is clearly gaining his knowledge of the church from Epaphras.

20. See especially the careful linguistic analysis of Roon, *Authenticity of Ephesians*.

ciliation of Jew and gentile in the church as an accomplished reality appears to some as impossible for the Paul of Rom 9–11; similarly, the elaborate table of household ethics in Eph 5:22–6:1 is thought to be incompatible with the Paul of 1 Corinthians, who seems to such interpreters as less conventional concerning domestic arrangements.[21]

There is a distinct possibility, however, that Ephesians was never intended to be simply or exclusively for believers in Ephesus. Some good early manuscripts lack the place name Ephesus in the greeting of the letter, having only "to the saints" (*tois hagiois*, 1:1),[22] while a number of other manuscripts add the word "all" to form "all the saints." These variations are especially intriguing, since the form of the Greek sentence calls out for a place name: "to the saints at ____ and faithful" (*tois hagiois tois ousin ____ kai pistois*).[23] The absence of a place name hardly seems accidental and could well have had a function. Taken together with the lack of personal names, the possibility arises that it was never intended to be a missive to one church alone, but was composed as a circular letter to be read aloud in several communities, with the name of the specific church inserted when the letter was read aloud in the assembly by the person who delivered it. This would help explain the magisterial and general tone of the composition: Paul was not addressing the issues peculiar to a single community but was writing in a manner that would give the letter pertinence for all his churches.

## Construals

Individually and collectively, this cluster of letters presents real problems. Why should such a personal note as Philemon, with so little apparent general appeal, be preserved and made part of the canon? Colossians is linked

21. This is not the place to enter into a full-scale discussion of these issues, except to say that the difficulties appear larger if one has already made up one's mind (or had one's perception shaped) to regard Ephesians as among the inauthentic letters, and seem smaller if one is open to the possibility of authenticity—at least in the larger sense of "Pauline authorship" that I have employed. For fuller discussion of Ephesians in this regard, see L. Johnson, *Writings of the New Testament*, 359–71; and for other perceptions on Ephesians, see Barth, *Ephesians*; Best, *Epistle to the Ephesians*; Lincoln, *Ephesians*; Schnackenburg, *Epistle to the Ephesians*.

22. See the original reading in P 46, Sinaiticus, and Vaticanus.

23. Santer, "Text of Ephesians i. 1"; Batey, "Destination of Ephesians," 101; Best, "Recipients."

to Philemon by a network of names, but if its authenticity is challenged on other grounds, could it be that this web of names was taken from Philemon by a pseudepigrapher to help authenticate Colossians as Pauline? It is certainly the case that ancient pseudonymous letters made use of biographical data to give plausibility to their efforts.[24] But what is puzzling in the present case is how so obscure a missive as Philemon should perform that function for a later audience. Who would know the letter or the people spoken of, especially Onesimus and Philemon themselves? And then Ephesians: it is unmistakably similar to Colossians in its style and outlook, while distinctive for its lack of local detail and having only a single substantive link to Philemon in its mention of Tychicus as news-bringer. Is there a hypothesis that adequately accounts for this strange combination of similarity and dissimilarity?

There are three basic positions. The first, seldom adopted today, is to dismiss all three letters as pseudonymous, perhaps as the same sort of elaborate literary hoax that is often ascribed to the Pastorals.[25] The second position maintains that Philemon is authentic—although there are few positive arguments made for that—but either Colossians or Ephesians (or both) is regarded as pseudonymous, with the relations among the letters explained on the basis of copying or imitation. The third position, for which I will argue here, is that all three letters are authored by Paul, in the sense I have already explained, and that the connections between the three letters are best understood when they are seen as parts of a multi-letter packet delivered by Tychicus.

If, as some scholars still maintain, Colossians is authentically Pauline,[26] the situation is considerably clarified: Philemon and Colossians were sent by Paul at the same time to the same place. The preservation of Philemon—and its ultimate canonization—is thereby explained; it is a valuable appendage to the more substantial missive to the Colossian church that was saved and gathered into the Pauline collection together with Colossians. That position, however, still fails to account for Ephesians.

---

24. See, e.g., Malherbe, *Cynic Epistles*.

25. F. C. Baur thought the authenticity of all three rose or fell together, and decided that they were all pseudonymous, calling Philemon "a Christian romance serving to convey a genuine Christian idea." *Paul the Apostle*, 2:1–44, 80–84.

26. See, e.g., Cannon, *Traditional Materials*. For the standard arguments against authenticity from the literary side, see E. Sanders, "Literary Dependence in Colossians," and from the side of theological coherence, see Lohse, "Pauline Theology." For a fuller treatment of Colossians as pseudepigraphic, see Kiley, *Colossians as Pseudepigraphy*.

An ingenious theory, based on the premise just stated, proposes Onesi-mus as the key figure in the production of Ephesians.[27] The early-second-century martyr Ignatius of Antioch, a fervent disciple of Paul (as we have seen), names in his letter to the Ephesians a certain Onesimus as bishop of that city in his day (Ign. *Eph.* 1.2, 2.1, 6.2). The theory proposes that this very Onesimus is the former slave returned by Paul to his owner, the subject of the Letter to Philemon, and suggests further that, upon reading Colossians, Onesimus undertakes the collection of all Paul's letters. More, having read those he collected, he borrows liberally from their substance if not their style and, in an act of filial loyalty to Paul, himself composes the compo-sition we know as Ephesians to be both a compendium of Paul's theology and an introduction to the collection of his letters as a whole. The theory is ingenious and attractive. It solves the issue of pseudonymity—Onesimus composed Ephesians—as well as the literary relation between Colossians and Ephesians: Onesimus simply borrowed from the letter best known to him when he was composing Ephesians.

The very concreteness of the hypothesis is its most attractive feature. Unfortunately, we cannot assume that the Onesimus named by Ignatius is the same as the Onesimus in Philemon. There is, moreover, no manuscript evidence to support the notion that Ephesians ever functioned as the intro-ductory letter to the Pauline collection. The theory also oversimplifies the stylistic and substantive similarities of Colossians and Ephesians.[28] Finally, there is no real reason to suppose that the Onesimus named in Philemon was capable of writing a composition like Ephesians, which is far from being simply a rehash of Colossians in light of other Pauline letters, and is, indeed, a composition of original and deep insight into the *mystērion tou theou*.

For all its weaknesses, however, the hypothesis grounds the three let-ters in real-life persons and circumstances rather than in a vague appeal to a later "Pauline school." It reminds us of the important realization that the Letter to the Colossians (at least) is part of the original epistolary context of Philemon, and both letters would probably have been understood by their first readers in light of each other. To make this specific: Philemon would not only be receiving back his slave together with Paul's delegate Tychicus, and reading the letter carried by that delegate; together with the rest of the Colossian community, he would hear Paul's explication in Colossians of the entailments of being a new kind of humanity in Christ.

---

27. See, e.g., Goodspeed, *Meaning of Ephesians*; Mitton, *Pauline Corpus*.
28. See Cadbury, "Dilemma of Ephesians 1"; Best, "Who Used Whom?"

Construing the compositions is made more difficult still when the inauthenticity of both Colossians and Ephesians is the premise. Now an account must be given of the similarity of the two letters (were they written by the same individual?) as well as their very real differences (including the odd fact that the use of names from Philemon was used in Colossians to certify a Pauline origin, but no need was felt to do the same with Ephesians). And if the literary relationship between the letters is imagined as an employment of an already pseudonymous Colossians by the pseudepigrapher of Ephesians, we are left with an even more elaborate scenario: a later member of the "Pauline school" imitates an earlier imitator of the Pauline manner.

A much more elegant hypothesis offers itself, in which the Pauline authorship is affirmed in the broad sense that I have employed in this book: they are all written under Paul's supervision and authority during his lifetime. In this case, they are all written when Paul is in prison with Epaphras; on the occasion of returning the slave Onesimus to his owner, letters are written to the local churches of Colossae and Laodicea (and perhaps others), as well as a circular letter to be read in any number of churches (including the church at Ephesus). This hypothesis enables us to make sense of the distinctive rhetorical character of the three letters that remain, and it makes the key figure to understanding the correspondence Paul's delegate Tychicus.

Here is a plausible reconstruction based on the evidence of the letters themselves. In captivity with Paul is Epaphras—he sends greetings to his community from Paul's side (Col 4:12). He is the founder of the community in Colossae: they have "recognized the gift of God in truth" from him (Col 1:6, author's translation), and he has reported to Paul their "love in the Spirit" (Col 1:7-8). Paul calls Epaphras his "beloved fellow-slave, who is a faithful servant of Christ in your behalf" (Col 1:7, author's translation) and repeats the designation of Epaphras as "a slave of Christ Jesus, who constantly struggles for you in prayers" (Col 4:12, author's translation). He also informs Paul about a crisis in his church concerning conflicts over the nature of true maturity, or perfection, information concerning which may have come from the slave Onesimus, who in some fashion has attached himself to Paul and has become a Christ-believer (Phlm 10-11).[29] Epaphras asks Paul to support his ministry in Colossae by writing a letter to be read aloud to

29. The number of theories concerning the exact character of the crisis is impressive; see, among others, Meeks and Francis, *Conflict at Colossae*; Arnold, *Colossian Syncretism*; Attridge, "On Becoming an Angel"; DeMaris, *Colossian Controversy*; Dunn, "Colossian Philosophy"; Evans, "Colossian Mystics," 188-205; Hooker, "False Teachers," 315-31.

his troubled community. Paul obliges, and uses the occasion of writing that letter to send Onesimus back to Philemon with what is, in effect, a letter of commendation. Thus, Philemon and Colossians arrive in the same place at the same time, and the personal letter is preserved because of its connection to the letter for the church.

At the same time, Paul composes a circular letter employing some of the themes and language of Colossians, but recasting them in a distinctive, more universal vision concerning God's work in the church as a whole. In this regard, Ephesians is to Colossians as Romans is to Galatians: convictions forged in the fire of local controversy are elevated to a meditation on how God, through Paul's mission among the gentiles, is revealing the mystery of his presence and power. This letter is to be delivered and read aloud to the circle of churches associated with Paul's ministry, though not necessarily founded by him. Tychicus therefore carries with him at least three or four, and possibly more, letters: (a) the letter commending Onesimus to his master; (b) the letter to be read to the Colossian church founded by Epaphras; (c) the letter to the local church at Laodicea (Col 4:16); (d) the circular letter that will be read aloud in various communities—name to be inserted—including the church at Ephesus. As he delivers and reads these letters, Tychicus will also report on news from Paul to each audience (Eph 6:21–22; Col 4:7–8).

This is an elegant hypothesis because it covers all the data in the simplest manner and answers satisfactorily the questions concerning the literary interrelationships of the extant letters, as well as the question why Philemon should have been preserved, collected, and canonized. The close geographical proximity of Ephesus, Colossae, Laodicea, and Hierapolis (Col 4:13) makes the theory more plausible, no matter where Paul may have been imprisoned. Moreover, the fact that Paul requests that the Colossians exchange their letter with the letter he sent to the Laodiceans (Col 4:16) provides evidence in this very collection of letters for the sort of practice I suggest. We know, furthermore, that Paul used his coworkers and delegates in this fashion (see, e.g., 1 Cor 4:17; 16:10–11; Phil 2:19–24; 1 Thess 3:1–7). The scenario provides a plausible sociological setting for those connected to Paul's "school." They helped in his correspondence, and they acted as emissaries to various gentile communities.

That this hypothesis is more than idle speculation is demonstrated by the analogy of the Johannine Letters, where we find the same combination of stylistic and thematic similarity, with rhetorical difference. First John is not a letter at all. It is a sermon or treatise—like Ephesians, lacking any personal

257

character or local reference—to be read aloud in an assembly. Second John is written for a local congregation, probably accompanying the "something" that the Elder had written. Third John is a straightforward personal note of commendation, addressed to the local leader Gaius in behalf of the Elder's delegate Demetrius (3 John 12). General treatise, cover letter for a local church, letter of commendation: the best explanation for the preservation of 2 and 3 John is that they were part of the same three-letter packet with 1 John.

## Paul's Voice in Philemon[30]

Despite its brevity, Philemon is far from a carelessly dashed-off note; it is, rather, a carefully crafted witness to an emerging Christian ethos, revealing its power to transform symbols (and attitudes) while struggling to transcend conventional—and therefore deeply entrenched—social forms. It also shows us a Paul whom we might not expect if we had read only letters in which Paul engaged in lengthy argument or harsh polemic. Paul in Philemon is perhaps unexpectedly diplomatic, urbane, and even witty, clearly as much at home in the mores of the ancient Mediterranean culture as he is in the new creation in Christ—an author who, if we did not have other evidence, we might never suspect had been raised as a Pharisaic Jew steeped in and fanatically dedicated to Torah; a Paul, indeed, who seems less concerned with *dikaiosynē* as the relationship between humans and God, and more concerned with *dikaiosynē* as righteous relations among humans. Philemon reveals a Paul who seeks, through the "soft power" of persuasion rather than the "hard power" of either Roman law or his own apostolic authority, to change both dispositions and behavior.[31]

Paul needs all the diplomatic skill at his disposal, for his situation is awkward. Let us accept the most logical reconstruction, in which Onesimus—by law the property of Philemon rather than a legal "person"—has run away from his master and joined up with Paul, perhaps even seeking refuge with the apostle. Under Paul's influence, in any case, he has become a Christian

---

30. Among works devoted specifically to Philemon, see J. H. Elliott, "Philemon and House Churches"; Winter, "Paul's Letter to Philemon"; Church, "Rhetorical Structure"; Barclay, "Dilemma of Christian Slave-Ownership"; Hock, "Support for His Old Age"; Lewis, "African-American Appraisal"; C. Martin, "Commercial Language"; Nordlin, "Onesimus Fugitivus."
31. I take the distinction from P. Collins, *Absolute Power*: hard power is institutional; soft power is rhetorical.

(Phlm 10). Philemon undoubtedly has the hard power of Roman law on his side. Under the strict dictates of that law, he can have Onesimus returned by force and severely punished or even killed—if he can find him. When Paul sets out to write Colossians to the church of which Philemon is a member, then, the subject of Onesimus awkwardly inserts itself. Not only could Paul, by a strict reading of Roman law, be guilty of harboring a runaway; he could also be accused of stealing Philemon's "property."

In Paul's eyes, it is clear that Onesimus should no longer be regarded simply as slave property. Before the Lord, with whom there is neither slave nor free, he is an equal. He is a brother in the faith (16). More than that, Paul sees himself as Onesimus's father in the faith, since he "gave him birth" through his conversion while in prison (10). Recognizing the reality of the law, Paul tells Philemon that he will repay him for whatever loss he has suffered (18). At the same time, however, he reminds Philemon of another truth: through the Pauline mission represented by Epaphras, Philemon himself has been given new life and freedom, so that Paul is actually Philemon's benefactor: "you owe me even yourself" (19, author's translation). Paul may owe Philemon monetary compensation, but Philemon owes Paul much more. In the sliding scale of benefaction, Paul's gift trumps Philemon's debt.

The situation, however, is even more complex. Onesimus has proven to be helpful to Paul in his bonds, and the apostle does not want to lose his assistance. He would like Philemon to send Onesimus back to rejoin Paul. Even though Paul's position is tenuous from a legal standpoint, he states that "in Christ" he could demand Philemon's compliance with his desire (8). In the realm of the Christian *oikoumenē*—which includes Philemon's and all other households in the larger Pauline communities—Paul is the "father" who can command obedience. If the game is to be played by the rules of social hierarchy, then even "in Christ" Paul holds the top cards. But he chooses not to go the route of hard power, even hard power "in the Lord." He prefers the path of persuasion. So he does not heavy-handedly demand submission to his wishes, but instead "appeals" to Philemon "on the basis of love" (9 NRSV). His remarks about being "an old man" or perhaps "ambassador" (*presbytēs/presbeutēs*) and a "prisoner of Christ Jesus" (9 NRSV) add a subtle, or perhaps not so subtle, level of emotional manipulation to his "appeal on the basis of love."[32] Paul clearly wants Philemon to read between the lines

---

32. "Old man" (*presbytēs*) has full manuscript support; the conjectured reading "ambassador" (*presbeutēs*) is an adaptation to the overall character of the letter and Paul's mission (see *presbeuō* in 2 Cor 5:20 and Eph 6:20).

and grant his desire, but he seems also to have left him little real choice. He does, however, provide a way out of the situation that will at once serve to meet his wish and also bring honor to Philemon, since he wants his desire to be met, not out of necessity, but willingly (14).

To fully appreciate Paul's rhetoric, we need to recognize his deployment of a number of clever puns. The first is based on the Greek name Onesimus, which means "useful." Paul tells Philemon that Onesimus had formerly been "useless" (*achrēstos*) to him, but now had become "useful" (*euchrēstos*, 11), since he had been "begotten" by Paul in the faith (10). This is actually a double pun, since the Greek *chrēstos* also suggests *christos* ("Christ"). Thus, before his conversion, Onesimus was "useless" (*achrēstos*) because he was "without Christ" (*a-chrēstos*). But now he is "useful" (*chrēstos*) because he is a "good Christian" (*euchrēstos*). In short, Onesimus had found his new and true identity in the gospel, as had Philemon himself. In Christ, Onesimus and Philemon are equals: Paul has begotten them both as their "father" and they are "beloved brothers" in the Lord. Philemon should therefore welcome him back, not with the punishment due a runaway slave, but as a beloved brother in the faith. Indeed, Paul wants him to receive Onesimus "as you would receive me" (17 RSV).

A second pun is suggested by the letter's thanksgiving, in which Paul remembers how Philemon had "refreshed the hearts of the saints" (*ta splanchna tōn hagiōn anapepautai dia sou*, Phlm 7). In light of Paul's language elsewhere (see 1 Cor 16:18; 2 Cor 7:13), we recognize code language for the hospitality and financial support that Philemon had made available to fellow believers from the resources of his household (e.g., Phlm 22). But when Paul speaks of returning Onesimus to Philemon, he virtually sighs, "I am sending my very heart" (*splanchna*, 12). The two levels of the pun come together in verse 20. Paul tells Philemon, "Yes, brother, I want some benefit from you [*sou onaimēn*, a pun on Onesimus] in the Lord [*en kyriō*]. Refresh my heart in Christ [*anapauson mou ta splanchna en Christō*]" (author's translation). He wants Onesimus ("his heart") returned to him, so that he can again do service to Paul in his chains for the good news, and this will be a service to Paul "in your behalf" (13). The return of Onesimus will be a gift to Paul and also a service of the good news in Philemon's behalf.

The force of this punning language rests on the premises of ancient benefaction, with its ideal of reciprocity between patron and client.[33] Phi-

---

33. The groundbreaking work is Danker, *Benefactor*; see also the essays in Satlow, *Gift in Antiquity*; for Paul specifically, see Barclay, *Paul and the Gift*, and Blanton, *Spiritual Economy*.

lemon is first praised for his patronage of the Christian movement. Paul then positions himself as Philemon's patron, by returning Onesimus to one who owes Paul his very life. But while Philemon is now the recipient of Paul's benefaction, he can again become a great patron of Paul's mission by allowing Onesimus to return in order to work for Paul and the mission "in behalf of" Philemon. No wonder Paul can write, "Confident of your obedience, I am writing to you, knowing that you will do even more than I say" (21 NRSV).

Paul has leveraged the protocols of beneficence, knowing that his own "giving" will necessitate the reciprocal "giving" of Philemon. In this dance, Paul and Philemon embody the sort of "equality" (*isotēs*) through reciprocity that Aristotle described as appropriate between those on different social levels who wished to be "friends."[34] Since in Greco-Roman culture "friends hold all things in common" (*tois philois panta koina*) and "friendship is fellowship" (*philia koinōnia*),[35] Paul appropriately applies language evoking such fellowship to household leaders in the Colossian church who provide financial support. Philemon is thus a "fellow worker" (*synergos*, 1), Archippus is a "fellow soldier" (*systratiōtē*, 2), and Epaphras is a "fellow prisoner" (*synaichmalōtos*, 23); the faith and love Philemon has shown to the Lord and all the saints is a "fellowship of his faith" (*koinōnia tēs pisteōs sou*, 6); he will show himself a "fellow/friend" (*koinōnos*) of Paul if he receives Onesimus as he would Paul himself (17).

Philemon reveals a Pauline voice that is personal, affectionate, and subtle, the voice of one at home in the social context of Greco-Roman culture and who understands the intricate ways in which social status and obligation was negotiated through notions of friendship involving reciprocity of gifts and honor. The letter also opens a small but light-filled window on the Pauline mission. We see how Paul worked together with a close network of fellow workers (2, 23-24), how these networks were nurtured through practices of benefaction (7), hospitality (22), the sending of delegates (Onesimus), and the writing of letters (Philemon). We see the "sister" Apphia as a leader in the household and probably in the household church, as well as the importance of households as the place for meeting (*tē kat' oikon sou ekklēsia*) (2; cf. Rom 16:5; 1 Cor 16:19). We see the community members as "holy ones"

---

34. See Aristotle, *Nicomachean Ethics* 8, 1-8.

35. Aristotle repeats many of the proverbial sayings in the *Nicomachean Ethics* 9.8.2. For the topos, see Hauck, "κοινος"; Dugas, *L'amitié antique*, 1-68; Eglinger, "Der Begriff der Freundschaft"; Bohnenblust, *Beiträge zum Topos peri filias*.

or "saints" (4, 7; cf. Rom 16:2; 1 Cor 1:2; 6:1–2; 16:15; 2 Cor 1:1; Phil 1:1). We find the fellowship (*koinōnia*) of the community to be one of faith and love (5–6) that is expressed through mutual service (13), reciprocal gift-giving (17; cf. Rom 15:27; 2 Cor 8:1–15; Phil 4:10–20), and prayer (3–7, 25).

Above all, we learn that this fellowship is not mere like-mindedness but is grounded by being "in Christ" (8, 20) and "in the Lord" (16). It transcends natural kinship relations and social stratification. Paul is a "father" to Onesimus because he converted him to the good news (10), so that Onesimus is now also a "beloved brother" to his master "both in the flesh and in the Lord" (16 RSV), and if a brother, then—within the frame of the good news—also a "fellow" or "friend" of his master,[36] whose service to Paul "in behalf of" Philemon (13) can even be regarded as an act of benefaction. Being "in the Lord" subverts and relativizes social locations but does not yet deny them (cf. 1 Cor 7:29–35).

Here, then, is the real reason why Philemon is and should be regarded as authentically Pauline, even if it lacks utterly any trace of teaching on righteousness or any citation of Scripture and, perhaps surprisingly, shows us an apostle totally at home within the conventions of Greco-Roman society. At every point, Philemon echoes important aspects of Paul's pastoral outlook and practice in other letters, and at no point does it contradict the evidence of the other canonical letters.

## Reading Philemon Together with Colossians

If, as I argue, Philemon was delivered together with the letter to be read aloud to the church in Colossae, then it makes perfect sense to ask how the two letters may have been heard by Philemon and his community. Colossians makes a strong argument against a competitive perfectionism in the church. Some in the Colossian congregation are seeking to "judge" others (Col 2:16) or "disqualify" them (2:18) on the basis of a higher status achieved through circumcision (2:11), or ascetic practices (2:20–23), or experiences

---

36. See Aristotle's struggle with this notion in *Nicomachean Ethics* 8.11.6–7: "For master and slave have nothing in common: a slave is a living tool, just as a tool is an inanimate slave. Therefore there can be no friendship with a slave as slave, *though there can be as human being: for there seems to be some room for justice in the relations of every human being with every other that is capable of participating in law and contrast, and hence friendship is possible with everyone so far as he is a human being*" (italics added). H. Rackham, *Nicomachean Ethics* LCL 2nd ed. (Cambridge: Harvard University Press, 1934).

of mysticism (2:18). In response, Paul insists on the adequacy of baptism (3:12–15) as incorporating all into the "fullness" of Christ and thereby also into the fullness of God's power and presence (2:4–9). Maturation, or "perfection" (*teleiōsis*), for the Colossians is to consist in an ever deeper insight into the mystery that has already been gifted them (1:6–11), and actions that flow from that new identity; God has already "qualified" them (1:12).

If religious status markers are not to cause rivalries and divisions among those who belong to Christ, neither should the markers of social status. Paul tells them, "You have taken off the old self with its practices and have put on the new self, which is being renewed, for knowledge, in the image of its creator. Here there is not Greek and Jew, circumcision and uncircumcision, barbarian, Scythian, slave, free; but Christ is all and in all [*panta kai en pasin Christos*]" (Col 3:9–11). Several aspects of this "unification," which resembles those in Gal 3:28 and 1 Cor 12:13,[37] deserve attention. First, the imagery of "taking off" and "taking on" identities as though they were clothes recalls the experience of baptism.[38] Second, the "self" (*anthrōpos*) that is being abandoned is expressed by certain practices that must also be relinquished—opening the way for practices more consistent with the identity of Christ being taken on. Third, the course of transformation is "into recognition" (*eis epignōsin*), a form of recognition that has both cognitive and moral dimensions (see Rom 1:28; 10:2). Fourth, the source and goal of renewal is the image of Christ, with the end point being a state wherein "Christ is all and in all" (cf. 1 Cor 15:28). Fifth, among the practices that must be changed are those expressing separation and alienation among humans: ethnic divisions (Greek/Jew), religious markings (circumcision/uncircumcision), negative cultural stereotypes (barbarians/Scythians), and social location and status (slave/free). Differences between humans are inevitable, but in Christ they are relativized by the reality of the "new humanity" being created according to the image of Christ. All sorts of people are not simply fully human, whatever their social location, but by baptism they are also brothers and sisters who seek to make "Christ all things in all things."

This reminder of the moral implications of baptism—even if it stood alone in Colossians—would provide a valuable contextualization for the return of Onesimus to Philemon "not only as a slave but as more than a

---

37. All three have the pairs Jew/Greek and slave/free. Only Gal 3:28 has "female/male." The pairing of barbarian/Scythian here has given rise to endless speculation, none of it terribly illuminating.

38. See Käsemann, "Primitive Christian Baptismal Liturgy."

slave, as a beloved brother" (author's translation), who is to be welcomed as though he were Paul himself (Phlm 16–17). But it does not stand alone. In the so-called table of household ethics in Col 3:18–4:1, the attention given to the relations between slaves and masters is more highly developed than the single lines given respectively to wives, husbands, children, and parents (3:18–21). Instruction given to slaves is the most elaborate: "Slaves, obey your human masters in everything, not only when being watched [*opthalmodoulia*], as currying favor [*hōs anthrōpareskoi*], but in simplicity of heart, fearing the Lord. Whatever you do, do from the heart [*ek psychēs*], as for the Lord and not for others, knowing that you will receive from the Lord the due payment of the inheritance [see 1:12]; be slaves of the Lord Christ. For the wrongdoer will receive recompense for the wrong he committed, and there is no partiality [*prosōpolēmpsia*]" (3:22–25). It would be anachronistic in the extreme to suppose that Paul here, or anywhere else for that matter, was in the position to abolish slavery within the empire or even within believing households. Such an expectation would be even more foolish in light of two aspects of Paul's outlook. The first is that, in light of the new creation, social differentiation, as gender and ethnicity, are among the *adiaphora* (things that are not of the essence). No more than eating and drinking or being circumcised or uncircumcised can a condition of being a slave or master affect one's place in God's kingdom, or in the life of the church. The second is that Paul understands Jesus himself in terms of the most profound and humbling form of service to humans as God's *doulos* (Phil 2:7). Indeed, Paul refers to himself also as God's *doulos* (Rom 1:1; Phil 1:1).

In this very letter, moreover, he calls Epaphras "our beloved fellow slave [*syndoulos*], who is a faithful servant [*diakonos*] of Christ in your behalf" (Col 1:7, author's translation), and "one of you, a slave [*doulos*] of Christ Jesus" (4:12); and he speaks of his delegate Tychicus as "beloved brother and faithful servant [*diakonos*] and fellow slave in the Lord [*syndoulos en kyriō*]" (4:7, author's translation). Could the relativization of status be made more overt? How can Philemon *not* receive Onesimus as "more than a slave, a beloved brother" when Paul, Epaphras, and Tychicus all bear the same designation of slave as Onesimus?

When we turn to the actual instructions for slaves in 3:22, we are struck first by the fact that Paul addresses slaves not as property but as persons with moral capacities and dispositions. His instruction does not deal with how masters are to "manage" their slaves, but with how slaves should conduct themselves as moral agents. Second, he refers to their masters "according to the flesh," indicating the subsidiary character of the authority under which slaves are placed: the primary point of reference for slaves, and the one for whom they do all that their masters order, is the Lord; their willingness to do what is ordered is real, but their motivation is their relationship with the Lord. Thus, whatever they do, they should do "from the soul" as to the Lord, not as those who serve only to please human owners. Third, their reward of an "inheritance" (see 1:12) will come from this same Lord, not their masters, just as their punishment will be, if they do injustice. Fourth, Paul asserts the principle "there is no respecter of persons" (*prosōpolēmpsia*) with God (see Rom 2:11; Eph 6:9; for *diastolē*, "distinction," see Rom 3:22; 10:12). Slaves are subject to divine judgment as are all others; what is determinative is not their social place but their internal dispositions, their "fear of the Lord."

There is no question that these instructions can be—and have been—read as a justification or at the very least a support for the institution of slavery. Christian slaveholders through the ages have employed this and other texts as scriptural proof of God's approval of human bondage. Read in context and with careful attention to Paul's actual language, however, the passage can also be read more liberatively: slaves are not property but persons; they share as heirs in the kingdom; with other believers, they have been "qualified" by God; the obedience they give to masters is relativized by their ultimate allegiance to God. Like other believers, they are called to serve above all the one who has liberated them as persons: "be slaves of the Lord Christ" (Col 3:24).

Read aloud in the church at Colossae, this admonition would have been heard by Philemon and other congregants as a call to moral reimagining, in the same manner as the statement that in Christ there is neither slave nor free, or the designation of Paul, Epaphras, and Tychicus as fellow slaves: Onesimus and others like him in bondage must now be seen, received, and engaged as equals, if not in the law of Rome, certainly in the kingdom of God (Col 1:13).

The lesson is driven home by Paul's short instructions to believers who are also slaveholders in Col 4:1: "Masters [*kyrioi*], treat your slaves justly and fairly, realizing that you too have a Master [*kyrios*] in heaven." The masters are reminded that their authority is not absolute. They cannot commit injustice toward those serving them, but must "do the righteous thing" (*to dikaion*). They cannot act arbitrarily, capriciously, or preferentially, but must "do the fair thing" (*tēn isotēta*). Those who are in the social position of slaves are not only persons with moral capacities, but they are to be treated by those in the social position of owners with the moral dispositions appropriate to persons. What Paul asks of Philemon for the slave who has become

Christian is even more: Philemon is to receive him as a beloved brother, and as Paul himself (Phlm 16–17).

Read together, Philemon and Colossians can be seen to reinforce each other, rhetorically. They also confirm that Paul characteristically—in this respect much more like Aristotle than like Plato—focuses on the transformation of human dispositions and attitudes, from which authentic structural change might occur but without which structural change would signify little, rather than on structural changes that may or may not be accompanied by a transformation of mind and heart.

## Reading Philemon Together with Ephesians

Even if Ephesians were written as a circular letter to be read aloud in a series of communities, we cannot be certain that it would have been read in the church at Colossae, or that Philemon would have heard this letter as he almost certainly heard (and been influenced by) Colossians upon the return of Onesimus to his household. We must therefore be more tentative in drawing thematic or rhetorical connections between Ephesians and Philemon. Nevertheless, since there is a high probability of their having been written and sent at the same time and circumstances, it would be foolish to ignore the connections that present themselves.

There is no need here to address the literary distinctiveness of Ephesians: its lengthy hypotactic sentences redolent with superlatives (in this respect even more of what we find in Colossians); its prayerful, even liturgical, tone; its cosmic consciousness; its engagement not with local circumstances but with the universal implications of the *mystērion* proclaimed by Paul and his associates; its distinctive way of developing characteristic Pauline emphases and metaphors.[39] It is, however, pertinent to remind ourselves of Paul's central argument in this letter, which is that God's work is one of reconciliation among humans: the condition of sin is one in which humans are alienated from God, which is expressed by alienation among humans. The prime example of such alienation is the hostility between Jew and gen-

---

39. For language, see O'Brien, "Ephesians I"; Kirby, *Ephesians, Baptism and Pentecost*. For cosmic dimensions, see Dahl, "Cosmic Dimensions"; Mussner, "Contributions"; Caird, *Principalities and Powers*. For thematic aspects of Ephesians, see Caragounis, *Ephesian Mysterion*; Cerfaux, "Revelation"; Meeks, "'In One Body,'" 209–21; Wild, "'Be Imitators of God'"; Best, *Essays on Ephesians*.

tile. By the death of Jesus, God has brought about a reconciliation between God and humans, which in turn is expressed by the reconciliation of Jew and gentile, who together form a new humanity. Jew and gentile have the same access to God in the Holy Spirit and form one body/house that is the dwelling place of God.

In Ephesians, Paul assigns the church—made up of persons who were once alienated from each other but are now reconciled—a cosmic function: the church is the place where the *mystērion* is realized, and where the presence and power of God in the world are made known: "To me, the very least of the holy ones, this grace was given, to preach to the Gentiles the inscrutable riches of Christ, and to bring to light for all what is the plan of the mystery hidden from ages past in God who created all things, so that the manifold wisdom of God *might now be known through the church* to the principalities and authorities in the heavens" (3:8–10, emphasis added). The church is where the gift of reconciliation is given, and the mandate of the church is to be the sign of such reconciliation in the world.

Much of the exhortation in Ephesians emphasizes the sort of moral dispositions and practices that enable the church to perform this revelatory function. After describing some of the behavioral characteristic of their former lives (4:17–19), Paul declares in 4:20–24: "That is not how you learned Christ, assuming that you have heard of him and were taught in him, as truth is in Jesus, that you should put away the old self of your former way of life, corrupted through deceitful desires, and be renewed in the spirit of your minds, and put on the new self, created in God's way in righteousness and holiness in truth." Paul's moral exhortations, consequently, emphasize those qualities that make for reconciliation among humans: not hostility and wrath, but compassion and mercy: "Do not grieve the Holy Spirit of God, with which you were sealed for the day of redemption. All bitterness, fury, anger, shouting, and reviling must be removed from you, along with all malice. And be kind to one another, compassionate, forgiving one another as God has forgiven you in Christ. So be imitators of God, as beloved children, and live in love, as Christ loved us and handed himself over for us as a sacrificial offering to God for a fragrant aroma" (4:30–5:2).

It is against this backdrop that Paul's instructions to members of the household are best understood. Paul wants the household to display the same reconciling attitudes and dispositions that express the reconciliation between God and humans at the cosmic level and the reconciliation between Jew and gentile at the social level. He assumes the established hierarchical arrangement of the ancient household, in which authority moves from the top down (husbands over wives, parents over children, masters over slaves) and obedience moves from the bottom up (slaves to masters, children to parents, slaves to masters). No more than in Philemon or in 1 Corinthians does Paul challenge a domestic structure that was widely regarded as "natural" and even as an order established by God—the notion that societal arrangements are "social constructions" lies many centuries in the future. Paul's rhetoric concerning these arrangements, however, is subtly subversive of the dominant dispositions and attitudes that pervaded these ancient social systems, and that gave those on the upper end of each binary absolute power over those at the lower end. In this regard, his opening command, "be subordinate to one another out of reverence for Christ [*en phobou Christou*]" (5:21) is the most important, since it (a) places all social arrangements and dynamics under the "fear of the Lord" and (b) stresses the mutuality or reciprocity of service: they are to be subordinate "to one another" (*allēlois*).

This christological context is most obvious in the instructions to husband and wives. On one side, wives are to be submissive to their husbands in every way as the church is to Christ (5:24) so that their submission is "as to the Lord" (5:22), because the husband is to the wife as Christ is to the church, the head who saves the church (5:23). On the other side, the instructions to husbands are much more elaborate, since Paul demands of them the specific disposition of *agapē* (self-donative love) that Christ showed toward the church when he gave himself as a sacrifice (5:25; see 5:1-2). Husbands are obliged to have such love toward their wives as toward their own bodies; the one showing such self-donative love toward his wife shows it to himself as well (5:28). The mention of the body enables Paul to think of the marriage relationship as analogous to the metaphor of the church as the body of Christ (5:29-30), indeed as more than a metaphor: the mystery of man and woman becoming one flesh is a symbolic expression of the relation between Christ and the church: "This is a great mystery, but I speak in reference to Christ and the church. In any case, each one of you should love his wife as himself, and the wife should respect [*phobein*] her husband" (5:32-33). If there is asymmetry in this instruction, it is one that falls on the dispositions required of the husband; while the wife is expected to respect and submit—not to all men, notice—to her husband (*tois idiois andrasin*), the husband is required to demonstrate toward his wife the same self-sacrificing love (*agapē*) of Christ, which goes considerably beyond the requirements of social convention.

The instruction to parents and children in Eph 6:1-4 is equally lenient when compared to ancient parallels. Children are to obey parents "in the

Lord" (*en kyriō*) as an act of righteousness (*touto estin dikaion*) and in the expectation of receiving (according to Exod 20:12) the promise of prospering and enjoying a long life when they fulfill this command of Torah (*entolē*). Their obedience is, in other words, not a mechanical submission to social obligation but the way to express righteousness according to Scripture. Children are moral agents. In turn, "fathers" (*hoi pateres*—not both parents, because we remember the structure of "hard power" in the ancient household) do not receive reinforcement of their absolute power over children, who, as Paul reminds us elsewhere, are, in that culture, no better than slaves (see Gal 4:1). Instead, Paul forbids expressions of wrath (*parorgizein*) and demands of them that they raise or nourish (*ektrephein*) their children with an education (*paideia)* and instruction (*nouthesia*) in the Lord (*en kyriō*). Here again, the greater weight of moral obligation and effort is demanded of those who are in the power positions. Reconciliation in the church—and in the world—must begin with reconciliation within the household, where differences in social status are ameliorated by greater vulnerability and generosity on the side of those with greater social power.

The instructions directed to slaves and masters are similar. He tells slaves in 6:5 to obey their masters "according to the flesh" (*kata sarka*) as to Christ (*hōs tō Christō*). The effect of this combination is to relativize the otherwise absolute subordination of slaves. The real "master/Lord" is Christ, in contrast to those humans who "possess" them. Thus, their obedience to human commands is a way of expressing obedience to Christ, "with fear and trembling" (cf. 2 Cor 7:15) and "simplicity of heart" (cf. Rom 12:8; 2 Cor 8:2; 9:11, 13; 11:3; Col 3:22). Slaves, like wives and like children, are moral agents and have the dignity of moral agents, rather than the mute and passive property of husbands, parents, and masters.

That this is the proper construal of Paul's opening command is made clear by the three remarkable qualifications that follow in 6:6–8. First, slaves are to show obedience, "not according to eye-service [*ophthalmodoulia*] in order to please humans [cf. Col 3:22], but as slaves of Christ doing the will of God from the soul [*ek psychēs*]" (author's translation). Second, they are to do this "with a disposition of benevolence [*eunoia*] performing service as to the Lord and not to humans" (author's translation). The NAB translates *met' eunoia* as "willingly," but the term in the broader culture bears definite associations with patronage and benefaction.[40] Paul subtly shifts the slave to

---

40. Aristotle sees it as a possible element in friendship but as lacking the intimacy that goes with true friendship; see *Nicomachean Ethics* 8.2.3–4, 9.5.1–4.

the position of a patron, whose service to the master is a form of gift. Finally, Paul provides the motivation: "Since you know [*eidotes*] that each one, if he does anything good, will receive a reward from the Lord, whether slave or free [*eite doulos eite eleutheros*]" (author's translation). Paul has effectively placed slaves and masters on the same moral/religious plane before the Lord. If slaves serve human masters, they do so as fully equal to free persons, making their acts of service a form of benefaction and a way of serving their true master, the Lord.

Remarkably, Paul's instructions to masters follow the same premise. They are to do "the same things" to their slaves (*ta auta pros autous*), which must mean that they are to act reciprocally and with the same understanding. Paul tells masters to "give up threatening" or, as the NABRE translates, "stop bullying" (*anientes tēn apeilēn*). Consistent with the entire moral teaching of Ephesians, the behaviors that express the hostility, wrath, and violence of the "old man" are to be replaced by attitudes of mercy and compassion. The motivation for masters is also a form of recognition: "since you know that their Lord and yours is in heaven and with him there is no respecting of persons [*prosōpolēmpsia*]" (author's translation). Masters and slaves will be judged by God by the same measure, because they are equal in his eyes; social status means nothing to God, a truth that ought to shape the perception of humans in diverse social positions. Paul's phrasing provides a subtle reminder to masters that a higher social position gives no advantage within the new humanity: it is "their Lord" that precedes "your Lord"!

## Conclusion

Reading Philemon as part of a three (or more) letter packet delivered by Tychicus when he returned the slave Onesimus to the household of Philemon in Colossae makes perfect sense of the literary relations among Philemon, Colossians, and Ephesians and provides an elegant hypothesis for the inclusion of this private letter in the canon: it came as a note saved together with those letters. It stands within the canon as a precious witness to the social and religious world of Paul the apostle, as he continued his ministry of reconciliation even when imprisoned.

When we read Philemon together with Colossians and Ephesians, moreover, we discover some of the benefits of reading the canonical Paul precisely as canonical: the two larger letters not only disclose the fuller theological and pastoral dimensions of Paul's ministry while in captivity; they also reveal how Paul's thought can be catalyzed by specific experiences and situations. And they also show how the same ambiguity concerning slavery and discipleship found in Philemon characterizes those letters as well: Paul does not challenge the social system of slavery any more than he seeks to dissolve the ethnic distinctions between Jew and gentile or the gender distinctions between husband and wife. But his vision of the "new humanity" and its accompanying dispositions and practices radically challenges the absolute character of those ancient social forms and opens the possibility of structural change and reform.

*Chapter 11*

# Paul, Oppressor or Liberator?

In the introduction to this book, I listed five reasons why Paul is of historical importance: (1) he was a persecutor of the church who, on the basis of a firsthand experience of the resurrected Jesus, became an apostle; (2) he founded and pastored—directly and through an extensive network of coworkers—communities of Christ-believers "from Jerusalem to Illyricum" (Rom 15:19); (3) he was one of the leaders and defenders of the mission to the gentiles as one that did not require circumcision and the observance of the law; (4) he was one of the first, and arguably the most influential, interpreters of the story of Jesus, not through a sustained narrative concerning his words and deeds, but through allusion to and application of a narrative pattern concerning Jesus as the one whose obedient faith in God was expressed through loving self-donation to other humans;[1] (5) he wrote letters to his communities and delegates, the collection of which formed the heart of the Christian canon and made Paul the apostle of historic, and not only historical, significance.[2]

As we have seen, his letters (and Acts) provide an abundance of evidence that Paul was a controverted figure even during his lifetime. It may not be possible to identify a set of Pauline "opponents" as an organized resistance to his mission, but both Acts and Paul's letters testify to a ministry punctuated by beatings, imprisonments, and other hardships, and it is clear from the letters that Paul's efforts were often misunderstood or (at least in his eyes) embraced in ways and with outcomes that he had not envisaged and that he did not approve. The statement that "those who liked Paul did

---

1. See esp. Hays, *Faith of Jesus Christ*.
2. The distinction is similar to, but not identical with, the scholarly distinction in German New Testament studies between *Historie* and *Geschichte*.

not understand him, while those who understood him did not like him" may be far too simple and broad,[3] but it serves to remind us that the very reason why Paul had to write letters was often due to troubled circumstances in his churches, and that sometimes those troubles involved himself.

The canonical Paul—the Paul whose letters have been read in the liturgy, preached, studied, and disputed through the centuries—has been, and continues to be, just as controversial as the historical Paul, perhaps even more controversial, because the canonical Paul has been read as Scripture, as the always compelling Word of God and not merely the correspondence of an ancient man, as the source and norm (together with other canonical writings) of Christian identity.[4] To the degree that identity has been challenged, we will find, so has the canonical Paul been challenged.

The earlier chapters of this book have had the aim of providing readers with the elements required for "constructing" Paul in the historical sense. I have considered the question of sources, his life and ministry, the shape of his correspondence, his place within early Christianity, his immersion in Judaism and Scripture, and his engagement with Greco-Roman culture. I have also ventured to identify some elements within the letters that always need to be appreciated: the role of both quotidian and extraordinary experience, and the ways that experience affects Paul's convictions, myths, symbols, and metaphors. Finally, I suggested that a "canonical" reading of Philemon in concert with Colossians and Ephesians both provides a historically plausible account of the three letters and deepens the Pauline "voice" revealed in Philemon.

But because the historic, canonical Paul remains so powerful (and for some so threatening) a figure even today, I think it is appropriate to conclude this volume with a consideration of the ways the canonical Paul has played a pivotal role within Christian history and a deeply divisive role in the last four centuries of that history. I begin with an initial and decisive argument concerning Paul in the second century between Marcion and Irenaeus, and indicate briefly how Paul was for over fifteen hundred years—especially for theologians—the "apostle of the church."[5] I then take up the challenges to

3. I cannot credit the witticism because I have no idea of its origin or original formulation.

4. See L. Johnson, "New Testament as the Church's Book."

5. My treatment leaves out the hostility shown Paul by Jewish Christians of the first centuries, because the little that can responsibly be said about it I have already indicated in chap. 1; it may have been real, it may have been vigorous, but it is impossible on the basis of the extant sources for the historian to provide a comprehensive assessment; see Lüdemann,

Paul (as representing classical Christianity) since the Enlightenment from a variety of perspectives, and respond to them point by point, before providing the reasons why I consider Paul to be the most liberating rather than the most oppressing voice within the canon.[6]

## Marcion and Irenaeus

For Marcion, who came from Sinope in Pontus to Rome ca. 150 with aspirations of being elected bishop of that city, and who, upon his failure in that venture, made a considerable success of his dualistic version of Christianity, especially in the East, Paul was the singular apostle who rightly grasped the message of Jesus and brought authentic salvation.[7] When Jesus spoke of God as his Father, he did not mean the creator God of the Jews but a previously unknown God who was involved not with material reality but with the spirits of humans. Using Paul's ten letters and an expurgated version of the Gospel of Luke as his textual basis,[8] and rejecting entirely the Old Testament

---

*Opposition to Paul.* Hostility toward or rejection of Paul, however, does not constitute an interpretation of Paul. My treatment here also leaves out of account the role of the canonical letters in Orthodox Christianity, although Paul certainly was read and celebrated as "the apostle" in the Eastern church as he was for centuries in the West; see, e.g., Mitchell, *Heavenly Trumpet.* Paul was appreciated as a source for distinctive Orthodox theological emphases: the transforming role of the Holy Spirit, the life of contemplation, and participation in the divine life (*theosis*); see Wallace, *Snatched into Paradise*; Gorman, *Inhabiting the Cruciform God*; Blackwell, *Christosis*; Christensen and Wittung, *Participation in the Divine Nature.* But in contrast to Western Christianity, the Orthodox tradition has for the most part lacked the demographic, linguistic, cultural, technological, and ideological disruptions that have shaped the way Paul has been read in the West; see the essays in Cunningham and Theokritoff, *Orthodox Christian Theology.* Plus, the history I sketch here is the one that immediately affects my readers and myself.

6. The material I map in the following pages has been surveyed in a different manner by Gray, *Paul as a Problem.*

7. I leave out of consideration here as well the positive view of Paul among gnostic writers of the second and third centuries, who shared—if in less dialectical fashion—the view of Paul espoused by Marcion; see Pagels, *Gnostic Paul.* The standard (admiring) reconstruction of Marcion's thought from the fragments of patristic polemic is Harnack, *Marcion.*

8. Although some think that Marcion did not know the Pastorals, it is difficult to construe Tertullian's use of *recusavit* in any sense other than "rejected" or "refused" (*Adversus Marcionem* 5.21). Marcion's acceptance of the ten other letters (making most use of Galatians and Romans and 2 Corinthians, to be sure) is powerful if indirect support for the position that the collection of at least Paul's letters was well established by the mid-second century; for discussion of Marcion's possible role as stimulator of the notion of canon, see BeDuhn,

writings—except as a foil—Marcion held a view of salvation that was simple and appealing. The true God was spiritual and sought to free human spirits from the shackles of materiality. Matter is bad, spirit is good. The dualism is absolute.[9] And it does not take an excess of experience to appreciate the appeal of a liberation from the all-too-frail body. Human imprisonment in materiality, however, is more than a cosmic accident. For Marcion it was the work of "the god of this world" whom Paul speaks of in 2 Cor 4:4 as blinding humans. Marcion sees Paul as referring precisely to the God of the Old Testament, who was a god of wrath as opposed to the god of mercy revealed by Jesus. In root and branch, Marcion's "gospel" is anti-Jewish, for if the Jews worship the God of creation, then they worship the source of all that is evil in the world. Paul's proclamation of what Jesus preached was made more complicated, however, by the fact that many calling themselves Christians actually opposed the good news of spiritual liberation and advocated a return to the law. Such "Judaizers" infiltrated Paul's gentile communities and tried to make Jesus continuous with the God of the Old Testament. Paul's battle against the Judaizers and the Jews was therefore a battle for the "truth of the gospel," which he alone held onto in all its purity—in contrast to the other Christian writings, which were corrupted by the Judaizing influence.

Marcion's approach is direct and powerful, presenting salvation in terms of an either/or, and Paul as an "over against" figure. He pits Paul alone against all other Christian writings, Paul alone against the Jews and Judaizers, Paul alone against the evil god of creation, Paul alone as champion of the battle of the spirit against the flesh—that is, all material reality (see, e.g., Gal 5:13-26). It is no wonder that his version of Christianity was popular among those who preferred their ideology simple and their salvation a liberation from the ambiguities and afflictions of the world. Although Marcion's sect eventually disappeared, it did so largely by being subsumed by other dualisms, such as those advanced by Valentinians and Manichaeans.[10] And Marcion's either/or approach to Paul had a powerful influence on subsequent interpreters, such as Augustine and Luther.

Irenaeus of Lyons (ca. 140-200 CE) is an indispensable source of knowledge concerning Marcion and other dualistic versions of Christianity, on

---

*First New Testament*; Campenhausen, *Formation of the Christian Bible*; McDonald, *Christian Canon*.

9. A selection of Marcion's *Antitheses* can be found in Meeks and Fitzgerald, *Writings of St. Paul*, 286-90; see also Vinzent, *Tertullian's Preface*.

10. See Lebreton, *Gnosticism, Marcionism and Manichaeism*; Peter Brown, *Body and Society*.

which he meticulously reported and which he mercilessly skewered in his five books known as *Against Heresies* (ca. 180).[11] Irenaeus also championed Paul, but in a manner clean contrary to Marcion, and by so doing he set the basic frame for all subsequent reading of Paul for the mainstream tradition of interpretation that followed. First, he read Paul as in concert with, rather than opposed to, the other writings of the canon; by stressing the consonance between Paul and the Old Testament (e.g., *Against Heresies* 3.16.3), he showed the continuity of God's revelation; by emphasizing Paul's understanding of Jesus as confirming of the Gospel accounts, he demonstrated the consistency of the Christian gospel; by placing Paul firmly within the story of Acts (which for the first time, so far as we know, was so vigorously deployed), he saw Paul's ministry as one in communication and cooperation with the other apostles. Using Paul's own words, he demonstrated the false character of Marcion's construction of Paul's place and Paul's position vis-à-vis both Scripture and the church.

Second, Irenaeus's way of reading Paul's letters established the fundamental principle of reading in context, rather than extracting texts at random to fit an ideological position. Time and again, Irenaeus calls attention to the grammar and syntax of Paul's sentences, as when he demonstrates from other examples how Paul's words in 2 Cor 4:4—so critical to Marcion's theory—ought to be read in quite a different way than Marcion proposes (*Against Heresies* 3.7.1–2), and when he shows—contrary to Marcion—that Paul's language about "flesh" and "spirit" ought to be read, not dualistically in the cosmological sense, but as describing two kinds of moral inclination (*Against Heresies* 5.9.1).[12] Not only is such contextual reading a corollary of taking seriously the material dimension of reality—the order and design of words must be construed just as the order and design of creation, if truth is to be found—but it rescues Paul's letters from a tendency to make them mean anything one wants. Irenaeus taught all subsequent generations the importance of grammar and syntax in exegesis.

Third, Irenaeus found in Paul the key to his own remarkable theological vision, which builds on the premise of the one God who creates all that exists as good and reveals himself truly through both testaments, and on the premise that Jesus (and Paul) represents this same living God who seeks the salvation of all and not just a few, desires the redemption of all real-

---

11. For the scant biographical details, see the admiring account of Irenaeus in Eusebius's *Ecclesiastical History*, book 5; for my own appreciation, see L. Johnson, "Irenaeus."

12. For other examples, see *Against Heresies* 3.15.9, 3.18.3, 3.22.1.

ity and not just human souls. He finds the Pauline key in Eph 1:10, which speaks of the recapitulation of all things through Christ (see *Against Heresies* 3.18.1, 4.34.1, 5.14.2, 5.21.2), and in Rom 5:12–21, which pictures Christ as the new Adam, who reverses the sad history of humanity since Adam's sin (see *Against Heresies* 3.23). Irenaeus thus pictures the process of revelation as God's pedagogical exercise, through which humans are prepared, despite all their inadequacy, to bear the image of God; thus his famous dictum, "The glory of God is a human being fully alive" (*Against Heresies* 4.34).[13] Christ represents the "recapitulation" of all creation and all of God's redeeming work; he is the "mature man" toward which all true faith tends, involving not only spirit but matter as well.

It was Irenaeus, in short, who constructed Paul as the canonical Paul, a construction that perdured for some fifteen hundred years. By so doing, and by his skill in linking scriptural interpretation to the teaching authority of the bishops in apostolic succession (see *Against Heresies* 3.3.1–4), Irenaeus also gave theological legitimation to what can be called classical Christianity. It was a singular and even spectacular achievement, seldom fully appreciated—and, as we shall see, in modernity much deplored. But for the great Christian theologians who followed Irenaeus, the basic elements of his synthesis were assumed.

## The Apostle of the Theologians

The reason why Paul's letters appeal so much to theologians should be obvious: they are filled with religious discourse that invites theological inquiry and lends itself to deployment in formal theological discussion. To the degree that Christian leaders in the patristic and medieval periods felt called on to articulate or defend the elements of the faith, Paul's letters proved, together with the Gospel of John, an invaluable, irreplaceable resource. For the largest part of Christian life and thought from late antiquity to the Reformation, the Irenaean synthesis that I have described held steady. Paul was preached as part of the canon, was used in theological discussions and debates together with other canonical writings, was commented on in the manner of other canonical writings, was regarded as authoritative and significant in the same measure as other writings in the canon.

13. English translation from Alexander Roberts and James Donaldson, eds. *ANF* 1 (Peabody, MA: Hendrickson, 1994).

Such is the case, for example, in the theological compositions of Thomas Aquinas (1225–74). Thomas used Paul everywhere and to great effect, and, while profoundly influenced by Augustine, found deep resonances between Paul and Aristotle, especially on questions of moral character and development (see, e.g., *Summa Theologiae* II, II, 47, 10 and II, II, 52, 1–2). He wrote perceptive commentaries in the scholastic manner on Paul's letters. In his theological works, when Thomas wrote "*apostolus dicit*" ("the apostle says"), he referred not to Peter or John but to the letters of Paul (see, e.g., *Summa Theologiae* II, 30, 2; III, 69). For Thomas, however, as for most other Christian theologians, Paul did not stand out as the distinctively important voice, as the pivotal figure, as the decisive vote. Paul was simply Scripture, with the same authority as James and John and Peter and, for that matter, the Gospels. All of them could be applied in equal fashion to whatever theological question was under discussion.[14]

But there is another line of development in which, while the Irenaean synthesis is assumed, Paul's voice does become more dominant and decisive, the critical and defining voice within the canon. Among these interpreters, in fact, something of the spirit of Marcion lingers, as the "over against-ness" of the apostle is emphasized more than the ways in which Paul stands among and in harmony with other witnesses. Among such interpreters of Paul, sharply defined theological positions derived from such readings of Paul tended to become more and more identified as defining of classical Christianity in the West.

The first in this series is Augustine of Hippo (354–430), who is important both in himself and for the huge impact he had on all subsequent Western theology. For Augustine, Paul had a direct and personal significance, as his *Confessions* attests: it was the reading of Rom 13:13–14, in response to a child's chant of "take and read," that led Augustine to abandon his dissolute ways and dedicate himself to the Christianity into which he had been baptized.[15] Augustine's consciousness of his strong sensuality and the errors to which it could lead, on one side, and his youthful flight to Manichaeism and then Platonism in the effort to free himself from his physical appetites, on the other side, had a lingering effect on the way he read Paul,[16] especially when

14. See, e.g., his discussion of Rom 3:21–26 in his *Commentary on Romans*, where Paul's exposition is amplified—we would probably say muted—by appeal to other canonical authorities from Hebrews to James.

15. Augustine, *Confessions* 8.12.

16. We can note how Rom 7 serves as the subtext to Augustine's inner struggles in *Confessions* 7.21 and 8.5.

he felt that his own experience of grace was implicitly being challenged by other Christian theologians.[17] When Augustine wrote polemically against the Manichaeans or against the sectarian Donatists, he used Paul much in the manner of Irenaeus, as a resource for asserting the goodness of creation, the continuity of divine revelation, the value of the body, and the unity of the church.[18]

It was in Augustine's conflict with the British monk Pelagius (ca. 360–418), however, that his reading of Paul became sharper and more tightly focused. The learned and ascetical Pelagius, who knew Greek as well as Latin, and who, unlike Augustine, had written a formal commentary on Romans as well as expositions on all thirteen of Paul's letters, was perceived by Augustine as advancing far too optimistic a view of the human potential for virtue apart from grace.[19] Guided by his own past experience, Augustine insisted that Paul taught original sin (reading the *in quo* of the Latin in Rom 5:12 as dispositive),[20] and understanding Paul's language about *epithymia* in Rom 7 as *concupiscentia*—human sexual desire such as he had grappled with—found there support for his view that humans could not simply do what God orders on their own power, but needed the remedy of grace for the power to do what is right.[21] Although these specific judgments about Paul are in fact exegetically suspect, it must be granted that Augustine was more correct about Paul overall than were Pelagius and his follower Caelestius. The fact that they came to Carthage between 410 and 415 when Augustine was in Hippo, and the fact that they were stubborn and able polemicists in their own right, meant that Augustine was pushed progressively to a harder position on the issue of (divine) grace and (human) works than he would otherwise have taken.

17. For an overview, see Canty, "Saint Paul in Augustine."

18. See, e.g., *On the Morals of the Catholic Church and on the Morals of the Manichaeans*; *On the Soul against the Manichaeans*; *Concerning the Nature of the Good against the Manichaeans*; *On Baptism against the Donatists*. For orientation, see Lee, *Augustine, Manichaeism, and the Good*; Meer, *Augustine the Bishop*.

19. For background, see G. Bonner, *Augustine*; Ferguson, *Pelagius*.

20. The Greek *eph' hō pantes* would be more accurately understood as "on account of which all"; Augustine and the subsequent Latin tradition understood *in quo* as referring to Adam, "in whom all have sinned."

21. Among Augustine's anti-Pelagian works, see *On the Spirit and the Letter*; *On Nature and Grace*; *On Man's Perfection in Righteousness*; *On the Grace of Christ and on Original Sin*; *On Grace and Free Will*; *On the Forgiveness of Sins*. We know of two Pelagian works of which Augustine (and other opponents) make mention: *On Nature* and *Defense of Freedom of the Will*.

In the Protestant Reformation of the sixteenth century, especially in the two main continental reformers, Martin Luther and John Calvin, Paul truly became the defining authority for Christian discipleship, and it was a Paul read as "over against" a Catholicism that was viewed as hopelessly corrupt. For Luther and Calvin, Paul was certainly "the Apostle" in a singular and contentious fashion. Simply because Luther is the more dramatic and impassioned figure, and the traits of Marcion and Augustine appear more noticeably in him, I will speak of Luther's Paul more than Calvin's, but it would be a great mistake to isolate Luther from Calvin and Zwingli and other continental reformers as interpreters of Paul.[22] They all participated in what was, in effect, the Pelagian controversy raised to an even greater pitch and with much more far-reaching consequences.

Like Augustine, Luther (1483–1546) read Paul in a highly personal fashion, finding especially in Galatians and Romans the "charter of Christian freedom" that liberated him from his guilt-ridden and works-righteous existence as a monk. But rather than read this Paul over against a single heresy, Luther pitted his Paul against the entire tradition of Western Christianity known as Catholicism, which he regarded as the source of his own previous torment and as a deep distortion of the good news proclaimed by Jesus and articulated by the apostle.[23]

Luther famously posed two powerful and opposing options: one based righteousness either on human works or on pure trust in God's forgiveness (works or faith); and one relied either on the entire apparatus of tradition (*traditio*), which choked the good news, or on the saving word of Scripture alone (*sola scriptura*). Fatefully, Luther not only read his own struggles in Rom 7 autobiographically, as Augustine also had, declaring that humans were incapable of pleasing God apart from grace (see *The Bondage of the Will*, 1525),[24] but he read Paul's struggles with Judaizers as the template for his own struggle against the works righteousness of medieval Catholicism. Once more, we find the tinge of Marcionism: now Paul is the champion of a good news defined in opposition to Judaism and Catholicism at once (they were, for Luther, much the same).

22. Calvin's reading of Romans was certainly consonant with Luther's, but in his *Commentary on Romans* and in the *Institutes of the Christian Religion*, his understanding of predestination (based especially on Rom 9–11) was especially influential in later Reformed theology; see, e.g., Raith, *Aquinas and Calvin on Romans*; Lane, "Calvin."

23. See Cameron, *Annotated Luther*; Hagen, *Luther's Approach*.

24. Written as a sharp rebuttal of Erasmus of Rotterdam (1466–1536), who had composed *On the Freedom of the Will* as an irenic yet critical response to Luther's earlier tracts.

So central was Paul for Luther's self-understanding and for the message of salvation by grace attained through faith that—in tension with the principle of *sola scriptura*—he declared Paul's letters as the heart of the New Testament: with the Gospel of John and 1 Peter, they "showed thee the Christ and taught thee all that is needful to know," leaving the other canonical compositions by comparison as "so much straw" (*Preface to the New Testament*, 1521).[25] Luther, then, had a true "canon within the canon," and the most important part of that reduced canon was the theology of Paul, found above all in Galatians and Romans.

Using Galatians and Romans as his chief sources, Luther elevated Paul to a position not utterly unlike Marcion's: the law's value was to reveal the hopelessness of the human condition; faith in the saving work of Christ, not all the machinery of sacraments and indulgences ("works") of late medieval Catholicism, made humans righteous. Paul was, in effect, the primary and essential definer of authentic Christianity. One could almost add "Paul alone" to "faith alone" and "Scripture alone"! It can be, and has been, argued that Luther's critical attack on the entire structure of Catholicism paved the way for the secularism that emerged in the West, although such a consequence would have been far from his own intentions.[26]

The history of theology following the sixteenth century is, to be sure, complex: Catholicism scarcely disappears, and Protestantism itself proves fissiparous in the extreme. It would require many volumes simply to sketch the theologies distinctive to all these various forms of Christianity. But I think it fair to say that the elevation of Paul accomplished by the sixteenth-century reformers remained in place over the next several centuries within Christianity itself. Certainly, the most influential Protestant theologians of the twentieth century each in their way grounded their thought squarely on Luther's and Calvin's Paul.

Ferdinand Christian Baur and Adolf Von Harnack, for example, celebrated Paul as the "second founder" of Christianity, who freed Jesus from his "Jewish particularity" and shaped a universal religion,[27] an accomplishment applauded by such Pauline stalwarts as Otto Pfleiderer,[28] Wilhelm Wrede,

---

25. For English translation, see E. Theodore Bachmann, ed., *Luther's Works: Word and Sacrament I* (Philadelphia: Fortress, 1960).

26. See Gregory, *Rebel in the Ranks*.

27. Baur, *Church History*; Harnack, *What Is Christianity?*; pertinent excerpts provided by Meeks and Fitzgerald, *Writings of St. Paul*, 399–408, 419–24.

28. Pfleiderer, *Religion and Historic Faiths*.

and Wilhelm Bousset.[29] It was his *Epistle to the Romans* (1918) that Karl Barth (1886–1968) used to shatter the smugness of late-nineteenth-century liberal Protestantism and introduce the dialectical theology that dominated theological debate for decades. It was in the Paul of Galatians and Romans—and in the Gospel of John—that Rudolf Bultmann (1884–1976) found the core of an existentialist vision of authentic existence, which for him resisted demythologization, simultaneously reducing all other canonical writings to mere sources for historical reconstruction.[30] And the "Protestant principle" so critical to the theology of Paul Tillich (1886–1965) was an abstraction whose basis was also Paul.[31]

What, then, is this Paul of the theologians that comes to define—at least in the eyes of its critics—classical Christianity? Several salient points can be noted. First, it is increasingly an abstraction called "Paul" rather than an engagement with specific letters, an abstraction drawn from a handful of letters and tending to focus on an embattled "religious personality." Second, Paul teaches the hopeless condition of humans, as captive to sin and law, whose rescue comes only from the power of God displayed in the cross of Christ. Third, Paul is the singular apostle who represents the "truth of the gospel" over against distortions connected with law and institutionalization. Fourth, baptism and the Lord's Supper are, in Paul's letters, preeminently the ritual activities that mediate the saving power of God, although other miracles also attest the truth of the good news. Fifth, Paul's Christology is as "high" and "from above" as the Gospel of John's, with Jesus being fully God's Son active in creation, the one sent in the form of a slave to rescue humans, the one exalted to God's right hand as Lord, the one who will return as Judge. Sixth, Paul's opponents represent Judaism, and authentic Christianity must be defined as "not Jewish," which means being defined also against Judaism's successors, above all Roman Catholicism, with its superstition, corruption, authoritarianism, clericalism, and proliferation of sacraments, sacramentals, pilgrimages, indulgences, miracle-working saints, and many-tentacled institutions. Other features could be mentioned, but these suffice to make the point. I only need to add that, for these major theological figures, all these elements are positive and good.[32]

29. Wilhelm Bousset produced the second edition of William Wrede's *Paul the Apostle*.

30. See the decisive review by Dahl, "Rudolf Bultmann's Theology."

31. See the frequent use of the term "Protestant principle"—in implicit contrast to the "theology of glory" associated with Catholicism—in Tillich, *Systematic Theology*.

32. See Westerholm, *Perspectives Old and New on Paul*. For a succinct treatment of the "old" Paul, see Schreiner, "Paul."

## The Case against Paul

To the very degree that Paul was taken by believers to define classical (creedal) Christianity, he became the chief target for those who despised classical (creedal) Christianity. Underlying the various charges against him is the often implicit, sometimes explicit premise that Paul rather than Jesus was the real founder of Christianity[33]—a premise whose falsity I showed in chapter 4. The case against the apostle therefore often involves a "good Jesus" / "bad Paul" contrast.

### *The Cultured Despisers*

It is not altogether unfair to call the Enlightenment of the seventeenth and eighteenth centuries the secularization of the Reformation, with "reason alone" replacing "faith alone," and "empirical evidence alone" replacing "Scripture alone." Luther's rejection of the episcopacy, monasticism, indulgences, and everything "superstitious" in the name of his distinctive reading of Galatians and Romans seemed, to those designating themselves as Deists, not nearly radical enough. Indeed, Paul was viewed as (in Thomas Jefferson's words) "the first corrupter of the doctrines of Jesus."[34] In Paul above all, the Deists found the source of all they detested in traditional Christianity— Protestant as well as Catholic. It was Paul, not Jesus, that made Christianity dogmatic, authoritarian, intolerant, sacramental, superstitious, mysterious, miraculous, illogical, a *religion* that worshiped Christ as a God rather than learned from Jesus as a wise teacher about God. David Hume's citing the case of a man raised from the dead as the supreme example of the impossibility of miracles was not casually chosen: the resurrection of Jesus, as preached by Paul, is at the very heart of classical Christianity.[35]

John Toland (1670–1722) argued in *Christianity Not Mysterious* (1696) that what was true in religion—its moral teaching—was not a matter of di-

33. By the end of the nineteenth century, to be sure, the effort to secure a Pauline "canon within the canon" had proven triumphant among scholars, precisely as a means to relieve some of these issues. For this process, see L. Johnson, *First and Second Letters to Timothy*, 42–54. The great advantage to the lovers of the "Lutheran" Paul is that they got to keep the letters that (in their view) contained him and be relieved of the embarrassing Pastorals!

34. Jefferson, *Letter to William Short*.

35. David Hume, *An Inquiry Concerning Human Understanding* (1748), esp. part 2, "On Miracles."

vine revelation but a matter of human nature, accessible through reason alone. Thomas Chubb declared that Paul was a liar[36] and anticipated all later quests for the historical Jesus—free of all supernatural accoutrements—in *The True Gospel of Jesus Christ* (1738). In 1820, the former American president Thomas Jefferson snipped out of his Bible all that appeared to him as superstitious, miraculous, and so forth (that is, all of Paul and much of the Gospels), and produced *The Life and Morals of Jesus Christ* as an appropriate moral guide to an enlightened gentleman from Virginia. All subsequent treatments of the "historical Jesus" continue the Enlightenment quest for a usable—that is, reasonable Jesus by eliminating anything supernatural in the Gospel accounts and ignoring Paul completely, unless it is to blame him for "Creedal Christianity," even when his letters offer significant evidence concerning the human Jesus.[37]

In the late nineteenth and early twentieth centuries, a new twist is put on the image of a despised but powerful second (or "real") founder of Christianity. Critics of Christianity like Friedrich Nietzsche and George Bernard Shaw read Paul's personality off the pages of his letters, regarding them not as carefully crafted examples of rhetoric but—in keeping with Romantic notions of literature—as the outpourings of a tortured soul. Paul's switch from persecutor to apostle of a sect he once tried to destroy can therefore be explained in terms of a psychopathology revealed on every page: Paul's malice, envy, hunger for power, and hostility toward the law were not eliminated but only transmuted by his baptism.[38] The Deist critique of classical Christianity as represented by Paul is now given an even sharper edge: Christianity is sick because it was created out of Paul's psyche, and Paul's psyche was sick.[39] Variations on this theme continue among the contemporary "new atheists," the enthusiastic adherents to evolutionary psychology who are generally kind to Jesus but view Paul as the villain whose unevolved pathologies undergird the resistance of believers to their thoroughly rational view of reality—if we except such invisible and personified entities as "selfish genes."[40]

---

36. *The Posthumous Works of Thomas Chubb* (London, 1748).

37. See L. Johnson, *Real Jesus*.

38. See the excerpts by Nietzsche, "The First Christian" (1880) and "The Jewish Dysangelist" (1888), and by Shaw, "The Monstrous Imposition upon Jesus" (1913), in Meeks and Fitzgerald, *Writings of St. Paul*, 408-14.

39. A milder form of psychological reductionism persists in writers such as Fromm, *Dogma of Christ*, and Rubenstein, *My Brother Paul*.

40. Among others, see Dawkins, *God Delusion* and *Selfish Gene*; Hitchens, *God Is Not*

*Jewish Detractors*

No group has a better case against the negative aspects of Christianity than the Jews, who have seen in the Shoah of the twentieth century a climax of centuries of Christian hostility and murder. Remarkably, not even the Holocaust has silenced anti-Jewish rhetoric and behavior, as the headlines, debates at the United Nations, and campus agitation daily attest.[41] It is clear that the Gospels provide ammunition enough for anti-Semitic dispositions and behaviors,[42] but among Jews, the "real Jesus" could be regarded as a teacher of Israel, even a prophet,[43] while Paul is regarded as the real culprit, the self-despising anti-Semitic Jew (see 1 Thess 2:14–16; 2 Cor 3:7–17; Phil 3:2–21; Gal 1–2; 1 Tim 1:3–17), who made a fundamental break with his heritage and thereby legitimated centuries of Jew-baiting and worse.

Such a reaction is understandable, given that a major strand of Pauline interpretation from Luther forward—more accurately, *the* major strand—tended to define Christianity in terms of its being "not Jewish," elevating Paul's polemic against Judaizers into an attack on an entire religious tradition, carrying forward into "normative Christianity" the Marcionist virus that infected the reading of Paul and identified Jews as "fleshly," "enslaved to law," and "haters of God."[44]

In light of this history, it is remarkable to find Jewish animus toward Paul to be so mild. Rabbi Leo Baeck considered that Paul never really understood Judaism as a "classical" religion—that is, guided by wise and life-enhancing precepts rather than feelings—because he was a "romantic" in matters religious, drawn to feelings and experiences. In contrast, Jesus (especially as depicted by Matthew) stood squarely within the classic Jewish tradition, making the sort of sane religious sense that Paul muddled in a quest for ecstasy.[45]

---

Great and *Portable Atheist*. For perceptive analysis, see Wolfe, *Hooking Up*, 17–112; Beattie, *New Atheists*.

41. See, e.g., Fackenheim, *Jewish Bible*; Lipstadt, *Denying the Holocaust*; Lipstadt, *History on Trial*.

42. E.g., Beck, *Mature Christianity*; J. Sanders, "Salvation of the Jews"; Bloom, "'Before Moses Was I Am.'"

43. See, e.g., Falk, *Jesus the Pharisee*; Vermes, *Jesus the Jew*.

44. The fact that New Testament scholarship is marked by anti-Jewish elements cannot be denied. See, e.g., Klein, *Anti-Judaism in Christian Theology*; E. Sanders, *Jesus and Judaism*, 23–52, 202. For specific examples, see Marxsen, *New Testament Foundations*; Hengel, "Der Jakobusbrief" (translation in Meeks and Fitzgerald, *Writings of St. Paul*, 242–53).

45. Baeck, "Faith of Paul."

*Feminist and Womanist Critics*

From *The Women's Bible* (1895/98) of Elizabeth Cady Stanton to Elizabeth Schüssler Fiorenza's *In Memory of Her* (1983), many women have found Paul's to be an oppressive voice: he is certainly androcentric and patriarchal, perhaps sexist, and possibly even misogynist.[46] Passages that flatly command women to be silent in the assembly (1 Tim 2:11–15; 1 Cor 14:33b–36), or to wear veils when praying or prophesying in the assembly (1 Cor 11:2–16); texts that call for women to be submissive to men in the household (Col 3:18; Eph 5:22–24), or that seem to define women by domestic roles (1 Tim 5:3–16; Titus 2:3–5), or that refer to women as "silly women" (*gynaikaria*, 2 Tim 3:6) fall within the category of texts that Phyllis Trible has memorably designated as biblical "texts of terror," passages supporting the dominance of males over females both in the church and in society.[47]

One way of managing this oppressive voice has been to distinguish between authentic and inauthentic letters: the authentic Paul—above all in Gal 3:28 and 1 Cor 7:1–40—is liberated and liberal regarding the "eschatological woman"; in contrast, the Paul of Colossians and Ephesians, and preeminently the Pastorals, not only is sexist in outlook but is actually opposed to women playing a public role.[48] The fatal flaw in this solution is that some passages within the authentic letters are as problematic as those in the letters deemed inauthentic (see 1 Cor 11:2–16; 14:33b–36; Rom 7:2–3). Having the evil author of the Pastorals interpolate such sexist passages into the authentic letters might be considered a solution, but it is a desperate one.[49]

Rather than grapple with the canonical letters at the exegetical level, some feminist (and womanist) writers exercise the thematic form of "canon within the canon" proposed by Rosemary Radford Ruether: only those texts that advance the liberation of women should be considered authoritative; those that do not can be relegated to the rubbish heap of history.[50] Schüssler Fiorenza, in turn, considers most of the New Testament corrupted by the sexism of its male authors, but finds, in her own reconstruction of a "woman-

---

46. See above all Schüssler Fiorenza, *In Memory of Her.*
47. Trible, *Texts of Terror.*
48. E.g., Scroggs, "Paul"; Bassler, "Widow's Tale."
49. See Wire, *Corinthian Women Prophets.*
50. Ruether, *Sexism and God-Talk.* The "rubbish heap of history" is, with permutations, a phrase used by Petrarch about ancient Roman ruins, borrowed by Trotsky for his Menshevik rivals, and used by a variety of politicians since.

defined" Jesus, the preacher of a Sophia/Wisdom version of good news, the redeemable nugget within the rubble of the canonical compositions.[51]

## Other Oppressed Objectors

Other groups who have sought liberation from various forms of social marginalization, while looking to the New Testament as inspiration or legitimation for such aspirations, have found the apostle Paul disappointing. Most notable in the history of the United States of America has been the plight of those (mostly of African or Caribbean descent) who were born or sold into slavery and, even when finally emancipated, had to struggle against societal attitudes and action that have perpetuated racism. In the debates between American abolitionists and slaveholders in the nineteenth century, slaveholders held the exegetical if not the moral advantage, since Scripture generally did not condemn slavery, and Paul was notoriously ambivalent.[52] On one side is the clear admonition for slaves to obey their masters (Eph 6:5–8; Col 3:22–25; 1 Tim 6:1–2; Titus 2:9–10). On the other side is the bold declaration that in Christ there is "neither slave nor free" (1 Cor 12:13; Gal 3:28; Col 3:11). In the middle is the ambivalence we have seen in the Letter to Philemon[53] and in 1 Cor 7:21–24.[54] The noted black spiritual teacher Howard Thurman narrates how his grandmother forbade reading Paul, because in her eyes he did nothing to help the slaves.[55] Paul has proven to be a deeply ambiguous witness to a freedom in Christ that requires a specific social expression.[56]

Not only female and black interpreters (as well as black female interpreters), but also readers who stand broadly within a liberation theology position—including Latino/a readers—find Paul in general too soft or vague on issues that are today regarded as paramount: imperialism, slavery, economic inequality.[57] Paul seems by far too domestic—indeed, far too "bourgeois" to

---

51. Schüssler Fiorenza, *Jesus*.

52. For a sense of the debates, see *Testimony of the General Assembly*; Spencer, *Fugitive Slave Law*; J. P. Thompson, *Teachings*; B. Green, *Chattel Principle*.

53. See, e.g., Johnson, Noel, and Williams, *Onesimus Our Brother*.

54. See Braxton, *Tyranny of Resolution*.

55. Thurman, *Jesus and the Disinherited*, 14.

56. E.g., Felder, *Stony the Road We Trod*; M. Brown, *Blackening of the Bible*; Wimbush, *Bible and African Americans*.

57. For a sample, see Segovia and Sugirtharajah, *Postcolonial Commentary*; Punt, *Postcolonial Biblical Interpretation*.

be regarded as a champion of social reformation. The Jesus who blesses the poor and denounces the rich seems a better source for liberative thought.[58]

Similarly, Christians belonging to what has come to be called the LGBT community—those who are lesbian, gay, bisexual, or transgender—find little cheer in Paul. Indeed, together with Leviticus 18, Paul's characterization of "same-sex love" as "against nature" in Rom 1:18–28 and his casual inclusion of homosexuals among sinners in 1 Cor 6:9 and 1 Tim 1:10 make his letters a much better source for prooftexts against the full inclusion and rights of persons other than heterosexual than as a support for such persons within the church.[59] Even when treated with hermeneutical kid gloves,[60] Paul's words are in no obvious sense supportive of LGBT people.

In sum, for many who call themselves enlightened, or who are female, Jewish, black, or homosexual, or who are passionately committed to social justice in the world, Paul seems a negative rather than a positive witness, an oppressor and not a liberator, one of the toxic places in the Bible that Christians need to read primarily with the hermeneutics of suspicion rather than the hermeneutics of generosity. Among Pauline detractors, however, the "cultured despisers" are substantively the most challenging, since they call into question the premises underlying all his letters—namely, that God acts in creation and has acted decisively through the resurrection of the crucified Messiah Jesus, and that this divine activity has been and can still be experienced through the power of the Holy Spirit. Denying these premises is truly basic. Other objections to Paul, by contrast, deal with one issue or another and, while important, do not cut to the heart of the Pauline correspondence: they are preoccupied with social relations more than the human relationship with God, or the way the good news hurts rather than heals the human spirit.

Before responding to some of these criticisms of Paul, I venture a few general observations concerning them. First, they generally derive from a "flat" reading of a passage, or a letter, or a cluster of letters. They seldom take up the canonical collection as a whole, seldom deal with the literary complexity it presents, seldom engage in a close reading of a Greek that is not always—or even often—easy to decipher. They operate, in short, with the false assumption that Paul is easy to understand and thus also easy to

---

58. Yoder, *Politics of Jesus*; Crossan, *Jesus*; Horsley, *Jesus*.

59. The most persistent academic critic defending the literal imperative of such texts is Gagnon, *Bible and Homosexual Practice*. The issues are joined by Gagnon and Via, *Homosexuality and the Bible*.

60. As, e.g., in Hays, *Moral Vision*; L. Johnson, *Scripture and Discernment*.

dismiss. Second, virtually all these critical stances assume that contemporary points of view and social realities are superior to those of Paul's age and to those held by Paul himself. It would be helpful if those scorning Paul's belief in angels would recognize that they talk easily about equally invisible and nonverifiable entities (see "selfish gene" above). It would be amusing, if it were not so tragic, to note that criticism of Paul's language about women and view of their place in the world has not been accompanied by the realization that the succeeding nineteen centuries had advanced very little beyond Paul, when compared to how Paul stood among his contemporaries on the subject. Third, constructions of Paul's "personality" lurk in the background, and sometimes the foreground, of critical stances. Certainly, among Paul's late-nineteenth-century "cultured despisers," the supposition that Paul had a sick or tortured psyche lay behind the position that, since he was the real founder of the Christian religion, Christians likewise were naturally neurotic. Similarly, Paul's views on women, or homosexuals, or Jews, are sometimes ascribed to a bent psychosexual or religious makeup.

## Reading Paul Responsibly

The first step here is to avoid anachronism, a vice especially grievous when indulged in by supposed practitioners of historical criticism. Paul's letters, it is true, emerge from a world very different—at least on the surface—from that of twenty-first-century seminary professors. But those professors would do well to remember that the basic structures and attitudes of that ancient world remained solidly in place for much of the world's population throughout history—and remains in place for much of the world's population still today. First-world academics need reminding that the political and religious views they represent have occupied only a tiny sliver of time and an even smaller portion of the world's population.

If we are shocked, for example, that Paul recommends respect for ruling authorities (Rom 13:1–7; 1 Tim 2:1–3; Titus 3:1), we must recognize that he adopts the same position as the majority of his fellow Jews. And he is far from being an advocate for Roman political ideology. For that matter, it is helpful to remember that the notion of leaders governing at the consent of the governed is a recent one, and only partially realized in the contemporary world. That there should be empires and imperial colonies was a commonplace of world history even through the twentieth century, at least for those who are not willfully blind to the ambitions and projects of the Austrian-

Hungarian, French, British, German, and Russian empires in the nineteen and twentieth centuries, and the Soviet/American versions in the twentieth and twenty-first centuries.

The same is true of human trafficking (to use the contemporary term) and slavery. As I suggested in an earlier chapter, slavery in the Greco-Roman world was more lenient at least in this, that it was neither racially defined nor permanent. But the capture, selling, transporting, and mistreatment of slaves has throughout history gone hand in hand with imperial conquest, political retribution, and economic opportunity: not only cotton in the Southern states, but diamonds in South Africa, wool and coal in England, opium in China, dams and railroads in Siberia and California, and sexual merchandising always and everywhere.

As in the case of empire, Paul was far from being a defender or advocate for the institution of slavery. My reading of Philemon in the context of Colossians and Ephesians (see chap. 10) shows how his language seeks to ameliorate rather than exacerbate such social inequality. But like his fellow moral philosopher Epictetus, Paul regarded such social conditions (including, for that matter, gender and ethnicity) as *adiaphora* (things that are not essential, that do not really matter in the long run). Paul had other fish to fry. His focus was not moving societal furniture around but recognizing how God was bringing about a new creation, which began in a renewed relationship with God. Everything else was secondary.

I hope I have already said enough about Paul as a Jew to dismiss the canard that he is in any fashion anti-Semitic—a fact recognized as well by contemporary Jewish scholarship.[61] But the other extreme should also be avoided. Paul is not "like every other Jew" of the first century, for Judaism in the first century was not yet the set and unified phenomenon it became after the fall of the temple and the composition of the Mishnah. In Jewish terms, Paul was extraordinary because of his claim to speak as a prophet—not only to his own people but also to the gentiles—of the God who was bringing a new humanity into existence through the paradoxical death and exaltation of his Son, Jesus. Nothing is more Jewish in Paul than his belief in the Holy Spirit; nothing so marks Paul off as a Jew than his insistence that this Holy Spirit was being experienced by him—and by gentiles—through a crucified Messiah.

---

61. Recent years have seen a spate of works by Jewish scholars with a more fine-grained historical contextualization of the apostle—accepting, to be sure, the critical judgments of New Testament critics on all important issues; see Segal, *Paul the Convert*; Boyarin, *Radical Jew*; Nanos, *Paul within Judaism*; Fredriksen, *Paul*.

As hurtful as Paul's words concerning homosexuality have been—hurtful because they are canonical and read as authoritative Scripture—a fair historical contextualization requires us to recognize three aspects of his language. First, they are incidental and nonthematic: same-sex love is not the topic of Rom 1:18–32; rebellion against God is the topic, and same-sex love is a convenient and conventional example.[62] Second, Greco-Roman culture generally was more accepting of same-sex relations than were Jews operating out of the background of Leviticus 18,[63] although mockery—especially of effeminacy—was not lacking;[64] Paul's perceptions on homosexuality were those of first-century Jews. Third, his language is remarkably mild when compared to roughly contemporary Jewish texts.[65]

As I suggested in an earlier chapter (chap. 7, "Paul and Greco-Roman Culture"), Paul's views on the household and domestic arrangements were conventional, not for his age alone, but for virtually every age and place in human history. It is again helpful to remind ourselves that women did not gain suffrage in England until the late nineteenth century, in the United States until 1920, and in some parts of Europe until much later in the twentieth century, and that the ability of women to work outside the home and farm—apart from the remarkable exception of female religious orders—was due largely to technological advances and the imperatives imposed by world war. What is today taken for granted in the twenty-first-century first world about the genders and their respective capabilities (and rights) would have astonished and even shocked ordinary members of the bourgeoisie two centuries ago, and remain alien to the perceptions of substantial parts of the world's population today.

It should be no shock, therefore, to read that Paul advises women to be submissive to their husbands in the household, or to run their households well, and to teach their daughters to love their husbands and children. His radical position concerning the equality of the genders applied mainly to the church: among the baptized there was no longer female and male (Gal 3:28). Paul recognized valuable female coworkers in the field and as heads of households where the assembly met. And apart from the difficult text in 1 Tim 2:15, Paul does not restrict women's identity to childbearing and domestic roles. In 1 Cor 7:1–40 he speaks to male and female directly

62. See Hays, *Moral Vision* and "Relations Natural and Unnatural."
63. See Cantarella, *Bisexuality in the Ancient World*.
64. See the graffiti and literary evidence in Williams, *Roman Homosexuality*.
65. See *The Sentences of Pseudo-Phocylides* for Hellenistic Jewish vituperation.

in terms of their mutual obligations. Where the ideal of equality and the conventions of culture are in tension—as they inevitably will be when an egalitarian movement meets in a household—Paul's androcentric anxiety is more pronounced, as when he forbids women to teach in the assembly, or when he requires of them (as is the custom in all the churches) that they be veiled when they pray or prophesy in the assembly.

But one should not miss the real point: the custom of veiling is just a custom; the action of females prophesying in the assembly is revolutionary. In contrast to later gnostic writings, which are sometimes applauded for the roles they assign women, but whose myths make the feminine the very ontological ground of error, Paul's sexism is functional and, as we have seen, ameliorable. Musonius Rufus, the Stoic teacher of Epictetus, is rightly praised for his essay *On the Education of Women.* By the standards of that day, it is truly enlightened: women have all the abilities that men have, so they should be educated in the same way, including the study of philosophy. But the conclusion of the essay is not that women so educated should become itinerant philosophers, but that they should be better managers of their household. One wonders what Musonius would have thought of Junia or Phoebe or Priscilla.

A more responsible reading of Paul, in short, does not ask Paul to solve problems he could not have seen as problems or to address issues that have become issues for some of the human population in the last three hundred years, above all when the incidental statements he made touching on such issues are at most tangential to the subjects that he truly seeks to address, having to do with the condition of human existence before the living God. Before turning to those (liberating) topics, or convictions, however, it may be good to caution ourselves against two other common assumptions running through the past three hundred years of Pauline rejection (standing in for the rejection of classical Christianity)—namely, a focus on Paul's psychology and an assumption that his letters are easy to understand (and dismiss).

I dealt earlier with the anachronistic premise that the Pauline letters are direct expressions of his personality. The assumption here is that we can account for Paul's thought through understanding his inner conflicts. Thus, his supposedly negative attitude toward sex is due to his own struggles with sensuality; the same struggles can be the basis for his suppression of women—they are so threatening. Thus, his hostility toward the law is owed to his inability to keep it perfectly himself. His pathologies did not disappear with his conversion but only took on new coloration. The basic problem with this way of reading is that it fails to take the actual texts adequately into account. As Krister Stendahl demonstrated a generation ago, the letters reveal nothing of a Pauline struggle with the law: Paul is, if anything, smug in his claims to having kept the law perfectly (see Phil 3:4–9; 2 Cor 5:11–13). Similarly, the "introspective" readings of Rom 7 by Augustine and Luther mistake Paul's use of a rhetorical trope for a personal confession.[66] As I have suggested earlier, what we find in Paul's letters is not the direct (and unconscious) expression of personality but the (conscious and deliberate) elements of logical argumentation. We read Paul, in short, not for personality but for rhetoric.

Finally, judgments concerning Paul, when they do not focus on his personality, tend to deal only with a handful of his letters (based on theories of inauthenticity), or on sections of his letters, in a manner that oversimplifies the process of their production or fails to acknowledge the ways in which an entire letter holds together. In a word, the difficult task of exegeting the entire Pauline collection is replaced by generalizations and by prooftexts drawn from only a fraction of his compositions. Any construal of Paul that rests on any such reduced textual basis ought to be regarded, for that very reason, as suspect. I would argue further that any effort to "fix" a Pauline theology—even if drawn from all the letters—ought to be seen as suspect, simply because the complex character of the canonical collection makes any effort to stabilize a single construal of Paul an impossibility.

Taking with full seriousness the four distinct dimensions of this correspondence, we begin to recognize that, rather than yield a single version of Paul's personality or thought, they present an arena for intense and diverse investigation that is open-ended and, for that reason, refreshing and renewing. The *anthropological* dimension of this literature reminds us that these are compositions written not as literary exercises but as expressions of the human impulse to seek meaning and as instruments of cultural formation within a nascent movement. The *historical* dimension alerts us to the specific ambience of this meaning-making process, not among the Trobriand Islanders or the Aborigines of Australia, but within the complex interactions among Jews, Greeks, and Romans that had gone on in the Mediterranean world over the course of centuries and was at its most intense just at the time when this new movement emerged, and which it needed to engage, not after centuries of separate maturation, but at once. The *literary* dimension demands of us that we take seriously the specific literary form of each letter: its epistolary genre, its modes of rhetoric, its mode of imaging the occasion that evoked

---

66. See Stendahl, "Apostle Paul"; Stowers, "Romans 7:7–25."

the composition and that it addressed. Most important of all, the *religious* dimension of Paul's canonical letters compels us to recognize that the subject that occupies Paul, and that he thinks ought to occupy his readers, is precisely how they should think about and act on the basis of the powerful experience of God that had touched them both individually and as communities.

## Paul as Liberator

By liberating Paul's letters from the shackles with which readers have bound them, we can see more clearly the elements within them that speak directly and powerfully to human liberation—not a liberation from this or that incidental inhibition but a liberation from the powers that seek to distort and destroy the image of God among humans, not simply a freedom from entrapment by human or cosmic forces but a freedom for a new way of existing according to this renewed image of God, with capacities and powers far exceeding our paltry imagination: "What eye has not seen, and ear has not heard, and what has not entered the human heart, what God has prepared for those who love him" (1 Cor 2:9 NABRE; see Isa 64:3).

Among many such elements, I single out here four that I find to be of particular importance, not only because they pervade the entire collection of Paul's canonical letters, and not only because they offer critical insight into what is of enduring importance in those letters, but also because each of them also challenges present-day readers to reconsider their own conceptions of Christian discipleship.

### God's Presence and Power in Creation

Everywhere, Paul's letters reveal the conviction that the living God brings the world into being and is powerfully present to his creation at every moment, above all in and through human bodies. The perceptions that God creates the world, speaks through the prophets, and raises the dead to life are all part of Paul's Jewish heritage, but for Paul such presence and power is active above all in the death and resurrection of Jesus, in his own experience (his transformation from persecutor to apostle), and in the experience of his readers, specifically the inclusion of gentiles in the people of God, the call of those who were nothing by the standards of the world to be members of the body of Christ. This conviction concerning the living God is the basis for all authentic hope for human liberation, for no human effort can accomplish what humans most need and desire; only God can and, on the evidence adduced by Paul, has lifted humans to genuine freedom. The truth that our hope rests in God alone bears with it a challenging corollary: our obedience of faith is also to be directed solely to the one who thus moves ahead of us in creation and calls us at every moment to step out of our secure human constructions and into the larger freedom of the world God is bringing into being. Such obedient faith demands of us a willingness to relinquish even our most beloved theological precedents and to be attentive and responsive to the one who transcends all precedents.

## The Transforming Power of the Spirit

In Paul's letters, the resurrected and exalted Jesus, who has become "life-giving spirit," is the source of God's presence and power among humans. The Holy Spirit empowers humans and transforms them according to the mind of Christ. It is of first importance to insist that this is not an abstract proposition but an existential reality, experienced in the lives of believers. The experience of power, as we have seen, is the central fact assumed and asserted in the canonical letters. Christ is not only the source of transforming power; he is the form toward which this power tends.

For Paul's letters, the incidental facts of the "historical" (better, "human") Jesus before his death are of less significance than his fundamental character as a human person: his faithful obedience toward God, even to death, and his loving self-donation to others, expressed above all by his death. This character, or "mind" or "image," is transportable and transferable in a way the *bruta facta* of Jesus's past never could be. And the transference is precisely what is accomplished by the Holy Spirit. The Spirit of Christ can change humans according to the image of Christ into a new humanity, in which humans seek to serve the living God through faithful obedience and seek to serve their fellow humans, thus fulfilling "the law of Christ" (Gal 6:2). Paul's letters, in short, do not focus on the activity of God in creation "out there," but on God's presence and power within his readers, individually and communally; they are where the "new creation" is coming into being (2 Cor 5:17). The work of the Holy Spirit is to replicate among believers the character of Jesus himself, which means replicating within them the freedom that is distinctively Christ's own.[67] This is liberation indeed.

67. L. Johnson, *Faith's Freedom.*

This dimension of Paul's letters also carries with it a direct challenge to conventional notions of discipleship. Reading his letters, we cannot be deceived into thinking that faith is a matter merely of belief, or that obedience is the following of prescriptions. It is a matter, rather, of transformation of character, of profound change from one way of being in the world (with its perceptions, dispositions, attitudes, and habits) into another way of being in the world (with perceptions, dispositions, attitudes and habits that derive from Jesus Christ and conform to his way of being in the world). Discipleship as transformation of character is perilous but also exhilarating, difficult but also liberating.

## The Church as God's Instrument

No careful reader of the canonical collection can miss the fact that Paul's preeminent interest is in the community more than the individual. Here again, his Jewish heritage is evident in the priority given to the integrity, the holiness, of the entire people. As a diaspora Jew, moreover, Paul naturally sought the stability and solidity of the *ekklēsia* as the local realization of the people God was calling out of the world. If Paul is rightly perceived as a shaper of character, he is best perceived as the shaper of communities of character. The "mind of Christ" that he inculcates is a communal "mind": all in the community are to show reciprocal dedication to service; all are to place the needs of others above their own. Those gifts and actions that "build" (edify) the community are to be preferred, even to those gifts, otherwise perfectly good, that serve only to build the self. The transforming power of the Holy Spirit is able to work in the world because the community is the somatic realization of the risen Jesus. Rather than a human association or club, they are the "temple of the Holy Spirit," and even more dramatically, they are "the body of Christ" in the world. The church reveals in its life the presence and power of God's Holy Spirit. The theme of Ephesians, that the church is the place in the world where God's reconciling world is made manifest, and that this is exactly the mission of the church, to make that reconciliation visible as a sort of sign to the world, is implicit in all the canonical letters.

That God's Holy Spirit works in and through a social organism is liberating in two ways. First, the individual believer is stimulated and strengthened in his or her own growth toward authentic liberation. The integrity of the church edifies the individual as the individual edifies the church.

Second, it is obvious that a Spirit-empowered community is a more pow-erful and effective instrument for the liberation of other humans than are the efforts of any individual. The challenge to believers in the proposition that the church is the instrument of God's liberating action is to learn to think and act communally rather than individualistically, to comprehend that salvation is about us and not simply me, to seek to build the church as a holy instrument of God rather than an obstruction to God's work.

### The Tension between the Ideal and the Real

From one perspective, Paul is the most utopian of ancient writers. He actually seeks to create communities in which ethnic, gender, and social distinctions do not become status markers for superior and inferior mem-bers, but opportunities for gift-giving across differences. From another perspective, Paul can be regarded as regressive precisely because he re-gards slavery, circumcision, being married or unmarried, and the like as *adiaphora*, things that do not ultimately matter in the sight of God. He challenges neither the empire nor the household, even as he envisages the *ekklēsia* as a fictive kinship system that works within but is not entirely to be conformed to empire and household. In several of the letters we see the tensions that are created by a utopian community existing within and over against traditional social structures. Paul certainly does not resolve these tensions within his correspondence. But it is precisely this irreso-lution that present-day readers ought to regard as liberating. In part, this is because Paul reveals to us the tensions that we might otherwise have missed were he to decide completely on the side of the (utopian) ideal or the (conventional) real. In part, it is because he helps us realize that the utopian ideal is always and inevitably going to stand in tension with human social structures, even though they may change from age to age, simply because the good news of God's rule can never simply be equated with any human institution.

Paul here liberates us precisely by the open-endedness of his letters. He frees us to recognize the need to identify our own social constraints and to address them with the challenge of the good news, knowing that we no more than Paul will be entirely able to harmonize the two. The tensions are precisely what liberate us for creative thought and engagement.

## Conclusion

Reading the canonical Paul responsibly—that is, by taking into full account the anthropological, historical, literary, and religious dimensions of his letters—we can see that much of the charge that Paul is an oppressive figure is based on distorted perspective and lack of full contextualization. At the same time, we become aware that the Pauline letters offer convictions that are profoundly challenging to present-day assumptions: the letters advance a radical vision of human life that is grounded in the experience of God's presence and power in the empirical world, a vision of life that offers an authentic liberation—not at the level of social arrangements but at the level of existence itself.

We learn from Paul's letters that the living God moves ahead of us in the world, calling to us in all the circumstances of our lives, demanding obedience to him alone. We learn that God's Holy Spirit given by the exalted Lord Jesus transforms us according to the mind of Christ. We learn that the church is the medium of God's presence, the body of Christ in service to the world. We learn that Christian identity is always and essentially unstable, having always to negotiate the vision of God's rule with the social structures of every age. Such realizations, I submit, are profoundly liberating and not in the least oppressive, and they all come to us through the canonical letters of Paul.

# BIBLIOGRAPHY

Achtemeier, Paul J. *The Quest for Unity in the New Testament Church: A Study in Paul and Acts*. Philadelphia: Fortress, 1987.

Afzal-Khan, Fawzia, and Kalpana Seshadri-Crooks, eds. *The Pre-occupation of Postcolonial Studies*. Durham, NC: Duke University Press, 2000.

Aland, Kurt. "The Problem of Anonymity and Pseudonymity in Christian Literature of the First Two Centuries." *JTS* 12 (1961): 39–49.

Alexander, Loveday. "Hellenistic Letter Forms and the Structure of Philippians." *JSNT* 12 (1989): 87–101.

Alexander, Philip S. *Mystical Texts*. Companion to the Qumran Scrolls 7. London: T&T Clark International, 2006.

Allan, John A. "The 'in Christ' Formula in the Pastoral Epistles." *NTS* 10, no. 1 (1963): 115–21.

Anderson, Charles P. "Hebrews among the Letters of Paul." *Studies in Religion* 5 (1975): 258–66.

Anderson, Graham. *The Second Sophistic: A Cultural Phenomenon in the Roman Empire*. London: Routledge, 1993.

Aquinas, Thomas. *Commentary on the Letter of Saint Paul to the Hebrews*. Latin/English Version of the Works of Saint Thomas Aquinas 41. Lander, WY: Aquinas Institute for the Study of Sacred Doctrine, 2012.

———. *Commentary on the Letter of Saint Paul to the Romans*. Latin/English Version of the Works of Saint Thomas Aquinas 37. Lander, WY: Aquinas Institute for the Study of Sacred Doctrine, 2012.

Arnold, Clinton F. *The Colossian Syncretism: The Interface between Christianity and Folk Belief at Colossae*. Grand Rapids: Baker, 1996.

Attridge, Harold W. *The Epistle to the Hebrews: A Commentary on the Epistle to the Hebrews*. Philadelphia: Fortress, 1989.

———. "On Becoming an Angel: Rival Baptismal Theologies at Colossae." Pages

481–98 in *Religious Propaganda and Missionary Competition in the New Testament World: Essays Honoring Dieter Georgi*, edited by Lukas Bormann, Kelly Tredici, and Angela Standhartinger. NovTSup 74. Leiden: Brill, 1994.

Aune, David E. "The Apocalypse of John and the Problem of Genre." *Semeia* 36 (1986): 65–96.

Badenas, Robert. *Christ, the End of the Law: Romans 10.4 in Pauline Perspective.* JSNTSup 10. Sheffield: JSOT Press, 1985.

Baeck, Leo. "The Faith of Paul." Pages 139–68 in *Judaism and Christianity: Essays.* New York: Jewish Publication Society of America, 1958.

Bailey, D. R. Shackleton. *Cicero.* New York: Scribner's Sons, 1927.

Bailey, John A. "Who Wrote II Thessalonians?" *NTS* 25 (1979): 131–45.

Barclay, John M. G. *Jews in the Mediterranean Diaspora: From Alexander to Trajan (323 BCE–117 CE).* Edinburgh: T&T Clark, 1996.

_____. *Paul and the Gift.* Grand Rapids: Eerdmans, 2015.

_____. "Paul, Philemon and the Dilemma of Christian Slave-Ownership." *NTS* 37 (1991): 161–86.

Barrett, C. K. "Things Sacrificed to Idols." *NTS* 11 (1965): 138–53.

Bartchy, S. Scott. *Mallon chrēsai: First-Century Slavery and the Interpretation of 1 Corinthians 7:21.* SBLDS 11. Missoula: Scholars Press, 1973.

Barth, Markus. *Ephesians: Translation and Commentary on Chapters 4–6.* 2 vols. AB 34. Garden City, NY: Doubleday, 1974.

Bassler, Jouette M. *1 Timothy, 2 Timothy, Titus.* Abingdon New Testament Commentary. Nashville: Abingdon, 1996.

_____. "The Widows' Tale: A Fresh Look at 1 Tim 5:3–16." *JBL* 103 (1984): 23–41.

Bates, W. H. "The Integrity of II Corinthians." *NTS* 12 (1965): 56–69.

Batey, Richard. "The Destination of Ephesians." *JBL* 82, no. 1 (1963): 101.

Bauer, Bruno. *Kritik der paulinischen Briefe.* Aalen: Scientia, 1972.

Bauer, Walter. *Orthodoxy and Heresy in Earliest Christianity.* Edited by Robert A. Kraft and Gerhard Krodel. 2nd ed. Philadelphia: Fortress, 1971.

Baur, F. C. *The Church History of the First Three Centuries.* Translated by Allan Menzies. London: Williams and Norgate, 1878.

_____. "Die Christuspartei in der korinthischer Gemeinde, der Gegensatz des paulinischen und petrinischen Christentum in der aeltesten Kirche, der Apostel Petrus im Rom." *Tübinger Zeitschrift für Theologie* 4 (1831): 61–206.

_____. *Die sogenannten Pastoralbriefe des Apostels Paulus aufs neue kritisch untersucht.* Stuttgart: J. G. Cotta'sche Verlagshandlung, 1835.

_____. *Paul the Apostle of Jesus Christ: His Life and Works, His Epistles and Teachings.* Translated by Allan Menzies. 2 vols. London: Williams and Norgate, 1875.

_____. *Paulus, der Apostel Jesu Christi: Sein Leben und Wirken, seine Briefe und seine Lehre: Ein Beitrag zu einer kritischen Geschichte des Urchristenthums.* Leipzig: Fues, 1866.

Beattie, Tina. *The New Atheists: The Twilight of Reason and the War on Religion.* New York: Orbis Books, 2007.

Beck, Norman. *Mature Christianity in the 21st Century: The Recognition and Repudiation of the Anti-Jewish Polemic of the New Testament.* London: Associated University Presses, 1985.

BeDuhn, Jason D. *The First New Testament: Marcion's Scriptural Canon.* Salem, OR: Polebridge, 2013.

Beetham, Christopher A. *Echoes of Scripture in the Letter of Paul to the Colossians.* Leiden: Brill, 2008.

Beker, Johan Christiaan. *Paul the Apostle: The Triumph of God in Life and Thought.* Philadelphia: Fortress, 1980.

Benedict XVI. *Saint Paul the Apostle.* Huntington, IN: Our Sunday Visitor, 2009.

Berchman, Robert M. *From Philo to Origen: Middle Platonism in Transition.* Brown Judaic Studies 69. Chico: Scholars Press, 1984.

Berger, Peter L., and Thomas Luckmann. *The Social Construction of Reality: A Treatise in the Sociology of Knowledge.* Garden City, NY: Doubleday, 1967.

Best, Ernest. *A Critical and Exegetical Commentary on the Epistle to the Ephesians.* International Critical Commentary. Edinburgh: T&T Clark, 1998.

_____. *Essays on Ephesians.* Edinburgh: T&T Clark, 1997.

_____. "Recipients and the Title of the Letter to the Ephesians: Why and When the Designation 'Ephesians'?" *ANRW* 25.4:3247–79.

_____. "Who Used Whom? The Relationship of Ephesians and Colossians." *NTS* 43 (1997): 72–96.

Betz, Hans Dieter. "2 Cor 6:14–7:1: An Anti-Pauline Fragment?" *JBL* 92 (1973): 88–108.

_____. *2 Corinthians 8 and 9: A Commentary on Two Administrative Letters of the Apostle Paul.* Translated by George W. MacRae. Hermeneia. Philadelphia: Fortress, 1985.

_____. *Galatians: A Commentary on Paul's Letter to the Churches in Galatia.* Philadelphia: Fortress, 1989.

_____. "Transferring a Ritual: Paul's Interpretation of Baptism in Romans 6." Pages 84–118 in *Paul in His Hellenistic Context*, edited by Troels Engberg-Pedersen. Minneapolis: Fortress, 1995.

Bianchi, Ugo, ed. *Le Origini dello Gnosticismo, Colloquio di Messina 13–18 Aprile 1966.* Leiden: Brill, 1967.

Bieler, Ludwig. *Theios anēr: Das bild des "göttlichen Menschen" in Spätantike und Frühchristentum*. Wien: O. Höfels, 1935.

Bird, Michael F. *An Anomalous Jew: Paul among Jews, Greeks, and Romans*. Grand Rapids: Eerdmans, 2016.

_____, ed. *Four Views on the Apostle Paul*. Grand Rapids: Zondervan, 2012.

_____. *Introducing Paul: The Man, His Mission and His Message*. Downers Grove, IL: IVP Academic, 2008.

Bjerkelund, Carl J. *Parakalô: Form, Funktion und Sinn der parakalô-Sätze in den paulinischen Briefen*. Oslo: Universitetsverlag, 1967.

Blackwell, Ben C. *Christosis: Engaging Paul's Soteriology with His Patristic Interpreters*. Grand Rapids: Eerdmans, 2016.

Blanton, Thomas R., IV. *A Spiritual Economy: Gift Exchange in the Letters of Paul of Tarsus*. New Haven: Yale University Press, 2017.

Bloom, Harold, ed. "'Before Moses Was I Am': The Original and Belated Testaments." *The Bible*. Modern Critical Views. New York: Chelsea House, 1987.

Blount, Brian K., Cain Hope Felder, Clarice J. Martin, and Emerson B. Powery, eds. *True to Our Native Land: An African American New Testament Commentary*. Minneapolis: Fortress, 2007.

Blumell, Lincoln H. "Scribes and Ancient Letters: Implications for the Pauline Epistles." Pages 208–26 in *How the New Testament Came to Be: The 35th Annual Sidney B. Sperry Symposium*, edited by Kent P. Jackson and Frank F. Judd. Salt Lake City: Deseret Book, 2006.

Boccaccini, Gabriele. *Beyond the Essene Hypothesis: The Parting of the Ways between Qumran and Enochic Judaism*. Grand Rapids: Eerdmans, 1998.

Boccaccini, Gabriele, and Carlos A. Segovia. *Paul the Jew: Rereading the Apostle as a Figure of Second Temple Judaism*. Minneapolis: Fortress, 2016.

Bohnenblust, Gottfried. *Beiträge zum Topos peri philias*. Berlin: Universitäts-Buchdruckerei Gustave Schade, 1905.

Bonner, Gerald. *Augustine and Modern Research on Pelagianism*. Villanova: Augustine Institute, Villanova University, 1972.

Bonner, Stanley. *Education in Ancient Rome: From the Elder Cato to the Younger Pliny*. Berkeley: University of California Press, 1977.

Borg, Barbara E. *Paideia: The World of the Second Sophistic*. Millennium Studies. Berlin: De Gruyter, 2004.

Boring, M. Eugene. "The Language of Universal Salvation in Paul." *JBL* 105 (1986): 269–92.

Bornkamm, Gunther. "On Understanding the Christ Hymn, Phil 2:6–11." Pages 112–22 in *Early Christian Experience*. New York: Harper & Row, 1969.

Bousset, Wilhelm. *Kyrios Christos: A History of the Belief in Christ from the Be-

*ginnings of Christianity to Irenaeus.* Translated by John E. Steely. Nashville: Abingdon, 1970.

_____. *What Is Religion?* Translated by Florence B. Low. London: T. Fisher Unwin, 1907.

Boyarin, Daniel. "Is Paul an 'Anti-Semite'?" Pages 136–57 in *A Radical Jew: Paul and the Politics of Identity.* Berkeley: University of California Press, 1994.

_____. *A Radical Jew: Paul and the Politics of Identity.* Berkeley: University of California Press, 1994.

Boys-Stones, George R. *Platonist Philosophy 80 BC to AD 250: An Introduction and Collection of Sources in Translation.* Cambridge Sourcebooks in Post-Hellenistic Philosophy. New York: Cambridge University Press, 2018.

Bradley, Guy, and John-Paul Wilson. *Greek and Roman Colonisation: Origins, Ideologies and Interactions.* Swansea, Wales: Classical Press of Wales, 2000.

Branham, R. Bracht. *Unruly Eloquence: Lucian and the Comedy of Traditions.* Cambridge, MA: Harvard University Press, 1989.

Branham, R. Bracht, and Marie-Odile Goulet-Cazé, eds. *The Cynics: The Cynic Movement in Antiquity and Its Legacy.* Berkeley: University of California Press, 1996.

Braxton, Brad Ronnell. *The Tyranny of Resolution: I Corinthians 7:1–24.* Dissertation Series of the American Schools of Oriental Research 181. Atlanta: Scholars Press, 2000.

Brooten, Bernadette J. "Paul's Views on Women and Female Homoeroticism." Pages 61–87 in *Immaculate and Powerful: The Female in Sacred Image and Social Reality*, edited by Clarissa W. Atkinson, Margaret R. Miles, and Constance H. Buchanan. Boston: Beacon, 1985.

Brosch, Joseph. *Charismen und Ämter in der Urkirche.* Bonn: P. Hanstein, 1951.

Brown, Michael Joseph. *Blackening of the Bible: The Aims of African American Biblical Scholarship.* African American Religious Life and Thought. Bloomsbury: T&T Clark, 2004.

Brown, Paul J. *Bodily Resurrection and Ethics in 1 Cor 15: Connecting Faith and Morality in the Context of Greco-Roman Mythology.* WUNT 2.360. Tübingen: Mohr Siebeck, 2014.

Brown, Peter. *The Body and Society: Men, Women, and Sexual Renunciation in Early Christianity.* 2nd ed. New York: Columbia University Press, 2008.

Brown, Raymond E. *An Introduction to the New Testament.* ABRL. New York: Doubleday, 1997.

_____. "Not Jewish Christianity and Gentile Christianity but Types of Jewish/Gentile Christianity." *CBQ* 45 (1983): 74–79.

Bultmann, Rudolf. *Der Stil der paulinischen Predigt und die Kynisch-stoische Diatribe*. Göttingen: Vandenhoeck & Ruprecht, 1910.

———. "New Testament and Mythology: The Problem of Demythologizing." Pages 1–44 in *New Testament and Mythology and Other Basic Writings*, edited by Schubert M. Ogden. Philadelphia: Fortress, 1988.

———. *Theology of the New Testament*. 2 vols. New York: Scribner, 1951.

Burke, Tony, and Brent Landau, eds. *New Testament Apocrypha: More Noncanonical Scriptures*. Grand Rapids: Eerdmans, 2016.

Byrne, Brendan. *Romans*. SP 6. Collegeville, MN: Liturgical Press, 1996.

Cadbury, Henry J. "The Dilemma of Ephesians 1." *NTS* 5 (1959): 91–102.

———. *The Making of Luke-Acts*. New York: Macmillan, 1927.

———. "'We' and 'I' Passages in Luke-Acts." *NTS* 3 (1957): 128–32.

Caird, G. B. *Principalities and Powers: A Study in Pauline Theology*. New York: Herder and Herder, 1961.

Callan, Terrance. "Pauline Midrash: The Exegetical Background of Gal 3:19b." *JBL* 99 (1980): 549–67.

Cameron, Euan. *The Annotated Luther: The Interpretation of Scripture*. Minneapolis: Fortress, 2017.

Campbell, Douglas A. "Christ and Church in Paul: A 'Post-New' Perspective." Pages 113–43 in Bird, *Four Views on the Apostle Paul*.

———. *The Deliverance of God: An Apocalyptic Rereading of Justification in Paul*. Grand Rapids: Eerdmans, 2009.

———. "An Echo of Scripture in Paul, and Its Implications." Pages 367–91 in Wagner, Rowe, and Grieb, *Word Leaps the Gap*.

Campenhausen, Hans von. *Ecclesiastical Authority and Spiritual Power in the Church of the First Three Centuries*. Translated by J. A. Baker. Stanford: Stanford University Press, 1969.

———. *The Formation of the Christian Bible*. Translated by J. A. Baker. Philadelphia: Fortress, 1972.

———. *Polykarp von Smyrna und die Pastoralbriefe*. Sitzungsberichte der Heidelberger Akademie der Wissenschaften, Philosophisch-Historische Klasse; Jahrgang 1951, Bericht 2 SHAW. Heidelberg: Winter, 1951.

Cannon, George E. *The Use of Traditional Materials in Colossians*. Macon, GA: Mercer University Press, 1983.

Cantarella, Eva. *Bisexuality in the Ancient World*. Translated by Cormac O. Cuilleanain. New Haven: Yale University Press, 1992.

Canty, Aaron. "Saint Paul in Augustine." Pages 115–42 in *A Companion to St. Paul in the Middle Ages*, edited by Steven Cartwright. Leiden: Brill, 2013.

Caragounis, Chrys C. *The Ephesian Mysterion: Meaning and Content*. ConBNT 8. Lund: C. W. K. Gleerup, 1977.

Castelli, Elizabeth A. *Imitating Paul: A Discourse of Power*. Literary Currents in Biblical Studies. Louisville: Westminster John Knox, 1991.

Cerfaux, Lucien. "Influence des Mystères sur le Judaisme alexandrin avant Philon." *Museón* 37 (1924): 29–88.

———. "The Revelation of the Mystery of Christ." Pages 402–38 in *Christ in the Theology of St. Paul*. New York: Herder and Herder, 1959.

Charlesworth, James H., ed. *The Old Testament Pseudepigrapha*. 2 vols. Garden City, NY: Doubleday, 1983.

Childs, Brevard S. *The Church's Guide for Reading Paul: The Canonical Shaping of the Pauline Corpus*. Grand Rapids: Eerdmans, 2008.

———. *Introduction to the Old Testament as Scripture*. Philadelphia: Fortress, 1979.

Christensen, Michael J., and Jeffery A. Wittung, eds. *Partakers of the Divine Nature: The History and Development of Deification in the Christian Traditions*. Madison, NJ: Fairleigh Dickinson University Press, 2007.

Chubb, Thomas. *The Posthumous Works of Thomas Chubb*. London, 1748.

Church, Frank Forrester. "Rhetorical Structure and Design in Paul's Letter to Philemon." *HTR* 71 (1978): 17–33.

Cicero. *Letters to Atticus*. Edited and translated by D. R. Shackleton Bailey. 4 vols. LCL. Cambridge, MA: Harvard University Press, 1999.

Clines, David J. A., and J. Cheryl Exum, eds. *The Reception of the Hebrew Bible in the Septuagint and the New Testament: Essays in Memory of Aileen Guilding*. Sheffield: Sheffield Phoenix, 2013.

Coggins, R. J. *Samaritans and Jews: The Origins of Samaritanism Reconsidered*. Atlanta: John Knox, 1975.

Cohen, Shaye. *From the Maccabees to the Mishnah*. 3rd ed. Louisville: Westminster John Knox, 2014.

Collins, John J. *The Apocalyptic Imagination: An Introduction to the Jewish Matrix of Christianity*. 3rd ed. Grand Rapids: Eerdmans, 2016.

———. *Apocalypticism in the Dead Sea Scrolls*. New York: Routledge, 1998.

———. "Pseudonymity, Historical Reviews, and the Genre of the Revelation of John." *CBQ* 39 (1977): 329–43.

Collins, Paul. *Absolute Power: How the Pope Became the Most Influential Man in the World*. New York: Public Affairs, 2008.

Collins, Raymond F. *Letters That Paul Did Not Write: The Epistle to the Hebrews and the Pauline Pseudepigrapha*. Wilmington, DE: Glazier, 1995.

Colson, F. H. "'Myths and Genealogies': A Note on the Polemic of the Pastoral Epistles." *JTS* 19, no. 74/75 (1918): 265–71.

Concannon, Cavan W. "The Acts of Timothy." Pages 395–405 in Burke and Landau, *New Testament Apocrypha*.

Conzelmann, H. "Paulus und die Weisheit." *NTS* 12 (1966): 231–44.

Cook, David. "The Pastoral Fragments Reconsidered." *JTS* 35 (1984): 120–31.

Copleston, Frederick. *A History of Philosophy*. Vol. 1, *Greece and Rome*. Garden City, NY: Doubleday, 1962.

Coutts, John. "The Relationship of Ephesians and Colossians." *NTS* 4 (1958): 201–7.

Cribiore, Raffaella. *Writing, Teachers, and Students in Graeco-Roman Egypt*. Atlanta: Scholars Press, 1996.

Cross, Frank Moore. *The Ancient Library of Qumran and Modern Biblical Studies*. 3rd ed. Minneapolis: Fortress, 1995.

Crossan, John Dominic. *The Historical Jesus: The Life of a Mediterranean Jewish Peasant*. San Francisco: HarperSanFrancisco, 1991.

―――. *Jesus: A Revolutionary Biography*. San Francisco: HarperSanFrancisco, 1994.

Crossan, John Dominic, and Jonathan L. Reed. *In Search of Paul: How Jesus's Apostle Opposed Rome's Empire with God's Kingdom*. San Francisco: HarperSanFrancisco, 2004.

Crouch, James E. *The Origin and Intention of the Colossian Haustafel*. FRLANT 109. Göttingen: Vandenhoeck & Ruprecht, 1972.

Cullmann, Oscar. *Baptism in the New Testament*. London: SCM, 1951.

Cunningham, Mary B., and Elizabeth Theokritoff. *The Cambridge Companion to Orthodox Christian Theology*. Cambridge Companions to Religion. Cambridge: Cambridge University Press, 2008.

Dahl, Nils Alstrup. "Contradictions in Scripture." Pages 159–77 in *Studies in Paul*.

―――. "Cosmic Dimensions and Religious Knowledge." Pages 57–75 in *Jesus und Paulus: Festschrift für Werner Georg Kümmel*, edited by E. Earle Ellis and Erich Grässer. Göttingen: Vandenhoeck & Ruprecht, 1975.

―――. "A Fragment and Its Context: II Cor 6:14–7:1." Pages 62–69 in *Studies in Paul*.

―――. "The Future of Israel." Pages 137–58 in *Studies in Paul*.

―――. "The Missionary Theology in the Epistle to the Romans." Pages 70–94 in *Studies in Paul*.

―――. "Paul and Possessions." Pages 22–39 in *Studies in Paul*.

―――. "Rudolf Bultmann's Theology of the New Testament." Pages 90–128 in *The Crucified Messiah and Other Essays*. Minneapolis: Augsburg, 1974.

―――. *Studies in Paul: Theology for the Early Christian Mission*. Philadelphia: Fortress, 1977.

Dalton, William J. "The Integrity of Philippians." *Bib* 60 (1979): 97–102.

Danker, Frederick W. *Benefactor: Epigraphic Study of a Graeco-Roman and New Testament Semantic Field*. St. Louis: Clayton, 1982.

Davies, Stevan L. *The Revolt of the Widows: The Social World of the Apocryphal Acts of the Apostles*. Carbondale: Southern Illinois University Press, 1980.

Davies, W. D. *Paul and Rabbinic Judaism: Some Rabbinic Elements in Pauline Theology*. Philadelphia: Fortress, 1980.

Dawkins, Richard. *The God Delusion*. Boston: Houghton and Mifflin, 2006.

_____. *The Selfish Gene*. Oxford: Oxford University Press, 2006.

De Giorgi, Andrea U. *Ancient Antioch: From the Seleucid Era to the Islamic Conquest*. New York: Cambridge University Press, 2016.

Deissmann, Adolf. *Light from the Ancient East*. Translated by Lionel R. M. Strachan. Grand Rapids: Baker, 1978.

_____. *Paul: A Study in Social and Religious History*. Translated by William E. Wilson. New York: Harper & Row, 1957.

DeMaris, Richard E. *The Colossian Controversy: Wisdom in Dispute at Colossae*. JSNTSup 96. Sheffield: Sheffield Academic, 1994.

Desai, Gaurav Gajanan, and Supriya Nair, eds. *Postcolonialisms: An Anthology of Cultural Theory and Criticism*. New Brunswick, NJ: Rutgers University Press, 2005.

Descamps, Albert. *Les Justes et La Justice dans les évangiles et le christianisme primitif hormis la doctrine proprement paulienne*. Gembloux: J. Duculot, 1950.

deSilva, David A. "Measuring Penultimate against Ultimate Reality: An Investigation of the Integrity and Argumentation of 2 Corinthians." *JSNT* 16, no. 52 (1993): 41–70.

Devenish, Philip E. "The So-Called Resurrection of Jesus and Explicit Christian Faith: Wittgenstein's Philosophy and Marxsen's Exegesis as Linguistic Therapy." *JAAR* 51 (1983): 171–90.

de Wette, Wilhelm Martin Leberecht. *An Historico-Critical Introduction to the Canonical Books of the New Testament*. Translated by Frederick Frothingham. 5th ed. Boston: Crosby, Nichols, 1858.

DeWitt, Norman Wentworth. *St. Paul and Epicurus*. Minneapolis: University of Minnesota Press, 1954.

Dibelius, Martin. "The Speeches in Acts and Ancient Historiography." Pages 138–85 in *Studies in the Acts of the Apostles*. Translated by Mary Ling. London: SCM, 1956.

Dibelius, Martin, and Hans Conzelmann. *The Pastoral Epistles: A Commentary on the Pastoral Epistles.* Edited by Helmut Koester. Translated by Philip Buttolph and Adela Yarbro. Hermeneia. Philadelphia: Fortress, 1989.

Dillon, John. *The Middle Platonists: 80 B.C. to A.D. 220.* Rev. ed. Ithaca, NY: Cornell University Press, 1996.

Dimant, Devorah. *History, Ideology and Bible Interpretation in the Dead Sea Scrolls: Collected Studies.* FAT 90. Tübingen: Mohr Siebeck, 2014.

Doering, Lutz. *Ancient Jewish Letters and the Beginnings of Christian Epistolography.* WUNT 298. Tübingen: Mohr Siebeck, 2012.

Dominik, William, and Jon Hall, eds. *A Companion to Roman Rhetoric.* Malden, MA: Blackwell, 2007.

Donfried, Karl P., ed. *The Romans Debate.* Rev. enl. ed. Peabody, MA: Hendrickson, 1991.

Dorey, Thomas Alan. *Cicero.* London: Routledge and Kegan Paul, 1965.

Doughty, Darrell J. "The Presence and Future of Salvation in Corinth." *ZNW* 66 (1975): 61–90.

Douglas, Mary. *Natural Symbols: Explorations in Cosmology.* New York: Pantheon, 2003.

Downey, Glanville. *Ancient Antioch.* Princeton: Princeton University Press, 1963.

Dube, Musa W., and R. S. Wafula, eds. *Postcoloniality, Translation, and the Bible in Africa.* Eugene: Pickwick, 2017.

Dugas, Ludovic. *L'amitié antique d'après les mœurs populaires et les théories des philosophes.* Paris: Félix Alcan, 1894.

Duncan, G. S. "Paul's Ministry in Asia—the Last Phase." *NTS* 3 (1957): 211–18.

Dunn, James D. G. "The Colossian Philosophy: A Confident Jewish Apologia." *Bib* 76 (1995): 153–81.

_____. *The Epistles to the Colossians and to Philemon.* NIGTC. Grand Rapids: Eerdmans, 1996.

_____. *The Theology of Paul the Apostle.* Grand Rapids: Eerdmans, 1998.

Dupont, Jacques. *The Sources of Acts: The Present Position.* Translated by Kathleen Pond. New York: Herder and Herder, 1964.

_____. *ΣΥΝ ΧΡΙΣΤΟΙ: L'union avec le Christ suivant saint Paul.* Bruges: Éditions de l'Abbaye de Saint-André, 1952.

Dupré, Louis K. *Symbols of the Sacred.* Grand Rapids: Eerdmans, 2000.

Du Toit, Andreas B. "Vilification as a Pragmatic Device in Early Christian Epistolography." *Bib* 75 (1994): 403–12.

Dyer, Keith D., and David J. Neville, eds. *Resurrection and Responsibility: Essays on Theology, Scripture, and Ethics in Honor of Thorwald Lorenzen.* Eugene: Pickwick, 2009.

Eastman, David L. "The Epistle of Pseudo-Dionysius the Areopagite to Timothy

Concerning the Deaths of the Apostles Peter and Paul." Pages 464–80 in Burke and Landau, *New Testament Apocrypha.*

Eglinger, Ruth. "Der Begriff der Freundschaft in der Philosophie: Eine historische Untersuchung." PhD diss., Basel, 1916.

Eichhorn, Johann Gottfried. *Einleitung in das Neue Testament.* Vol. 3, pt. 1. Leipzig: Weidmanischen Buchhandlung, 1812.

Eisenbaum, Pamela. *Paul Was Not a Christian: The Original Message of a Misunderstood Apostle.* New York: HarperCollins, 2009.

Ellingworth, Paul. *The Epistle to the Hebrews.* NIGTC. Grand Rapids: Eerdmans, 1993.

Elliott, J. K., ed. *The Apocryphal New Testament: A Collection of Apocryphal Christian Literature in an English Translation.* Oxford: Clarendon, 1993.

Elliott, John H. "Philemon and House Churches." *TBT* 22 (1984): 145–50.

Elliott, Neil. *The Arrogance of Nations: Reading Romans in the Shadow of Empire.* Minneapolis: Fortress, 2008.

Ellis, E. Earle. *The Old Testament in Early Christianity: Canon and Interpretation in the Light of Modern Research.* Grand Rapids: Baker, 1992.

_____. *Paul's Use of the Old Testament.* Grand Rapids: Eerdmans, 1957.

_____. "Traditions in the Pastoral Epistles." Pages 237–53 in *Early Jewish and Christian Exegesis: Studies in Memory of William Hugh Brownlee*, edited by Craig A. Evans and William F. Stinespring. Atlanta: Scholars Press, 1987.

Engberg-Pedersen, Troels. *Cosmology and Self in the Apostle Paul: The Material Spirit.* New York: Oxford University Press, 2010.

_____. *Paul and the Stoics.* Louisville: Westminster John Knox, 2000.

Evans, Craig A. "The Colossian Mystics." *Bib* 63 (1982): 188–205.

Evans, Craig A., and James A. Sanders, eds. *Paul and the Scriptures of Israel.* JSNTSup 83. Sheffield: Sheffield Academic, 1993.

Evans, Craig A., and H. Daniel Zacharias, eds. *Early Christian Literature and Intertextuality.* 2 vols. London: T&T Clark, 2009.

Fackenheim, Emil L. *The Jewish Bible after the Holocaust: A Re-reading.* Bloomington: Indiana University Press, 1990.

Falk, Harvey. *Jesus the Pharisee: A New Look at the Jewishness of Jesus.* New York: Paulist, 1983.

Fanon, Frantz. *The Wretched of the Earth.* Translated by Constance Farrington. New York: Grove Wiedenfeld, 1963.

Fee, Gordon D. *The First Epistle to the Corinthians.* NICNT. Grand Rapids: Eerdmans, 1987.

_____. *God's Empowering Presence: The Holy Spirit in the Letters of Paul.* Peabody, MA: Hendrickson, 1994.

Ferguson, John. *Pelagius: A Historical and Theological Study*. New York: AMS Press, 1978.

Fiensy, David A., and James Riley Strange, eds. *Galilee in the Late Second Temple and Mishnaic Periods*. 2 vols. Minneapolis: Fortress, 2014–15.

Finkelstein, Louis. *The Pharisees: The Sociological Background of Their Faith*. 2 vols. 3rd ed. Philadelphia: Jewish Publication Society of America, 1962

Fiore, Benjamin. *The Function of Personal Example in the Socratic and Pastoral Epistles*. AnBib 105. Rome: Pontifical Biblical Institute, 1986.

Fischel, Henry A., ed. *Essays in Greco-Roman and Related Talmudic Literature*. New York: KAV, 1977.

_____. *Rabbinic Literature and Greco-Roman Philosophy: A Study of Epicurea and Rhetorica in Early Midrashic Writings*. StPB 21. Leiden: Brill, 1973.

Fitch, John G., ed. *Seneca*. Oxford Readings in Classical Studies. New York: Oxford University Press, 2008.

Fitzgerald, John T., ed. *Friendship, Flattery, and Frankness of Speech: Studies on Friendship in the New Testament World*. NovTSup 82. Leiden: Brill, 1996.

Fitzmyer, Joseph A. *Romans: A New Translation with Introduction and Commentary*. AB 33. New York: Doubleday, 1992.

Flint, Peter W., and James C. VanderKam, eds. *The Dead Sea Scrolls after Fifty Years. A Comprehensive Assessment*. 2 vols. Leiden: Brill, 1998.

Foster, Ora Delmer. *The Literary Relations of "The First Epistle of Peter" with Their Bearing on the Date and Place of Authorship*. New Haven: Yale University Press, 1913.

Francis, Fred O. "Humility and Angelic Worship in Col 2:18." *Studia Theologica* 16 (1962): 109–34.

Fredriksen, Paula. *Paul: The Pagans' Apostle*. New Haven: Yale University Press, 2017.

Freire, Paulo. *Pedagogy of the Oppressed*. 30th anniversary ed. Translated by Myra Bergman Ramos. New York: Continuum, 2000.

Friesen, Steven J. *Twice Neokoros: Ephesus, Asia, and the Cult of the Flavian Imperial Family*. Religions in the Graeco-Roman World 116. Leiden: Brill, 1993.

Friesen, Steven J., Daniel N. Schowalter, and James C. Walters, eds. *Corinth in Context: Comparative Studies on Religion and Society*. NovTSup 134. Leiden: Brill, 2010.

Fromm, Erich. *The Dogma of Christ: And Other Essays on Religion, Psychology and Culture*. New York: Rinehart and Winston, 1963.

Funk, Robert Walter. "The Apostolic Presence." Pages 81–102 in *Parables and Presence: Forms of the New Testament Tradition*. Philadelphia: Fortress, 1982.

Gagnon, Robert A. J. *The Bible and Homosexual Practice: Texts and Hermeneutics.* Nashville: Abingdon, 2001.

Gagnon, Robert A. J., and Dan O. Via. *Homosexuality and the Bible: Two Views.* Minneapolis: Fortress, 2003.

Gamble, Harry A., Jr. *The Textual History of the Letter to the Romans: A Study in Textual and Literary Criticism.* Grand Rapids: Eerdmans, 1979.

Ganzevoort, R. Ruard, Maaike de Haardt, and Michael Scherer-Rath, eds. *Religious Stories We Live By: Narrative Approaches in Theology and Religious Studies.* Boston: Brill, 2014.

García Martínez, Florentino, and Julio Trebolle Barrera. *The People of the Dead Sea Scrolls: Their Writings, Beliefs and Practices.* Translated by Wilfred G. E. Watson. Leiden: Brill, 1995.

Garnsey, Peter, and Richard Saller, eds. *The Roman Empire: Economy, Society and Culture.* Berkeley: University of California Press, 1987.

Gärtner, Bertil. *The Temple and the Community in Qumran and the New Testament: A Comparative Study in the Temple Symbolism of the Qumran Texts and the New Testament.* Cambridge: Cambridge University Press, 1965.

Gench, Frances Taylor. *Encountering God in Tyrannical Texts: Reflections on Paul, Women, and the Authority of Scripture.* Louisville: Westminster John Knox, 2015.

George, Roji T. *Paul's Identity in Galatians: A Postcolonial Appraisal.* New Delhi: Christian World Imprints, 2016.

Georgi, Dieter. *The Opponents of Paul in 2 Corinthians: A Study of Religious Propaganda in Late Antiquity.* Rev. ed. Philadelphia: Fortress, 1986.

———. *Remembering the Poor: The History of Paul's Collection for Jerusalem.* Nashville: Abingdon, 1992.

Goldstein, Jonathan. "Jewish Acceptance and Rejection of Hellenism." Pages 2:64–87 in *Jewish and Christian Self-Definition*, edited by E. P. Sanders. Philadelphia: Fortress, 1980.

Goodenough, Erwin R. *By Light, Light: The Mystic Gospel of Hellenistic Judaism.* New Haven: Yale University Press, 1935.

———. *Jewish Symbols in the Greco-Roman Period.* 13 vols. New York: Pantheon, 1953.

Goodfellow, Charlotte E. *Roman Citizenship: A Study of Its Territorial and Numerical Expansion from the Earliest Times to the Death of Augustus.* Lancaster, PA: Lancaster Press, 1935.

Goodspeed, Edgar J. *The Meaning of Ephesians.* Chicago: University of Chicago Press, 1933.

Gorman, Michael J. *Apostle of the Crucified Lord: A Theological Introduction to Paul and His Letters*. 2nd ed. Grand Rapids: Eerdmans, 2017.

_____. *Inhabiting the Cruciform God: Kenosis, Justification, and Theosis in Paul's Narrative Soteriology*. Grand Rapids: Eerdmans, 2009.

Goulder, Michael D. "The Pastor's Wolves: Jewish Christian Visionaries behind the Pastoral Epistles." *NovT* 38 (1996): 242–56.

Gray, Patrick. *Paul as a Problem in History and Culture: The Apostle and His Critics through the Centuries*. Grand Rapids: Baker Academic, 2016.

Grayston, Kenneth, and Gustav Herdan. "The Authorship of the Pastorals in the Light of Statistical Linguistics." *NTS* 6 (1959): 1–15.

Green, Beriah. *The Chattel Principle: The Abhorrence of Jesus Christ and the Apostles, or, No Refuge for American Slavery in the New Testament*. New York: American Anti-Slavery Society, 1839.

Green, Peter. *Alexander to Actium: The Historical Evolution of the Hellenistic Age*. Reprint ed. Berkeley: University of California Press, 1990.

Gregory, Brad S. *Rebel in the Ranks: Martin Luther, the Reformation, and the Conflicts That Continue to Shape Our World*. New York: HarperOne, 2017.

Grenfell, Bernard P., and Arthur S. Hunt, eds. *The Oxyrhynchus Papyri*. Vol. 73. London: Egypt Exploration Fund, 1898.

Grieb, Katherine. *The Story of Romans: A Narrative Defense of God's Righteousness*. Louisville: Westminster John Knox, 2002.

Griffith-Jones, Robin. *The Gospel According to Paul: The Creative Genius Who Brought Jesus to the World*. San Francisco: HarperSanFrancisco, 2004.

Gross, Alan G., and Arthur E. Walzer, eds. *Rereading Aristotle's Rhetoric*. Carbondale: Southern Illinois University Press, 2008.

Gruenwald, Ithamar. *Apocalyptic and Merkavah Mysticism*. Arbeiten zur Geschichte des antiken Judentums und des Urchristentums 14. Leiden: Brill, 1980.

Gunderson, Erik, ed. *The Cambridge Companion to Ancient Rhetoric*. New York: Cambridge University Press, 2009.

Gundry, Robert Horton. "The Form, Meaning, and Background of the Hymn Quoted in 1 Tim 3:16." Pages 203–22 in *Apostolic History and the Gospel: Biblical and Historical Essays Presented to F. F. Bruce on His 60th Birthday*, edited by W. Ward Gasque and Robert P. Martin. Grand Rapids: Eerdmans, 1970.

Gunkel, Hermann. *The Influence of the Holy Spirit: The Popular View of the Apostolic Age and the Teaching of the Apostle Paul* [1888]. Translated by Roy A. Harrisville and Philip A. Quanbeck. Philadelphia: Fortress, 1979.

Habinek, Thomas. *Ancient Rhetoric and Oratory*. Malden, MA: Blackwell, 2005.

Hadas, Moses. *Hellenistic Culture: Fusion and Diffusion.* New York: Norton, 1959.

Hafemann, Scott J. *Paul, Moses, and the History of Israel: The Letter/Spirit Contrast and the Argument from Scripture in 2 Corinthians 3.* Peabody, MA: Hendrickson, 1996.

Hagen, Kenneth. *Luther's Approach to Scripture as Seen in His "Commentaries" on Galatians, 1519–1538.* Tübingen: Mohr Siebeck, 1993.

Hamilton, Edith, and Huntington Cairns, eds. *The Collected Dialogues of Plato: Including the Letters.* Translated by Lane Cooper. Princeton: Princeton University Press, 1989.

Han, Paul. *Swimming in the Sea of Scripture: Paul's Use of the Old Testament in 2 Corinthians 4:7–13:13.* LNTS 519. London: Bloomsbury, 2014.

Hanson, Anthony Tyrrell. *Studies in Paul's Technique and Theology.* Grand Rapids: Eerdmans, 1974.

Harink, Douglas. *Paul among the Postliberals.* Grand Rapids: Brazos, 2003.

Harland, Philip. *Associations, Synagogues, and Congregations: Claiming a Place in Ancient Mediterranean Society.* Minneapolis: Fortress, 2003.

Harlow, Barbara, and Mia Carter, eds. *Imperialism and Orientalism: A Documentary Sourcebook.* Malden, MA: Blackwell, 1999.

Harnack, Adolf von. *Marcion: The Gospel of the Alien God.* Translated by John E. Steely. Eugene: Wipf & Stock, 2007.

_____. *What Is Christianity? Lectures Delivered in the University of Berlin during the Winter-Term 1899–1900.* Translated by Thomas Bailey Saunders. New York: Harper, 1901.

Harris, Horton. *The Tübingen School.* Oxford: Clarendon, 1975.

Harrison, James R. "The Apostle Paul and the Spiral of Roman Violence." Pages 119–48 in *Bridges in New Testament Interpretation: Interdisciplinary Advances,* edited by Neil Elliott and Werner H. Kelber. Minneapolis: Fortress, 2018.

Harrison, P. N. *The Problem of the Pastoral Epistles.* London: Oxford University Press, 1921.

Hart, David Bentley, trans. *The New Testament: A Translation.* New Haven: Yale University Press, 2017.

Hartin, Patrick J. *James and the "Q" Sayings of Jesus.* Sheffield: JSOT Press, 1991.

Hatch, Edwin. *The Influence of Greek Ideas and Usages upon the Christian Church.* London: Williams and Norgate, 1897.

Hauck, Frederick. "κοινός." In *TDNT* 3:789–809.

Hauerwas, Stanley. *A Community of Character: Toward a Constructive Christian Social Ethic.* Notre Dame, IN: University of Notre Dame Press, 1981.

Hauerwas, Stanley, and L. Gregory Jones, eds. *Why Narrative? Readings in Narrative Theology.* Grand Rapids: Eerdmans, 1989.

Hauge, Matthew Ryan, and Andrew W. Pitts, eds. *Ancient Education and Early Christianity*. LNTS 553. New York: Bloomsbury, 2016.

Hayes, John H., and Sara R. Mandell. *The Jewish People in Classical Antiquity: From Alexander to Bar Kochba*. Louisville: Westminster John Knox, 1998.

Hays, Richard B. "Christ Prays the Psalms: Paul's Use of an Early Christological Convention." Pages 122–36 in *The Future of Christology: Essays in Honor of Leander E. Keck*, edited by Wayne A. Meeks and Abraham J. Malherbe. Minneapolis: Fortress, 1993.

———. *The Conversion of the Imagination: Paul as Interpreter of Israel's Scripture*. Grand Rapids: Eerdmans, 2005.

———. *Echoes of Scripture in the Letters of Paul*. New Haven: Yale University Press, 1993.

———. *The Faith of Jesus Christ: The Narrative Substructure of Galatians 3:1–4:11*. SBLDS 56. Chico: Scholars Press, 2002.

———. *The Moral Vision of the New Testament: Community, Cross, New Creation*. San Francisco: HarperSanFrancisco, 1996.

———. "Relations Natural and Unnatural: A Response to John Boswell's Exegesis of Romans 1." *Journal of Religious Ethics* 14 (1986): 184–215.

Hedrick, Charles W. "Paul's Conversion/Call: A Comparative Analysis of the Three Reports in Acts." *JBL* 100 (1981): 415–32.

Heitmüller, Wilhelm. "Zum Problem Paulus und Jesus." *ZNW* 13 (1912): 320–37.

Hemer, Colin J. *The Book of Acts in the Setting of Hellenistic History*. Edited by Conrad H. Gempf. WUNT 49. Tübingen: Mohr Siebeck, 1989.

Hengel, Martin. *Crucifixion in the Ancient World and the Folly of the Cross*. Philadelphia: Fortress, 1977.

———. "Der Jakobusbriefe als antipaulinische Polemik." Pages 248–78 in *Tradition and Interpretation in the New Testament: Essays in Honor of E. Earle Ellis for His 60th Birthday*, edited by Gerald F. Hawthorne and Otto Betz. Grand Rapids: Eerdmans, 1987.

———. *Judaism and Hellenism: Studies in Their Encounter in Palestine during the Early Hellenistic Period*. Translated by John Bowden. 2 vols. Philadelphia: Fortress, 1974.

———. *The Zealots*. Translated by David Smith. Edinburgh: T&T Clark, 1989.

Henning, Meghan. *Educating Early Christians through the Rhetoric of Hell: "Weeping and Gnashing of Teeth" as Paideia in Matthew and the Early Church*. WUNT 2.382. Tübingen: Mohr Siebeck, 2014.

Hersbell, J. P. "The Stoicism of Epictetus: Twentieth Century Perspectives." *ANRW* 36.3:148–63.

Hickling, Colin J. A. "A Problem of Method in Gospel Research." *Religious Studies* 10, no. 3 (1974): 339–46.

Hitchens, Christopher. *God Is Not Great: How Religion Poisons Everything.* New York: Twelve Books, 2007.

_____, ed. *The Portable Atheist: Essential Reading for the Nonbeliever.* Cambridge: Da Capo, 2007.

Hock, Ronald F. *The Social Context of Paul's Ministry: Tentmaking and Apostleship.* Minneapolis: Augsburg, 1995.

_____. "A Support for His Old Age: Paul's Plea in Behalf of Onesimus." Pages 67–81 in *The Social World of the First Christians: Essays in Honor of Wayne A. Meeks,* edited by L. Michael White and O. Larry Yarbrough. Minneapolis: Fortress, 1995.

Holladay, Carl R. *Fragments from Hellenistic Jewish Authors.* 5 vols. Society of Biblical Literature Texts and Translations 39, Pseudepigrapha 13. Atlanta: Society of Biblical Literature, 1983.

_____. *Introduction to the New Testament: Reference Edition.* Waco: Baylor University Press, 2017.

_____. "Jewish Responses to Hellenistic Culture." Pages 139–63 in *Ethnicity in Hellenistic Egypt,* edited by Per Bilde. Aarhus: Aarhus University Press, 1992.

_____. "Paul and His Predecessors in the Diaspora." Pages 429–60 in *Early Christianity and Hellenistic Culture: Comparative Studies in Honor of Abraham J. Malherbe,* edited by John T. Fitzgerald, Thomas H. Olbricht, and L. Michael White. NovTSup 110. Leiden: Brill, 2003.

_____. *Theios Aner in Hellenistic Judaism: A Critique of the Use of This Category in New Testament Christology.* SBLDS 40. Chico: Scholars Press, 1977.

Holmberg, Bengt. *Paul and Power: Structure of Authority in the Primitive Church as Reflected in the Pauline Epistles.* Philadelphia: Fortress, 1978.

Holtz, Barry W. "Midrash." Pages 177–211 in *Back to the Sources: Reading the Classic Jewish Texts,* edited by Barry W. Holtz. New York: Summit Books, 1984.

Holtzmann, Heinrich Julius. *Die Pastoralbriefe, kritisch und exegetisch behandelt.* Leipzig: Englemann, 1880.

_____. *Lehrbuch der historisch-kritischen Einleitung in das neue Testament.* 3rd ed. Freiburg: Mohr Siebeck, 1892.

Hooker, Morna D. "Were There False Teachers in Colossae?" Pages 315–31 in *Christ and Spirit in the New Testament: Studies in Honour of Charles Francis Digby Moule,* edited by Barnabas Lindars and Stephen S. Smalley. Cambridge: Cambridge University Press, 1973.

Horace. *Satires, Epistles and Ars Poetica.* Translated by Henry Rushton Fairclough. Cambridge, MA: Harvard University Press, 1924.

Horsley, Richard A. "'How Can Some of You Say That There Is No Resurrection of the Dead?' Spiritual Elitism in Corinth." *NovT* 20 (1978): 203–31.

_____. *Jesus and the Politics of Roman Palestine*. Columbia: University of South Carolina Press, 2014.

_____, ed. *Paul and Empire: Religion and Power in Roman Imperial Society*. Valley Forge: Trinity Press International, 1997.

Horsley, Richard A., with John S. Hanson. *Bandits, Prophets, and Messiahs: Popular Movements at the Time of Jesus*. San Francisco: Harper & Row, 1985.

Hunt, Arthur S., and J. Gilbart Smyly, eds. *The Tebtunis Papyri*. London: Oxford University Press, 1933.

Hurtado, Larry W. *Lord Jesus Christ: Devotion to Jesus in Earliest Christianity*. Grand Rapids: Eerdmans, 2005.

Hylen, Susan E. *A Modest Apostle: Thecla and the History of Women in the Early Church*. New York: Oxford University Press, 2015.

Isaac, Benjamin. *Empire and Ideology in the Graeco-Roman World: Selected Papers*. Cambridge: Cambridge University Press, 2017.

Jackson, Hugh. "The Resurrection Belief of the Earliest Church: A Response to the Failure of Prophecy?" *Journal of Religion* 55, no. 4 (1975): 415–25.

Jaeger, Werner. *Paideia: The Ideals of Greek Culture*. 3 vols. New York: Oxford University Press, 1943.

Jefferson, Thomas. "Letter to William Short." April 13, 1820. https://founders .archives.gov/.

Jellicoe, Sidney. *Studies in the Septuagint: Origins, Recensions, and Interpretations: Selected Essays, with a Prolegomenon*. New York: KAV, 1973.

Jeremias, Joachim. *Central Message of the New Testament*. New York: Charles Scribner's Sons, 1965.

_____. "Paul and James." *Expository Times* 66 (1955): 368–71.

Jervell, Jacob. *Luke and the People of God: A New Look at Luke-Acts*. Minneapolis: Augsburg Fortress, 1972.

_____. *The Unknown Paul: Essays on Luke-Acts and Early Christian History*. Minneapolis: Augsburg Fortress, 1984.

Jewett, Robert. "The Agitators and the Galatian Congregation." *NTS* 17 (1971): 198–212.

_____. *A Chronology of Paul's Life*. Philadelphia: Fortress, 1979.

_____. "Conflicting Movements in the Early Church as Reflected in Philippians." *NovT* 12 (1970): 362–90.

_____. *Dating Paul's Life*. London: SCM, 1979.

_____. "The Epistolary Thanksgiving and the Integrity of Philippians." *NovT* 12 (1970): 40–53.

_____. *Romans: A Commentary*. Hermeneia. Minneapolis: Fortress, 2007.

Jobes, Karen H., and Moisés Silva. *Invitation to the Septuagint*. Grand Rapids: Baker Academic, 2000.

Johnson, Luke Timothy. "1 Timothy 1:1–20: The Shape of the Struggle." Pages 383–406 in *Contested Issues in Christian Origins and the New Testament: Collected Essays*. NovTSup 146. Leiden: Brill, 2013.

_____. *The Acts of the Apostles*. SP 5. Collegeville, MN: Liturgical Press, 1992.

_____. *Among the Gentiles: Greco-Roman Religion and Christianity*. ABRL. New Haven: Yale University Press, 2009.

_____. "The Authority of the New Testament in the Church: A Theological Reflection." Pages 87–99 in *Conservative, Moderate, Liberal: The Biblical Authority Debate*, edited by Charles R. Blaisdell. St. Louis: CBP Press, 1990.

_____. "The Bible's Authority for and in the Church." Pages 67–72 in *Engaging Biblical Authority: Perspectives on the Bible as Scripture*, edited by William P. Brown. Louisville: Westminster John Knox, 2007.

_____. *Brother of Jesus, Friend of God: Studies in the Letter of James*. Grand Rapids: Eerdmans, 2004.

_____. *The Creed: What Christians Believe and Why It Matters*. New York: Doubleday, 2004.

_____. *Faith's Freedom: A Classic Spirituality for Contemporary Christians*. Minneapolis: Fortress, 1990.

_____. *The First and Second Letters to Timothy*. AB 35A. New Haven: Yale University Press, 2001.

_____. *First Timothy, Second Timothy, Titus*. John Knox Preaching Guides. Atlanta: John Knox, 1987.

_____. "Friendship with the World and Friendship with God: A Study of Discipleship in James." Pages 202–20 in *Brother of Jesus, Friend of God*.

_____. "God Was in Christ: 2 Corinthians 5:19 and Mythic Language." Pages 216–23 in *Myth and Scripture: Contemporary Perspectives on Religion, Language, and Imagination*, edited by Dexter E. Callender Jr. SBLSBS 78. Atlanta: SBL Press, 2014.

_____. *The Gospel of Luke*. SP 3. Collegeville, MN: Liturgical Press, 1990.

_____. *Hebrews: A Commentary*. New Testament Library. Louisville: Westminster John Knox, 2006.

_____. *Invitation to the Letters of Paul: Ephesians, Colossians, Pastorals*. Invitation to the New Testament. Garden City, NY: Doubleday, 1980.

_____. "Irenaeus: Teacher of the Church." *Ligourian* 95, no. 4 (2007): 20–23.

_____. "Isaiah the Evangelist." *Milltown Studies* 48 (2001): 88–105.

_____. "James' Significance for Early Christianity." Pages 1–23 in *Brother of Jesus, Friend of God*.

_____. "John and Thomas in Context: An Exercise in Canonical Criticism." Pages 284–309 in Wagner, Rowe, and Grieb, *Word Leaps the Gap*.

_____. *The Letter of James: A New Translation with Introduction and Commentary*. AB 37A. Garden City, NY: Doubleday, 1995.

_____. *Letters to Paul's Delegates: 1 Timothy, 2 Timothy, Titus*. New Testament in Context. Valley Forge, PA: Trinity Press International, 1996.

_____. *The Literary Function of Possessions in Luke-Acts*. SBLDS 39. Missoula: Scholars Press, 1977.

_____. "Meals Are Where the Magic Is." Pages 137–79 in *Religious Experience in Earliest Christianity*.

_____. *Miracles: God's Presence and Power in Creation*. Louisville: Westminster John Knox, 2018.

_____. "The New Testament as the Church's Book." Pages 525–46 in *Writings of the New Testament*.

_____. "The New Testament's Anti-Jewish Slander and the Conventions of Ancient Polemic." *JBL* 108 (1989): 419–41.

_____. "The Paul of the Letters: A Catholic Perspective." Pages 65–96 in Bird, *Four Views on the Apostle Paul*.

_____. *Prophetic Jesus, Prophetic Church: The Challenge of Luke-Acts to Contemporary Christians*. Grand Rapids: Eerdmans, 2011.

_____. *Reading Romans: A Literary and Theological Commentary*. New York: Crossroad, 1997.

_____. *The Real Jesus: The Misguided Quest for the Historical Jesus and the Truth of the Traditional Gospels*. San Francisco: Harper San Francisco, 1996.

_____. "The Reception of James in the Early Church." Pages 45–60 in *Brother of Jesus, Friend of God*.

_____. *Religious Experience in Earliest Christianity: A Missing Dimension in New Testament Study*. Minneapolis: Fortress, 1998.

_____. "The Rise of Church Order." Pages 155–72, 303–5 in *Beyond Bultmann: Reckoning a New Testament Theology*, edited by Bruce W. Longenecker and Mikeal C. Parsons. Waco: Baylor University Press, 2014.

_____. "Ritual Imprinting and the Politics of Perfection." Pages 69–104 in *Religious Experience in Earliest Christianity*.

_____. "Rom 3:21–26 and the Faith of Jesus." *CBQ* 44 (1982): 77–90.

_____. *Scripture and Discernment: Decision Making in the Church*. Nashville: Abingdon, 1996.

_____. *Septuagintal Midrash in the Speeches of Acts.* Pere Marquette Lecture 33. Milwaukee: Marquette University Press, 2002.

_____. "The Social Dimensions of Sōtēria in Luke-Acts and Paul." Pages 520–36 in *Society of Biblical Literature Seminar Papers,* edited by Eugene H. Lovering. Atlanta: Scholars Press, 1993.

_____. "Ways of Being Jewish in the Greco-Roman World." Pages 111–29, 326–43 in *Among the Gentiles: Greco-Roman Religion and Christianity.* ABRL. New Haven: Yale University Press, 2009.

_____. *The Writings of the New Testament: An Interpretation.* 3rd ed. Minneapolis: Fortress, 2010.

Johnson, Luke Timothy, and Wesley H. Wachob. "The Sayings of Jesus in the Letter of James." Pages 431–50 in *Authenticating the Words of Jesus,* edited by Bruce D. Chilton and Craig A. Evans. New Testament Tools and Studies 28.1. Leiden: Brill, 1999.

Johnson, Mark. *Moral Imagination: Implications of Cognitive Science for Ethics.* Chicago: University of Chicago Press, 1983.

_____, ed. *Philosophical Perspectives on Metaphor.* Minneapolis: University of Minnesota Press, 1981.

Johnson, Matthew V., James A. Noel, and Demetrius K. Williams, eds. *Onesimus Our Brother: Reading Religion, Race, and Slavery in Philemon.* Paul in Critical Contexts. Minneapolis: Fortress, 2012.

Jones, Christopher P. *Plutarch and Rome.* Oxford: Clarendon, 1971.

Jones, F. Stanley. "The Pseudo-Clementines: A History of Research." *Second Century* 2 (1982): 1–33, 63–96.

Jootsen, Jan, and Peter J. Thomson, eds. *Voces Biblicae: Septuagint Greek and Its Significance for the New Testament.* Leuven: Peeters, 2007.

Josephus. *Antiquities of the Jews.* Translated by H. St. J. Thackery. LCL. Cambridge, MA: Harvard University Press, 1958.

Joubert, Stephan. *Paul as Benefactor: Reciprocity, Strategy and Theological Reflection in Paul's Collection.* WUNT 2.124. Tübingen: Mohr Siebeck, 2000.

Judge, E. A. "The Early Christians as a Scholastic Community." *Journal of Religious History* 1 (1960): 4–15, 125–37.

Juel, Donald H. *Messianic Exegesis.* Minneapolis: Fortress, 1987.

Kalmar, Ivan D. *Early Orientalism: Imagined Islam and the Notion of Sublime Power.* Routledge Islamic Studies. London: Routledge, 2011.

Kamudzandu, Israel. *Abraham Our Father.* Minneapolis: Fortress, 2013.

Karrer, Martin, Siegfried Kreuzer, and Marcus Sigismund, eds. *Von der Septuaginta zum Neuen Testament: Textgeschichtliche Erörterungen.* Berlin: De Gruyter, 2010.

Karris, Robert J. "The Background and Significance of the Polemic of the Pastoral Epistles." *JBL* 92 (1973): 549–64.

Käsemann, Ernst. *Perspectives on Paul.* Translated by Margaret Kohl. Philadelphia: Fortress, 1971.

_____. "A Primitive Christian Baptismal Liturgy." Pages 149–68 in *Essays on New Testament Themes.* Philadelphia: Fortress, 1964.

_____. "Principles of Interpretation of Romans 13." Pages 196–216 in *New Testament Questions of Today.* Philadelphia: Fortress, 1969.

Kazen, Thomas. *Issues of Impurity in Early Judaism.* ConBNT. Winona Lake, IN: Eisenbrauns, 2010.

Kennedy, George A. *Classical Rhetoric and Its Christian and Secular Tradition from Ancient to Modern Times.* 2nd ed. Chapel Hill: University of North Carolina Press, 1999.

Kennedy, Valerie. *Edward Said: A Critical Introduction.* Oxford: Blackwell, 2000.

Kern, F. H. *Der Charakter und Ursprung des Briefes Jacobi.* Tübingen: Fues, 1835.

Kidd, R. M. "Titus as Apologia: Grace for Liars, Beasts, and Bellies." *Horizons in Biblical Theology* 21 (1999): 185–209.

Kiley, Mark. *Colossians as Pseudepigraphy.* Sheffield: JSOT Press, 1987.

Kilpatrick, George D. "Galatians 1:18 *historesai Kephan.*" Pages 144–49 in *New Testament Essays: Studies in Memory of Thomas Walter Manson, 1893–1958,* edited by A. J. B. Higgins. Manchester: Manchester University Press, 1959.

Kirby, John C. *Ephesians, Baptism and Pentecost: An Inquiry into the Structure and Purpose of the Epistle to the Ephesians.* London: SPCK, 1968.

Klein, Charlotte. *Anti-Judaism in Christian Theology.* Translated by Edward Quinn. Philadelphia: Fortress, 1985.

Klijn, A. F. J. "Paul's Opponents in Philippians III." *NovT* 7 (1965): 278–84.

Knight, George W. *The Faithful Sayings in the Pastoral Letters.* Grand Rapids: Baker, 1979.

Knox, John. *Chapters in a Life of Paul.* Nashville: Abingdon, 1950.

Knudsen, Rachel Ahern. *Homeric Speech and the Origins of Rhetoric.* Baltimore: Johns Hopkins University Press, 2014.

Koch, Dietrich-Alex. *Die Schrift als Zeuge des Evangelium: Untersuchungen zur Verwendung und zum Verstaendnis der Schrift bei Paulus.* Beiträge zür historischen Theologie 69. Tübingen: Mohr Siebeck, 1986.

Koester, Helmut, ed. *Ephesos, Metropolis of Asia: An Interdisciplinary Approach to Its Archaeology, Religion, and Culture.* HTS 41. Valley Forge, PA: Trinity Press International, 1995.

_____. *Introduction to the New Testament.* 2 vols. Philadelphia: Fortress, 1980.

_____. "The Purpose of the Polemic of a Pauline Fragment." *NTS* 8 (1962): 317–32.

Kolenkow, Anitra Bingham. "Paul and His Opponents in 2 Cor 10–13: Theioi Andres and Spiritual Guides." Pages 351–74 in *Religious Propaganda and Missionary Competition in the New Testament World: Essays Honoring Dieter Georgi*, edited by Lukas Bormann, Kelly Tredici, and Angela Standhartinger. NovTSup 74. Leiden: Brill, 1994.

Kondoleon, Christine, ed. *Antioch: The Lost Ancient City.* Princeton: Princeton University Press, 2000.

Kraftchick, Steven, "Ethos and Pathos Arguments in Galatians Five and Six: A Rhetorical Analysis." PhD diss., Emory University, 1985.

Kraus, Wolfgang, R. Glenn Wooden, and Florian Wilk, eds. "The Letters of Paul as Witness to and for the Septuagint Text." *Septuagint Research: Issues and Challenges in the Study of the Greek Jewish Scriptures.* SCS 53. Atlanta: Society of Biblical Literature, 2005.

Kümmel, Werner Georg. *Introduction to the New Testament.* Translated by Howard Clark Kee. Nashville: Abingdon, 1975.

Kurz, William S. "Kenotic Imitation of Paul and Christ in Phil 2 and 3." Pages 105–26 in *Discipleship in the New Testament*, edited by Fernando F. Segovia. Philadelphia: Fortress, 1985.

Kyrychenko, Alexander. *The Roman Army and the Expansion of the Gospel.* BZNW 203. Berlin: De Gruyter, 2014.

Lacey, Walter Kirkpatrick. *Cicero and the End of the Roman Republic.* London: Hodder & Stoughton, 1978.

Lake, Kirsopp, trans. *The Apostolic Fathers.* LCL. Cambridge, MA: Harvard University Press, 1912.

Lakoff, George. *Women, Fire, and Dangerous Things: What Categories Reveal about the Mind.* Chicago: University of Chicago Press, 1987.

Lakoff, George, and Mark Johnson. *Metaphors We Live By.* Chicago: University of Chicago Press, 1980.

Lane, Anthony N. S. "Calvin." Pages 285–97 in *The Blackwell Companion to Paul*, edited by Stephen Westerholm. Oxford: Blackwell, 2011.

Lane Fox, Robin J. *Brill's Companion to Ancient Macedon.* Brill's Companions in Classical Studies 1. Leiden: Brill, 2011.

Lang, Mabel L. *Cure and Cult in Ancient Corinth: A Guide to the Asklepieion.* Princeton: American School of Classical Studies at Athens, 1977.

Lau, Te-Li. *The Politics of Peace.* NovTSup 133. Leiden: Brill, 2009.

Layton, Bentley, ed. *The Rediscovery of Gnosticism.* 2 vols. Leiden: Brill, 1980–81.

Lebreton, Jules. *Gnosticism, Marcionism, and Manichaeism*. London: Catholic Truth Society, 1956.

Lee, Kam-Lun Edwin. *Augustine, Manichaeism, and the Good*. Patristic Studies 2. New York: Peter Lang, 1999.

Lee, Yeong Mee, and Yoon Jong Yoo, eds. *Mapping and Engaging the Bible in Asian Cultures: Congress of the Society of Asian Biblical Studies 2008 Seoul Conference*. Korea: The Christian Literature Society of Korea, 2009.

Levenson, Jon D. *Resurrection and the Restoration of Israel: The Ultimate Victory of the God of Life*. New Haven: Yale University Press, 2006.

Levine, Amy-Jill, ed. *Feminist Companion to Paul: Authentic Pauline Writings*. Feminist Companion to the New Testament and Early Christian Writings. New York: Continuum, 2004.

_____, ed. *The Jewish Annotated New Testament*. New York: Oxford University Press, 2011.

Lewis, Lloyd. "An African-American Appraisal of the Paul-Philemon-Onesimus Triangle." Pages 232–46 in *Stony the Road We Trod: African American Biblical Interpretation*, edited by Cain Hope Felder. Minneapolis: Fortress, 1991.

Lewis, Naphtali, and Meyer Reinhold. *Roman Civilization: Selected Readings*. 3rd ed. 2 vols. New York: Columbia University Press, 1990.

Lieberman, Saul. *Greek in Jewish Palestine, Hellenism in Jewish Palestine*. New York: The Jewish Theological Seminary of America, 1994.

Lieu, Judith M. *Marcion and the Making of a Heretic: God and Scripture in the Second Century*. Cambridge: Cambridge University Press, 2017.

Lincoln, Andrew T. *Ephesians*. WBC 42. Grand Rapids: Zondervan, 1990.

Lipstadt, Deborah E. *Denying the Holocaust: The Growing Assault on Truth and Memory*. New York: Free Press, 1993.

_____. *History on Trial: My Day in Court with David Irving*. New York: Ecco, 2005.

Lohse, Eduard. *Colossians and Philemon*. Edited by Helmut Koester. Translated by William R. Poehlmann and Robert J. Karris. Hermeneia. Philadelphia: Fortress, 1988.

_____. "Pauline Theology in the Letter to the Colossians 1." *NTS* 15, no. 2 (1969): 211–20.

Loisy, Alfred. *The Birth of the Christian Religion and the Origins of the New Testament*. New York: University Books, 1962.

_____. *L'évangile et l'église*. Paris: Picard, 1902.

Long, A. A. *Hellenistic Philosophy: Stoics, Epicureans, Sceptics*. 2nd ed. London: Duckworth, 1986.

Long, A. A., and D. N. Sedley. *The Hellenistic Philosophers*. 2 vols. Cambridge: Cambridge University Press, 1987.

Longenecker, Bruce W., and Todd D. Still. *Thinking Through Paul: A Survey of His Life, Letters, and Theology*. Grand Rapids: Zondervan, 2014.

Longenecker, Richard N. "Ancient Amanuenses and the Pauline Epistles." Pages 281–97 in *New Dimensions in New Testament Study*, edited by Richard N. Longenecker and Merrill C. Tenney. Grand Rapids: Zondervan, 1974.

_____. "The 'Faith of Abraham' Theme in Paul, James, and Hebrews: A Study in the Circumstantial Character of New Testament Teaching." *Journal of the Evangelical Theological Society* 20 (1977): 203–12.

_____, ed. *Life in the Face of Death: The Resurrection Message of the New Testament*. Grand Rapids: Eerdmans, 1998.

_____. *Paul, Apostle of Liberty*. 2nd ed. Grand Rapids: Eerdmans, 2015.

Lucie-Smith, Alexander. *Narrative Theology and Moral Theology: The Infinite Horizon*. Burlington, VT: Ashgate, 2007.

Lüdemann, Gerd. *Opposition to Paul in Jewish Christianity*. Translated by M. Eugene Boring. Minneapolis: Fortress, 1989.

_____. *Paul, Apostle to the Gentiles: Studies in Chronology*. Translated by F. Stanley Jones. Philadelphia: Fortress, 1984.

_____. *Resurrection of Jesus: History, Experience, Theology*. Minneapolis: Fortress, 1994.

Lull, David J. *The Spirit in Galatia: Paul's Interpretation of PNEUMA as Divine Power*. Chico: Scholars Press, 1980.

Lütgert, Wilhelm. *Die Irrlehrer der Pastoralbriefe*. Beiträge zur Förderung christlicher Theologie; 13. Bd., 3. Heft. Gütersloh: Bertelsmann, 1909.

Luther, Martin. "Preface to the New Testament (1522)." Page 362 in *Luther's Works*, vol. 35, *Word and Sacrament I*, edited by E. Theodore Bachmann. Philadelphia: Fortress, 1960.

_____. "Sermons on the Sum of Christian Life: 1 Tim 1:5–7." Pages 259–87 in *Luther's Works*, vol. 51, *Sermons I*, edited by Helmut T. Lehmann, translated by John W. Doberstein. Philadelphia: Muhlenberg, 1959.

Lutz, Cora E. *Musonius Rufus, "The Roman Socrates."* Yale Classical Studies 10. New Haven: Yale University Press, 1947.

Maccoby, Hyam. *Jesus the Pharisee*. London: SCM, 2003.

_____. *The Mythmaker: Paul and the Invention of Christianity*. New York: Barnes & Noble, 1998.

MacDonald, Dennis R. "Virgins, Widows, and Paul in Second Century Asia Minor." Pages 1:165–84 in *1979 Society of Biblical Literature Seminar Papers*, edited by Paul J. Achtemeier. Missoula: Scholars Press, 1979.

MacDonald, Margaret Y. *Colossians and Ephesians*. SP 17. Collegeville, MN: Liturgical Press, 2000.

Mack, Burton L. *Who Wrote the New Testament? The Making of the Christian Myth*. San Francisco: HarperCollins, 1995.

MacMullen, Ramsay. *Enemies of the Roman Order: Treason, Unrest, and Alienation in the Empire*. New York: Routledge, 1992.

_____. *Roman Social Relations, 50 BC to AD 284*. New Haven: Yale University Press, 1974.

Magness, Jodi. *The Archaeology of Qumran and the Dead Sea Scrolls*. Studies in the Dead Sea Scrolls and Related Literature. Grand Rapids: Eerdmans, 2003.

Malherbe, Abraham J. *Ancient Epistolary Theorists*. Atlanta: Scholars Press, 1988.

_____. "Ancient Epistolary Theory." *Ohio Journal of Religious Studies* 5 (1977): 3–77.

_____, ed. *The Cynic Epistles: A Study Edition*. Vol. 12. Resources for Biblical Studies. Missoula: Society of Biblical Literature, 1977.

_____. *The Letters to the Thessalonians: A New Translation with Introduction and Commentary*. AB 32B. New York: Doubleday, 2000.

_____. *Moral Exhortation: A Greco Roman Sourcebook*. Library of Early Christianity. Philadelphia: Westminster, 1986.

_____. *Paul and the Popular Philosophers*. Philadelphia: Fortress, 1989.

_____. *Paul and the Thessalonians: The Philosophic Tradition of Pastoral Care*. Philadelphia: Fortress, 1987.

_____. "A Physical Description of Paul." Pages 165–70 in *Paul and the Popular Philosophers*.

_____. "'Seneca' on Paul as Letter Writer." Pages 414–21 in *The Future of Early Christianity: Essays in Honor of Helmut Koester*, edited by Birger A. Pearson. Philadelphia: Fortress, 1991.

_____. *Social Aspects of Early Christianity*. 2nd ed. Philadelphia: Fortress, 1983.

Mangold, Wilhelm. *Die Irrlehrer der Pastoralbriefe: Eine Studie*. Marburg: Elwertsche Universitätsbuchhandlung, 1856.

Marchal, Joseph A. *The Politics of Heaven: Women, Gender, and Empire in the Study of Paul*. Paul in Critical Contexts. Minneapolis: Fortress, 2008.

Marks, Herbert. "Pauline Typology and Revisionary Criticism." *JAAR* 52 (1984): 71–92.

Marrou, H. I. *A History of Education in Antiquity*. Translated by George Lamb. New York: Sheed and Ward, 1956.

Marshall, I. Howard. *Luke: Historian and Theologian*. Grand Rapids: Zondervan, 1970.

Martin, Clarice J. "The Rhetorical Function of Commercial Language in Paul's Letter to Philemon (Verse 18)." Pages 321–37 in *Persuasive Artistry: Studies in New Testament Rhetoric in Honor of George A. Kennedy*, edited by Duane F. Watson. JSNTSup 50. Sheffield: Sheffield Academic Press, 1991.

Martin, Dale B. *The Corinthian Body*. New Haven: Yale University Press, 1995.

_____. *Slavery as Salvation: The Metaphor of Slavery in Pauline Christianity*. New Haven: Yale University Press, 1990.

Martin, Ralph P. *Carmen Christi: Philippians 2:5–11 in Recent Interpretation and in the Setting of Early Christian Worship*. Grand Rapids: Eerdmans, 1983.

_____. *Ephesians, Colossians, and Philemon*. Louisville: John Knox, 1992.

Martin, Troy W. *By Philosophy and Empty Deceit: Colossians as Response to a Cynic Critique*. Sheffield: Sheffield Academic Press, 1996.

Marxsen, Willi. *Introduction to the New Testament*. Translated by G. Buswell. 3rd ed. Philadelphia: Fortress, 1968.

_____. *New Testament Foundations for Christian Ethics*. Minneapolis: Fortress, 1993.

_____. *The Resurrection of Jesus of Nazareth*. Translated by Margaret Kohl. Philadelphia: Fortress, 1970.

Mason, John P. *The Resurrection According to Paul*. Lewiston, NY: Mellen, 1993.

May, James M., ed. *Brill's Companion to Cicero: Oratory and Rhetoric*. Leiden: Brill, 2002.

Mayor, Joseph B. *The Epistle of Saint James*. London: Macmillan, 1913.

McAuley, David. *Paul's Covert Use of Scripture: Intertextuality and Rhetorical Situation in Philippians 2:10–16*. Eugene: Pickwick, 2015.

McDonald, Lee Martin. *The Biblical Canon: Its Origin, Transmission, and Authority*. Peabody, MA: Hendrickson, 2007.

McLay, R. Timothy. *The Use of the Septuagint in New Testament Research*. Grand Rapids: Eerdmans, 2003.

Meade, David G. *Pseudonymity and Canon: An Investigation into the Relationship of Authorship and Authority in Jewish and Earliest Christian Tradition*. Grand Rapids: Eerdmans, 1987.

Meeks, Wayne A. *The First Urban Christians: The Social World of the Apostle Paul*. New Haven: Yale University Press, 1983.

_____. "'In One Body': The Unity of Humanity in Colossians and Ephesians." Pages 209–21 in *God's Christ and His People: Studies in Honour of Nils Alstrup Dahl*, edited by Jacob Jervell and Wayne A. Meeks. Oslo: Universitetsforlaget, 1977.

_____, ed. *The Writings of St. Paul*. Norton Critical Edition. New York: Norton, 1981.

Meeks, Wayne A., and John T. Fitzgerald, eds. *The Writings of St. Paul.* 2nd ed. Norton Critical Edition. New York: Norton, 2007.

Meeks, Wayne A., and Fred O. Francis, eds. *Conflict at Colossae: A Problem in the Interpretation of Early Christianity Illustrated by Selected Modern Studies.* Rev. ed. SBLSBS 4. Missoula: Scholars Press, 1975.

Meer, Frederick van der. *Augustine the Bishop.* New York: Sheed and Ward, 1961.

Meier, John P. *A Marginal Jew: Rethinking the Historical Jesus.* 5 vols. New York: Doubleday, 1991.

Mellor, Ronald. *Augustus and the Creation of the Roman Empire: A Brief History with Documents.* New York: Macmillan, 2006.

Metzger, Bruce M. "Literary Forgeries and Canonical Pseudepigrapha." *JBL* 91 (1972): 3–24.

Meyer, Ben F. "The Pre-Pauline Formula in Rom 3:25–26a." *NTS* 29 (1983): 198–208.

Meyer, Roland. *La Vie après la Mort: Saint Paul, Défenseur de la Résurrection.* Pensée Chrétienne. Lausanne: Belle Riviere, 1989.

Millar, Fergus. *The Roman Empire and Its Neighbors.* 2nd ed. London: Duckworth, 1981.

Miller, James D. *The Pastoral Letters as Composite Documents.* Cambridge: Cambridge University Press, 1997.

Mitchell, Margaret M. *The Heavenly Trumpet: John Chrysostom and the Art of Pauline Interpretation.* Tübingen: Mohr Siebeck, 2000.

_____. "New Testament Envoys in the Context of Greco-Roman Diplomatic and Epistolary Conventions: The Example of Timothy and Titus." *JBL* 111 (1992): 641–62.

_____. *Paul and the Rhetoric of Reconciliation: An Exegetical Investigation.* Louisville: Westminster John Knox, 1991.

_____. *Paul, the Corinthians and the Birth of Christian Hermeneutics.* Cambridge: Cambridge University Press, 2012.

Mitton, Charles Leslie. *Ephesians.* New Century Bible. Grand Rapids: Eerdmans, 1976.

_____. *The Formation of the Pauline Corpus of Letters.* London: Epworth, 1955.

_____. "The Relationship between 1 Peter and Ephesians." *JTS* 1 (1950): 67–73.

Moo, Douglas J. *The Epistle to the Romans.* NICNT. Grand Rapids: Eerdmans, 1996.

Moore, George Foot. *Judaism in the First Centuries of the Christian Era.* 2 vols. New York: Schocken Books, 1927.

Moore, Stephen D. *Empire and Apocalypse: Postcolonialism and the New Testament.* The Bible in the Modern World. Sheffield: Sheffield Phoenix, 2006.

_____. *God's Beauty Parlor: And Other Queer Spaces in and Around the Bible.* Contraversions: Jews and Other Differences. Stanford: Stanford University Press, 2002.

Moore, Stephen D., and Fernando F. Segovia. *Postcolonial Biblical Criticism: Interdisciplinary Intersections.* London: T&T Clark, 2007.

Mor, Menachem, and Friedrich V. Reiterer, eds. *Samaritans: Past and Present.* Berlin: De Gruyter, 2010.

Mossman, Judith. *Plutarch and His Intellectual World.* London: Duckworth, 1997.

Moule, C. F. D. *The Epistles of Paul the Apostle to the Colossians and to Philemon: An Introduction and Commentary.* Cambridge: Cambridge University Press, 1962.

Moulton, H. K. *Colossians, Philemon, and Ephesians.* London: Epworth, 1963.

Moyise, Steve. *Paul and Scripture: Studying the New Testament Use of the Old Testament.* London: SPCK, 2010.

Munck, Johannes. "The Judaizing Gentile Christians." Pages 87–134 in *Paul and the Salvation of Mankind.* Translated by Frank Clarke. Richmond: John Knox, 1959.

Münderlein, Gerhard. "Die Überwindung der Mächte: Studien zu theologischen Vorstellungen des apokalyptischen Judentums und bei Paulus." PhD diss., University of Zürich, 1971.

Munoz, Kevin A. "How Not to Go Out of the World: 1 Corinthians 14:13–25 and the Social Foundations of Early Christian Expansion." PhD diss., Emory University, 2008.

Murphy-O'Connor, Jerome. "The Non-Pauline Character of 1 Corinthians 11:2–16?" *JBL* 95 (1976): 615–21.

_____. *Paul: A Critical Life.* Oxford: Clarendon, 1996.

_____. *St. Paul's Corinth: Texts and Archaeology.* Collegeville, MN: Liturgical Press, 2003.

Mussner, Franz. "Contributions Made by Qumran to the Understanding of the Epistle to the Ephesians." Pages 159–78 in *Paul and the Dead Sea Scrolls*, edited by Jerome Murphy-O'Connor and James H. Charlesworth. New York: Crossroad, 1990.

Nanos, Mark D. "A Jewish View." Pages 159–93 in Bird, *Four Views on the Apostle Paul.*

_____. *The Mystery of Romans: The Jewish Context of Paul's Letters.* Minneapolis: Fortress, 1996.

_____. *Paul within Judaism: Restoring the First-Century Context to the Apostle.* Minneapolis: Fortress, 2015.

Nasrallah, Laura, Charalambos Bakirtzis, and Steven J. Friesen, eds. *From Ro-*

*man to Early Christian Thessalonikē: Studies in Religion and Archaeology.* HTS 64. Cambridge, MA: Harvard University Press, 2010.

Neusner, Jacob. "The Formation of Rabbinic Judaism: Yavneh (Yamnia) from A.D. 70 to 100." *ANRW* 19.2:3–42.

———. *From Politics to Piety: The Emergence of Pharisaic Judaism.* Englewood Cliffs, NJ: Prentice-Hall, 1973.

———. *The Rabbinic Traditions about the Pharisees before 70.* Leiden: Brill, 1971.

Newsom, Carol A., Sharon H. Ringe, and Jacqueline E. Lapsley, eds. *Women's Bible Commentary.* 3rd rev. ed. Louisville: Westminster John Knox, 2012.

Neyrey, Jerome H. *Paul, in Other Words: A Cultural Reading of His Letters.* Louisville: Westminster John Knox, 1990.

Nickle, Keith F. *The Collection: A Study in Paul's Strategy.* London: SCM, 1966.

Nicolet-Anderson, Valerie. *Constructing the Self: Thinking with Paul and Michel Foucault.* WUNT 324. Tübingen: Mohr Siebeck, 2012.

Nordling, John G. "Onesimus Fugitivus: A Defense of the Runaway Slave Hypothesis in Philemon." *JSNT* 13 (1991): 97–119.

Nortwick, Thomas Van. *Imagining Men: Ideals of Masculinity in Ancient Greek Culture.* Westport, CT: Praeger, 2008.

Nussbaum, Martha C. *The Therapy of Desire: Theory and Practice in Hellenistic Ethics.* Princeton: Princeton University Press, 1964.

O'Brien, Peter T. *Colossians–Philemon.* WBC. Grand Rapids: Zondervan, 1982.

———. "Ephesians I: An Unusual Introduction to a New Testament Letter." *NTS* 25 (1979): 504–16.

———. *Introductory Thanksgivings in the Letters of Paul.* NovTSup 49. Leiden: Brill, 1977.

Ogilvie, Robert M. *The Romans and Their Gods in the Age of Augustus.* New York: Norton, 1970.

Öhler, Markus, ed. *Aposteldekret und antikes Vereinswesen: Gemeindschaft und Ordnung.* Tübingen: Mohr Siebeck, 2011.

Olson, Alan. *Myth, Symbol, and Reality.* Boston University Studies in Philosophy and Religion. Notre Dame, IN: University of Notre Dame Press, 1980.

Pagels, Elaine H. *The Gnostic Paul: Gnostic Exegesis of the Pauline Letters.* Philadelphia: Fortress, 1975.

Pastor, Jack, Pnina Stern, and Menahem Mor. *Flavius Josephus: Interpretation and History.* Leiden: Brill, 2011.

Patterson, Orlando. *Slavery and Social Death: A Comparative Study.* Cambridge, MA: Harvard University Press, 1982.

Pearson, Birger A. "1 Thessalonians 2:13–16: A Deutero-Pauline Interpolation." *HTR* 64 (1971): 79–94.

<br>

*Bibliography*

_____. *The Pneumatikos-Psychikos Terminology in 1 Corinthians.* SBLDS 12. Missoula: Scholars Press, 1973.

Pervo, Richard I. "The Acts of Titus." Pages 406–15 in Burke and Landau, *New Testament Apocrypha.*

_____. *Dating Acts: Between the Evangelists and the Apologists.* Salem, OR: Polebridge, 2006.

_____. *The Pastorals and Polycarp: Titus, 1–2 Timothy, and Polycarp to the Philippians.* Salem, OR: Polebridge, 2016.

_____. *Profit with Delight: The Literary Genre of the Acts of the Apostles.* Philadelphia: Fortress, 1987.

Peters, Melvin K. H. "Septuagint." In *ABD* 5:1093–104.

Petersen, Norman R. *Literary Criticism for New Testament Critics.* Philadelphia: Fortress, 1978.

_____. *Rediscovering Paul: Philemon and the Sociology of Paul's Narrative World.* Philadelphia: Fortress, 1985.

Pfleiderer, Otto. *Das Urchristentum: Seine Schriften und Lehren in geschichtlichen Zusammenhang.* Berlin: Georg Reimer, 1902.

_____. *Religion and Historic Faiths.* Translated by Daniel A. Huebsch. London: T. Fisher Unwin, 1907.

Philo. *Philo.* Vol. 1. Translated by F. H. Colson and G. H. Whitaker. LCL. Cambridge, MA: Harvard University Press, 1931.

Plevnik, Joseph. *Paul and the Parousia: An Exegetical and Theological Investigation.* Peabody, MA: Hendrickson, 1997.

Pliny the Younger. *Complete Letters.* Translated by Peter G. Walsh. New York: New York University Press, 2009.

Plümacher, Eckhard. *Lukas als hellenistischer Schriftsteller: Studien zur Apostelgeschichte.* SUNT 9. Göttingen: Vandenhoeck & Ruprecht, 1972.

Pollard, Nigel. *Soldiers, Cities, and Civilians in Roman Syria.* Ann Arbor: University of Michigan Press, 2000.

Pollard, T. E. "The Integrity of Philippians." *NTS* 13 (1966): 57–66.

Porter, Stanley E. *The Apostle Paul: His Life, Thought, and Letters.* Grand Rapids: Eerdmans, 2016.

Porter, Stanley E., and Andrew W. Pitts. *The Language of the New Testament: Context, History, and Development.* Leiden: Brill, 2031.

Porter, Stanley E., and Christopher D. Stanley, eds. *As It Is Written: Studying Paul's Use of Scripture.* Atlanta: Society of Biblical Literature, 2008.

Praeder, Susan Marie. "The Problem of First Person Narration in Acts." *NovT* 29 (1987): 193–218.

329

Punt, Jeremy. *Postcolonial Biblical Interpretation: Reframing Paul*. Leiden: Brill, 2013.

Rahtjen, B. D. "The Three Letters of Paul to the Philippians." *NTS* 6 (1960): 167–73.

Raith, Charles, II. *Aquinas and Calvin on Romans: God's Justification and Our Participation*. Oxford: Oxford University Press, 2014.

Rajak, Tessa. *Josephus: The Historian and His Society*. Philadelphia: Fortress, 1984.

Ramsay, William M., and Mark Wilson. *St. Paul the Traveler and Roman Citizen*. London: Hodder & Stoughton, 1925.

Reale, Giovanni. *A History of Ancient Philosophy*. Translated by John R. Catan. 4 vols. Albany: State University of New York Press, 1985.

Redalié, Yann. *Paul après Paul: Le temps le Salut, la morale selon les épîtres à Timothée et à Tite*. Monde de la Bible 31. Geneva: Labor et Fides, 1994.

Reed, Jeffrey T. *A Discourse Analysis of Philippians: Method and Rhetoric in the Debate over Literary Integrity*. JSNTSup 136. Sheffield: Sheffield Academic, 1997.

Reinders, Eric. *Borrowed Gods and Foreign Bodies: Christian Missionaries Imagine Chinese Religion*. Berkeley: University of California Press, 2004.

Reitzenstein, Richard. *Hellenistic Mystery-Religions: Their Basic Ideas and Significance*. Translated by John E. Steely. 3rd ed. Pittsburgh: Pickwick, 1978.

Renan, Ernest. *The Life of Jesus*. Translated by John Haynes Holmes. New York: Modern Library, 1927.

Rensberger, David K. "As the Apostle Teaches: The Development of the Use of Paul's Letters in Second-Century Christianity." PhD diss., Yale University, 1981.

Reumann, John. "Philippians 3.20–21—a Hymnic Fragment?" *NTS* 30 (1984): 593–609.

Rhoads, David M. *Israel in Revolution, 6–74 C.E.: A Political History Based on the Writings of Josephus*. Philadelphia: Fortress, 1976.

Richard, Earl J. *First and Second Thessalonians*. SP 11. Collegeville, MN: Liturgical Press, 1995.

Richards, E. Randolph. *Secretary in the Letters of Paul*. WUNT 2.42. Tübingen: Mohr Siebeck, 1991.

Ricoeur, Paul. *Freud and Philosophy: An Essay on Interpretation*. Translated by Denis Savage. Terry Lectures. New Haven: Yale University Press, 1977.

Robbins, Vernon K. *The Tapestry of Early Christian Discourse: Rhetoric, Society and Ideology*. New York: Routledge, 1996.

Robinson, James M., ed. *The Nag Hammadi Library in English*. San Francisco: Harper & Row, 1977.

Robinson, James M., and Helmut Koester, eds. *Trajectories through Early Christianity*. Philadelphia: Fortress, 1979.

Robinson, John A. T. *Redating the New Testament*. Philadelphia: Westminster, 1978.

Roller, Otto. *Das Formular der paulinischen Briefe: Ein Beitrag zur Lehre vom antike Briefe*. Beiträge zur Wissenschaft vom Alten und Neuen Testament 5–6. Stuttgart: Kohlhammer, 1933.

Roon, A. van. *The Authenticity of Ephesians*. NovTSup 39. Leiden: Brill, 1979.

Roose, Hannah. "2 Thessalonians as Pseudepigraphic Reading Instruction for 1 Thessalonians: Methodological Implications and Exemplary Illustration of an Intertextual Concept." Pages 133–51 in *The Intertextuality of the Epistles: Explorations of Theory and Practice*, edited by Thomas L. Brodie, Dennis R. MacDonald, and Stanley E. Porter. Sheffield: Sheffield Phoenix, 2006.

Rosen, Ralph Mark, and Ineke Sluiter, eds. *Andreia: Studies in Manliness and Courage in Classical Antiquity*. Mnemosyne, Biblioteca Classica Batava, Supplementum 238. Boston: Brill, 2003.

Rosner, Brian S. *Paul, Scripture, and Ethics: A Study of 1 Corinthians 5–7*. Grand Rapids: Baker, 1994.

Rowland, Christopher. *The Open Heaven: A Study of Apocalyptic in Judaism and Early Christianity*. London: SPCK, 1982.

Rubenstein, Richard L. *My Brother Paul*. New York: Harper & Row, 1972.

Ruether, Rosemary R. *Sexism and God Talk: Toward a Feminist Theology*. Boston: Beacon, 1983.

Rüsen-Weinhold, Ulrich. *Der Septuagintapsalter im Neuen Testament: Eine textgeschichtliche Untersuchung*. Neukirchen-Vluyn: Neukirchener, 2004.

Russell, D. S. *The Method and Message of Jewish Apocalyptic*. Philadelphia: Westminster, 1964.

Sacchi, Paolo. *Jewish Apocalyptic and Its History*. Translated by William J. Short. Sheffield: Sheffield Academic, 1990.

Safrai, Shmuel. "Education and the Study of Torah." Pages 2:945–70 in *The Jewish People in the First Century: Historical Geography, Political History, Social, Cultural and Religious Life and Institutions*, edited by Shmuel Safrai and Menaḥem Stern. Compendia Rerum Iudaicarum ad Novum Testamentum. Philadelphia: Fortress, 1987.

Said, Edward W. *Orientalism*. New York: Pantheon, 1978.

Saldarini, Anthony J., and James C. VanderKam. *Pharisees, Scribes and Saddu-*

*cees in Palestinian Society: A Sociological Approach*. Grand Rapids: Eerdmans, 2001.

Salmon, Edward Togo. *Roman Colonization under the Republic*. London: Thames and Hudson, 1969.

Sampley, J. Paul. *"And the Two Shall Become One Flesh": A Study of Traditions in Ephesians 5:21–33*. Cambridge: Cambridge University Press, 1971.

_____, ed. *Paul in the Greco-Roman World: A Handbook*. Harrisburg, PA: Trinity Press International, 2003.

Sanders, E. P. *Jesus and Judaism*. Philadelphia: Fortress, 1985.

_____. *Judaism: Practice and Belief 63 BCE–66 CE*. Philadelphia: Trinity Press International, 1992.

_____. "Literary Dependence in Colossians." *JBL* 85 (1966): 28–45.

_____. *Paul and Palestinian Judaism: A Comparison of Patterns of Religion*. Philadelphia: Fortress, 1977.

_____. *Paul: The Apostle's Life, Letters, and Thought*. Minneapolis: Fortress, 2015.

Sanders, Jack T. *Ethics in the New Testament*. Philadelphia: Fortress, 1975.

_____. "The Salvation of the Jews in Luke-Acts." Pages 104–28 in *Luke-Acts: New Perspectives from the Society of Biblical Literature Seminar*, edited by Charles H. Talbert. New York: Crossroad, 1984.

Sandmel, Samuel. *The Genius of Paul: A Study in History*. Philadelphia: Fortress, 1979.

Santer, Mark. "The Text of Ephesians i. 1." *NTS* 15 (1969): 247–48.

Satlow, Michael, ed. *The Gift in Antiquity*. Chichester, UK: Blackwell, 2013.

Sauter, Gerhard, and John Barton, eds. *Revelation and Story: Narrative Theology and the Centrality of Story*. Burlington, VT: Ashgate, 2000.

Sawyer, John F. A. *The Fifth Gospel: Isaiah in the History of Christianity*. Cambridge: Cambridge University Press, 1996.

Schechter, Solomon. *Aspects of Rabbinic Theology*. New York: Schocken Books, 1961.

Schewel, Benjamin. *Seven Ways of Looking at Religion: The Major Narratives*. New Haven: Yale University Press, 2017.

Schiavone, Aldo. *Spartacus*. Translated by Jeremy Carden. Cambridge, MA: Harvard University Press, 2013.

Schiffman, Lawrence H. *Reclaiming the Dead Sea Scrolls: The History of Judaism, the Background of Christianity, the Lost Library of Qumran*. Philadelphia: Jewish Publication Society of America, 1994.

Schleiermacher, Friedrich. *Über den sogenannten Ersten Brief des Paulos an den Timotheos: Ein Kritisches Sendschreiben an J. C. Gass*. Berlin: Realschulbuchhandlung, 1807.

Schlier, Heinrich. *Principalities and Power in the New Testament*. Quaestiones Disputatae 3. New York: Herder and Herder, 1961.

Schmidt, Daryl. "1 Thess 2:13–16: Linguistic Evidence for an Interpolation." *JBL* 102 (1983): 269–79.

Schmidt, Karl L. "ἐκκλησία." In *TDNT* 3:513–18.

Schmithals, Walter. *Gnosticism in Corinth*. Translated by J. Steely. Nashville: Abingdon, 1971.

——. *Paul and the Gnostics*. Translated by John E. Steely. Nashville: Abingdon, 1972.

Schnackenburg, Rudolf. *Epistle to the Ephesians: A Commentary*. Translated by Helen Heron. Edinburgh: T&T Clark, 1991.

Schnelle, Udo. *Apostle Paul: His Life and Theology*. Grand Rapids: Baker Academic, 2005.

Schoeps, Hans-Joachim. *Paul: The Theology of the Apostle in the Light of Jewish Religious History*. Translated by Harold Knight. Philadelphia: Westminster, 1961.

Scholem, Gershom G. *Jewish Gnosticism, Merkabah Mysticism, and Talmudic Tradition*. New York: The Jewish Theological Seminary of America, 1961.

——. *Major Trends in Jewish Mysticism*. New York: Schocken Books, 1961.

Schopen, Gregory. *Bones, Stones, and Buddhist Monks: Collected Papers on the Archaeology, Epigraphy, and Texts of Monastic Buddhism in India*. Studies in the Buddhist Traditions. Honolulu: University of Hawaii Press, 1997.

Schowalter, Daniel, and Steven J. Friesen, eds. *Urban Religion in Roman Corinth: Interdisciplinary Approaches*. HTS 53. Cambridge, MA: Harvard University Press, 2005.

Schreiner, Thomas R. "Paul: A Reformed Reading." Pages 19–47 in Bird, *Four Views on the Apostle Paul*.

——. *Paul, Apostle of God's Glory in Christ: A Pauline Theology*. Downers Grove, IL: IVP Academic, 2006.

Schubert, Paul. *Form and Function of the Pauline Thanksgivings*. Berlin: Toeplemann, 1939.

Schürer, Emil. *A History of the Jewish People in the Time of Jesus Christ*. Edited by Geza Vermes, Fergus Millar, Martin Goodman, Matthew Black, and Pamela Vermes. Edinburgh: T&T Clark, 1973.

Schüssler Fiorenza, Elisabeth. *In Memory of Her: A Feminist Theological Reconstruction of Christian Origins*. New York: Crossroad, 1983.

——. *Jesus: Miriam's Child, Sophia's Prophet: Critical Issues in Feminist Christology*. New York: Continuum, 1994.

Schwegler, Albert. *Das nachapostolische Zeitalter in den Hauptmomenten seiner Entwicklung*. Tübingen: Fues, 1846.

Schweitzer, Albert. *The Mysticism of Paul the Apostle*. New York: Seabury, 1931.

———. *Paul and His Interpreters: A Critical History*. Translated by William Montgomery. New York: Schocken Books, 1964.

Schweizer, Eduard. *The Letter to the Colossians: A Commentary*. Translated by Andrew Chester. Minneapolis: Augsburg, 1982.

———. "σῶμα." In *TDNT* 7:1025–41.

Scott, Bernard Brandon. *The Trouble with Resurrection: From Paul to the Fourth Gospel*. Salem, OR: Polebridge, 2010.

Scott, Matthew. *The Hermeneutics of Christological Psalmody in Paul*. New York: Cambridge University Press, 2014.

Scroggs, Robin. "Paul and the Eschatological Woman." *JAAR* 40 (1972): 283–303.

Sebeok, Thomas A., ed. *Myth: A Symposium*. Bloomington: Indiana University Press, 1965.

Segal, Alan F. *Paul the Convert: The Apostolate and Apostasy of Saul the Pharisee*. New Haven: Yale University Press, 1990.

Segovia, Fernando F., and R. S. Sugirtharajah, eds. *A Postcolonial Commentary on the New Testament Writings*. The Bible and Postcolonialism 13. London: T&T Clark, 2009.

Seneca. *Epistles*. Translated by Richard Mott Gummere. 3 vols. LCL. Cambridge, MA: Harvard University Press, 1917.

Sharples, R. W. *Stoics, Epicureans and Sceptics: An Introduction to Hellenistic Philosophy*. New York: Routledge, 1996.

Sherwin-White, Adrian Nicholas. *The Roman Citizenship*. Oxford: Clarendon, 1973.

———. *Roman Society and Roman Law in the New Testament*. Oxford: Oxford University Press, 1963.

Smail, William M. *Quintilian on Education*. Classics in Education 28. New York: Teachers College Press, 1966.

Smallwood, E. Mary. *The Jews under Roman Rule: From Pompey to Diocletian; A Study in Political Relations*. Leiden: Brill, 1976.

Smith, Abraham. *Comfort One Another: Reconstructing the Rhetoric and Audience of 1 Thessalonians*. Louisville: Westminster John Knox, 1995.

Smith, Jonathan Z. *Drudgery Divine: On the Comparison of Early Christianities and the Religions of Late Antiquity*. Chicago: University of Chicago Press, 1990.

———. "Fences and Neighbors: Some Contours of Early Judaism." Pages 1–13,

135–39 in *Imagining Religion: From Babylon to Jonestown*. Chicago: University of Chicago Press, 1982.

Smith, Morton. "Observations on Hekaloth Rabbati." Pages 142–60 in *Biblical and Other Studies*, edited by Alexander Altmann. Cambridge, MA: Harvard University Press, 1963.

Spencer, Ichabod. *Fugitive Slave Law: The Religious Duty of Obedience to Law; A Sermon Preached in the Second Presbyterian Church in Brooklyn, Nov 4, 1850*. New York: M. W. Dodd, 1850.

Spicq, Ceslas. *L'Épître aux Hébreux*. Etudes bibliques. Paris: Gabalda, 1952.

Spong, John Shelby. *Resurrection: Myth or Reality?* San Francisco: HarperSanFrancisco, 1994.

Stanley, Christopher D., ed. *The Colonized Apostle: Paul in Postcolonial Eyes*. Minneapolis: Fortress, 2011.

_____, ed. *Paul and Scripture: Extending the Conversation*. Atlanta: Society of Biblical Literature, 2012.

_____. *Paul and the Language of Scripture: Citation Technique in the Pauline Epistles and Contemporary Literature*. Cambridge: Cambridge University Press, 1992.

Stanley, David M. "Paul's Conversion in Acts: Why Three Accounts?" *CBQ* 15 (1953): 315–38.

Stegman, Thomas. *The Character of Jesus: The Linchpin to Paul's Argument in 2 Corinthians*. AnBib 138. Rome: Pontifical Biblical Institute, 2005.

Stemberger, Günter. *Jewish Contemporaries of Jesus: Pharisees, Sadducees, Essenes*. Translated by Allan W. Mahnke. Minneapolis: Fortress, 1995.

Stendahl, Krister. "The Apostle Paul and the Introspective Conscience of the West." Pages 78–96 in *Paul among Jews and Gentiles and Other Essays*. Philadelphia: Fortress, 1976.

Sterling, Gregory E. *Historiography and Self-Definition: Josephos, Luke-Acts, and Apologetic Historiography*. NovTSup 64. Leiden: Brill, 2005.

Stone, I. F. *The Trial of Socrates*. Boston: Little, Brown, 1988.

Stowers, Stanley K. *The Diatribe and Paul's Letter to the Romans*. SBLDS 57. Chico, CA: Scholars Press, 1981.

_____. *Letter Writing in Greco-Roman Antiquity*. Philadelphia: Westminster, 1986.

_____. "Romans 7:7–25 as Speech-in-Character (Prosopopoiia)." Pages 180–202 in *Paul in His Hellenistic Context*, edited by Troels Engberg-Pedersen. Minneapolis: Fortress, 1995.

_____. "Social Typification and the Classification of Ancient Letters." Pages 78–89 in *The Social World of Formative Christianity and Judaism: Essays in*

*Tribute to Howard Clarke Kee*, edited by Jacob Neusner and Peder Borgen. Philadelphia: Fortress, 1988.

Strange, James F., and Thomas R. W. Longstaff, eds. *Excavations at Sepphoris*. Brill Reference Library of Judaism 22. Leiden: Brill, 2006.

Strauss, David Friedrich. *The Life of Jesus: Critically Examined*. Edited by Peter C. Hodgson. Philadelphia: Fortress, 1975.

Strecker, Georg. *Das Judenchristentum in den Pseudoklementinen*. Texte und Untersuchungen 70.5. Berlin: Akademie, 1958.

Strenski, Ivan. *Four Theories of Myth in Twentieth-Century History: Cassirer, Eliade, Levi Strauss and Malinowski*. Iowa City: University of Iowa Press, 1987.

Stroup, George W. *The Promise of Narrative Theology*. London: SCM, 1984.

Suh, Michael K. W. "Power and Peril in Corinth: 1 Corinthians 5:1–13, 10:1–33, and 11:17–34 as Temple Discourse." PhD diss., Emory University, 2018.

Sumney, Jerry L. *Identifying Paul's Opponents: The Question of Method in 2 Corinthians*. JSNTSup 40. Sheffield: Sheffield Academic, 1990.

_____. *Paul: Apostle and Fellow Traveler*. Nashville: Abingdon, 2014.

_____. *Servants of Satan, False Brothers and Other Opponents of Paul*. JSNT 188. Sheffield: Sheffield Academic, 2000.

_____. "Those Who 'Pass Judgment': The Identity of the Opponents in Colossians." *Bib* 74 (1993): 366–88.

Sweetman, Rebecca J., ed. *Roman Colonies in the First Century of Their Foundation*. Oxford: Oxbow, 2011.

Swinson, L. Timothy. *What Is Scripture? Paul's Use of* Graphē *in the Letters to Timothy*. Eugene: Wipf & Stock, 2014.

Talbert, Charles H. *Ephesians and Colossians*. Grand Rapids: Baker Academic, 2007.

_____. *What Is a Gospel? The Genre of the Canonical Gospels*. Philadelphia: Fortress, 1977.

Tappenden, Frederick S. *Resurrection in Paul: Cognition, Metaphor, and Transformation*. Atlanta: SBL Press, 2016.

Tarn, William W. *Hellenistic Civilization*. 3rd rev. ed. New York: World Publishing, 1952.

Tcherikover, Victor. *Hellenistic Civilization and the Jews*. Translated by Shimon Appelbaum. New York: Athenaeum, 1970.

Telbe, Mikael. "The Sociological Factors behind Phil 3:1–11 and the Conflict at Philippi." *JSNT* 55 (1994): 97–121.

*Testimony of the General Assembly of the Presbyterian Church in the United States of America on the Subject of Slavery AD 1858*. Philadelphia: Presbyterian Publishing, 1858.

Thiselton, Anthony C. *The First Epistle to the Corinthians*. NIGTC. Grand Rapids: Eerdmans, 2000.

———. *The Living Paul: An Introduction to the Apostle's Life and Thought*. Downers Grove, IL: IVP Academic, 2009.

———. "The Logical Role of the Liar Paradox in Titus 1:12, 13: A Dissent from the Commentaries in the Light of Philosophical and Logical Analysis." *Biblical Interpretation* 2 (1994): 207–23.

———. "Realized Eschatology at Corinth." *NTS* 24 (1978): 510–26.

Thomas, Christine M. *The Acts of Peter, Gospel Literature, and the Ancient Novel: Rewriting the Past*. New York: Oxford University Press, 2003.

Thompson, James W. *The Beginnings of Christian Philosophy: The Epistle to the Hebrews*. Catholic Biblical Quarterly Monograph Series 13. Washington, DC: Catholic Biblical Association of America, 1982.

Thompson, Joseph P. *Teachings of the New Testament on Slavery*. New York: J. H. Ladd, 1856.

Thurman, Howard. *Jesus and the Disinherited*. Boston: Beacon, 1949.

Tiede, David Lenz. *The Charismatic Figure as Miracle Worker*. Society of Biblical Literature Dissertation Series. Missoula: Society of Biblical Literature for the Seminar on the Gospels, 1972.

Tillich, Paul. *Systematic Theology*. 3 vols. Chicago: University of Chicago Press, 1967.

Tilling, Chris. *Beyond Old and New Perspectives on Paul: Reflections on the Work of Douglas Campbell*. Eugene: Cascade, 2014.

Tinsley, Annie. *A Postcolonial African American Re-reading of Colossians: Identity, Reception, and Interpretation under the Gaze of Empire*. Postcolonialism and Religions. New York: Palgrave Macmillan, 2013.

Tomson, Peter J. *Paul and the Jewish Law: Halakha in the Letters of the Apostle to the Gentiles*. Minneapolis: Fortress, 1991.

Townsley, Gillian. *The Straight Mind in Corinth: Queer Readings across 1 Corinthians 11:2–16*. Atlanta: SBL Press, 2017.

Trible, Phyllis. *Texts of Terror: Literary-Feminist Readings of Biblical Narratives*. Philadelphia: Fortress, 1984.

Trobisch, David. *Paul's Letter Collection: Tracing the Origins*. Minneapolis: Fortress, 1994.

Ulansey, David. *The Origins of the Mithraic Mysteries: Cosmology and Salvation in the Ancient World*. New York: Oxford University Press, 1991.

Ulrich, Eugene, and James C. VanderKam, eds. *The Community of the Renewed Covenant*. Notre Dame, IN: University of Notre Dame Press, 1994.

Urbach, Ephraim E. *The Sages*. Translated by Israel Abrahams. Jerusalem: Magnes, 1975.

Urbainczyk, Theresa. *Roman Slavery*. New York: Oxford University Press, 2011.

Urban, Wilbur Marshall. *Language and Reality: The Philosophy of Language and the Principles of Symbolism*. New York: Routledge, 2013.

van der Horst, Pieter Willem. *The Sentences of Pseudo-Phocylides: With Introduction and Commentary*. SVTP 4. Leiden: Brill, 1978.

van Unnik, W. C. *Tarsus or Jerusalem: The City of Paul's Youth*. Translated by George Ogg. London: Epworth, 1962.

_____. "'With Unveiled Face', an Exegesis of 2 Corinthians III 12–18." *NovT* 6 (1963): 153–69.

Van Voorst, Robert E. *The Ascents of James: History and Theology of a Jewish-Christian Community*. Atlanta: Scholars Press, 1989.

Vawter, F. Bruce. "The Colossians Hymn and the Principle of Redaction." *CBQ* 33 (1971): 62–81.

Vermes, Geza. *Jesus the Jew*. New York: Macmillan, 1973.

Veyne, Paul, ed. *A History of Private Life*. Vol. 1, *From Pagan Rome to Byzantium*. Translated by Arthur Goldhammer. Cambridge, MA: Harvard University Press, 1987.

Vielhauer, Philipp. "Zum 'Paulinismus' der Apostelgeschichte." *Evangelische Theologie* 10 (1950): 1–15.

Vinzent, Markus. *Tertullian's Preface to Marcion's Gospel*. Leuven: Peeters, 2016.

Von Hendy, Andrew. *The Modern Construction of Myth*. Bloomington: Indiana University Press, 2002.

Voss, Barbara L., and Eleanor Conlin Casella, eds. *The Archaeology of Colonialism: Intimate Encounters and Sexual Effects*. New York: Cambridge University Press, 2011.

Vries, Johannes de, and Martin Karrer. *Textual History and the Reception of Scripture in Early Christianity*. SCS 60. Atlanta: Society of Biblical Literature, 2013.

Wachsmuth, Curt, Otto Hense, and Curt Stobaeus. *Ioannis Stobaei Anthologium*. 5 vols. Zürich: Weidmann, 1999.

Wagner, J. Ross. *Heralds of the Good News: Isaiah and Paul in Concert in the Letter to the Romans*. NovTSup 101. Leiden: Brill, 2008.

_____. *Reading the Sealed Book: Old Greek Isaiah and the Problem of Septuagint Hermeneutics*. FAT 88. Tübingen: Mohr Siebeck, 2013.

Wagner, J. Ross, C. Kavin Rowe, and A. Katherine Grieb, eds. *The Word Leaps the Gap: Essays on Scripture and Theology in Honor of Richard B. Hays*. Grand Rapids: Eerdmans, 2008.

Wakefield, Andrew Hollis. *Where to Live: The Hermeneutical Significance of Paul's Citations from Scripture in Galatians 3:1–14*. Atlanta: Society of Biblical Literature, 2003.

Walaskay, Paul W. *"And So We Came to Rome": The Political Perspective of St. Luke*. Society for New Testament Studies Monograph Series 49. New York: Cambridge University Press, 1983.

Wall, Robert. "The Jerusalem Council (Acts 15:1–21) in Canonical Context." Pages 93–101 in *From Biblical Criticism to Biblical Faith: Essays in Honor of Lee Martin McDonald*, edited by William H. Brackney and Craig A. Evans. Macon, GA: Mercer University Press, 2007.

Wallace, James Buchanan. *Snatched into Paradise (2 Cor 1–10): Paul's Heavenly Journey in the Context of Early Christian Experience*. BZNW 179. Berlin: De Gruyter, 2011.

Wason, Brandon. "'All Things to All Men': Paul as Orator in Acts." PhD diss., Emory University, 2017.

Watson, Francis. "Scripture in Pauline Theology: How Far Does It Go?" *Journal of Theological Interpretation* 2 (2008): 181–92.

Weiss, Johannes. *Earliest Christianity*. Edited by Frederick C. Grant. New York: Harper & Row, 1959.

Welles, Charles Bradford. *Royal Correspondence in the Hellenistic Period*. New Haven: Yale University Press, 1934.

Wernik, Uri. "Frustrated Beliefs and Early Christianity: A Psychological Enquiry into the Gospels of the New Testament." *Numen* 22, no. 2 (1975): 96–130.

Westerholm, Stephen. *Perspectives Old and New on Paul: The "Lutheran" Paul and His Critics*. Grand Rapids: Eerdmans, 2003.

Wheelwright, Philip E. *Metaphor and Reality*. Bloomington: Indiana University Press, 1962.

White, Devin L. *Teacher of the Nations: Ancient Educational Traditions and Paul's Argument in 1 Corinthians 1–4*. BZNW 227. Berlin: De Gruyter, 2017.

White, John Lee. *The Form and Function of the Body of the Greek Letter: A Study of the Letter-Body in the Non-Literary Papyri and in Paul the Apostle*. SBLDS 2. Missoula: Scholars Press, 1972.

_____. *Light from Ancient Letters*. Philadelphia: Fortress, 1986.

Whitehead, Alfred North. *Symbolism: Its Meaning and Effect*. New York: Capricorn Books, 1959.

Wiesinger, August. *Biblical Commentary on St. Paul's Epistles to the Philippians, to Titus, and the First to Timothy*. Translated by John Fulton. Edinburgh: T&T Clark, 1851.

Wild, Robert A. "'Be Imitators of God': Discipleship in the Letter to the Ephesians." Pages 127–43 in *Discipleship in the New Testament*, edited by Fernando F. Segovia. Philadelphia: Fortress, 1985.

_____. "The Warrior and the Prisoner: Some Reflections on Ephesians 6:10–20." *CBQ* 46.1984 (1985): 284–98.

Wilk, Florian. "The Letters of Paul as Witnesses to and for the Septuagint Text." Pages 253–71 in *Septuagint Research: Issues and Challenges in the Study of the Greek Jewish Scriptures*, edited by Wolfgang Kraus and R. Glenn Wooden. SCS 53. Atlanta: Society of Biblical Literature, 2006.

Wilken, Robert Louis. *The Spirit of Early Christian Thought: Seeking the Face of God*. New Haven: Yale University Press, 2005.

Williams, Craig A. *Roman Homosexuality*. Oxford: Oxford University Press, 2010.

Williams, Guy. *The Spirit World in the Letters of Paul the Apostle: A Critical Examination of the Role of Spiritual Beings in the Authentic Pauline Epistles*. FRLANT 31. Göttingen: Vandenhoeck & Ruprecht, 2009.

Wilson, A. N. *Paul: The Mind of the Apostle*. New York: Norton, 1998.

Wilson, John F. *Rediscovering Caesarea Philippi: The Ancient City of Pan*. Malibu: Pepperdine University Press, 2001.

Wimbush, Vincent L. *African Americans and the Bible: Sacred Texts and Social Textures*. Eugene: Wipf & Stock, 2012.

_____. *The Bible and African Americans*. Minneapolis: Fortress, 2003.

Wink, Walter. "The Hymn of the Cosmic Christ." Pages 235–45 in *The Conversation Continues: Studies in Paul and John in Honor of J. Louis Martyn*, edited by Beverly R. Gaventa and Robert T. Fortna. Nashville: Abingdon, 1990.

Winter, Sara C. "Paul's Letter to Philemon." *NTS* 33 (1987): 1–15.

Wire, Antoinette C. *The Corinthian Women Prophets: A Reconstruction through Paul's Rhetoric*. Minneapolis: Fortress, 1990.

Witherington, Ben, III. *1 and 2 Thessalonians: A Socio-Rhetorical Commentary*. Grand Rapids: Eerdmans, 2006.

_____. "The Influence of Galatians on Hebrews." *NTS* 37 (1991): 146–52.

_____. *Isaiah Old and New: Exegesis, Intertextuality, and Hermeneutics*. Minneapolis: Fortress, 2017.

_____. *The Letters to Philemon, the Colossians, and the Ephesians: A Socio-Rhetorical Commentary on the Captivity Epistles*. Grand Rapids: Eerdmans, 2007.

_____. *Paul's Letter to the Philippians: A Socio-Rhetorical Commentary*. Grand Rapids: Eerdmans, 2011.

Wolfe, Tom. *Hooking Up*. New York: Farrar, Straus and Giroux, 2010.

Wolfson, Harry Austryn. *Philo: Foundations of Religious Philosophy in Judaism,*

*Christianity, and Islam.* 2 vols. Cambridge, MA: Harvard University Press, 1947.

Wolter, Michael. *Die Pastoralbriefe als Paulustradition.* FRLANT 146. Göttingen: Vandenhoeck & Ruprecht, 1988.

Woodruff, Paul. "Rhetoric and Tragedy." Pages 92–107 in *The Oxford Handbook of Rhetorical Studies,* edited by Michael J. MacDonald. New York: Oxford University Press, 2017.

Wrede, William. *Paul.* Translated by Edward Lummis. Boston: American Unitarian Association, 1908.

_____. *Paul the Apostle.* Tübingen: Mohr Siebeck, 1907.

Wright, N. T. *The New Testament and the People of God.* Christian Origins and the Question of God 1. London: SPCK, 1992.

_____. "Paul and Empire." Pages 285–97 in *The Blackwell Companion to Paul,* edited by Stephen Westerholm. Oxford: Blackwell, 2011.

_____. *Paul and the Faithfulness of God.* Christian Origins and the Question of God 4. Minneapolis: Fortress, 2013.

_____. *Paul: In Fresh Perspective.* Minneapolis: Fortress, 2009.

Yadin, Yigael. *Masada: Herod's Fortress and the Zealots' Last Stand.* Translated by Moshe Pearlman. New York: Random House, 1966.

Yamauchi, Edwin. *Pre-Christian Gnosticism: A Survey of the Proposed Evidence.* Grand Rapids: Eerdmans, 1973.

Yoder, John Howard. *The Politics of Jesus.* 2nd ed. Grand Rapids: Eerdmans, 1994.

Young, Frances M. *Biblical Exegesis and the Formation of Christian Culture.* Grand Rapids: Baker Academic, 2002.

Young, Robert J. C. *Postcolonialism: A Very Short Introduction.* Oxford: Oxford University Press, 2003.

Zimmermann, Johannes. *Messianische Texte aus Qumran: Koeniglich, priesterliche und prophetische Messiasvorgestellung in den Schriftfunden von Qumran.* WUNT 2.104. Tübingen: Mohr Siebeck, 1998.

# INDEX OF AUTHORS

# INDEX OF SUBJECTS

# INDEX OF SCRIPTURE AND OTHER ANCIENT SOURCES

| | | | | | |
|---|---|---|---|---|---|
| 1:6 | 101 | 1:12–20 | 104 | 21:8 | 104 |
| 1:7 | 100n23 | 1:18 | 104 | 21:14 | 104 |
| 1:12 | 101, 101n26 | 2:1–3:22 | 103 | 22:3 | 104 |
| 1:16 | 101 | 2:6 | 103n30 | 22:6 | 104 |
| 1:18 | 101, 101n26 | 2:10 | 101n26 | 22:7 | 104 |
| 1:19 | 101 | 2:14–15 | 103n30 | 22:9 | 104 |
| 2:1 | 100, 101, 101n26 | 2:20 | 104 | 22:15 | 104 |
| 2:2 | 100 | 3:3 | 104 | 22:17 | 104 |
| 2:5 | 100, 101 | 3:11 | 104 | | |
| 2:7 | 100 | 3:20 | 104 | **DEUTEROCANON-** | |
| 2:9 | 101n26 | 3:21 | 104 | **ICAL WORKS** | |
| 2:14 | 101 | 4:4 | 104 | | |
| 2:14–26 | 33, 100 | 4:10 | 104 | **Tobit** | |
| 2:15 | 101 | 5:6–14 | 104 | 4:13 | 152n33 |
| 2:17 | 101 | 5:8 | 104 | | |
| 2:18 | 101 | 6:9 | 104 | **Judith** | |
| 2:20 | 101 | 6:10 | 104 | 8:25 | 152n33 |
| 2:22 | 101 | 7:3 | 104 | 10:18 | 153n35 |
| 2:24 | 101 | 7:14 | 104 | 12:8 | 152n30 |
| 2:26 | 101 | 8:3 | 104 | | |
| 3:1 | 101 | 8:4 | 104 | **Wisdom of Solomon** | |
| 3:9 | 100n23 | 10:7 | 104 | 1:3 | 151n26 |
| 4:10 | 100n23 | 11:8 | 104 | 1:5 | 152n29 |
| 4:15 | 100n23 | 11:10 | 104 | 1:16 | 151n26, 152n28 |
| 5:4 | 100n23 | 11:11–12 | 104 | 2:4 | 152n33 |
| 5:7 | 100n23, 101 | 11:18 | 104 | 2:16 | 152n32 |
| 5:8 | 100, 100n23, 101 | 12:10 | 104 | 2:17 | 151n26 |
| 5:10 | 101 | 12:11 | 104 | 2:19 | 151n26 |
| 5:11 | 100n23, 101 | 13:7 | 104 | 3:5 | 152n28 |
| 5:14 | 100, 100n23, 101 | 13:16 | 104 | 3:9 | 152n33, 153n34 |
| 5:15 | 100n23, 101 | 14:4 | 101n26, 104 | 4:15 | 153n34 |
| | | 14:12 | 104 | 6:4 | 152n28 |
| **2 Peter** | | 15:3 | 104 | 6:18 | 152n33 |
| 1:1–2 | 70n27 | 16:6 | 104 | 6:20 | 152n28 |
| 3:15 | 33 | 17:6 | 104 | 8:16 | 152n33 |
| 3:15–16 | 19n2, 33 | 17:14 | 104 | 9:12 | 152n28 |
| | | 18:20 | 104 | 9:17 | 152n29 |
| **2 John** | | 18:24 | 104 | 10:10 | 152n28 |
| 7 | 117n62 | 19:2 | 104 | 12:2 | 152n33 |
| | | 19:7–9 | 104 | 12:7 | 152n28 |
| **3 John** | | 19:10 | 104 | 12:12 | 152n32 |
| 12 | 258 | 19:18 | 104 | 12:26 | 151n26, 152n28 |
| | | 21:1 | 104 | 14:1 | 150n22 |
| **Revelation** | | 21:2 | 104 | 14:1–28 | 186n104 |
| 1:1 | 104 | 21:3 | 104 | 14:11 | 150n22 |
| 1:8 | 104 | 21:4 | 104 | 14:12 | 150n22, 152n32 |
| 1:9 | 103 | 21:5 | 104 | 14:30 | 150n22 |